BEHIND THE MIRROR
AIMÉ MAEGHT AND HIS ARTISTS

BONNARD, MATISSE, MIRÓ
CALDER, GIACOMETTI, BRAQUE

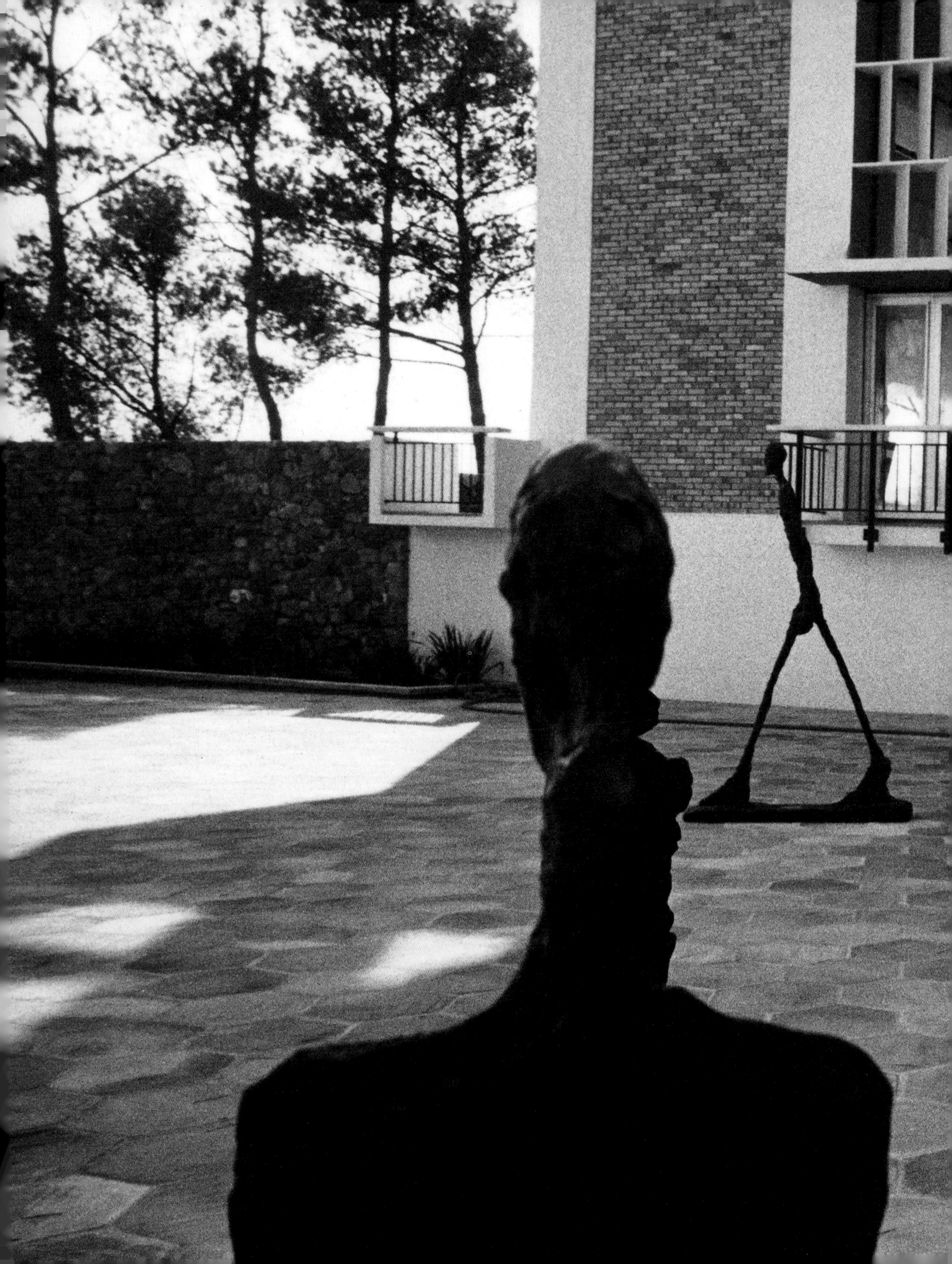

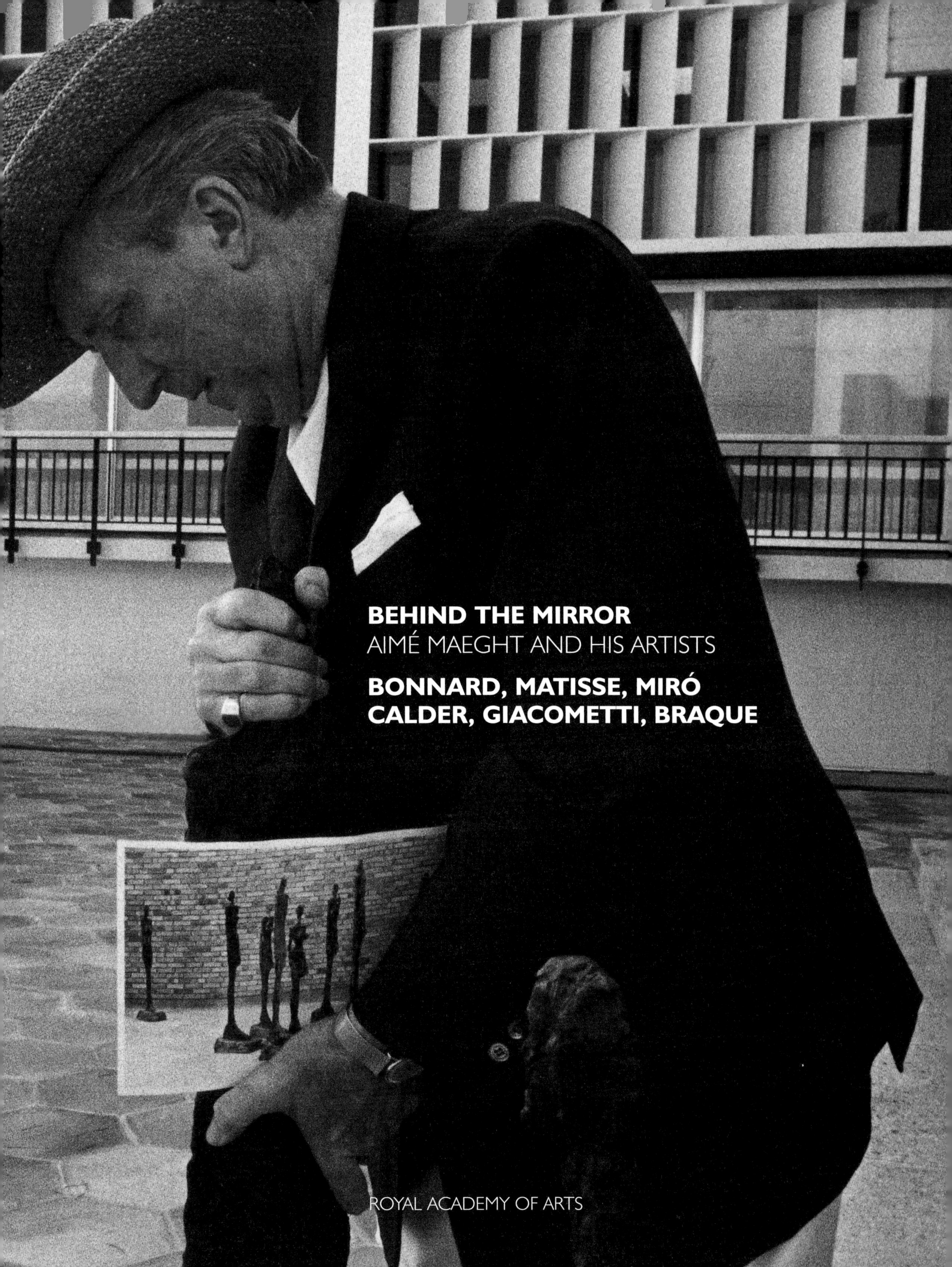

BEHIND THE MIRROR
AIMÉ MAEGHT AND HIS ARTISTS
BONNARD, MATISSE, MIRÓ
CALDER, GIACOMETTI, BRAQUE

ROYAL ACADEMY OF ARTS

First published on the occasion
of the exhibition 'Miró, Calder, Giacometti,
Braque: Aimé Maeght and His Artists'

Royal Academy of Arts
4 October 2008 – 2 January 2009

Sponsored by

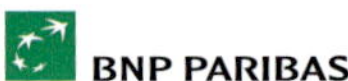 BNP PARIBAS

The Royal Academy of Arts is grateful to
Her Majesty's Government for agreeing to
indemnify this exhibition under the National
Heritage Act 1980, and to Resource, The
Council for Museums, Archives and
Libraries, for its help in arranging the
indemnity.

EXHIBITION CURATOR
Ann Dumas

EXHIBITION ORGANISATION
Caroline McCarthy

**PHOTOGRAPHIC AND COPYRIGHT
CO-ORDINATION**
Miranda Bennion

CATALOGUE
Royal Academy Publications
Lucy Bennett
David Breuer
Sophie Oliver
Peter Sawbridge
Sheila Smith
Nick Tite

Design: Luke Herriott
Colour origination: DL Repro Ltd

Printed in Italy by Printer Trento

ACKNOWLEDGEMENTS
In addition to those mentioned in the President's Foreword on page 7, the curator of the exhibition
would like to acknowledge with gratitude the assistance of the following individuals:
Philippa Baker, Cloé Barnard-Guelle, Marie-Pierre Bathany, Ema Bonifacic, Cathy Cordova,
Michel Enrici, Fairhurst Ward Abbotts, Sophie Hicks, Jim Hollands, Mariko Kuroda, Fernanda
Lanzara, Véronique de Lavenne, Florence Monnier, Philippe de Montebello, Helly Nahmad,
Francis Parmentier, Magnus Sweeney, Gary Tinterow.

EDITORIAL NOTE
Unless otherwise stated in the captions, all works in the exhibition have been lent by the Maeght
family, Paris, or the Fondation Marguerite et Aimé Maeght, Saint-Paul. Full lender credits appear
in the List of Works in the Exhibition on pages 171–2.
All measurements are given in centimetres, height before width before depth.
Illustrations not otherwise captioned: pages 2–3: detail of cat. 134; page 6: detail of cat. 37; page 8:
Georges Braque (1882–1963), *La Nuit, la faim*, text by Georges Ribemont-Dessaignes, 1960,
cover (cat. 94); pages 10–11: Aimé Maeght and his beloved dog Asco (1946–1965) and
Giacometti's *Dog* (*Le Chien*) on the day of the opening of the Fondation Marguerite et Aimé
Maeght, 28 July 1964; endpapers: detail of cat. 135.

CONTENTS

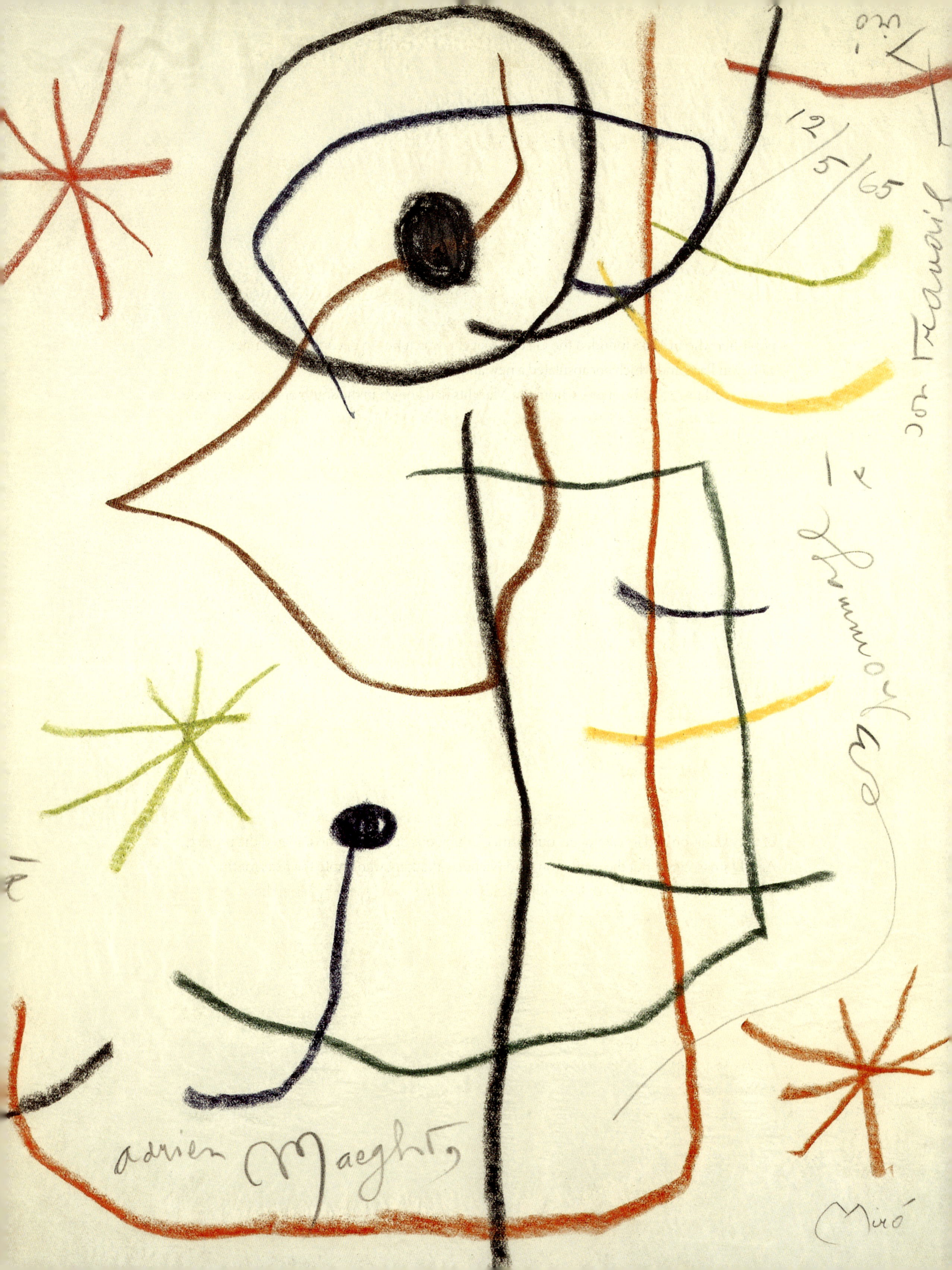

12/5/65
adrien Maeght
Miró

PRESIDENT'S FOREWORD

This exhibition presents a selection of outstanding works from the Fondation Marguerite et Aimé Maeght at Saint-Paul in the south of France, and from the collection of the Maeght family in Paris. At the heart of the show is Aimé Maeght, the remarkable dealer, patron and publisher who in 1945 founded the Galerie Maeght, which was to become the premier gallery in Paris and which encapsulated a new and bold spirit in art.

Matisse and Bonnard, whom the Maeghts had known in the south of France, provide a prelude to the exhibition. Braque's rich and sombre late canvases and Giacometti's disturbing and timeless solitary figures evoke the darker side of post-war Paris. By contrast, Miró's exuberant and poetic abstract paintings and the brilliantly coloured floating shapes of Calder's mobiles explode with *joie de vivre*. This is the first exhibition to explore the work of these four artists in the context of their close personal relationship with the Maeght family and the Galerie Maeght. Later, the Fondation Marguerite et Aimé Maeght, which opened in 1964 and in whose creation all four played an active role, continued this close co-operation. Aimé encouraged his artists to explore the creative possibilities of printmaking, and the results are demonstrated here by an impressive variety of prints by all four artists. His love of contemporary literature brought together poets and artists, and the result was a succession of beautifully produced limited-edition *livres d'artistes* (artists' books), as well as the periodical *Derrière Le Miroir*, an issue of which accompanied each exhibition.

The Royal Academy owes an enormous debt of gratitude to the Maeght family: to Aimé's son Adrien and his children Isabelle, Yoyo, Florence and Jules, who are actively engaged in running the Fondation and the Galerie Maeght today, and who have generously agreed to lend over 120 works.

We also extend our grateful thanks to those who have contributed to the realisation of the exhibition and its catalogue: our former Exhibitions Secretary, who initiated the project; Ann Dumas, curator of the exhibition; and Nicholas Watkins, who wrote the texts for the catalogue. We would also like to thank two additional lenders to the exhibition: the Metropolitan Museum of Art, New York, and the Nahmad Collection, Switzerland.

We are immensely grateful to our sponsor, BNP Paribas. Long-time supporters of the Royal Academy, they are sponsoring an exhibition for the first time and we are delighted to work with them. We would also like to thank Mr Rabih Hage for his generous contribution.

We sincerely hope that this exhibition of works by four highly individual international artists who worked together in the unique context of the Galerie Maeght and the Fondation Marguerite et Aimé Maeght will deepen our public's appreciation of this vital period in the history of modern art.

Sir Nicholas Grimshaw CBE
President, Royal Academy of Arts

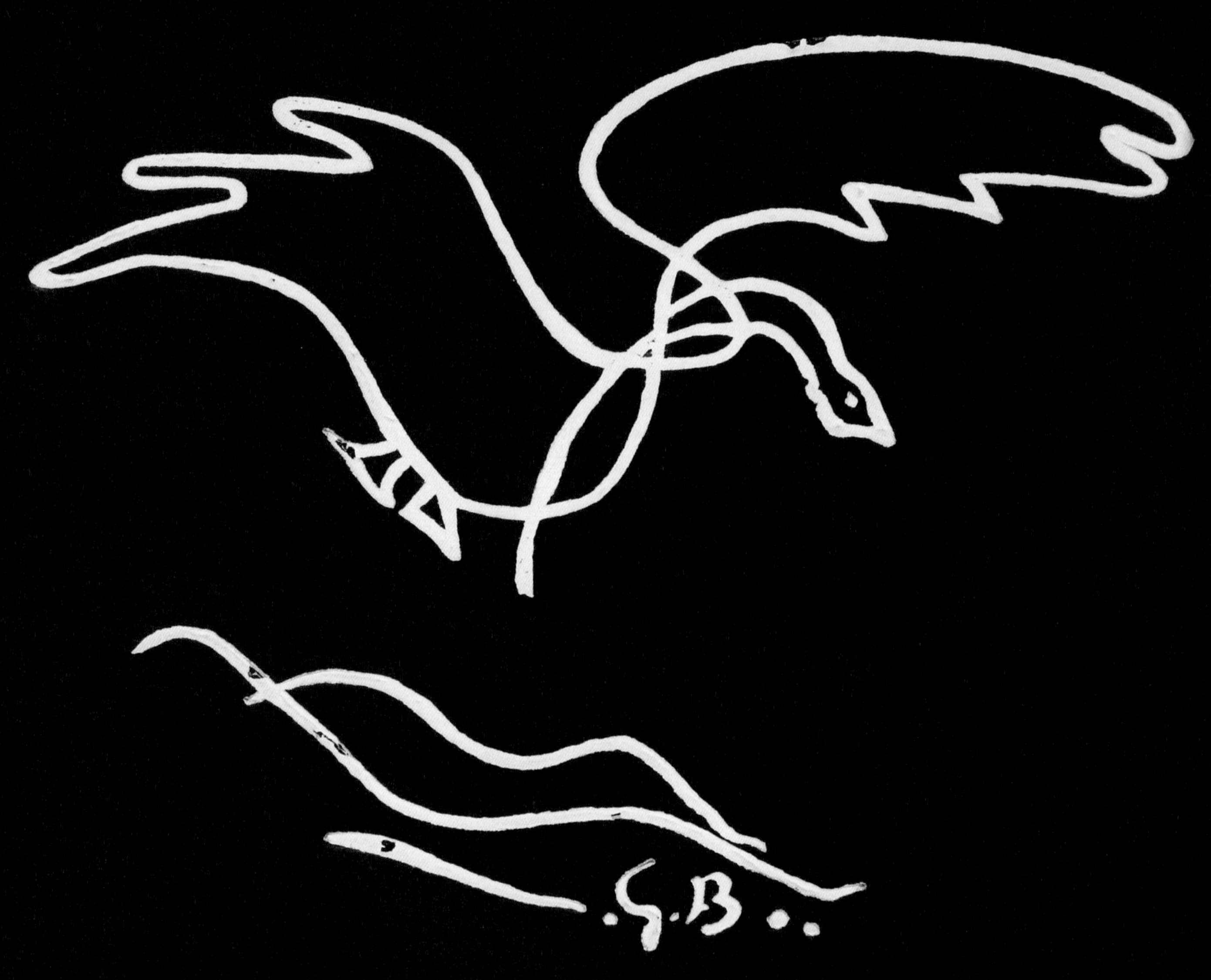

SPONSOR'S PREFACE

BNP Paribas is proud to sponsor 'Miró, Calder, Giacometti, Braque: Aimé Maeght and His Artists' at the Royal Academy of Arts. This exhibition of works by an international group of distinguished artists witnesses Aimé Maeght's outstanding contribution to art in mid-twentieth-century France.

United by a bold new spirit of innovation that defined the art-world in post-war Paris, the artists represented by Maeght brought to their work values that resonate strongly with people today. Originality and innovation are universal values at the foundation of all progress. Evident in the works of art in this exhibition, they are also reflected in the partnership that underpins the relationships that we have with our clients.

This is the first exhibition that BNP Paribas has sponsored at the Royal Academy of Arts and we are pleased to be working with this acclaimed institution. Through our sponsorship we hope to inspire visitors, clients and colleagues alike with the same creativity that marked Aimé Maeght and the artists that he worked with. We also hope that our partnerships with local charities and schools will enable as many people as possible from the community to enjoy the exhibition and the stimulation that it will provide.

Ludovic de Montille
BNP Paribas, UK CEO

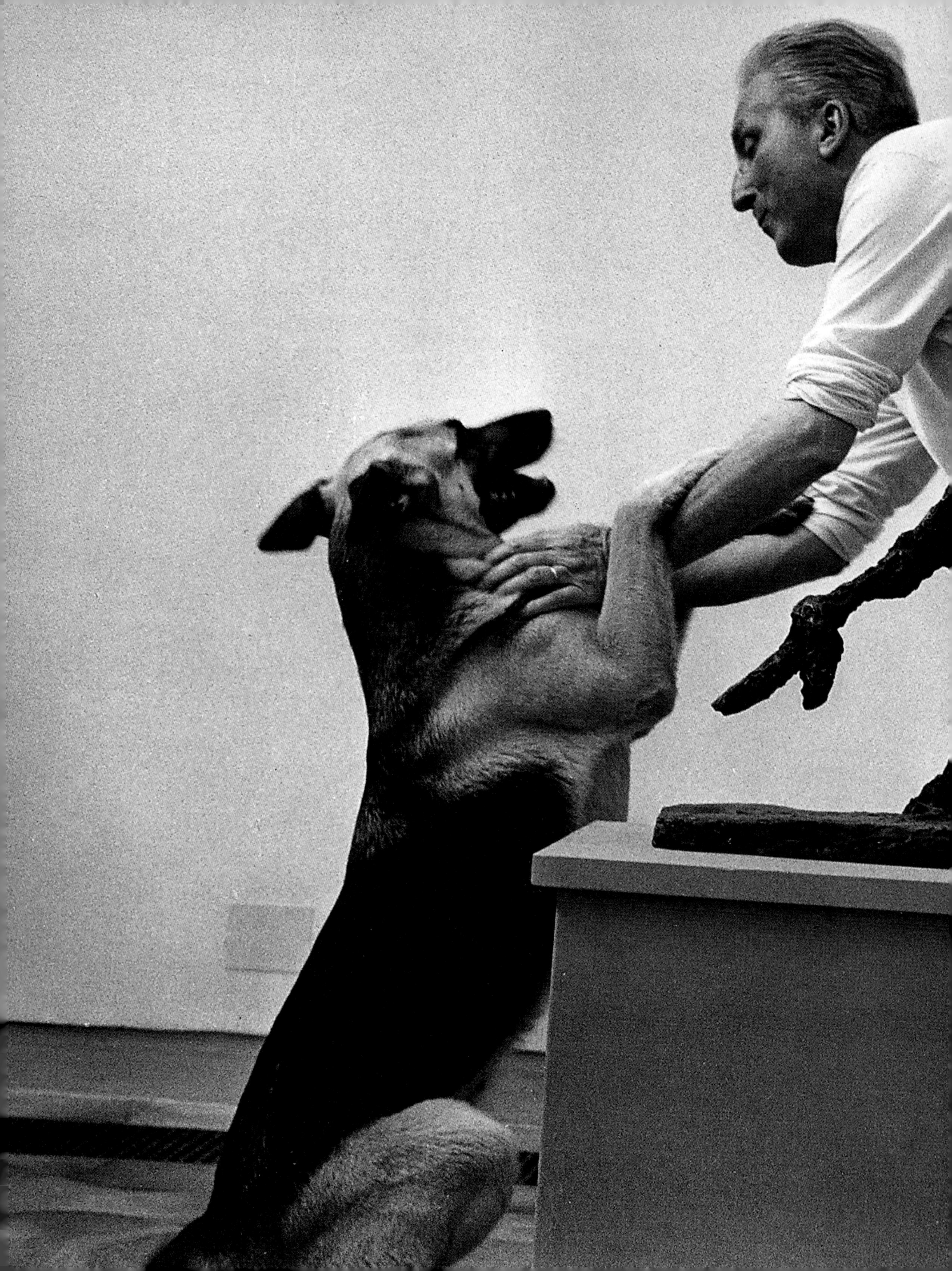

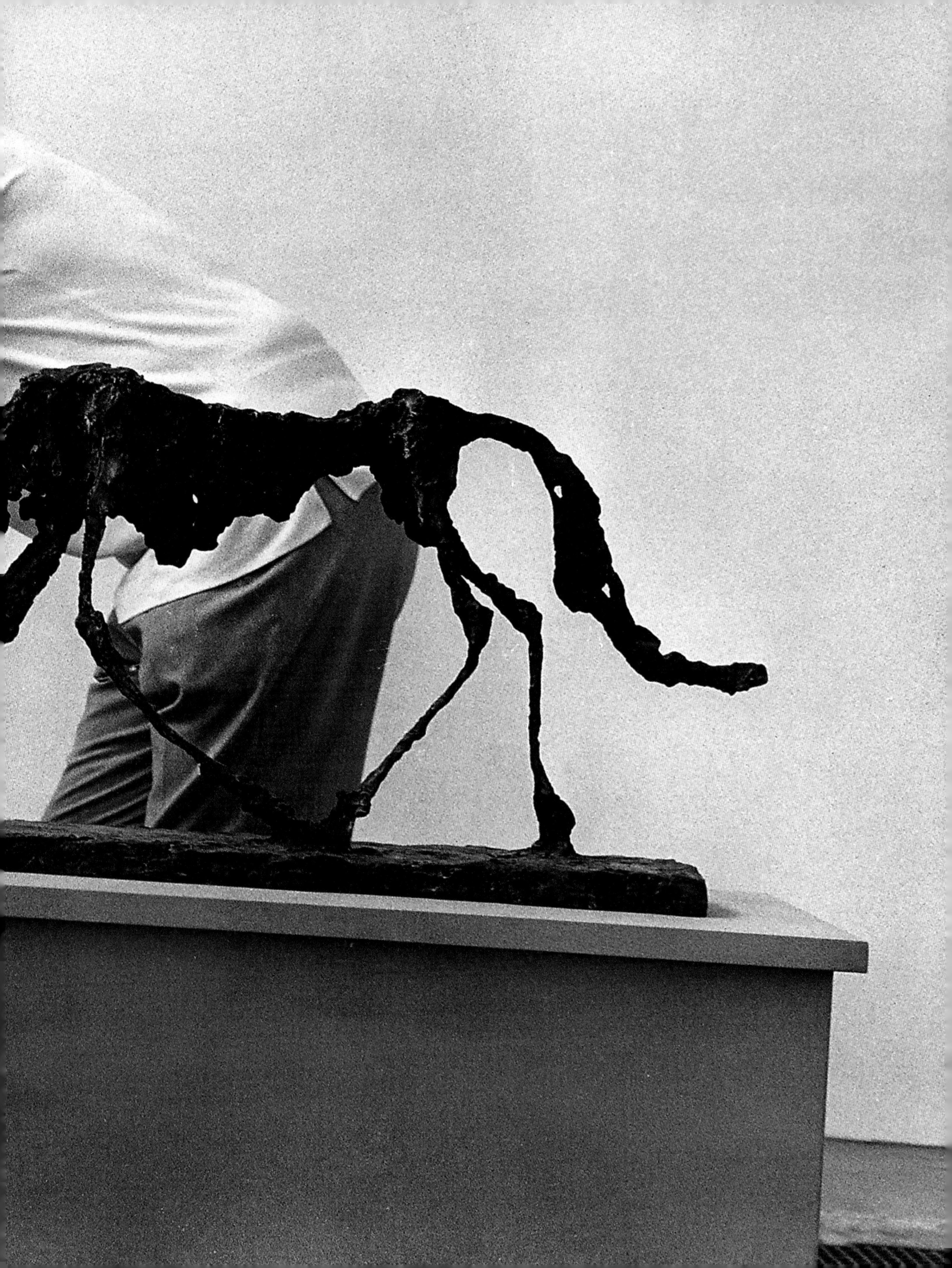

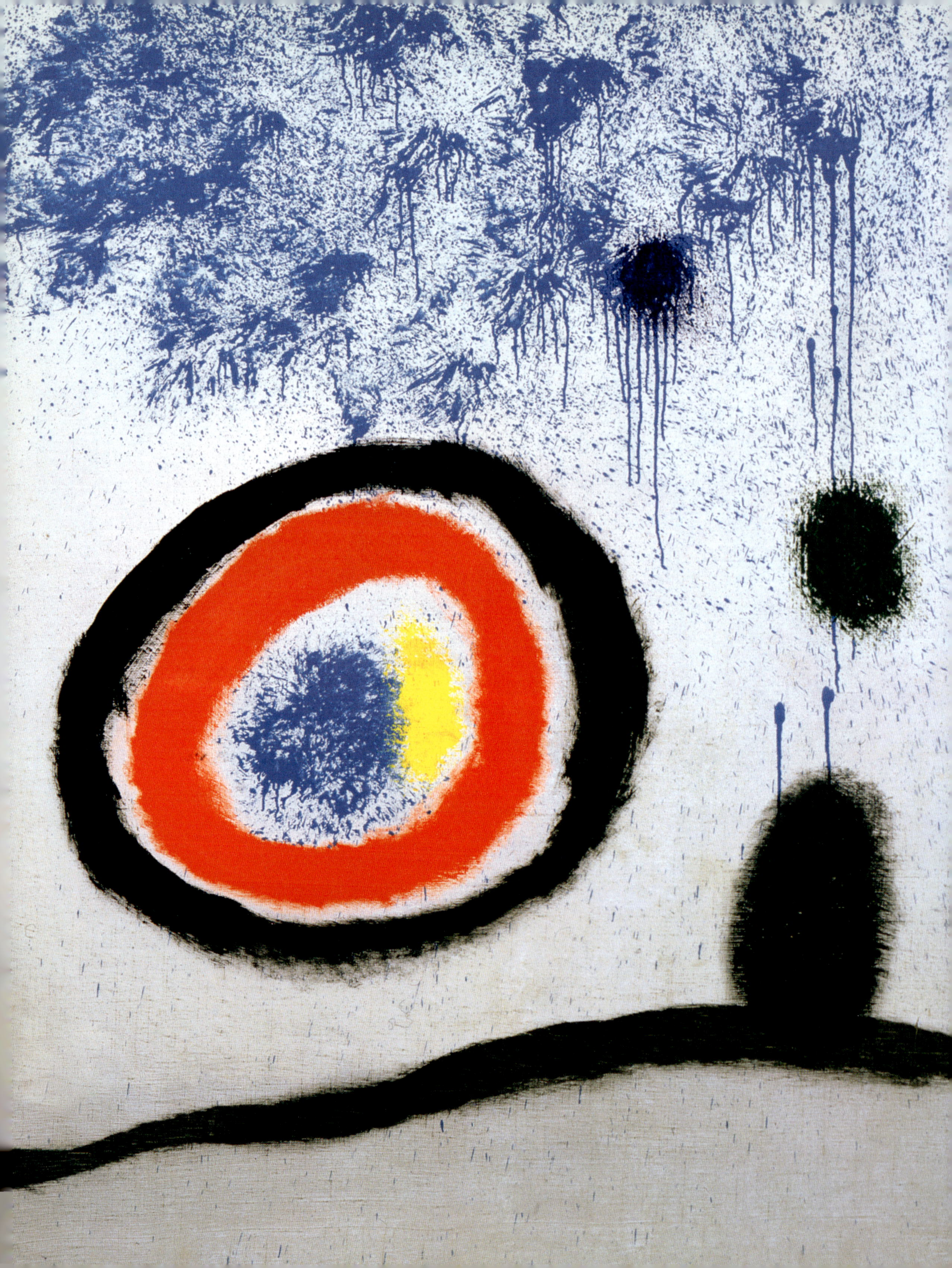

AIMÉ MAEGHT AND HIS ARTISTS

Nicholas Watkins

The name Maeght is synonymous with the emergence of the major modern art gallery in post-World War II Paris and with the creation of the Fondation Marguerite et Aimé Maeght, a novel temple complex dedicated to modern art, on a hill outside Saint-Paul in the south of France. However, for Aimé Maeght, the founder of the business, the family's publishing enterprise ranked as one of his proudest achievements. Trading under the name of Arte-Adrien Maeght, it gained an international reputation for its graphic editions and beautifully produced reviews, catalogues and books promoting and popularising Maeght artists. Ably supported by his wife, Marguerite, Aimé Maeght had a genius for publicity coupled with the vision, ambition and financial clout to take mid-to-late-career artists into the big time while also promoting a younger pan-European generation. His gallery on Paris's Rive Droite was no Ambroise Vollard-style dusty sanctuary for the initiated but a modern dealing emporium to compete with the major American galleries, complete with large exhibition spaces and small private rooms.

Aimé knew how to look after and spoil his artists, and even the most ascetic and reclusive found it difficult to resist him. The gallery stable was soon virtually a Who's Who of leading artists. Much as other dealers and artists might have resented Maeght's success, he was definitely a presence on the Parisian dealing scene – a force to be reckoned with.

With his profound love of art and poetry, Aimé wanted both the Galerie and Fondation Maeght to act as meeting places for artists, poets and writers. He and Marguerite kept open house. Braque, like most of Aimé's artists, became a personal friend of the family, as numerous personal gifts and portraits of the Maeghts testify. Braque stood witness at the wedding of the Maeghts' elder son, Adrien (b. 1930), to his wife, Paule. Pierre Bonnard drew Marguerite alone (cat. 3) and with the Maeghts' son Bernard (born 1942) (cat. 6). Adrien filmed Henri Matisse drawing his mother (cat. 7) – an inscrutable Madonna-like presence filling the format. Giacometti drew Aimé (cat. 81) and painted Marguerite (cat. 82). Alexander Calder's signature in the visitors' book is accompanied by a felt-tip sketch of Florence (cat. 123), one of the Maeghts' three daughters. On the tragic death of Bernard in 1953 at the age of eleven, Braque and Léger suggested that the Maeghts should build a centre for the living arts in his memory.[1] Although the Maeght family went on to support a younger generation of artists, Bonnard,

FIG. 1
Joan Miró (1893–1983), *The Birth of Day I* (*Naissance du jour I*), 1964 (detail of cat. 34). Oil on canvas, 146 x 113.5 cm

Matisse, Braque, Giacometti, Miró and Calder remained at the heart of their gallery and the Fondation Maeght's collection, and the dialogue between their respective *oeuvres* forms the subject of this exhibition.

Aimé Maeght (1906–1981), a war orphan, was born in the north of France and trained as a master lithographer at the Ecole des Beaux-Arts in Nîmes. He and his wife, Marguerite (1909–1977), from a family of dealers and printers, were married in Cannes in 1928 and together started Arte in 1936 – a printing studio and advertising agency also selling radios and modern furniture designed by Aimé, along with a few paintings by local artists in the shop window. The Maeghts emerged as dealers during World War II. With Aimé away in the army, Marguerite was no longer able to run the printing studio and so she sold the paintings that had been brought in to be reproduced in lithography.[2] Aimé in turn displayed considerable initiative, running paintings for clients between the occupied zone in the north and the 'free' zone in the south. In addition, he had the good fortune to befriend and cater for the needs of two distinguished modern masters, Bonnard and Matisse, who were cut off, anxious and lonely in their studio-homes in Le Cannet and Nice. Essential provisions were increasingly difficult to obtain. Bonnard's anxiety was compounded by the death of his beloved Marthe on 26 January 1942. He wrote to Matisse in February: 'Six days ago we buried her in Le Cannet cemetery. You can imagine my grief and my solitude, filled with bitterness and worry about the life I may be leading from now on.'[3] Aimé kept him going with supplies and emotional support.

Matisse came round to Aimé, finding him useful, especially after the threat of Allied bombing forced the artist's evacuation from Nice to the Villa Le Rêve in Vence in 1943, the same year that the Maeghts were obliged to leave Cannes and seek refuge at a farm in Vence. Aimé drove Bonnard to see Matisse and generally acted as a go-between. After Marguerite Duthuit, Matisse's daughter, had spent a fortnight with her father in January 1945 as she recovered from being hideously tortured by the Gestapo, it was Aimé who drove her back to Paris in his comfortable car. Matisse came to acknowledge that the quality of the pictures Aimé was exhibiting in his shop in Cannes had been transformed and predicted him a possible future as a successful dealer.[4]

To make the big time, Aimé knew that he had to open a gallery in Paris. Bonnard introduced him to a dealer who wanted to close down his gallery, and Aimé decided to buy it. Although Matisse agreed to be the subject of the inaugural exhibition, which opened on 6 December 1945 (fig. 3), he wanted to be free to go beyond easel painting and explore new decorative dimensions without being tied down to a contract.[5] Aimé's kindness to Marguerite Duthuit paid off when she introduced him to Georges Braque – the only major modern master temporarily out of contract and wanting to move dealers.

Aimé took a tremendous gamble starting a gallery in 1945. The trading situation in Paris was challenging as the nation faced continuing violence, material deprivation and political uncertainty. The Fall of France and the Occupation were

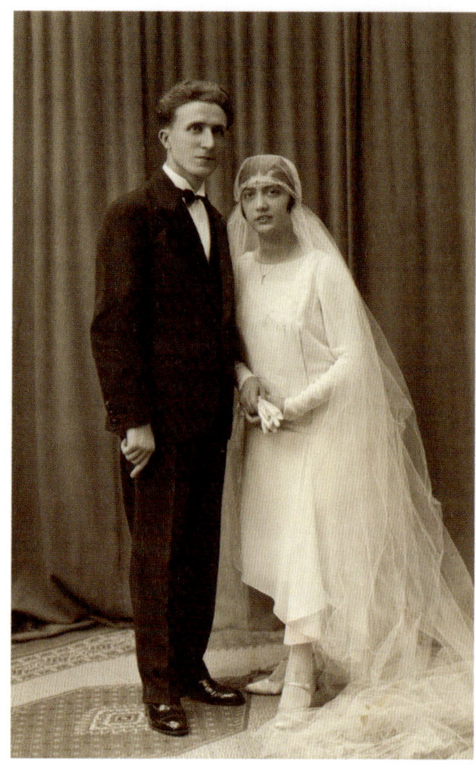

FIG. 2
Aimé and Marguerite Maeght at their wedding in Cannes, 1928

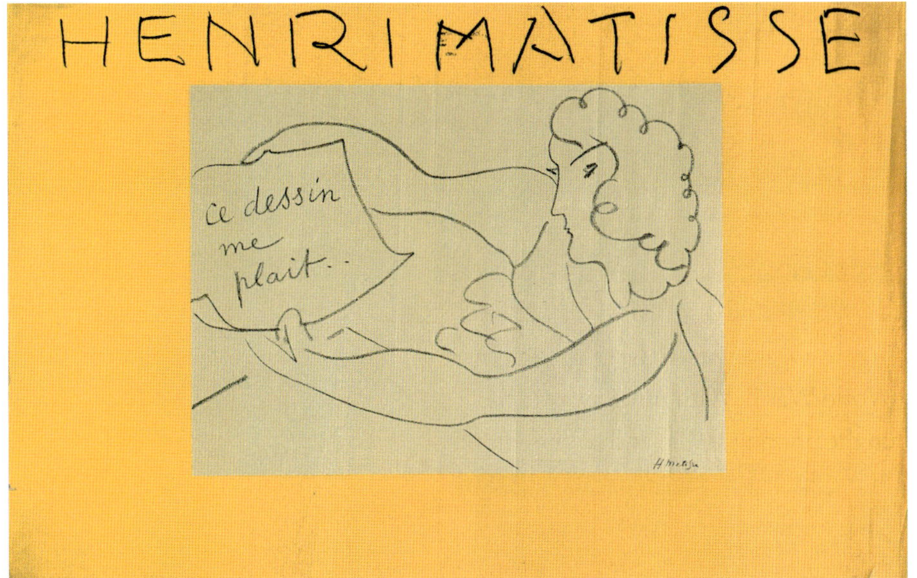

inevitably linked with a general cultural collapse. No single artistic style emerged to dominate the period, and competing salons opened in Paris to champion their various causes. The communists adopted a form of Social Realism as their official style. With the support of the Salon des Réalités Nouvelles and the Galerie Denise René, international Constructivism emerged as the only movement seriously concerned with building a better tomorrow. The Surrealists in exile in the United States during the war had been discredited: nothing they had dreamt up could compete with the reality of the death camps. The new heroes for a generation coming to terms with violence, alienation and loss were the Existentialists, led by such literary giants as Jean-Paul Sartre, who had been prominent in the Resistance. For the post-war generation, the classical figurative style had been closed off by the Nazis and tainted as a vocabulary of oppression. Drawing on Dada iconoclasm, Surrealist automatism, Paul Klee and alternative sources such as tribal and psychotic art, artists as varied as Wols, Bram and Geer van Velde, Antonin Artaud, Henri Michaux, Jean Dubuffet, Hans Hartung, Pierre Soulages and Jean Fautrier – often loosely grouped under the label 'Informel' and many of whom Maeght was to exhibit in exhibitions for young artists called 'Les Mains éblouies' – worked in styles ranging from expressive gestural abstraction to primitivist Art Brut figuration. Nicolas de Staël stood slightly outside this group in his reworking of Braque-like themes drawn from reality in a sensually articulated *matière*.

Picasso's status as the premier artist remained undisputed. Courted by both sides of the political divide, he nailed his colours to the mast in October 1945 by joining the Communist Party. John Richardson has attributed Braque's continued alienation from Picasso to the fact that Braque had drifted towards the opposite political pole, sympathising with the decidedly right-wing war veterans' association the Croix-de-Feu.[6] Meanwhile, in the catalogue of the 'Picasso–Matisse' exhibition at the Victoria and Albert Museum in 1945, Picasso, represented by contemporary work and by reproductions of both *Guernica*

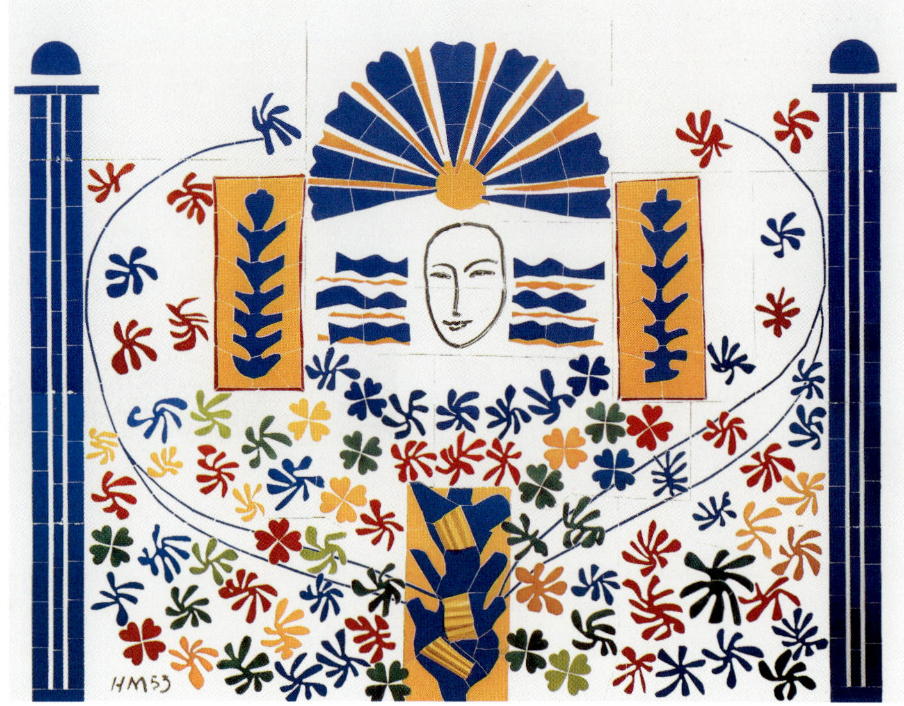

FIG. 4
Henri Matisse (1869–1954), *Apollo*, 1953.
Ceramic tile, ground marble, and plaster,
334 x 425 cm. Toledo Museum of Art, Ohio.
Purchased with funds from the Libbey
Endowment, gift of Edward Drummond
Libbey, 1983.40

(1937, Museo Reina Sofia, Madrid) and *The Charnel House* (1945, Museum of
Modern Art, New York), was held up as a moral conscience of the age for dealing
head-on with the theme of violence, whereas Matisse, with a selection of paintings
from throughout his career, was taken to exemplify the seductive charm of the
French tradition. Stung by this distinction, Matisse discovered in the paper cut-
out process a way of uniting line and colour in a truly innovative decorative art
that came to a conclusion in 1948–51 at the Chapel of the Rosary, Vence, and in
1953 in the glorious ceramic mural *Apollo* (fig. 4). Picasso moved on to Matisse's
ground but in a different mode. After staying in Paris during the Occupation as a
symbol of resistance, he moved to the south in the summer of 1946 and, having
been loaned the vast salon of the Château Grimaldi in Antibes, took up where
Matisse had left off in 1906 with *The Joy of Life* (*La joie de vivre*) (1905–06, Barnes
Foundation, Merion, Pennsylvania), and embarked on a series of Dionysian murals
with classical figures cavorting before a schematised Mediterranean landscape of
sand, sea and sky.

One of Aimé's great strengths as a dealer was that he fully understood
and supported his artists' aspirations to go beyond small-scale easel painting into
mural-sized paintings, ceramics, stained glass, prints and illustrated books. In
1946, 1951 and 1958 the Galerie Maeght staged a series of exhibitions entitled
'Sur quatre murs', which were specifically designed to promote contemporary
mural-sized paintings in the decoration of modern rooms. Among the artists
featured were Jean Bazaine, Braque, Marc Chagall, Giacometti, Léger, Matisse,
Miró, Picasso, Georges Rouault and Pierre Tal-Coat. Maeght artists produced
site-specific works for the Fondation Maeght when it opened, and mural-sized
paintings, ceramics and mosaics became a feature of the permanent collection.

Aimé, who was one of the first to exhibit Abstract Expressionism in Europe, responded to the scale of the new American painting by demonstrating the continuance of a vital European modern tradition of large-scale painting. Bonnard's pastoral *Summer* (*L'Eté*) (1917; cat. 1) combines the classical with the contemporary in a Rococo evocation of happiness, *un rêve de bonheur*, set in the French countryside. Decorative projects such as ceramic murals and stained glass engendered by Matisse's paper cut-outs were complemented by a series of large-scale independent drawings on paper, for example *The Bush* (*Le Buisson*) (1951; cat. 10), in which he pantheistically came to identify with the growth, death and regeneration of trees – his final metaphor for a life lived through creation.

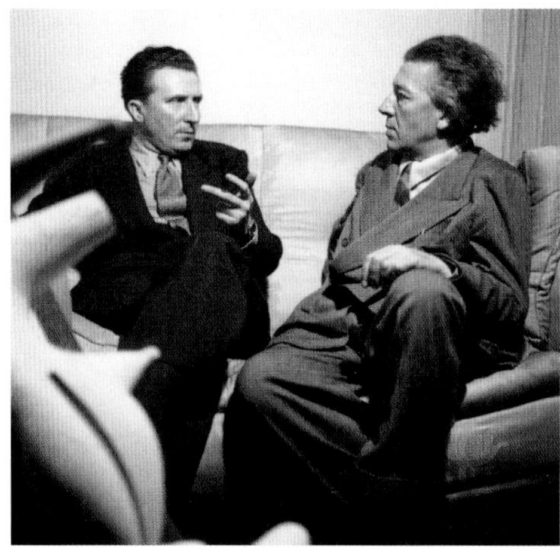

Faced with this plethora of post-war styles, the Maeghts evolved the highly successful strategy of structuring their business around a group of well-established artists and then varying the programme with exhibitions devoted to younger artists and with shows and publications with a historical theme. The prime example was the 'Exposition internationale du surréalisme en 1947', organised by André Breton (fig. 5) and Marcel Duchamp, which established the gallery's radical chic reputation. It may also have confirmed Aimé in his belief in the link between art and poetry.

The backbone of established artists – Miró, Giacometti, Calder and Chagall – had been nurtured and given an identity in the American market by Matisse's son Pierre. The Pierre Matisse Gallery opened in New York in 1931. Miró first exhibited there in 1932. Giacometti made his debut with Matisse in 1937. Chagall was first included in a group exhibition, 'Artists in Exile', in March 1942, along with Amedée Ozenfant, Fernand Léger, Jacques Lipchitz, André Masson, Ossip Zadkine, Yves Tanguy, André Breton and Piet Mondrian, then given a solo exhibition later that year. Stressful as the relationship between Matisse and Maeght became, Pierre acknowledged that his artists wanted the European exposure that Aimé was happy to provide.[7] These older artists proved essential to the survival of the Galerie Maeght, as younger artists often did not sell.[8]

With his background in lithography, printing and advertising, Aimé also saw publishing activities as an integral part of his business. It was his chosen *métier*. Gallery artists were encouraged to produce prints and limited-edition books. Each major exhibition was accompanied by an issue of the Maeghts' in-house periodical, *Derrière Le Miroir*, featuring essays by leading writers, coupled with original lithographs. These served as souvenirs and at the same time promoted Maeght artists by providing the texts to frame their critical reception. Issues of *Derrière Le Miroir* soon became collectors' items.

No other contemporary gallery could match the Maeghts' publications. They produced a succession of literary reviews devoted to the arts and commissioned and published monographs on their artists. The directors of the Galerie Maeght were respected literary figures. The first, the young poet Jacques Kober, whose *Le Vent des épines* (1947) was illustrated by Braque, Bonnard and Matisse, initiated the review *Pierre à feu* in 1944. Matisse's striking cover for the

1947 edition (fig. 29, page 40) established a benchmark for other artists in its integration of text, colour and image, the central explosive crown of abstracted black and blue palm branches blasting the letters and two whale-like red and green shapes to the periphery.

The Maeghts used the lithographers Mourlot Imprimeurs and other specialist graphic workshops before developing their own facilities, staffed by skilled technicians, where artists could explore and combine different graphic media. The artists built up essential creative relationships with the specialist technicians. Braque, for instance, working with the master lithographer Henri Deschamps at Mourlot, took infinite pains to achieve a precise tonal balance between colours, as can be seen in the restrained, very beautiful lithograph *Teapot and Lemons* (*Théière et citrons*) (1949; cat. 99), with the suggestively spouted black teapot set off by two fragrant lemons against a grey background.[9] Miró, on the other hand, liked to juxtapose different media for expressive effect, the raw impact of a burning red planet in aquatint, for instance, against an incised engraving line weaving into space. His immense lithographs (cats 110–12) acquired the status of easel paintings – but at an accessible price.

Adrien Maeght, a skilled printer in his own right, inherited his father's interests, opening his own gallery in Paris in 1956 at 42 rue de Bac. In 1964 he created the printing house Arte-Adrien Maeght. It was Adrien who encouraged Calder to adapt his metalworking procedure to printmaking by welding cut-metal shapes on to copper printing plates and then inking them.[10] With their combined energies and enthusiasm, the Maeghts soon became the largest publishers of original graphics in the world.

It may well have been Bonnard who awakened Aimé's interest in the possibilities of fine-art graphics. In 1936 the artist brought in a poster for printing to L'Imprimerie Robaudy in Cannes, where Aimé was working, and complimented him on his judicious balance of 'the beige and the red with the flesh tone'.[11] Bonnard had first made his name as a graphic artist when his lithograph poster *France-Champagne* appeared on the streets of Paris in March 1891, and he went on to design the poster for the avant-garde *La Revue blanche* (1894; fig. 6), which served as a model for Aimé's subsequent reviews, as he acknowledged with his *La Revue blanche* exhibition at the Galerie Maeght in 1966.

Bonnard's first illustrated book of lithographs, *Parallèlement* (1900), commissioned by Vollard, went against the fashion for crisply defined woodcut images and broke new ground in achieving an equivalent for Paul Verlaine's often highly erotic poems. Softly sensual pink lines caress the forms of a female nude in a sequence of recumbent poses: tossed back in ecstasy over the poem 'Séguidille' (fig. 7); splayed out on her front underneath 'Auburn'; and both sitting up and collapsed on crumpled bed sheets beneath 'L'Eté', her love-befuddled head lost in a hazy cloud.[12]

Although poorly received at the time, *Parallèlement* set a standard that was rivalled only in the 1930s, when publishers and major artists again took up the

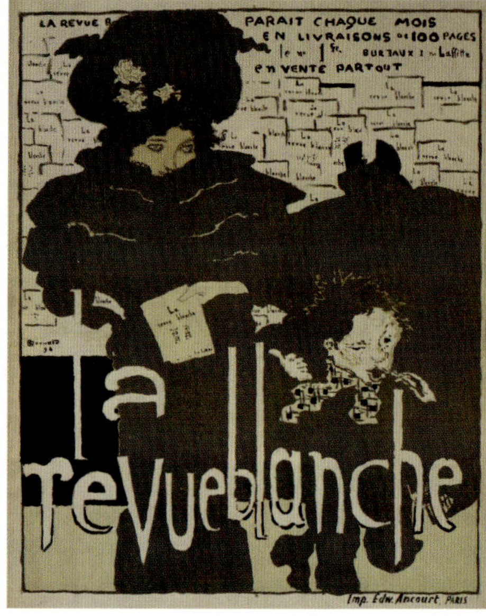

FIG. 6
Pierre Bonnard (1867–1947), poster for
La Revue blanche, 1894. Lithograph in four
colours, 81 x 62.5 cm. The Metropolitan
Museum of Art, New York. Purchase, gift of
Joy. E Feinberg of Berkeley, California, 1986
(1986.1081)

challenge of producing illustrated books. The young Swiss publisher Albert Skira commissioned Matisse to illustrate an edition of the poems of Stéphane Mallarmé, and Picasso to illustrate Ovid's *Metamorphoses* in 1930. Both artists employed a highly refined classical style of line drawing that set the tone of the 1930s. Mallarmé's diamond-like perfection found a direct equivalent in Matisse's etching style. Not to be outdone, Vollard went on to commission illustrated books from Picasso and Braque that reveal their very different responses to classicism. Picasso's so-called 'Vollard Suite' (1930–37) employed classical mythology as a vehicle with which to explore in a linear language emotional extremes, passionate love and violence. Braque selected a pre-classical archaic text of the eighth century BC, Hesiod's *Theogony*, to cut back to the origins of Western culture, with the figures emerging as in a creation myth from a lilting network of encircling lines. Vollard was killed in a car crash in 1939 and Aimé bought the plates and published a deluxe edition of *Theogony* in 1955 (cat. 92).

Reviews and limited-edition illustrated books were the ideal media for Aimé to put into practice his collaborative ideal of writers working with artists. Pierre Reverdy, whose review, *Nord–Sud*, set Miró on the path to Paris, bridged the divide between Braque's earlier poet mentors, Mallarmé, Guillaume Apollinaire and Max Jacob, and a post-World War II generation of writers. He collaborated with Braque on two illustrated books, *Une Aventure méthodique* (1950) and *La Liberté des mers*, published by Maeght Editeur in 1959 (cat. 93). Jean Paulhan, a former editor of *La Nouvelle Revue française*, published *Braque le Patron* in 1946, based on his first-hand experience of watching Braque moving between his canvases 'like a gardener between his plants'.[13] This stimulated the interest of a younger generation. Francis Ponge wrote nine essays on Braque, and *Cinq Sapates* (1950) – a book of prose poems with five Braque illustrations. The poet René Char developed a close working relationship with the artist, contributing essays on him for issues of *Derrière Le Miroir* in 1947 and 1950 and collaborating with him on a series of illustrated books, culminating in *Lettera Amorosa*, published in 1963, shortly before the artist's death.[14] On his return to Paris in 1945, Giacometti attracted a circle of writers. Jean Genet's *L'Atelier de Giacometti* and an essay on him by Jean-Paul Sartre came out in the May 1954 issue of *Derrière Le Miroir*. Poetry and friendship with poets remained a constant source of inspiration for Miró. He first met Tristan Tzara and Pierre Reverdy in 1921 and began to illustrate, working on books by Benjamin Péret and Alice Paalen. Jacques Prévert, the polymath author, poet and scriptwriter and a Maeght favourite, collaborated on two of the Maeghts' greatest illustrated books: Calder's *Fêtes* (1971; cat. 97) and Miró's *Adonides* (1975; cat. 98).

Aimé's recruitment of Braque, the quintessential French modern master with the credentials to match Picasso and Matisse, was a major coup. His invention, with Picasso, of Cubism stands as the most revolutionary innovation in twentieth-century art, weaning artists away from a dependence on the object and permitting a wealth of associations in the interplay of created form. For

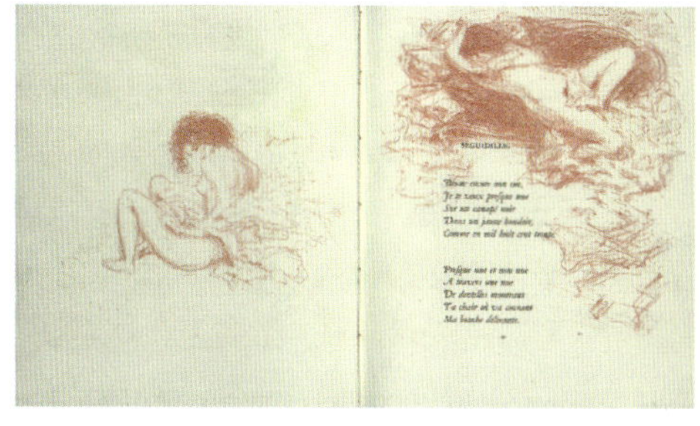

Pierre Bonnard (1867–1947), 'Séguidille', from *Parallèlement*, text by Paul Verlaine, 1900. Lithograph printed in rose ink, 30.5 x 25 cm. The Metropolitan Museum of Art, New York. The Elisha Whittelsey Collection, the Elisha Whittelsey Fund, 1970 (1970.713)

Braque, Cubism was concerned not so much with new ways of giving a multiplicity of information about the formal properties of objects as with 'research into space', best carried out in the controlled conditions of the studio and the still-life arrangement.[15] Like musical notes, forms had to be limited and the palette restricted in order to explore the sonority of their relationships in space. Braque described this space as 'tactile, even manual'.[16] The key event in Braque's development of Cubism, and the linchpin of his future art, was his discovery in September 1912 of the *papier collé* (literally 'glued paper') technique, which brought colour back into his work. The break made it stilted and also acted as a catalyst in his increasingly complex art of relationships between the resonant impact of *matière* – the experience of the physical reality of the painted surface, of shape and colour – and the 'illusion' of what is represented or just suggested.

By 1945, Braque's status as one of the leading French modern masters, along with Matisse, was assured. He won the first prize for a foreign artist at the Venice Biennale in 1948, and in 1953 was commissioned by the Louvre to paint a ceiling decoration for the Salle Henri II (see fig. 8). In a sense, as the co-originator of Cubism, his achievements had been written into the annals of modern art. But in another more profound way his suffering and near death in the trenches of World War I and his continuing to work against all odds during World War II turned him into an icon for a post-war generation similarly isolated, alienated and obsessed both with the metaphysical and with the nature of their own creativity. Far from slowing down he went on to create some of the greatest paintings in the history of European art.

Four themes dominated: billiard tables, ateliers or studios, birds and landscapes. The nine large *Ateliers* (see fig. 9), Braque's masterpieces, are his culminating meditations on the nature of a life lived through making art. Their principal subject is not the external. The viewer's journey into breadth is interrupted by overplays of successive veiled and overt allusions, palimpsests of previous forms, memories and observations. Space no longer exists as a finite entity. Air and light are drained into pigment, voids, acting as black holes absorbing matter. Nothing is given a concrete reality. In a highly revealing statement to John Richardson, Braque explained: 'I have made a great discovery: I no longer believe in anything. Objects don't exist for me except insofar as a rapport exists between them or between them and myself. When one attains this harmony, one reaches a sort of intellectual non-existence – what one can only describe as a sense of peace – which makes everything possible and right.'[17] In pursuing a transcendental path, with all the paradoxes and contradictions that this implied for an arch Cubist with a classical bent, Braque found reassurance in and parallels with Eastern religions. According to Alex Danchev, Braque's biographer, Braque had a long-standing love of the *Tao Te Ching*.[18] He illustrated not only the Tibetan saint Milarepa's *Songs* in a book published by Maeght in 1950 but also a special edition of *Zen in the Art of Archery* (*Le Zen dans l'art chevaleresque du tir à l'arc*), published in 1960, which included a selection of his own aphorisms.[19]

FIG. 8

Georges Braque painting a ceiling decoration for the Salle Henri II at the Louvre, Paris, 1953

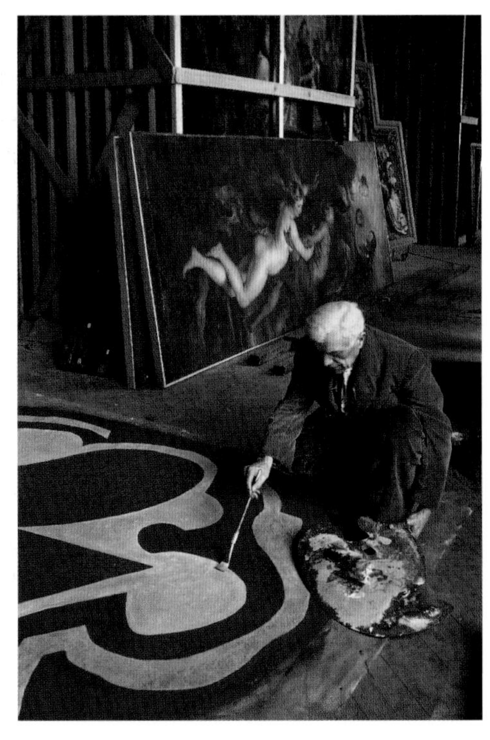

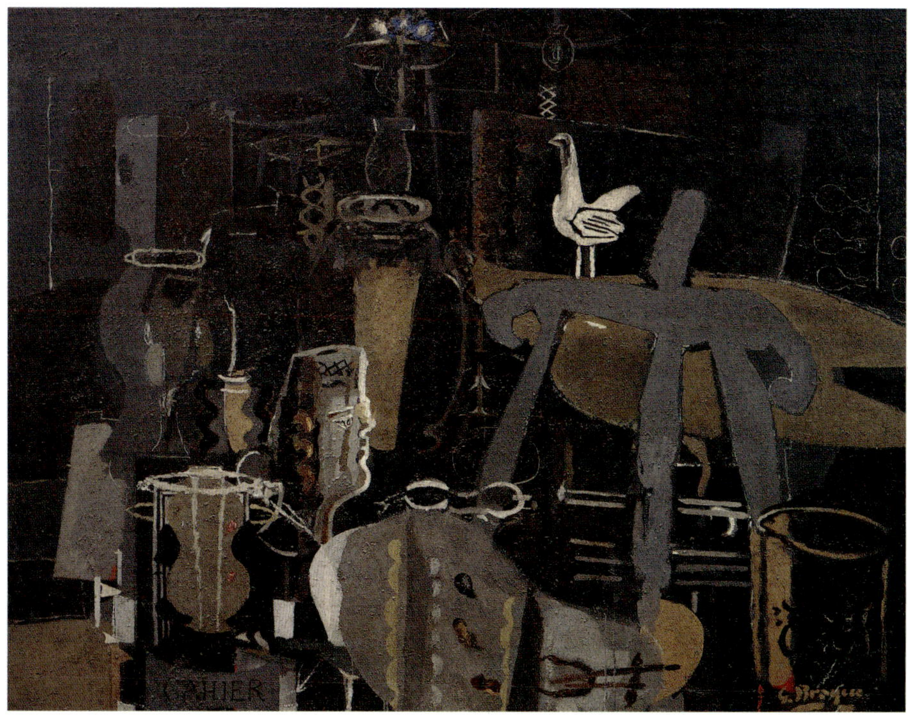

FIG. 9
Georges Braque (1882–1963), *Atelier VI*, 1950–51. Oil on canvas, 130 x 162.5 cm. Fondation Marguerite et Aimé Maeght, Saint-Paul

The strange birds suspended in flight across the studio are not to be read as literal symbols: their meaning and function changes from painting to painting, and they also appear as the central subject of a separate series of works. Are they metaphors for artistic aspiration, harbingers of death or signs of the human spirit? It is significant that Braque chose a bird for the stained-glass window in St Bernard's Chapel at the Fondation Maeght (fig. 10).

In Alberto Giacometti the Galerie Maeght acquired post-war Paris's artist of the moment, who had been adopted by the leading Existentialist writers as their principal image-maker. He answered their need for an artist who could encapsulate Braque's sombre, introspective mood and sense of mortality in a novel figurative art dealing overtly, as they saw it, with the predicament of an alienated, isolated generation coming to terms with the violence and destruction of the war. His lonely, attenuated figures are both living presences and, in the context of post-war Paris, Greek funeral stelae reborn, the war memorials of our time. Jean-Paul Sartre himself provided the catalogue essay for the Giacometti exhibition at the Pierre Matisse Gallery in New York in 1948. 'At first glance,' he observed, 'we seem to be up against the fleshless martyrs of Buchenwald.'[20] No other artist seemed quite as relevant. On going to Paris in 1947, the young English critic David Sylvester noted a dearth of exciting new art, with the exception of the current work of Giacometti. Imported copies of the Matisse Gallery catalogue, with the essay by Sartre and studio photographs by Patricia Matisse, passed 'with a sort of reverence from hand to hand'.[21]

What is now known is the extent to which Giacometti was complicit in the construction of his own myth, inviting writers to his studio, feeding them insights into his work and even annotating their texts. His tiny, dark studio at 46

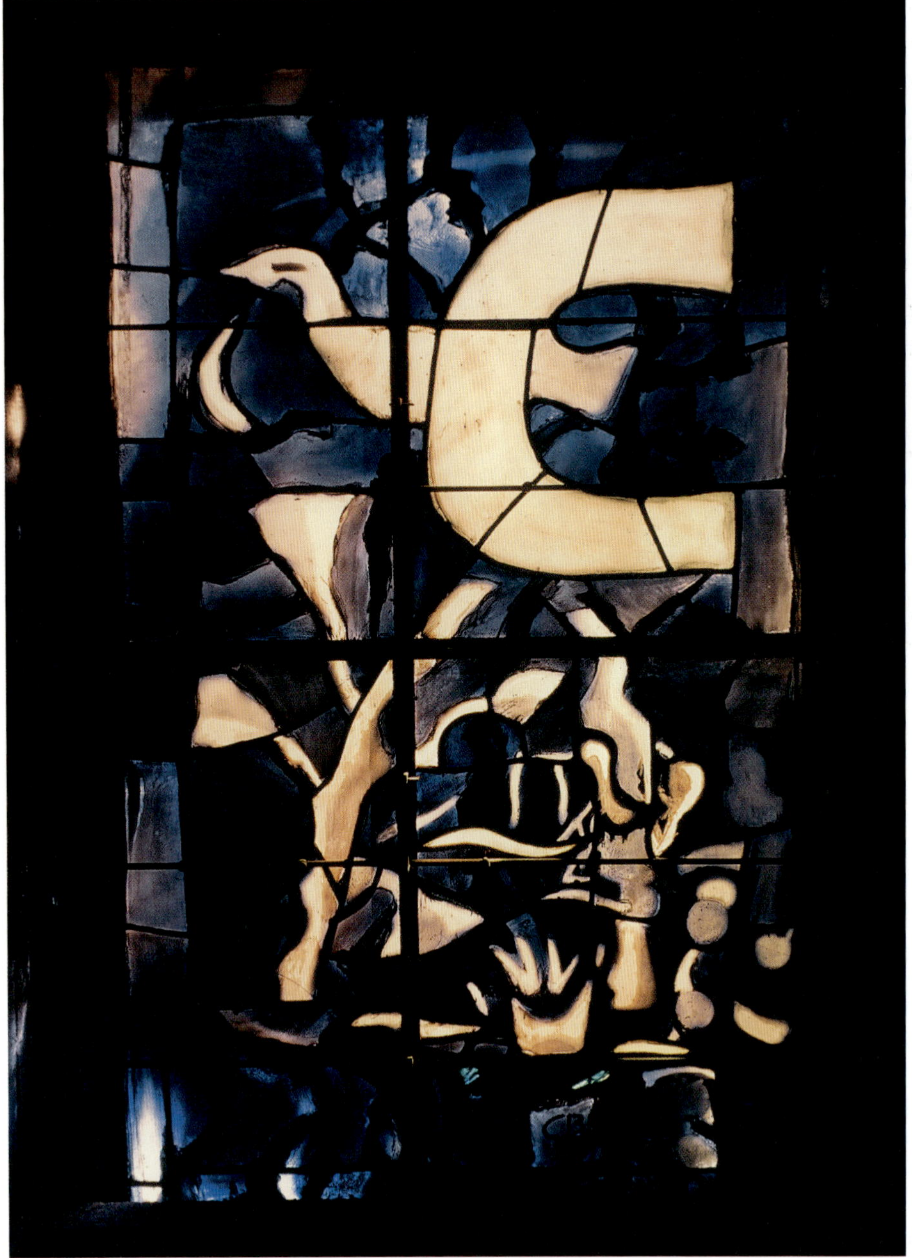

rue Hippolyte-Maindron, into which he moved in December 1926, became
a shrine, peopled by his cult figures, where the influential were initiated. Jean
Genet, in his essay on the studio, promulgated analogies with temples, worship
and mortality. With Giacometti's figures placed in a bedroom, 'the bedroom
becomes a temple'. To the dead, Giacometti's work 'communicates knowledge
of the solitude of each being and of each thing, and that this solitude is our surest
glory'. Recognising that the origins of the standing solitary female figures lay in
Giacometti's experiences in his favourite brothels, Genet explained, 'He entered
these places almost like a worshipper. He went there so as to see himself kneeling
before some implacable and distant divinity.'[22]

    The signing of Joan Miró brought something new to the Galerie
Maeght. The sacerdotal gloom of Braque and Giacometti's studios was replaced

by Miróland – an airy cosmos inhabited by a phantasmagoria of primordial creatures, a modern Altamira opened out against the sky. The transition to light symbolised a testament of faith in the future. With his passion for poetry and interest in graphic art, Miró was just the artist Aimé wanted for his gallery. Having been introduced to Miró by André Breton at the Galerie Maeght's Surrealist exhibition in 1947, Aimé gave Miró an exhibition in Paris the following year.

Miró knew both Braque and Giacometti and had close links with the American Alexander Calder, another addition to the gallery stable, while at the same time his work appealed to a younger generation of European and American abstract–symbolist image-makers. When Miró began his annual sojourns in Paris in 1920, Braque was among the modern masters he most admired.[23] Between 1920 and 1925, Miró's art rapidly evolved from the detailed realism of his early masterpiece *The Farm* (*La masia*) (1921–22, National Gallery of Art, Washington, D.C.) – which acts as a key to his subsequent cast of creatures – to, in *The Tilled Field* (*Terra llaurada*) (1923–24, Solomon R. Guggenheim Museum, New York), a new, more synthetic form of realism stimulated by recent developments in Paris. In a letter dated 10 August 1924, from his family's farm at Montroig near Tarragona, to the ethnographer and Surrealist writer Michel Leiris, Miró described his continued move away from external reality: 'My latest canvases are conceived like a bolt from the blue, absolutely detached from the outer world (the world of men who have two eyes in the space below their forehead).'[24] Nature is reduced to a system of signs. Woman in *Maternity* (*Maternité*) (1924, Scottish National Gallery of Modern Art, Edinburgh) is represented by just four elements precariously balanced at the end of crossed wires floating in space. Day-to-day contact with André Masson in Paris and his meeting with the poets Louis Aragon, André Breton and Philippe Soupault, the founders of Surrealism in 1924, confirmed and encouraged Miró's development of a hybrid art floating between painting and poetry.

Miró's transition to the dream paintings (cat. 12) was of immense significance for both Giacometti and Calder in their parallel moves away from external reality and traditional modes of representation. It was through Miró that Giacometti was attracted to Surrealism – the dissident Surrealism of Georges Bataille, Michel Leiris and the rue Blomet set rather than the more doctrinaire official version of Breton. 'Miró', Giacometti told the critic Pierre Schneider, 'was utter freedom. Something lighter, more aerial, more disengaged than I had ever seen. In a way, it was sheer perfection.'[25] The two artists remained lifelong friends. Specific characteristics, such as Miró's employment of stage-like bases in his object–sculptures to suggest self-contained worlds, were developed into major features of Giacometti's art (cat. 61). It is interesting to note that Michel Leiris compared of Miró's process of dematerialising the object to the spiritual exercise of a Tibetan ascetic – 'In this way, first the physical then the metaphysical void, the absolute, is comprehended'.[26]

Calder and Miró first met in 1928 and remained close friends until Calder's death in 1976. Initially trained as an engineer, Calder, whose father and grandfather were sculptors, went on to study at the Art Students' League in New York from 1923 until 1926, when he moved to Paris. He made an instant name for himself in avant-garde circles with his mechanical toy *Circus* (1926–31, Whitney Museum of American Art, New York), with which he performed in Paris and New York. On one level the *Circus* relates to Léger's interest in machine culture, but on another it has much in common with Miró, with whom Calder shared an interest in toys, folk cultures, the playful, the crude and the burlesque. In the longer term, a profound awareness of the planetary rhythms of the universe was, for both, a principal source of inspiration.

Miró's lifelong passion for folk art can be seen in the context of a general revival of interest by the Catalans in their native folk art. His teacher, José Pasco, wanted to revitalise the Catalan tradition. Above all, it was Antonio Gaudí who revealed to Miró the possibilities of a popular art form that drew on the past. Gaudí's Parque Güell (*c.* 1900–14), with its undulating benches faced with a mosaic of ceramic fragments containing a galaxy of sun and moon images, was being built during Miró's youth in Barcelona.[27]

Calder similarly drew extensively on childhood memories: gazing up at the night sky, San Francisco cable cars, folk festivals.[28] He was much taken by Miró's *Carnival of Harlequins* (*Le Carnaval d'Arlequin*) (1924–25; fig. 11), in which the normal hierarchies of scale and species are reversed in a crazy dance orchestrated by a festive flea. However, it was a meeting with Piet Mondrian in the latter's studio in 1930 that set Calder on the revolutionary path of balancing abstract shapes of colour suspended in space, 'floating' or 'drifting' like planetary models of the universe. When they were exhibited for the first time in Paris in 1931, at the Galerie Percier, Marcel Duchamp christened the moving sculptures 'mobiles' and Jean Arp's reference to the stationary wire abstractions as 'stabiles' was also adopted by Calder.[29] The close connection between Calder and Miró soon became lodged in the public domain. The headline of one review in 1936 of Calder's second exhibition at the Pierre Matisse Gallery read 'Calder's "Mobiles" are like living Miró abstractions'.[30]

After a hiatus of four years, Calder and Miró met up again in April 1937 at Varengeville-sur-Mer in Normandy, at the home of the American architect Paul Nelson, who had designed Braque's summer studio-home there in 1930. That spring they collaborated for the first time, on the Spanish Pavilion at the World's Fair in Paris. Commissioned by the Spanish Republican government to promote their embattled cause, the pavilion was designed by Josep Lluís Sert, the future architect of Miró's studio in Mallorca (fig. 12), the Fondation Marguerite et Aimé Maeght, and the Fundació Joan Miró in Barcelona. Miró's mural, *The Reaper (Catalan Peasant in Revolt)* (*Le Faucheur*), does not survive but Calder's *Mercury Fountain*, designed to bring attention to the plight of the Almadén mercury mines, besieged by Franco's forces, was given to the Fundació Miró.

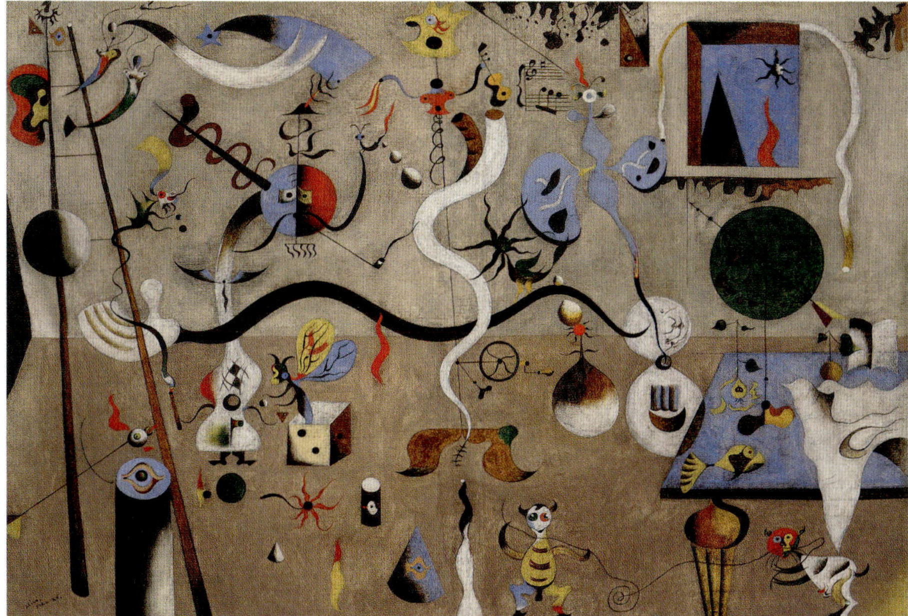

Cut off in Varengeville for the rest of the Spanish Civil War, Miró could only dream of returning home. Braque was a frequent visitor. The sight of crows in flight above the Normandy countryside inspired Miró's series of paintings on the theme, literally entitled *Flight of a Bird over the Plain* (*Le Vol de l'oiseau sur la plaine*). In an interview with James Johnson Sweeney, the organiser of his retrospective exhibition at the Museum of Modern Art, New York, in 1941, Miró recalled: 'Night, music and the stars began taking on an increasingly important role in the formation of my painting.'[31] His glorious *Constellation* series (1939–41; see cat. 46), begun at Varengeville and completed in Spain after his flight from France in 1940, marked, with its cast of creatures migrating across the cosmos in an abbreviated linear language, both the end of a terrible decade and a new beginning.

Miró's return to the Mediterranean and refuge in Barcelona and Mallorca, his mother's birthplace, constituted a quest for artistic and spiritual renewal, and it was during this period that he explored ideas that Aimé Maeght helped him to achieve on a large scale. His 'Working Notes 1941–42' contain a virtual agenda. He wanted somehow to get back to the origins of art through the physical experience of media: kneading clay, watching the drift of a wash, allowing brush marks to suggest signs for women, birds and animals. From watching Braque at work in his Varengeville studio, Miró learned that creation could begin with the building up of a ground. He wanted to explore ceramic and graphic techniques and to develop through his native folk tradition a monumental public art, 'a truly phantasmagoric world of living monsters'.[32] Working with clay and experimenting with ceramics under the direction of the master potter Josep Lloréns Artigas, he produced a whole series of maquettes, some of which were later enlarged into monumental sculptures. Renewal for Miró also meant sexual regeneration. The emphasis is on genitalia, penises and gaping vaginas, stressing their connection with primitive fertility gods and goddesses. 'Remember', Miró wrote in his 'Working

Notes', 'that in primitive, non-decadent races the sex organ was a magic sign of which man was proud, far from feeling the shame that today's decadent races feel.'[33] Many of these ceramic sculptures were first exhibited at the Galerie Maeght.

In 1948 Miró completed a mural for the Gourmet Restaurant of the Terrace Plaza Hotel, Cincinnati, and Calder made a *mobile* for the lobby. From 1955 to 1958 Miró collaborated with Lloréns Artigas on two large-scale ceramic walls for the new UNESCO building in Paris. In *Derrière Le Miroir* he described these ceramic murals as stemming from the caves of Altamira, Catalan Romanesque frescoes and Gaudí, and compared Lloréns Artigas to an alchemist whose researches into clays, sandstone enamels and colours were a 'true act of creation'.[34] But his first opportunity to combine ceramics and sculpture on a large scale in a total environment, a Miróland, came with the commission to contribute to the Fondation Marguerite et Aimé Maeght at Saint-Paul.

On Léger's advice, Aimé looked at foundations in the United States – notably the Barnes Foundation outside Philadelphia, with Matisse's mural of dancers rising and falling in the rhythm of the lunettes above the French windows in the main hall; the Phillips Collection in Washington, D.C., with its outstanding selection of modern masters; and the Solomon R. Guggenheim Museum, its innovative signature building by Frank Lloyd Wright still, at the time, under construction in New York. But Aimé came up with something new. His foundation was going to be more than just a repository for the family collection in a magnificent setting. It had to act as a creative centre for the arts, with space for temporary exhibitions, poetry readings and music, as well as including a library and accommodation. In fact, he envisaged a temple dedicated to a new religion: modern art. Picasso had set the ball rolling in 1949 when he gave his entire summer's output to the Château Grimaldi at Antibes. Renamed the Musée Picasso, it became the first in a succession of shrines dedicated to the modern masters whose work would attract cultural tourists to the Côte d'Azur in great numbers.[35]

Braque and Léger's initial suggestion of a foundation as a memorial to the Maeghts' young son Bernard, who had died of leukaemia in 1953, was given substance when the potential site on a hill outside Saint-Paul overlooking the sea revealed a little ruined chapel dedicated to St Bernard. It was therefore fitting that Braque was subsequently commissioned to provide the design for the stained-glass window of a new chapel on the site, featuring a mysterious white bird drifting through deep violet (fig. 10). However, it was Josep Lluís Sert and Joan Miró who were undoubtedly the principal inspirations behind the Fondation Maeght. Aimé was deeply impressed by Sert's new studio for Miró, similarly located on a hill overlooking the Mediterranean, at Cala Mayor just outside Palma de Mallorca. Its crisp, white, concrete architecture framed surfaces of local stone and terracotta, with a roof rounded to suggest either waves or the curved wings of gliding gulls silhouetted against the pine trees and sky above the sea. The whole seemed to Aimé to be so appropriate to a Mediterranean setting that he commissioned

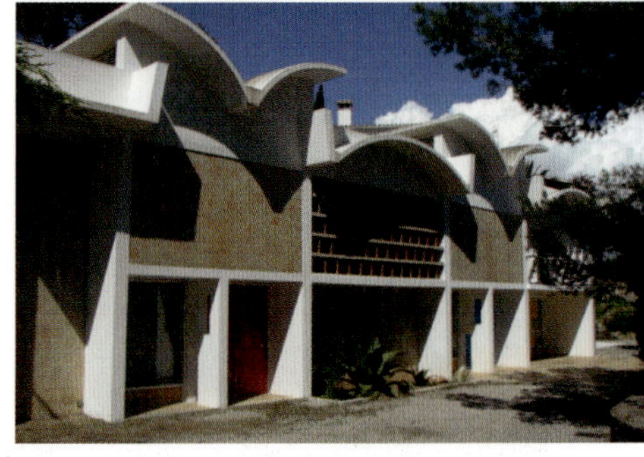

FIG. 12
Joan Miró's studio at Cala Mayor, Mallorca, designed by Josep Lluís Sert, 1956

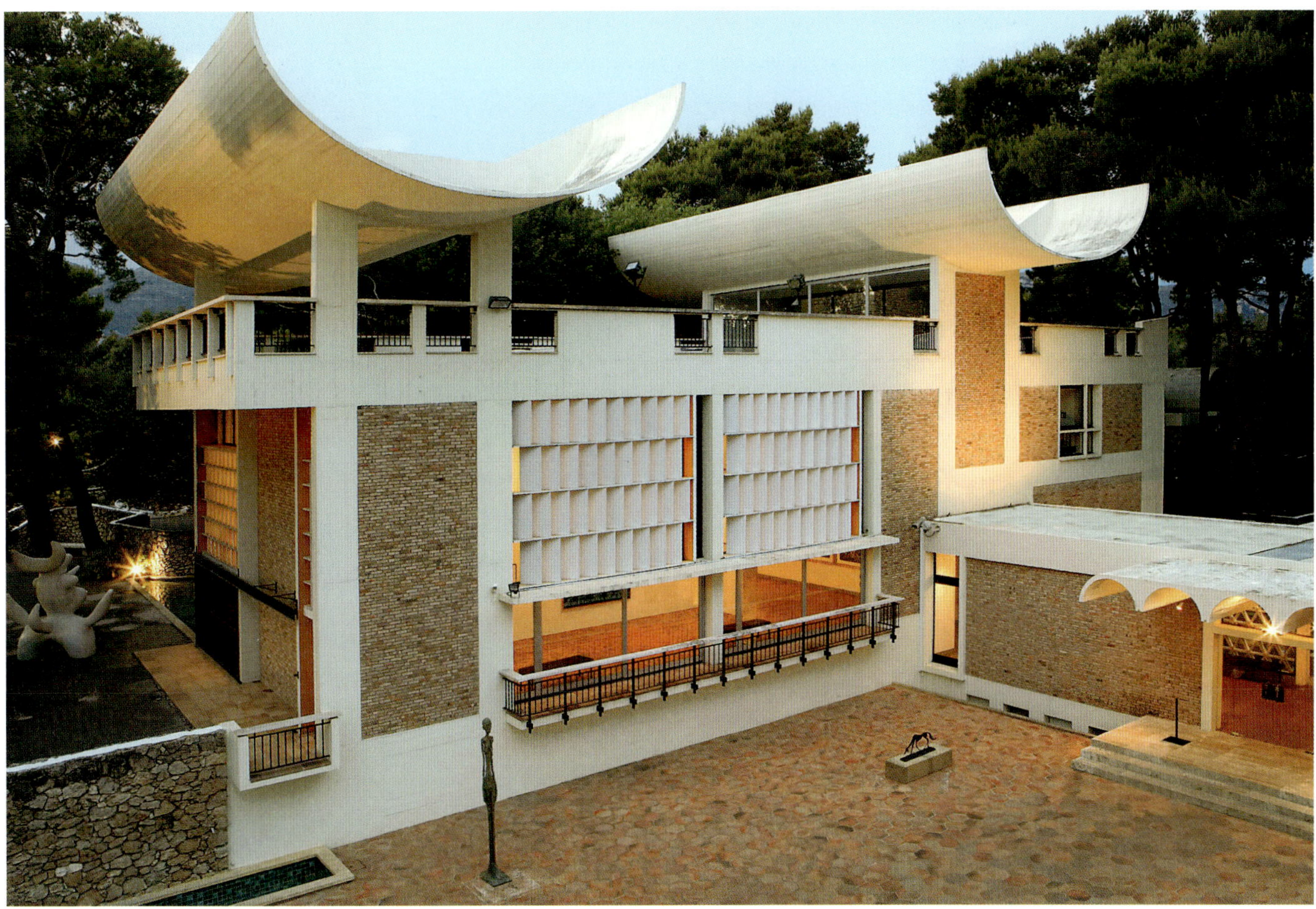

Sert to design his foundation.[36] Construction began in 1960 (see fig. 33, page 44) and the official inauguration by André Malraux took place on 28 July 1964.

Sert's Fondation Maeght crowning a hill outside Saint-Paul is a masterpiece (fig. 13). The seemingly conflicting ambitions of temple site, modern art centre and Mediterranean walled hill village are brilliantly reconciled in a sequence of interlocking courtyards, terraces, ponds and gardens, complete with a labyrinth. Great care was taken to maintain a connection with the original site and the local vernacular: pine trees were preserved and incorporated into the design, the bricks were specially baked from local clay, and a typical Provençal wall was built round the garden, facing the *ville perchée* of Saint-Paul. Sert, who at the time of the commission in 1957 was working for his former teacher, Le Corbusier, on the Carpenter Center for the Visual Arts at Harvard University, continued at the Fondation Maeght the university monastic tradition of building around quadrangles. The names 'Mairie' (town hall) for the main administration and exhibition block and 'Cloister' for the building opposite with its sequence of galleries are a reminder of the Fondation's divergent origins.

Jan Birksted argues in *Modernism and the Mediterranean: The Maeght Foundation* (Aldershot, 2004) that, in addition, it was the great Minoan temple of Knossos on the island of Crete – dedicated to bull worship and the myth of the terrifying bull–man, the Minotaur, incarcerated in the labyrinth – that provided the overriding inspiration for both Sert's building and Miró's iconographic programme.[37] The white concrete roofs of the Mairie are swept up like the crescent horns of Miró's signature sculptures *Moon Bird* (*L'Oiseau lunaire*) and *Sun Bird* (*L'Oiseau solaire*) (both 1968), the presiding deities of his *Labyrinth* (see fig. 14). The source of both the giant white *Moon Bird*, cut out of Carrara marble, and *Sun Bird* lies in a little *siurell* – a Mallorcan penny whistle in the form of a bull. Miró believed these could be traced back, via the Phoenician occupation of the neighbouring island of Ibiza, to the pre-Tanagra terracottas of Greece and the Eastern Mediterranean, which served not only as cult objects and votive offerings at shrines and funerals but also as toys. It is typical of his view of the past that he should see the *siurells* and, by extension, his own art as belonging to an ancient tradition of magical image-making that survived only in the form of folk art.[38]

Miró collaborated with Sert and Llorens Artigas on the construction of the *Labyrinth*, the principal installation at the Fondation Maeght. Our staggered journey up, or down, the *Labyrinth* takes us on a primordial path of mythological awakening. The ovoid, pebble-like, white Carrara marble *Woman with Hair Down* (*Femme à la chevelure défaite*) (1968) rests on a rock in the middle of a little pond, flanked by the rampant *Moon Bird* – phallic horns erect, ready for action – on one side, and *Sun Bird*, silhouetted on a plinth above the rampart, on the other, symbolising, Birksted suggests, the myth of Ariadne, who was associated with the moon. In addition, the ritual marriage of the ruler of Crete and the moon-priestess of Knossos 'seems to have been understood as one between Sun and Moon'.[39] At the end of the terrace, a totemic figure with a circular sun–moon hole for a head, holding an eponymous *Pitchfork* (*La Fourche*) (1963; fig. 33) like a five-pronged wind vane, signals a trajectory across the sky. Up the steps on the terrace above, the fertility *Goddess* (*Déesse*) (1963), split open to reveal a giant vagina, gapes at the enormous ceramic *Egg* (*L'Œuf*) (1963), glazed with the cosmological signs of sun and moon, in the middle of another small pond. Further along the terrace, the ceramic *Sundial* (*Cadran solaire*) (1973), with red, yellow, green and blue islands floating in a celestial firmament between black clouds and the surrounding white base, encapsulates the rhythms of earth, air, fire and water in essential form and acts as a cosmological compass. The biomorphic *Arch* (*L'Arc*) (1963), complete with bull's horns, crescent moons, solar circles and phallic protuberances, ends the earthly path through the *Labyrinth* and frames the sky. In *Derrière Le Miroir* the philosopher Henri Maldiney described it as 'the large living door, separating beast and man'.[40]

Sert managed to accommodate the individual vision of each of the main artists and show their work to best advantage. Giacometti was allocated the central courtyard (figs 15 and 16), framed on three sides by the Mairie, the Cloister and the entrance corridor that connects them. The fourth side is open to the sky and the pine trees, which now obscure the distant view of the sea. The courtyard takes on the appearance of one of Giorgio de Chirico's city squares, activated by the mysterious presences of Giacometti's *Standing Woman*

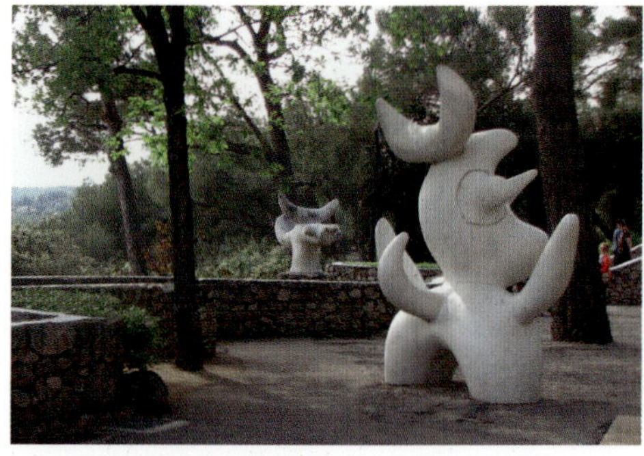

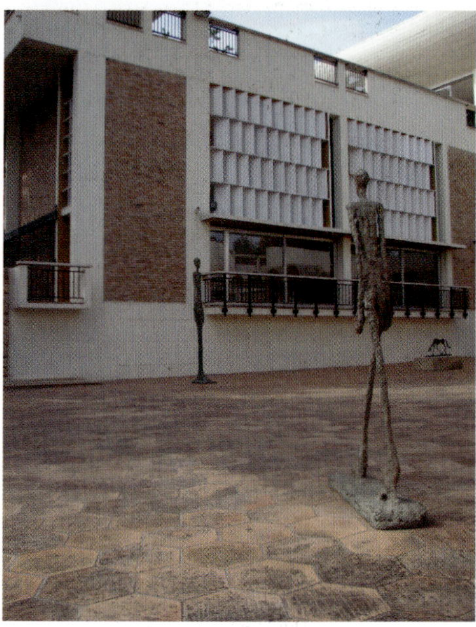

Joan Miró's *Labyrinth* at the Fondation Maeght, showing, in the foreground, *Moon Bird* (*L'Oiseau lunaire*) and, in the background, *Sun Bird* (*L'Oiseau solaire*), both 1968

The Giacometti courtyard at the Fondation Maeght, with *Walking Man II* (*L'Homme qui marche II*), 1960, in the foreground

(*Femme Debout*) *I* (cat. 86) and *II*, *Walking Man* (*L'Homme qui marche*) *I* (cat. 87) and *II* and *Bust* (*Buste*), all made in 1960 for the abortive commission for the Chase Manhattan Bank Plaza in New York. These are amplified by *Dog* (*Le Chien*) (1957; cat. 74) – Giacometti's canine alter ego – *The Cube* (*La Cube*) (1934–35) and a scaled-down version of *Women of Venice* (*Femmes de Venise*) (1956). The origin of *Bust* may well lie in a Roman bust of the Emperor Constantine in the Vatican Museums, but Giacometti's skeletal figures undermine the whole notion of self-confident classical statues dominating the surrounding space.[41] The essentially fragile and vulnerable sentinel figures *Standing Woman I and II* both command attention and yet remain distant. *Walking Man I and II* are driven pilgrims condemned to pace with remorseless strides. The ceiling of the gallery in the Cloister devoted to Giacometti was, on his advice, kept low to accentuate his smaller figures.

The Braque room looks out through a wall-to-ceiling glass window on to his pond mosaic *Fish* (*Les Poissons*) (1963; fig. 17), which recalls the decorations of Roman public baths – a reminder of his abiding interest in classical culture as a structuring French inheritance. The overall theme of the mosaic decorations is a unifying whiteness. In Chagall's *The Lovers* (*Les Amoureux*) (1964–65) the couple float free from isolated patches of colour to unite in marriage, just as all the colours of the image blend in the overall lightness of white. Pierre Tal-Coat's boundary wall *Mosaic Mural* (1963–64), inspired by the prehistoric cave paintings at Lascaux and Chinese graphic signs, playing against a fluctuating field of greys and whites, serves both to enclose space and also to open up the imagination. Calder's great black *stabile, Reinforcements* (*Les Renforts*) (1963; fig. 42, page 65) in the entrance garden, both phantom presence and archaic horseman resurrected in a modern form, chimes in with a general theme running through the architecture and commissioned works: a renaissance of the archaic in a contemporary temple dedicated to the arts.

The Maeghts' move beyond the founding generation of established modern masters included not only leading representatives of a pan-European post-war generation but also such outstanding Francophile Americans as Ellsworth Kelly, who first exhibited at the Galerie Maeght in 1958. Fascinated by the fragmentation, energy and identity of the separate forms in stained-glass windows, by the ceramic mosaics of Gaudí's Parque Güell, and by Picasso's Cubism and Matisse's paper cut-outs, Kelly went on to create a stunning art of shaped abstract forms interacting with and defining space.[42] His strikingly reduced design of a simple blue disk balanced by black lettering against white for an edition of *Derrière Le Miroir* devoted to his work (no. 110, October–November 1958) is one of the most successful of all the Maeght covers. Kelly still visits Saint-Paul and paints canvases inspired by colours found in the Fondation Maeght's garden: blue for the sky, yellow for the mimosas and red for other flowers.[43]

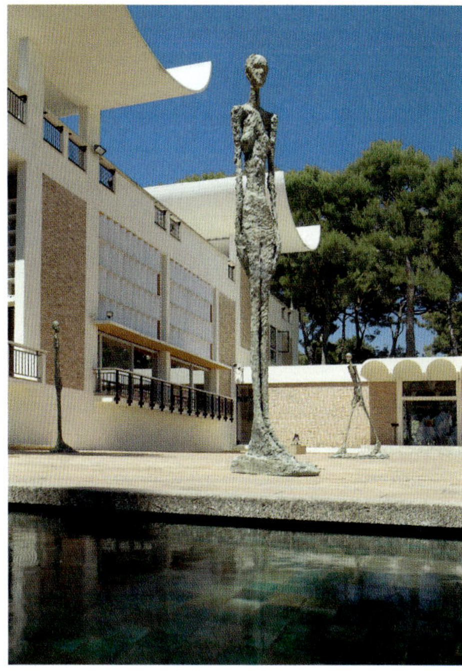

The Giacometti courtyard with *Standing Woman I* (*Femme debout I*) in the foreground

Of the loosely grouped Informel painters, Jean Bazaine, Jean-Paul Riopelle, Bram and Geer van Velde, Hans Hartung, Jean Dubuffet and Paul Rebeyrolle were all exhibited at the gallery and a Nicolas de Staël retrospective was staged at the Fondation Maeght in 1972. Karel Appel and Pierre Alechinsky, two of the leading lights of Cobra – one of the most vital of the post-war pan-European movements – were given a joint exhibition at the Fondation in 1982–83.

The Catalan–Basque connection fostered by Miró and Llorens Artigas continued with the painter Antoni Tàpies and the sculptor Eduardo Chillida, and in 1974 a branch of the Galerie Maeght opened in Barcelona. Though very different, the work of both artists grew out of a dialogue with materials. Chillida, a Maeght artist par excellence, is a prime example of an outstandingly gifted self-taught artist who drew extensively on the modern masters, classical Greek architecture and Oriental art to produce something radically new. After studying architecture in Madrid, he moved to Paris in 1948 and met Constantin Brancusi, Giacometti and Braque. Brancusi helped him to realise the torso in architectural terms, seeing the spaces between limbs 'like gaps between rocks', while Giacometti explained to him that 'to construct a feeling of the immensity of space you had to use a very small figure'.[44] Braque saw one of Chillida's sculptures at the Galerie Maeght and liked it so much that he contacted the Basque artist and gave him one of his series of *Birds*. A Braque bird operates both as image and object shaping space – a lesson Chillida never forgot. Miró opened up to him an expanded conception of space, the planetary rhythms of the universe, and the elements, earth, air, fire, water'.[45] Working with the Maeght facilities in collaboration with the technicians, Chillida produced both his special *terre chamottée* clay-ceramic sculptures and etchings such as those for Jorge Guillén's poem 'Más Allá'.

By the time of Marguerite's death in 1977 and Aimé's in 1981, the Maeght family enterprises had come a long way from the founding of Arte in Cannes. Their gallery and foundation countered America's post-war artistic hegemony and provided a platform for established artists and a younger generation to exhibit and meet. They supported their artists' aspiration to go beyond easel painting and traditional sculptures and explore other media, notably ceramics and graphics, and the building of the Fondation Maeght provided an opportunity for these artists to work and exhibit on a large scale. They helped to perpetuate the perception of Paris as the international centre of graphic art. Leading American galleries found it difficult to sell prints, so the Maeghts had taken a considerable risk in developing substantial graphic facilities with highly skilled technicians working directly with their artists. The sheer scale of the publishing venture Arte established an international benchmark. They produced a succession of literary reviews on the arts written by leading contemporary writers, and commissioned and published monographs on their artists. They published whole series of limited graphic

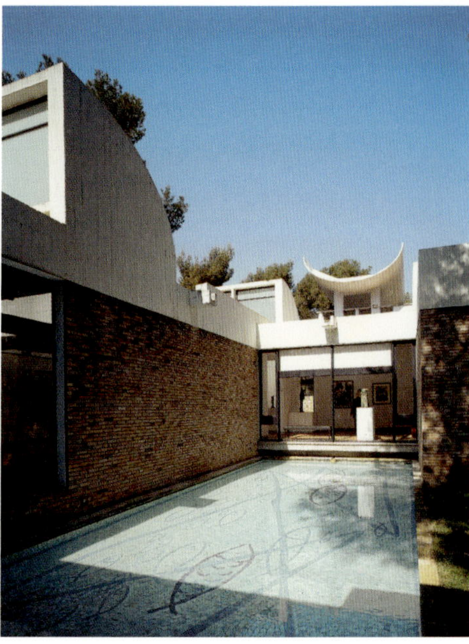

FIG. 17
Georges Braque (1882–1963), *Fish* (*Les Poissons*), 1963. Mosaic, 1214 x 460 cm. Made by Lino Melano for the Fondation Maeght

editions and married artist with poet in beautifully produced books. Their move
into art films brought a new dimension to the documentation and promotion of
their artists. The establishment of the Fondation Maeght created a new
relationship between private enterprise and state patronage in the commissioning
and promotion of contemporary art. The thousands of visitors trooping round
the Maeghts' temple to modern art each summer bear witness to the success of
a remarkable family's enterprise and their lasting contribution.

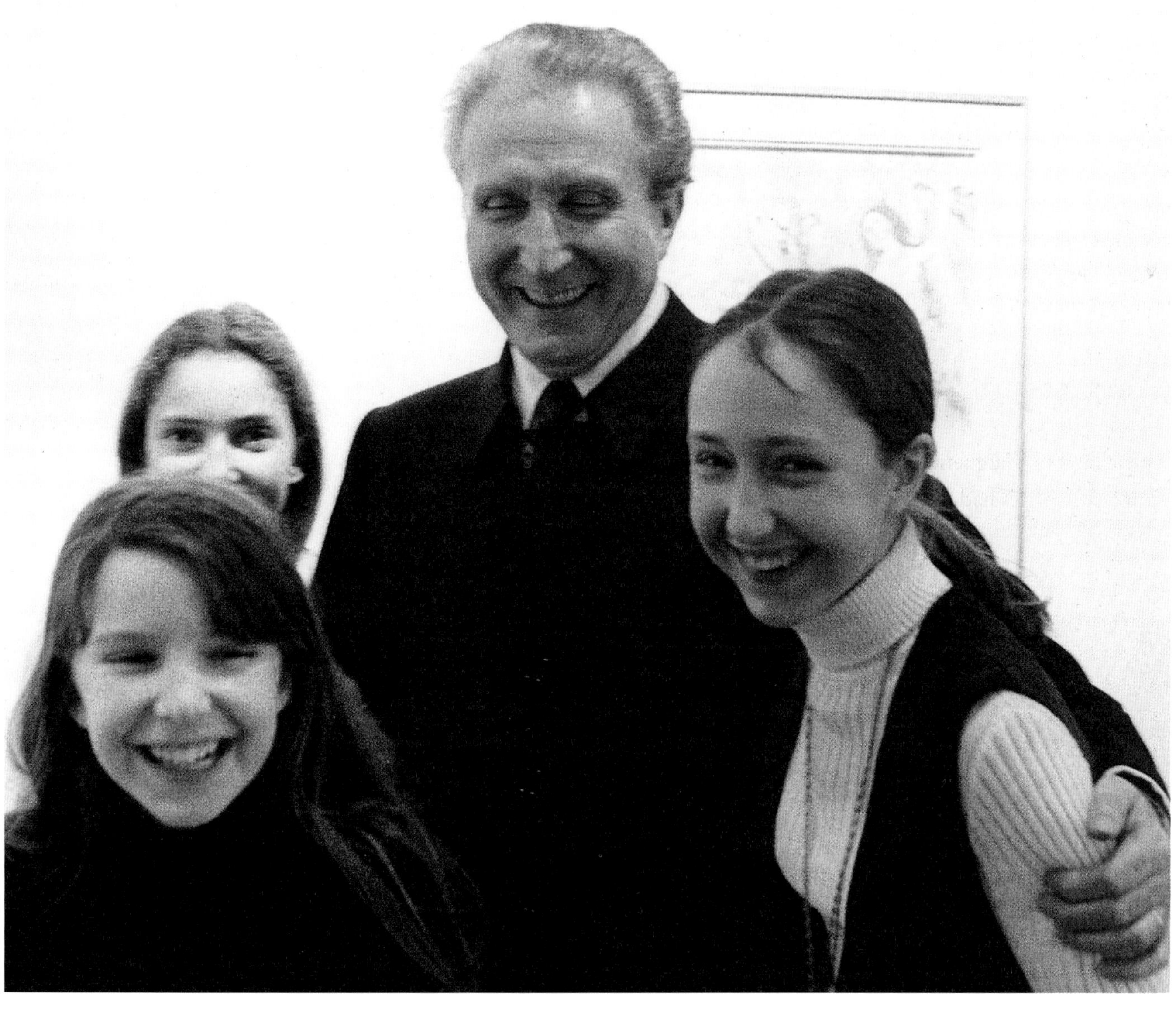

Aimé with, from left to right, Yoyo,
Florence and Isabelle Maeght at
the Fondation Maeght

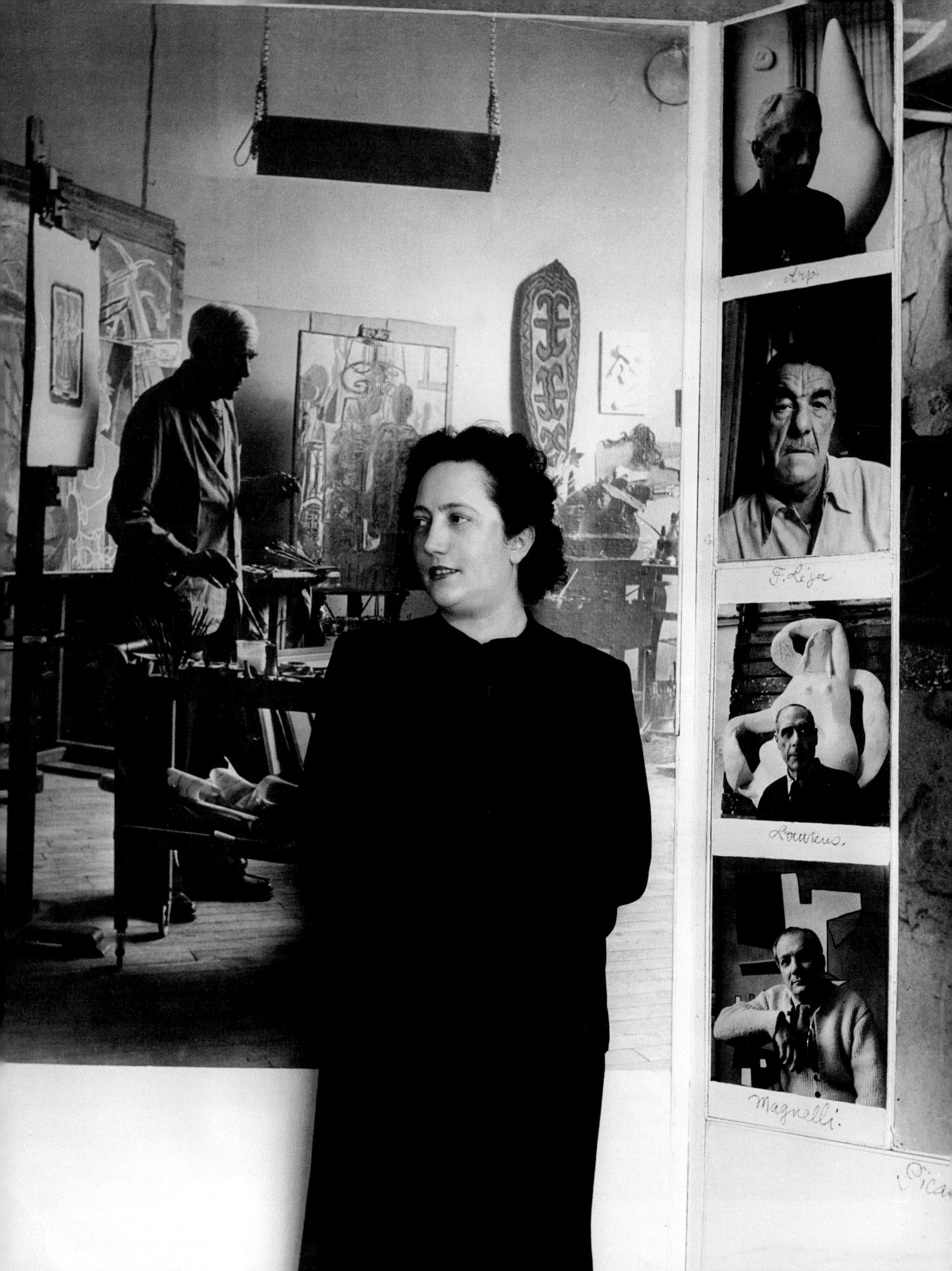
Arp.
F. Léger
Laurens.
Magnelli.
Picasso

'LET THE STONE MAKE FIRE'

Ann Dumas in conversation with Isabelle and Yoyo Maeght

Ann Dumas: Your grandfather was one of the leading figures of modern art in the twentieth century. Immediately after World War II and just over a year after the Liberation of Paris, he founded the Galerie Maeght, which became one of the city's most adventurous and experimental galleries. But I believe the origins of this great adventure began much earlier, in the 1930s in Cannes?

Isabelle Maeght: My grandfather, Aimé, was born in northern France, in Hazebrouck. World War I left my great-grandmother a widow with four children. They were evacuated by the Red Cross to Les Cévennes in the south, where she intended to be a maid on a farm. When they arrived at the station, nobody wanted a woman with four children, but a farmer, Milou Berbiguier, arrived late and immediately fell in love with her. Two years later they were married.

Aimé's stepfather sent him to the *école normale* and then to art school, where he studied lithography and obtained a diploma. He found a job at the Imprimerie Robody in Cannes. Aimé's landlady told him about a choir, explaining that he should follow a certain girl to find his way to the rehearsal. So he did, and the girl turned round and slapped him! It was my grandmother, Marguerite, the daughter of the biggest trader in Cannes. She and Aimé married two years later and started Arte, a little shop on rue des Belges (see fig. 22).

Aimé was a very good lithographer. Bonnard said he was the best lithographer he ever had. There is a letter in which he says that Maeght is the only one who knows how to mix colours to make the colour of skin. When my grandfather went to Toulon during World War II, my grandmother ran the shop and the printmaking studio, but there was no printer, no lithographer.

AD: So she sold furniture. And I believe she also sold radios?

IM: Yes. Without the printmaking studio she had to make some money. So there were radios, there was furniture designed by my grandfather, and some paintings. And there was a Bonnard in the printmaking studio that my grandfather had been asked to reproduce, so she hung that. One day an elegant man asked how much it was. As she didn't know if Bonnard wanted to sell it, she quoted an enormous price. The man agreed. She ran to Bonnard and told him that she had made a great mistake, but he said, 'That's a very good price. If you want more paintings, take them, and here's a percentage for you.'

AD: Your sister's book says that Marguerite went to see Bonnard with a wheelbarrow to put his paintings in! She was obviously a real character with

FIG. 19
Marguerite Maeght in front of portraits of (clockwise from left) Georges Braque, Jean Arp, Fernand Léger, Henri Laurens and Alberto Magnelli

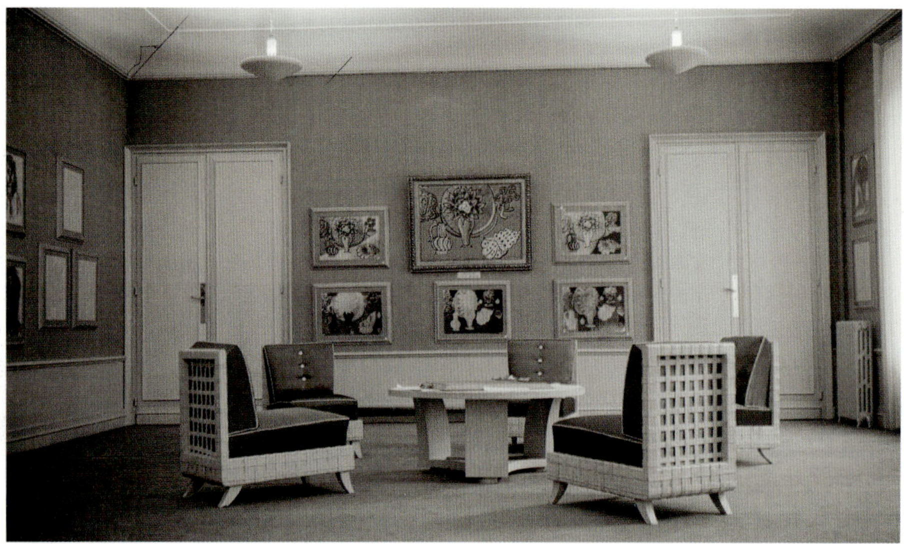

great energy. I read that she was described as 'the ant who makes things happen' –
'ant' because she was very small.

IM: Yes. My grandmother had her feet on the ground. She ran the gallery really.
She was charming, had lots of character and loved artists. And artists really loved
her. My grandfather was a visionary, more of a technician. If my grandmother
said, 'Aimé, no way,' that was that.

AD: I believe that later Aimé considered his meeting with Bonnard at this time
to have been the turning point of his life?

IM: Absolutely. Bonnard had no children and decided to adopt my grandfather.
Unfortunately he died before he could. During the war, Bonnard worried a lot
about his paintings [which he had been forced to leave behind in Paris when he
fled to the south after the Occupation]. As my grandfather had been born in the
north, he had the right to go there during the war. So he went to Paris and painted
washes on canvases, covering the paintings beneath. When he arrived in Cannes,
he would remove the wash, and underneath it was a Bonnard!

My grandparents and father, Adrien, had to flee Cannes during the war
because my grandfather had printed fake papers for the Resistance. He worked
with the Resistance leader Jean Moulin, who had opened the Galerie Romanet
in Nice to have a reason to be in the south. As my grandmother was born in
Cannes, she knew everybody. In 1943 the chief of police called her to tip her off
that the Gestapo were coming. So they ran away with just my father and Bernard
and a few things to Vence.

AD: Where Matisse was living.

IM: Exactly. My grandmother met Matisse at the doctor's, and he asked if he
might make her portrait. My grandmother refused, thinking he wanted to do a
nude. He explained that he was Matisse and he made this wonderful charcoal
drawing (cat. 7) and they became very close. For my father, Matisse was like an

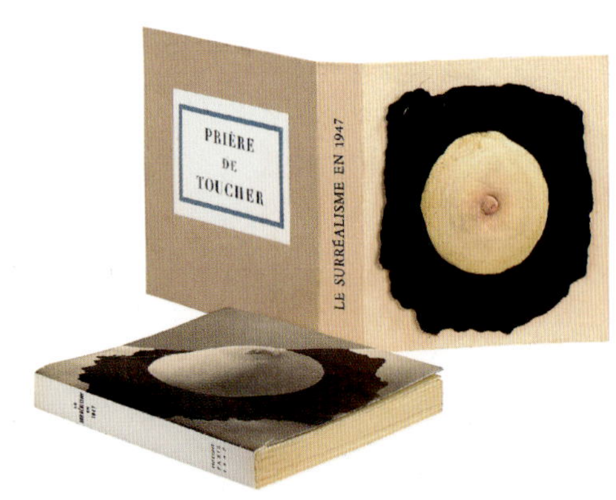

uncle. Matisse and Bonnard were my grandfather's two godfathers for art. After the war, Bonnard wanted to go to Paris, so he went with my grandfather and they spent one month together there, sharing the same hotel room. My grandfather said that, during this period, he learned an enormous amount from Bonnard. The two became really close, more as a father and son than an artist and his dealer.

Bonnard and Matisse suggested that my grandfather should have the Paris gallery. Bonnard said, 'I have to go to a dealer who owes me some money, so let's go together'. So Matisse, Bonnard and my grandfather met André Schoeller, who was in a very bad way. Schoeller said, 'If I knew some idiot who would buy my gallery, I would sell it immediately'. Bonnard turned to my grandfather and said, 'Aimé, you have the face of the perfect idiot'. So they bought the gallery. Matisse said he would like to make the opening exhibition (fig. 20). They didn't tell my grandmother. A month later, she found out but said nothing. The three of them were wondering how to tell her when suddenly she said at dinner, 'So you've bought a gallery. Now we have to do something with it.'

Artists needed good dealers just after the war. Many [dealers] were Jewish and had run away to America during the war or just before the war, or disappeared. And, you know, all the artists had run away from France too. A lot felt that, with Maeght, they had found a dealer but they had also found a family.

AD: As the two founding artists, Matisse and Bonnard, were both from the south, like Aimé and Marguerite, there must have been a sense of Mediterranean hospitality.
IM: Absolutely. My grandparents brought all these artists from the south into contact with poets. The first director of the gallery, Jacques Kober, was a poet. Kober introduced them to more poets and through the poets they met artists and it went on like that.

AD: So they allowed things to evolve from this very sociable ambience that they created? The atmosphere in Paris in the period following the Liberation must have been exciting.
IM: It was, but there was rationing and there were restrictions. But there was a will to rebuild, to show the world that France was still strong. There was a lot of excitement around the exhibitions.

AD: The 'Exposition internationale du surréalisme en 1947' at the Galerie Maeght was a remarkable event. André Breton, one of the founding members of the Surrealist movement in the 1920s, had gone to America, like many of the Surrealist artists during the war, and he had returned to Paris. Your grandfather travelled to New York shortly after the war and met Marcel Duchamp. They came back to France and decided to look back at what Surrealism had been.
IM: Because for everybody Surrealism was over. During these years, Surrealism had become more intellectual than concrete. All the artists did special things for this exhibition (fig. 25). Miró made *Superstition* (cat. 18), and there's a

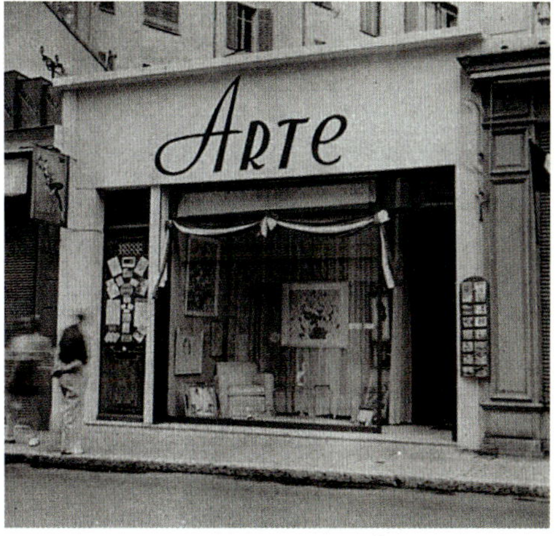

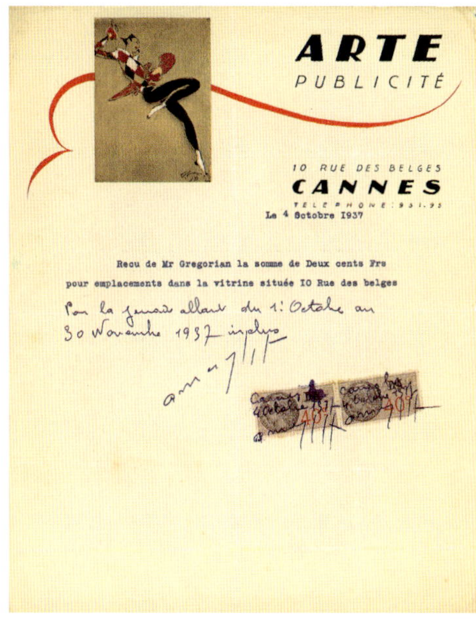

FIG. 22
Arte shopfront, Cannes, 1939 (cat. 118)

FIG. 23
Stationery for Arte Publicité (cat. 119)

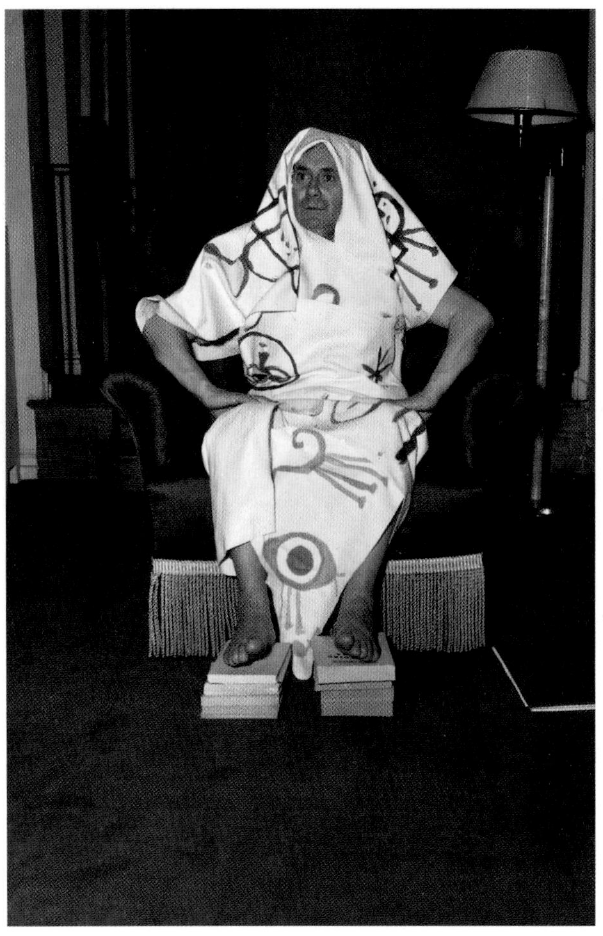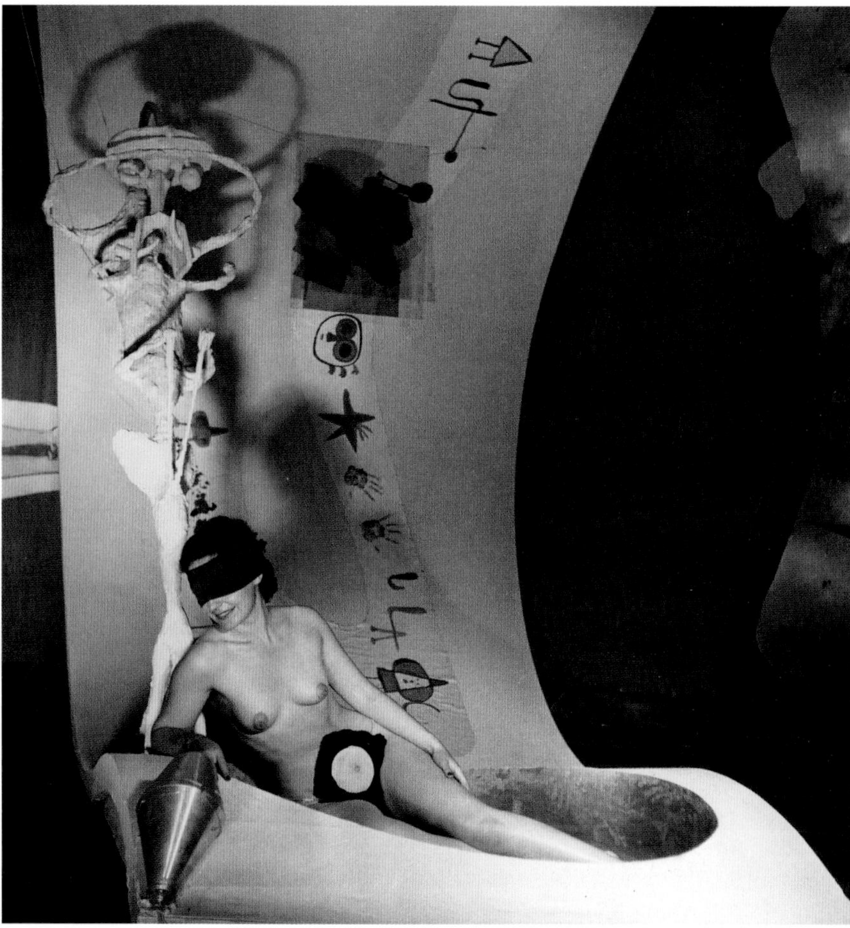

photograph of him wearing it (fig. 24). Hans Bellmer made the *Hôtel de superstition*. The catalogue is fabulous (see fig. 21).

AD: The one with the cover by Marcel Duchamp with a plastic breast, which says 'Please touch'?
IM: Yes. Duchamp bought the breasts at an army surplus shop in America (they were good for troop morale!) and he sent them to Paris to make the cover. They were rolled into a tube and my father, who was sixteen, went to the airport to collect it. The Customs people opened the tube and all the breasts burst out!

Giacometti said that grandmother made the most Surrealist gesture. A lot of little things went wrong during the installation, and my grandmother said the exhibition was cursed because of an upside-down crucifix that appeared in the 'Salle des superstitions'. So she sent my father to ask the priest for some holy water and, at midnight, she blessed the exhibition!

AD: Did the show establish the gallery's exciting, avant-garde character?
IM: Yes, and it was important too, because it led to my grandfather meeting Calder and Miró. Miró had no dealer, and Calder had a dealer but didn't want to work with him any more. And immediately they all got on so well together. The first time he showed his plasters to my grandfather, Giacometti said, 'Which one

do you want to cast?' My grandfather said, 'All of them. We will cast all of them immediately.' For us, if we work together with an artist it's because we love the work. Giacometti found in my grandfather somebody who believed in him, who accepted him and his art.

Also, they provided a printmaking studio for all these artists. It was the end of the war, a time of reconstruction. My grandfather remarked, 'Right, we have 200,000 flats to rebuild in France. There's a minimum of four walls in each.'

AD: Of course. People would need art to put on those walls, and prints are a very democratic medium, because they allow people who don't have a lot of money to buy art.
IM: That was the idea.

AD: Would you tell me about the relationships with the four artists who were especially important in the story: Miró, Calder, Braque and Giacometti? I believe that Braque was very close to the family, especially you when you were a child (see fig. 26).
IM: Yes, Braque was one of the most important people in the world for us. He was a witness at my parents' wedding. He was very tall, with white hair, blue eyes – really elegant, even wearing sports clothes. I was really in love with him.

AD: How old were you at this point?
IM: I was eight when he died. I was the only one allowed to go into his studio. My sisters were furious, very jealous. When he died Mme Braque wanted me to attend the national funeral, which took place at the Louvre. It was the first time that I was confronted with the fact that my friend was no longer there. I couldn't believe that M. Braque, with all that elegance and strength, could be in that box.

AD: We are showing Braque and Giacometti together here because we feel there is a relationship between their work: an existential feeling, a sense of texture.
IM: They had a lot of respect for one another. And Giacometti wrote a wonderful text about Braque (cat. 136, not illustrated). I think there are parallels in their work. Giacometti was really a Cubist without knowing Cubism. Braque created Cubism and afterwards said 'No more Cubism'. They both changed the way they worked, and for that, I think, they respected each other.

AD: There's a beautiful drawing by Giacometti of Braque on his deathbed (fig. 47, page 101). Now, if we move on to Miró and Calder, they seem to have a similar visual relationship, and they were close friends. They were both friends of the poet Jacques Prévert as well. Do you have strong memories of Miró and Calder from your youth?
IM: I was thirty when Miró died. He was a small man, extremely elegant: he bought his clothes in London. He had light in his eyes. Each exhibition was a revelation. He was the master of all his mediums. For Braque, painting was more important, and Giacometti was wonderful in sculpture, painting and drawing, but everybody knows

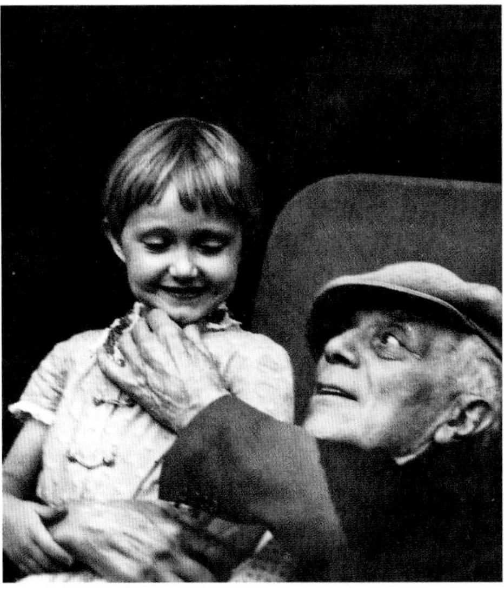

FIG. 26
Georges Braque and Isabelle Maeght, Varengeville, 1963

him for his sculpture. For Miró, everybody knows him for everything, like Picasso.

AD: When your father's younger brother, Bernard, was ill with leukaemia, I understand that Calder brought his *Circus* pieces and performed just for him?

IM: Yes, and Matisse made a wonderful drawing of a burning bush (cat. 10) for him and said, 'It's a bush just for you, to give you power'. And when my grandmother had her heart operation – she was the first to have a pacemaker fitted in France – she wanted Matisse's bush in the operating theatre!

AD: Did your grandparents' gallery and your parents' gallery on the rue du Bac exist together?

IM: Yes, for a time. My grandparents' gallery was founded in 1945, and the gallery on rue du Bac was founded in 1956 by my parents, and remains there to this day.

AD: Meanwhile your grandfather was still running his gallery. In which year did that close?

IM: In 1981, when he died. The rue du Bac gallery opened with an exhibition of Giacometti drawings. Then there was a Prévert show of collages. Jean Cocteau and all the Maeght artists attended the opening and all the people from Editions Gallimard. Poor people came for the art and rich people too; it was very mixed. And even if you were M. Braque, you talked to a young artist. Now it's a bit different.

AD: You mentioned earlier that your grandfather was very supportive of his artists. I believe that he bought Braque's entire production. When did he do that?

IM: Yes. His buying of Braque began in 1948. And we had exclusivity on Miró, except in America. In America it was Pierre Matisse, as with Giacometti. But with all the other artists we showed, there was an exclusive arrangement.

AD: There's a record of this life you have been describing, with the artists and the parties, in the films that your grandfather and your father made. They always had cameras and made home-made movies. Your father also commissioned professional films of artists at work.

IM: Yes. For example, the only film in which you see Bonnard moving was made by my father when he was twelve (cat. 137). We have Matisse doing a portrait of my grandmother (see cat. 7). We have around 300 movies. Some are in bad condition – they are seventy years old! – so we are restoring them. One of the first colour films that my father had made is a movie about Matisse making the cut-outs (cat. 138). It's the first colour film showing Matisse.

AD: You and your sister Yoyo run the gallery today. What is your vision for the future?

IM: For us, the gallery is the Maeghts and the artists. We work in the same way as before. We still have the printmaking studio. And we have studios for artists who live in Paris, but also for artists who come to Paris. The difference between

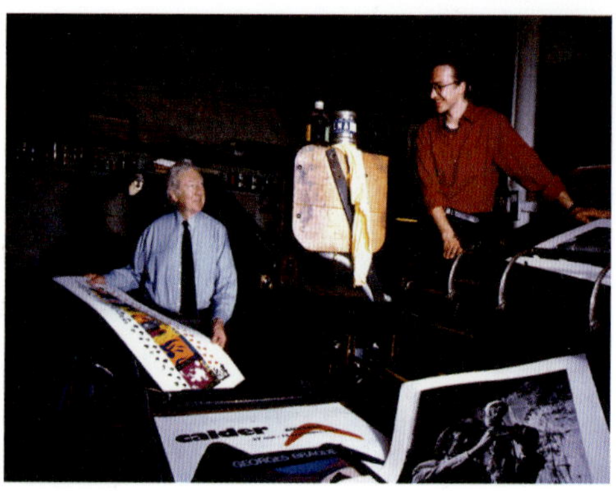

FIG. 27
Adrien and Jules Maeght at the Arte printing house, 1994 (cat. 122)

us and other galleries is that other galleries specialise in a kind of work, a kind of artist. We have artists from Miró to Chagall, Kandinsky to Léger to Riopelle – we have all sorts.

We continue with the idea that an artist can't work truthfully if he has money problems. We arrange accounts to buy canvas, paint and brushes, pay for electricity bills, air tickets. If an artist has problems paying his bills, he will make commercial work that is easy to sell, lacking in sincerity. We give the artist the space, money and materials. And the technicians who work in the printmaking studio are at the artist's disposal to help him find the right way to express himself.

With our work – and I think that we are the only gallery that does it – we help artists to be themselves, to be powerful, to be strong enough.

§

Ann Dumas: Is it true to say that the Galerie Maeght is as well known for producing original artists' prints and limited edition *livres d'artistes* as it is for dealing in modern pictures?
Yoyo Maeght: Yes. It was very important for my grandfather to find the perfect tool to promote the artist.

AD: Something exceptional about Aimé Maeght was his deep interest in literature and his aim to fuse art and poetry – to publish unpublished literary texts and to illustrate them with original prints, thus bringing his artist and writer friends together in joint collaborations. The Galerie Maeght became a crossroads of the literary and artistic worlds of Paris.
YM: Yes. The artists' books were the result of the relationship between the people in my grandparents' life. The ideas for the books arose from discussions around a table, on vacations, during a trip. No commissions. My grandfather always told me that it is vital to mix with people. He said, 'If you take Picasso and leave him alone in the desert, he won't become Picasso, even with all the talent, all the gifts he has.'

AD: I see that he founded a literary group called 'Pierre à feu' with the young poet Jacques Kober and in 1944 published the first issue of a review with the same title. Your sister has told us that Kober was also the first director of the gallery. It's interesting that your grandfather should have chosen a poet.
YM: My grandfather's talent was to recognise not what a person is but what he could be. He understood very quickly that photography had removed art's need to represent a subject or a person. So, with the end of representational painting after the Impressionists, what we see is the soul of the artist. And who is more capable to understand the soul of an artist than a poet?

AD: Kober attracted many important contemporary writers to the gallery.
YM: Yes, but at that moment there weren't many people publishing poetry.

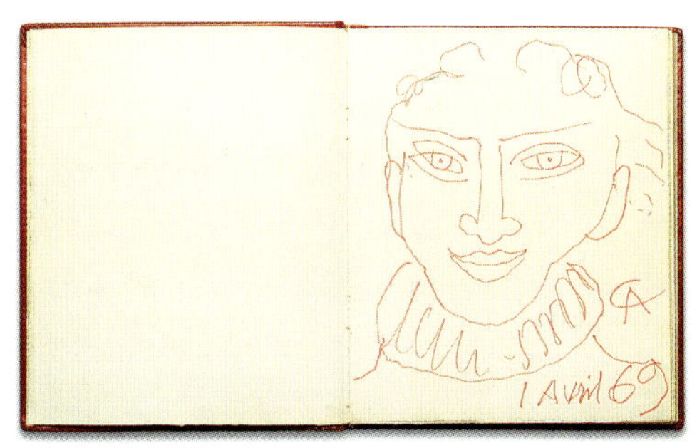

FIG. 28
Florence Maeght's visitors' book, with a felt-tip drawing of Florence by Alexander Calder, 1969 (cat. 123)

AD: I understand that Kober invented some of the titles of the journals produced by the gallery?

YM: Yes, *Derrière Le Miroir* and *Pierre à feu* (see fig. 29). I love the title *Pierre à feu.*

AD: How would you translate it?

YM: 'Let the stone make fire' – like prehistoric man did. To make a spark, to ignite something. It was a reference to the past and also to future creation.

AD: This literary connection was also important to a number of the gallery's artists. The idea of poetic metaphor, free association and word play – a legacy of Surrealism – extended into the process of making visual art, especially for Miró and Calder. Miró once said he liked the idea of starting with a word and seeing where it would take him. Do you think that Miró and Calder play with forms and shapes in this open-ended way, rather in the way that these poets were playing with words?

YM: Yes. When I was about seven, Duke Ellington came to play at the Fondation Maeght (see fig. 30), and we were listening to him rehearsing, and he created a piece of music called 'Blues for Miró'. I was talking with Miró – we were all alone in the *Labyrinth*! – and Miró told me: 'You see on the piano there are so few notes. Mozart and Duke Ellington use the piano, and the same notes, and they can create an infinitude of music.' Only twenty-six letters in the alphabet and Prévert can make so many words from them. It's the same in painting: only three colours and black and white, and we can create infinity. With so few elements, Miró told me, each artist can create a new world.

AD: The most famous journal produced by the Galerie Maeght was *Derrière Le Miroir,* with 253 issues produced between 1946 and 1982. Each issue was also the catalogue of an exhibition, with original lithographs by the artist. Many artists made original lithographs for *Derrière Le Miroir.*

YM: Yes. The first issue, on the subject of 'Le Noir est une couleur', was a great failure. But my grandfather wasn't too discouraged. My father, Adrien, controlled all the issues after he established his own printmaking studio. It was too difficult at that time to take photos to illustrate the works in the shows and, in any case, the paintings were often not finished two days before the exhibition. What my father wanted was to preserve the memory of the exhibition. An original lithograph is not a reproduction of a drawing or a painting. Even if it is small, you retain 'le geste' – the movement of the hand of the artist – at the right scale, even if it is very simple. It is better than the reproduction of a painting in a book. The artists all loved this idea because they could create something.

AD: So it brought out very good work?

YM: Yes, a direct record of what they were doing at that moment, with no filter. And all 253 issues are original creations: the layout, the way the paper is folded,

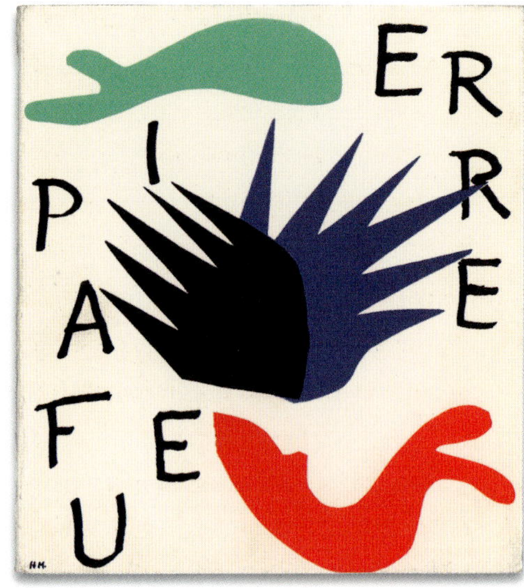

FIG. 29
Henri Matisse (1869–1954), *Deep Mirrors (Miroirs profonds)*, on the cover of *Pierre à feu*, 1947. 24 x 21 cm (cat. 124)

the way it is printed – sometimes in relief, sometimes on glossy paper, sometimes with the text in the middle of a drawing, sometimes a very simple page with only one word. For each exhibition, copies always arrived just a few hours before the opening. Everyone in the gallery – even my grandfather – saw the issue for the first time then!

AD: He must have had some idea of what it contained?
YM: No! The artists used to go into my father's printmaking studio and do whatever they wanted. There was no mock-up, no approval from my grandfather. My father printed them and my grandfather gave him complete authority.

AD: So it was almost a kind of spontaneous production?
YM: Yes. My father controlled the quality, but also he brought many ideas.

AD: Other magazines were produced too: *Pierre à feu*, which we spoke about, but also *Argile* and *L'Ephémère* (see fig. 31).
YM: *L'Ephémère* was published by the Fondation Maeght. My grandmother said that, because we published many posters and books about our artists, we needed a bookshop. There were no bookshops in museums then. And my father said that, to enlarge the Fondation's public, the Fondation should have catalogues. They were quite unknown then. So that's why he opened his printmaking studio at that time.

You create something, you bring it to the public, but the public wants a souvenir of the experience. It might be a lithograph, signed and numbered, or a postcard, a poster or a catalogue. So that's why my family wanted the Fondation to have its own publications.

AD: So was *L'Ephémère* primarily a literary journal, or did it publish art and poetry?
YM: Mostly poetry, with a few pages of art in black and white.

AD: So it was quite different from *Derrière Le Miroir?*
YM: Yes. *Argile* was a literary magazine too.

AD: It's unusual for a man who was an art dealer to be so active in literature.
YM: But on his passport Aimé described himself as a publisher. When we asked him what his job was, he always answered that he was a publisher.

AD: Let's talk now about the *livres d'artistes*. Rather like Ambroise Vollard, the great artists' book and print publisher of the early twentieth century, Aimé encouraged his artists to take up printmaking and book illustration, often pushing them to experiment with techniques that they may not have experienced otherwise. This was a role taken on by your father, Adrien, as you have mentioned. It seems that it was their aim to foster artists' ideas and then to give them the freedom to pursue their work with financial support.
YM: Not with financial support. Support means you know the cost. Instead the

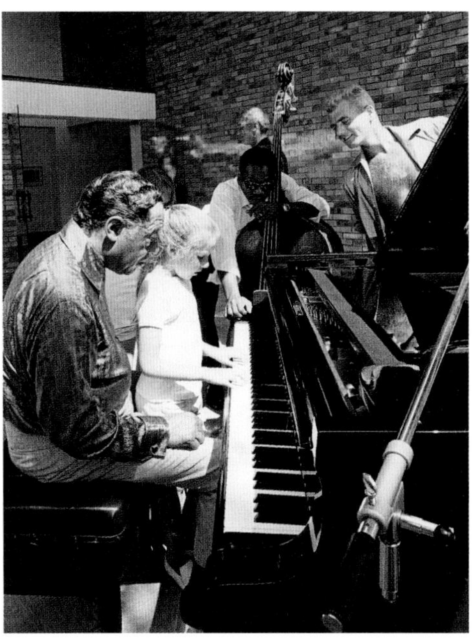

FIG. 30
Duke Ellington with Yoyo Maeght at the
Fondation Marguerite et Aimé Maeght, 1966

artists were given total freedom. That's why we published small books and huge ones. Some have only two or three original lithographs, others twenty or thirty.

AD: So it was entirely up to the artist what he felt he wanted to do?

YM: Yes, and it was not illustration of a text: it was a collaboration. One of my favourite books was *Adonides* (cat. 98), a collaboration between Miró and Prévert. When you see the text and the images, which are mixed together on the same page, impossible to separate, the letters turn around the lithographs. It took several years to create this book and several years to print it. My grandfather brought Miró and Prévert together to do a book. Prévert wrote the text and Miró said 'No, it's not a good text'. Miró wrote a letter to my grandfather and asked him to find a painting he had done in 1925, and made a small sketch of the painting: 'It's a totally blue painting, with a small planet in the corner. If you find it, show it to Prévert. This painting is a good starting point for Prévert's text.' My grandfather found the painting and showed it to Prévert, and Prévert and Miró started a new book, and it became *Adonides*. It took them about fifteen years to finish the book they had to do together. Unfortunately Prévert died a month before its publication, and it is for that reason that his signature was stamped in the copies. My grandfather signed the book with Miró. And we still have that Miró painting (cat. 12).

AD: I read in *Derrière Le Miroir* that Aimé said: 'A book is like a total work of art. It has an architecture, the characters are like the stones, the paper is its material, and the illustrations are the decorations of this edifice.'

YM: Yes. My grandfather made no mistakes in architecture, no mistakes in design. I can believe he said that. A book has to be something that feels right. It's a collaboration between a writer, a painter and some technicians, and the chemistry has to succeed. Without the technicians, you can't make the book. My grandfather, who had been a technician in a printmaking studio, knew this.

I love my father who prints all these books. He is very proud to be able to say that no printer can say 'I printed that book'.

AD: Another thing that Aimé once said about art publishing was that it was 'to fix a moment', but that this does not mean that publishing it brings it to a standstill and blocks it. Once the book is closed, the adventure continues. I find that a very appealing idea.

YM: Publishing means spreading ideas, bringing something to other people. If you asked me how I would define my grandfather, I would say he was a 'diffuser'. You can be a perfect publisher, you can produce a beautiful book, but what is important is to bring it to the public. Something published for two people is not interesting. What is important is to give the public the chance to buy a book by an unknown poet: an unknown book.

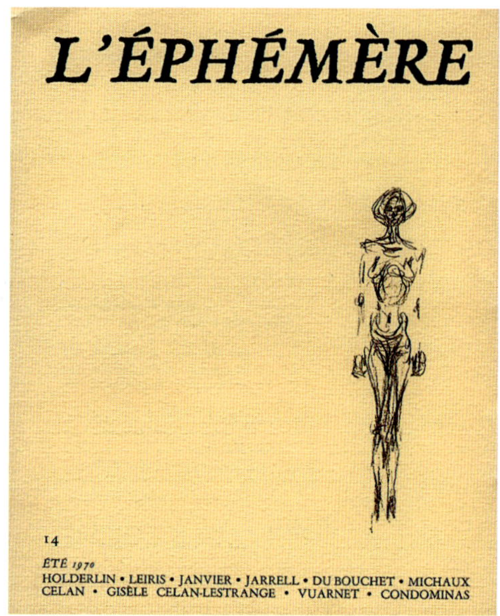

FIG. 31
L'Ephémère, 14 (Summer 1979), Maeght Editeur, Paris

AD: There is another wonderful book by Miró, *Parler seul* (cat. 96), with text by Tristan Tzara, whom I think Miró had known in the 1920s when they were both part of the Surrealist movement when Miró first came to Paris.

YM: Yes. It has many pages. It was one of the first books my grandfather published, in 1948–50. I looked at all the pages very often as a child. You know, Tzara wrote this text while he was in a psychiatric hospital. Our favourite room was my grandfather's library. We were allowed to touch all the books. We never damaged anything.

AD: Braque's books suggest a darker mood: *La Nuit, la faim* (cat. 94) and *La Liberté des mers* (cat. 93). How would you describe the character of Braque's *livres d'artistes?*

YM: Yes, they are different. I remember, even though I was very young, how calm and slow Braque was. Everything was very quiet in his house, in his studio, in his life, even in Varengeville. His books are the same: they are peaceful. The text of *La Liberté des mers* is by Pierre Reverdy. Some of the illustrations don't look like Braque's. If you looked at them without knowing who the artist was, you might think they were the work of a contemporary artist. They're not typical of his work, but they are emblematic of his soul. 'Dans ce livre, Braque se livre'! – 'In this book Braque gives of himself'.

AD: And there's a book that Calder made images for, with text by Prévert, called *Fêtes* (fig. 32 and cat. 97).

YM: Yes. Actually, Calder didn't like lithography very much. As he was in my father's printmaking studio, my father found him a different technique. Calder was a genius at cutting metal. My father gave him some copper and Calder cut some triangles, circles, spirals, stars, a sun, and stuck these pieces of copper on to another copperplate to make a relief. So Calder created a sculpture to make a book. It's like a print of a sculpture. He used the same 'geste' that he would have used to make a *mobile*.

AD: So your father was really encouraging these artists, pointing out new directions for them?

YM: Not to find a new way: he wanted the artist to find the right way.

AD: Miró made some remarkable prints in his seventies – those very large-scale, colourful prints that have almost the same impact as some of his paintings (see cats 110–12).

YM: Yes, and Miró was not a big man. You need courage, physically, to work at such a scale. The boldness of the colours! And the audacity of his inventiveness! It was not because he had large paper that he made such big prints. My father had to find a way to enable him to make larger prints because his work needed this size.

AD: Can you tell me a bit about Giacometti's zincographs?

YM: What is important in Giacometti's drawings is the swiftness of 'le geste',

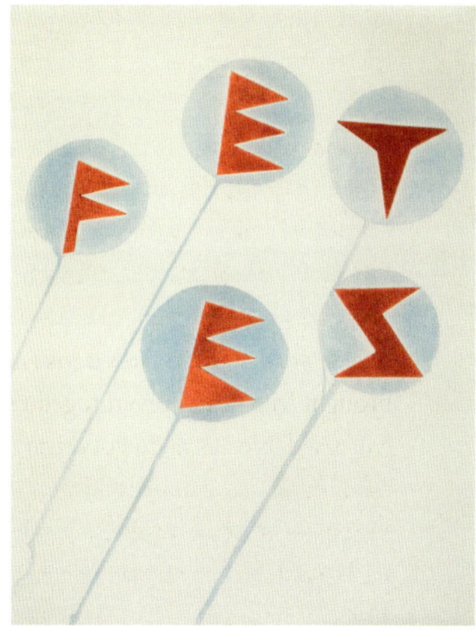

FIG. 32
Alexander Calder (1898–1976), *Fêtes*, text by Jacques Prévert, 1971, cover (cat. 97)

and that is preserved perfectly in the prints. If Giacometti had used a technique where the pen was resisted, he might have lost his vitality. First he worked on tracing paper and afterwards it was transferred to the metal.

AD: Could you tell me about the publishing and the printmaking activities of the gallery today?

YM: Yes. We still have our own printmaking studio for our artists. The difficulty with using an outside studio is that it would limit our artists' horizons. An outside studio would want to fix a price for a certain technique and quantity at the outset, and that technique and quantity might not be right for the artist.

AD: Now I'd like to ask you about the Fondation Maeght in Saint-Paul. The idea of creating a foundation for artists was a remarkable idea and something that no art dealer had ever done. How did it come about?

YM: In 1952 the gallery was seven years old and already famous. So my grandfather felt that he had realised his ambition. Then Bernard died. Remember, many artists, not only at the Galerie Maeght but also all over the world, had no children. Others had plenty and didn't take care of them. Family life held no interest for them; they were focused on work. And Braque said something horrible to my grandfather: 'If you only touch life, you have failed. You have to make something out of life.'

AD: Something that goes beyond the present?

YM: Something immortal. Bernard's death was such a trauma for my family that my grandfather responded to the idea of the Fondation immediately and said 'Right, it's a project' – something to get away from that trauma. Immediately he talked about it to Miró. My grandfather remembered that he had seen the Spanish Pavilion built in 1937 for the Paris World's Fair by the Catalan architect Josep Lluís Sert, and Miró said he would introduce him to Sert. My grandfather went to America and returned with Sert. They decided first to make perfect rooms in which to exhibit contemporary art. Léger also was very excited about the project, saying: 'You have to make a place for us, the artists. I will come with my colours and brushes, to paint even the rocks!' (see figs 33 and 34)

AD: The degree to which artists were actually involved in the design of the building is exceptional.

YM: Yes. The parameters were to respect the artists and to respect nature. Don't forget, this was after the death of a child. Some of the walls go around the trees.

AD: Rather like Prévert's text turning round Miró's images?

YM: Yes. That's lovely. And what was exciting in this project was to talk about it before it opened. Remember that there was no contemporary building made specifically to hold art in France at the time. The idea was that the public could

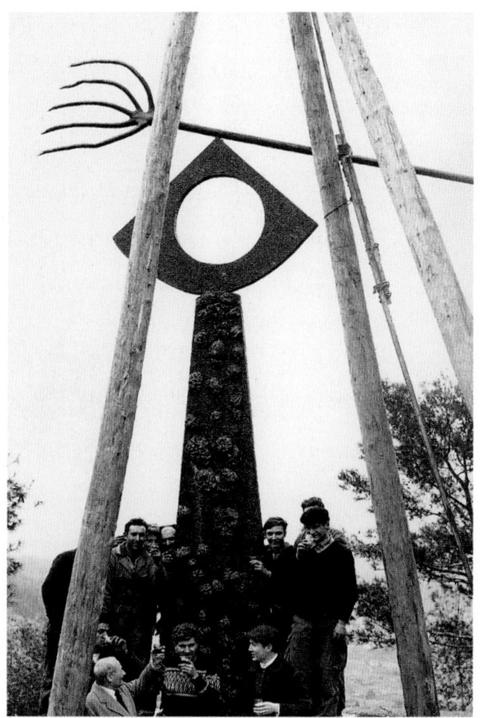

FIG. 33
Joan Miró's *Pitchfork* (*La Fourche*), shown during construction of the Fondation Marguerite et Aimé Maeght, Saint-Paul, 1963

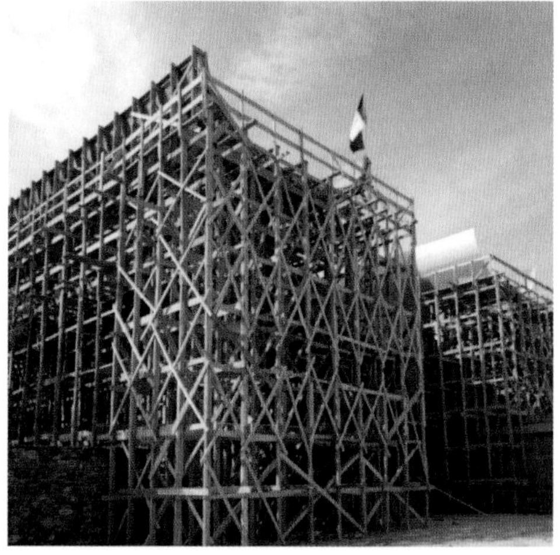

FIG. 34
The construction of the Fondation Maeght, Saint-Paul, 1963

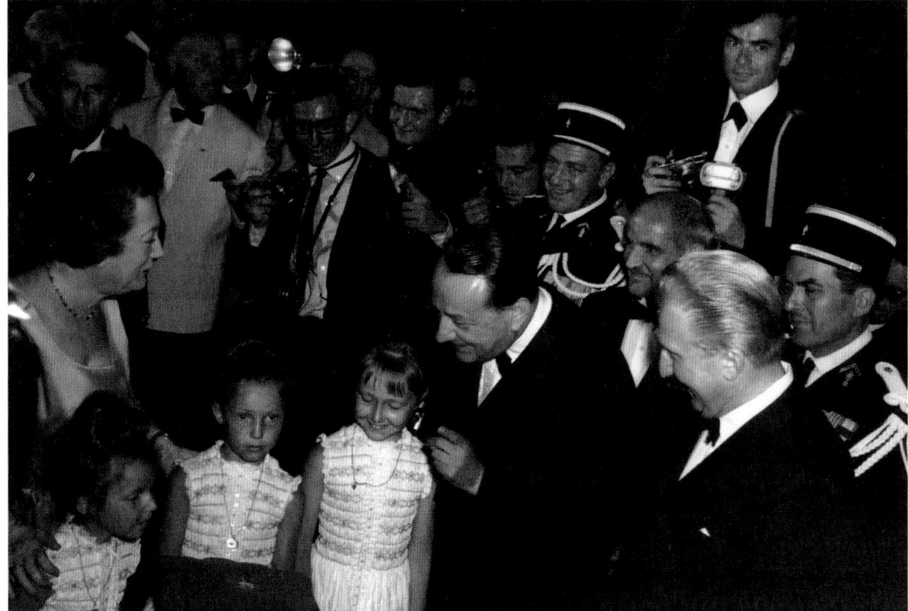

come to see how the artists wanted their work to be shown. For example,
in the courtyard, the Giacomettis have no plinths; they stand on the ground.
And Giacometti painted them to be very close to the colour of the ground.

AD: Yes, in an ochre to pick up the colour of the Mediterranean light. I believe
at the opening André Malraux, Charles de Gaulle's minister of culture, stressed
in his inaugural speech that the Fondation was very much a living museum?
YM: Yes. On the opening night, instead of waiting for the guests at the door of
the Fondation, my grandfather took his three granddaughters – I was five years
old, Florence seven and Isabelle nine – to be the first to receive Malraux (see
fig. 35). Why? He did this as if to say 'We do this today but what is important
is tomorrow'. 'Pierre à feu': it's the same.

At this moment, he could have stopped, but he went on. He encouraged
us – never told us – to love art, music and books, of course. His great success
was not in having done things, but in getting other people to do them.

AD: Could we talk about the building and the site of the Fondation? You
mentioned that your artists were involved from the beginning, so your
grandfather and Sert worked closely with Giacometti, Braque and Miró. You
have Miró's *Labyrinth*, you have the Giacometti sculpture courtyard and the
Braque pool, which are all very strong elements of the building. Jan Birksted's
Modernism and the Mediterranean: The Maeght Foundation (Aldershot, 2004) talks
about the strong feeling of the Mediterranean in the concept of the building
and how it was important to make the outdoor and indoor spaces interact.
YM: The Fondation is built like a typical southern French village. First, you have
the wall surrounding it. For me, the most important piece of art in the Fondation
is Pierre Tal-Coat's curving mosaic wall in the first field. So, you are inside the

Fondation, you are surrounded by a wall, but it is not a barrier, rather a work of art that is an integral part of the conception. We are safe inside, but we are not locked inside. The first door of the Fondation is less than a metre high. This is very important: it signifies that the Fondation is not sacred.

After the first field, as in a French village in the Middle Ages, there's a drawbridge over the water. Then the windows are very small – because it is so sunny – and they never look outside. And every room has an opening on to nature.

I have a favourite place in the Fondation, of course. When you look at Braque's pool, on the patio, here you have big pine trees and walls made of brick. It is like an embodiment of the idea of 'pierre à feu'. My grandfather asked a factory nearby to reopen especially to make the bricks. He wanted all the materials to come from the area, from the south of France. When you look at this patio, you have the water (Braque's pool), the fire (the bricks), the trees and the sky. Can you imagine making a sculpture here? It's like purgatory: you succeed or you fail. The Fondation is like that. People say, 'At the Fondation you can hang anything and it becomes beautiful.' I say, 'No. It's not a jewellery box.' The Fondation doesn't make works of art look better; it is a prism to look through.

AD: Birksted also makes the point that classical mythology is one of the inspirations for the building: the labyrinth is remade in a modern way by Miró with his magical creatures. There's a classical feel to the Giacometti courtyard. Do you think this was deliberately thought out by your grandfather and Sert?
YM: Yes. Everything in the Fondation was decided for a reason, from Miró's *Labyrinth* to the doors. The letters show that they thought about everything, down to the last detail.

My grandfather was close to Georges Pompidou, who came to visit several times before he became president and of course when he was president. When he saw the Fondation, he saw a place that was not a museum for dead art but a living place with music, art, a permanent collection and exhibitions, a theatre. Thirteen years after the opening of the Fondation, the Centre Pompidou opened in Paris.

AD: So the Fondation was an inspiration for the Centre Pompidou?
YM: Of course.

AD: And finally, what are your ambitions for the future of the Fondation?
YM: For the Fondation it is very simple. We accept, in my family, that it is a real foundation, that nothing belongs to us any more. We gave it all to the public, not to the state. Our aim is to find a way that the Fondation can survive – survive us, of course, but also for several centuries more – with the same principles. So we must find money, independence and bring people to understand our mission. The mission is not to exhibit famous artists: it is to support creation – to bring to the public some artists that we like. We don't ask you to like them, we ask you to know them. And then you make your choice. That's all.

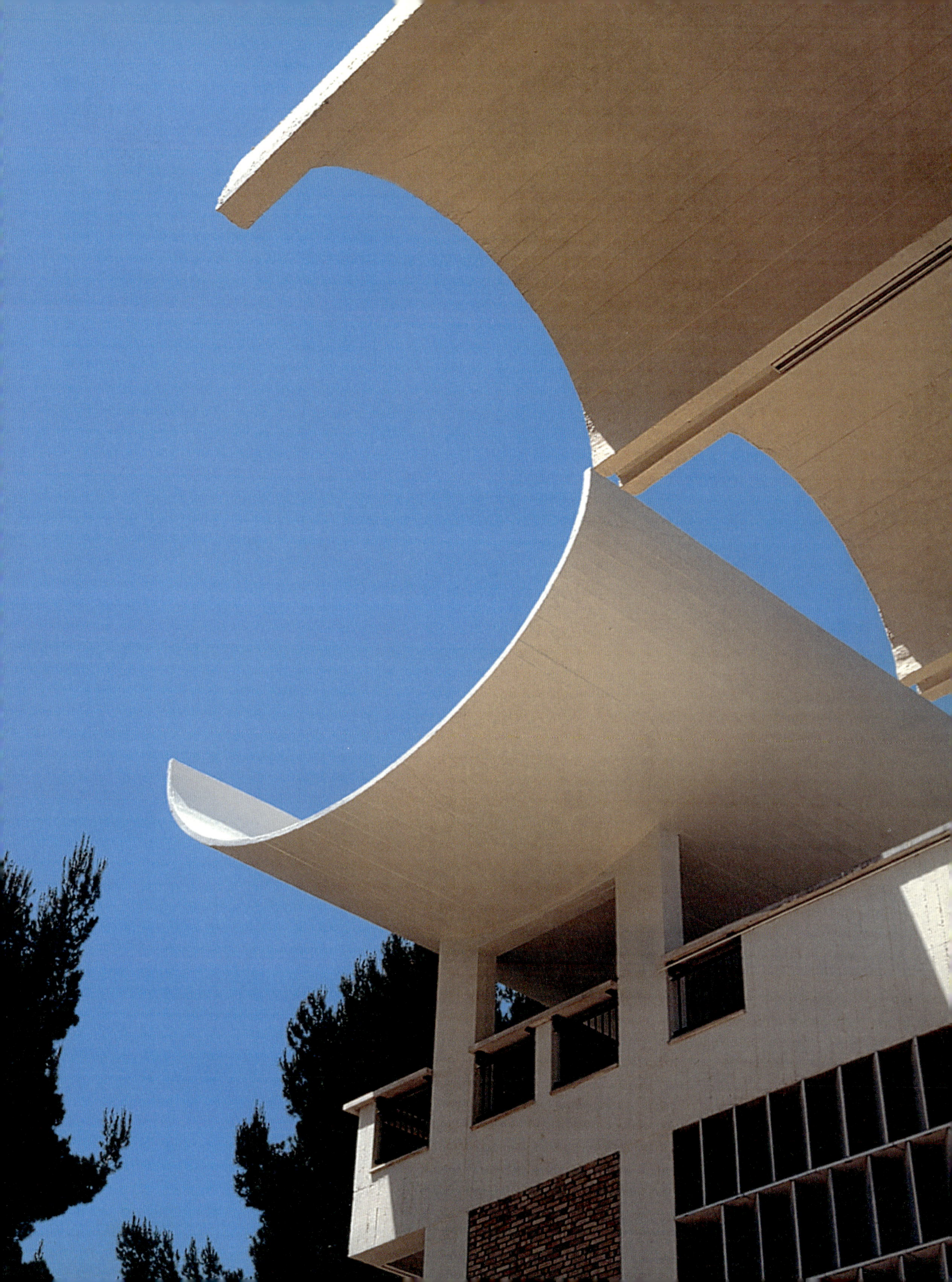

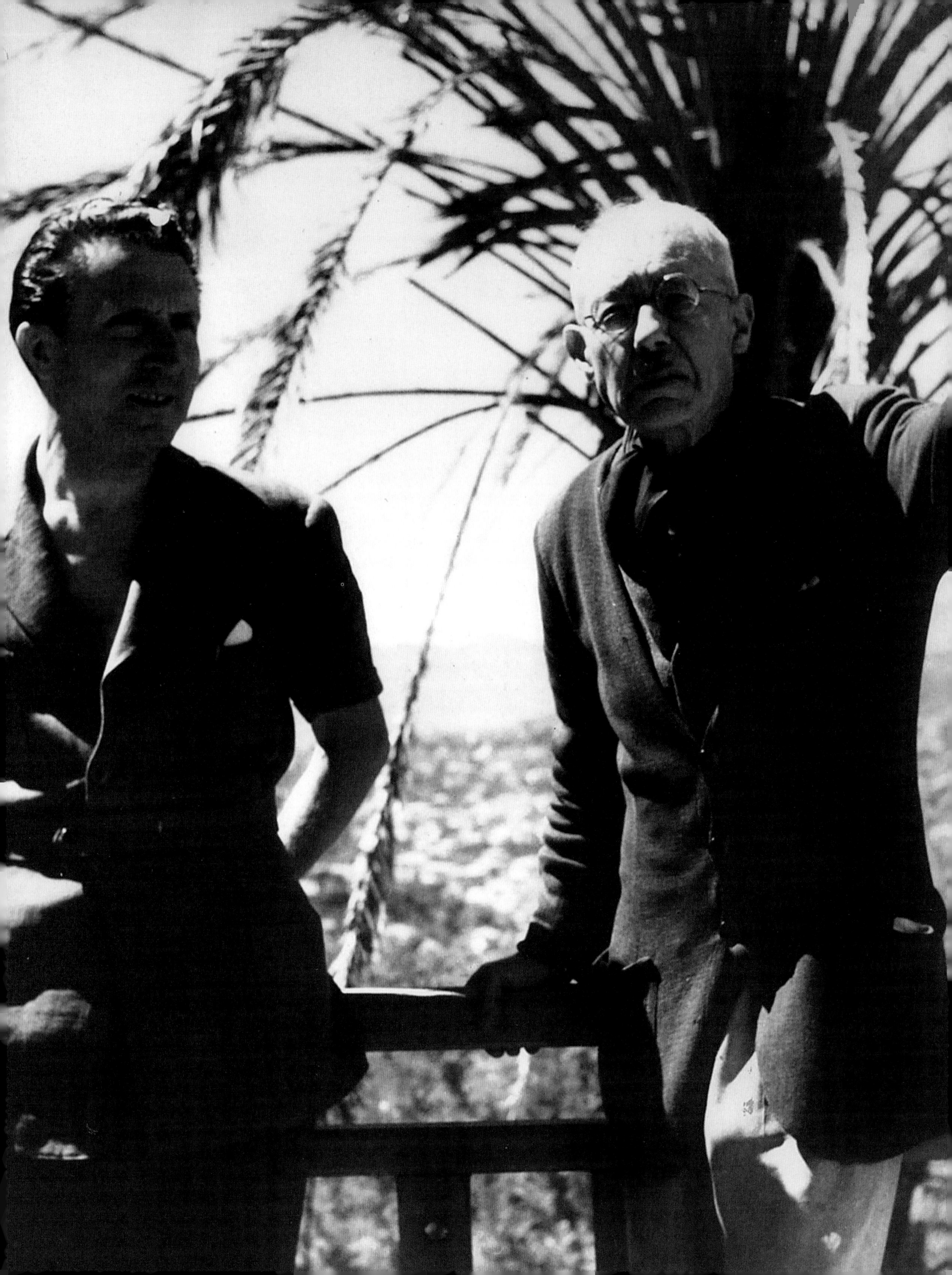

BONNARD AND MATISSE

BONNARD AND MATISSE

Pierre Bonnard (1867–1947) and Henri Matisse (1869–1954), Aimé
and Marguerite Maeght's acknowledged mentors in starting their gallery
in Paris in 1945, provided the example of two very great artists whose
achievements went far beyond small-scale easel painting to include grand
decorative projects, tapestries, ceramics, stained glass, prints and illustrated
books. Large decorative commissions required special treatment.
Bonnard's enormous *Summer (L'Eté)* (1917; cat. 1) is a case in point. It
was commissioned by his Swiss patrons, the Hahnlosers, for an office in
their house in Winterthur. In a letter to Mme Hedy Hahnloser-Buhler
dated 26 July 1917, Bonnard commented on the large surface to be
covered – more than double the size he had envisaged – which required
'subjects that are more decorative than expressive'. He went on to describe
what he had in mind: 'Two naked figures are placed in a small valley
surrounded by trees, and in the foreground there are modern characters –
sleeping figures and young girls.'[1] The composition is literally banded into
different times, blending the past with the present in a glorious light-filled
landscape, into which the figures appear woven as in a Rococo tapestry.

In numerous drawings made from the balcony and terrace of his
little house at Vernonnet (see cat. 4), Bonnard had rehearsed the idea of a
foreground platform overlooking the ever-changing spectacle of his garden
and the wooded island in the Seine beyond. But for Bonnard a decorative
painting demanded the universal and the timeless. To drop down into a
decorative landscape was to drift back in time to a pastoral idyll, to the
legendary era of human innocence on the isle of Lesbos described by
Longus in *Daphnis and Chloe* (late second or early third century AD),
which Bonnard himself had illustrated for an edition commissioned by
Ambroise Vollard and published in 1902. In the Prologue, Longus
describes his discovery in a wood of a painting of lovers, which he decides
to emulate in words 'as an offering to Love and the Nymphs and Pan, and
as a source of pleasure for the human race – something to heal the sick
and comfort the afflicted, to refresh the memory of those who have been
in love and educate those who have not'.[2]

Bonnard could recover and give life to the past only through his
memories of people and places in the present. The two naked women in
the centre of the clearing in *Summer* look as though they have come from
Matisse's great idyll *The Joy of Life (La joie de vivre)* (1905–06, Barnes
Foundation, Merion, Pennsylvania). The landscapes of Normandy and
his childhood home in the Dauphiné became Bonnard's Lesbos.[3] As he
and his companion, Marthe, whom he married in 1925, had no children,
he strung his surrogate family – his sister with his nephews and niece –
across the foreground. His love of children and his interest in the

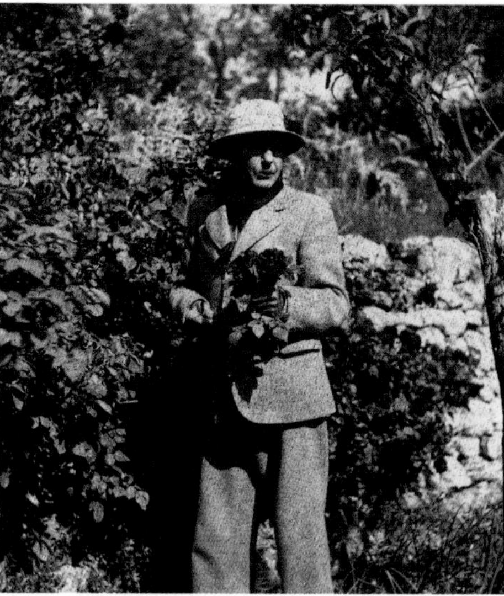

FIG. 37
Pierre Bonnard at Villa La Chance,
Cannes, 1943

Page 48: Pierre Bonnard and Aimé Maeght
(cat. 125)

mother–child relationship were perpetuated in his drawings of Marguerite Maeght and her son Bernard (cats 5 and 6), who tragically died in 1953. He drew Marguerite as a quattrocento Madonna looking down as though at a child (cat. 3).

Bonnard and Matisse, in their different ways, depended upon women to generate the necessary emotional atmosphere for them to make art. In the 1920s, Bonnard's studio-home became a place of both refuge and confinement. Marthe acted as his jailor and muse, and her jealous presence is felt whenever he painted other women. *Young Girl Reclining (Jeune fille étendue)* (1921; cat. 2) looks on with wary sadness. Was she a lover or a memory of Marthe as a young woman?

Drawing became Matisse's favourite medium following his operation for stomach cancer in 1941, which left him a virtual invalid, confined either to bed or to a wheelchair for the rest of his life. Where Bonnard's tentative marks, dots, dashes, hatching and lines felt out the figure in relation to the atmosphere of the setting, Matisse, through preliminary shaded charcoal drawing of his model, arrived at a point where he could encapsulate form with an emphatic contour. The strength of Marguerite Maeght's character is brought out by the strength of the contours of his drawing (cat. 7). The structural dialogue between armchair and seated model became the subject of *Seated Nude (Nu assis)* (1944; cat. 9), the model's curled-up left leg and raised right arm merging with the armchair, just as her extended right leg takes on the supporting role of the armchair's erased right leg.

Matisse's absorption with drawing also found an outlet in a succession of books that he designed and illustrated.[4] Charles Baudelaire, for whose *Les Fleurs du mal* he provided drawings in a 1946 edition, remained one Matisse's lifelong icons and he treated him as such in *Blessing to Baudelaire (Bénédiction à Baudelaire)* (1944; cat. 8). The paper cut-out process that became the sole medium out of which his coloured album, *Jazz* (1943–46, published in 1947) was created, released a new-found feeling for the autonomy and expressive power of his pictorial elements within a pervasive field of light. This led to a series of large independent brush drawings that assume the status of major decorative works in their own right. The subject of trees, which became a structuring theme in his decoration of the Chapel of the Rosary in Vence (1948–51), led to the Maeghts' *The Bush (Le Buisson)* (1951; cat. 10). 'An artist must possess Nature,' Matisse reminded young artists in 1948. 'He must identify himself with her rhythm, by efforts that prepare for the mastery by which he will later be able to express himself in his own language.'[5]

NW

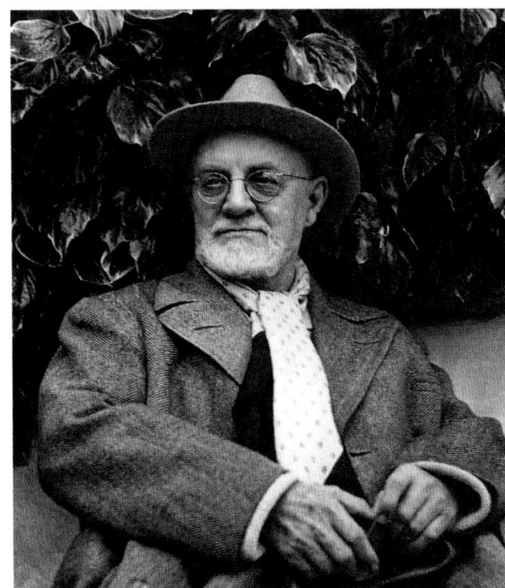

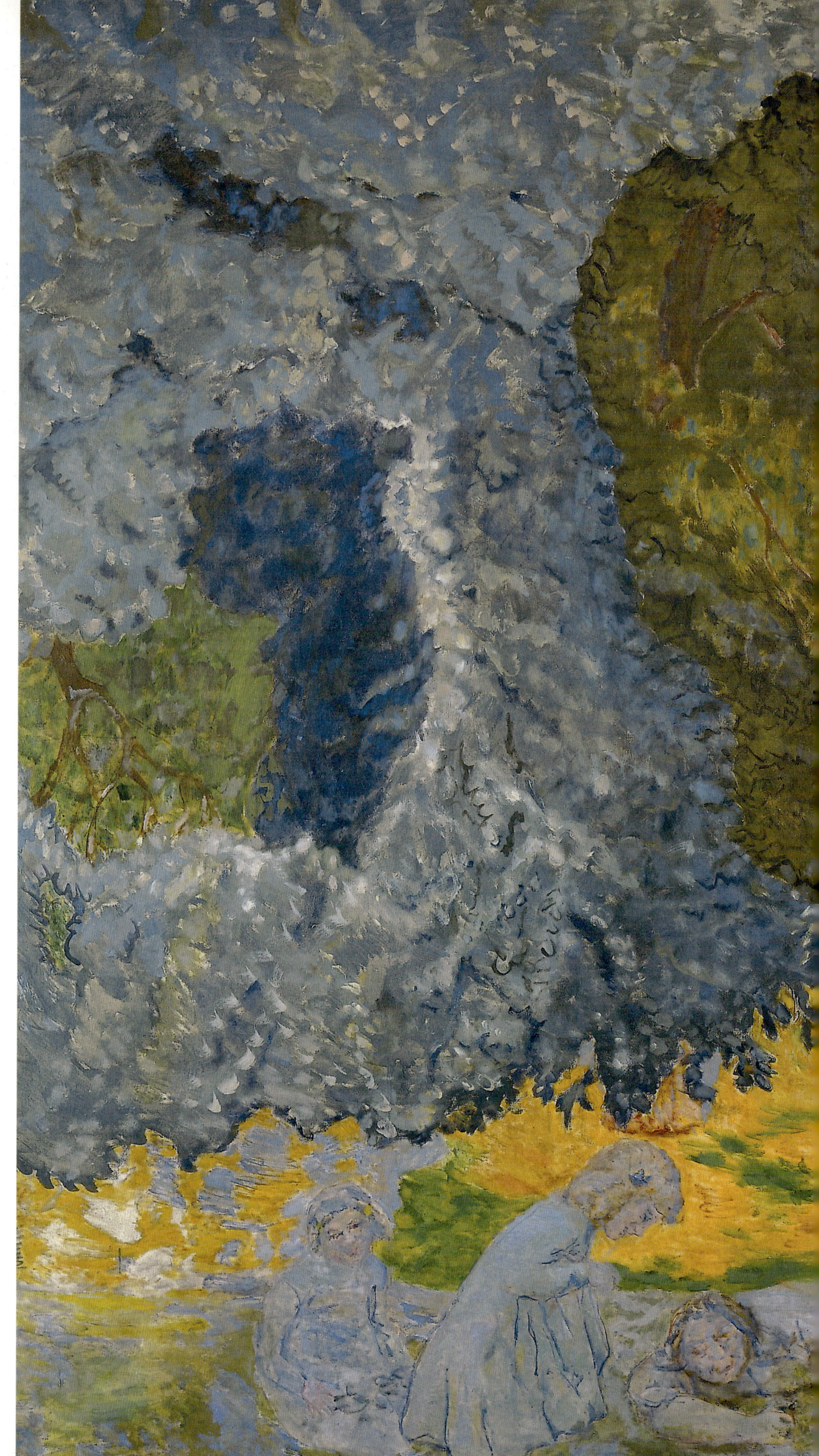

CAT. 1
Pierre Bonnard (1867–1947)
Summer (L'Eté), 1917
Oil on canvas, 260 x 340 cm

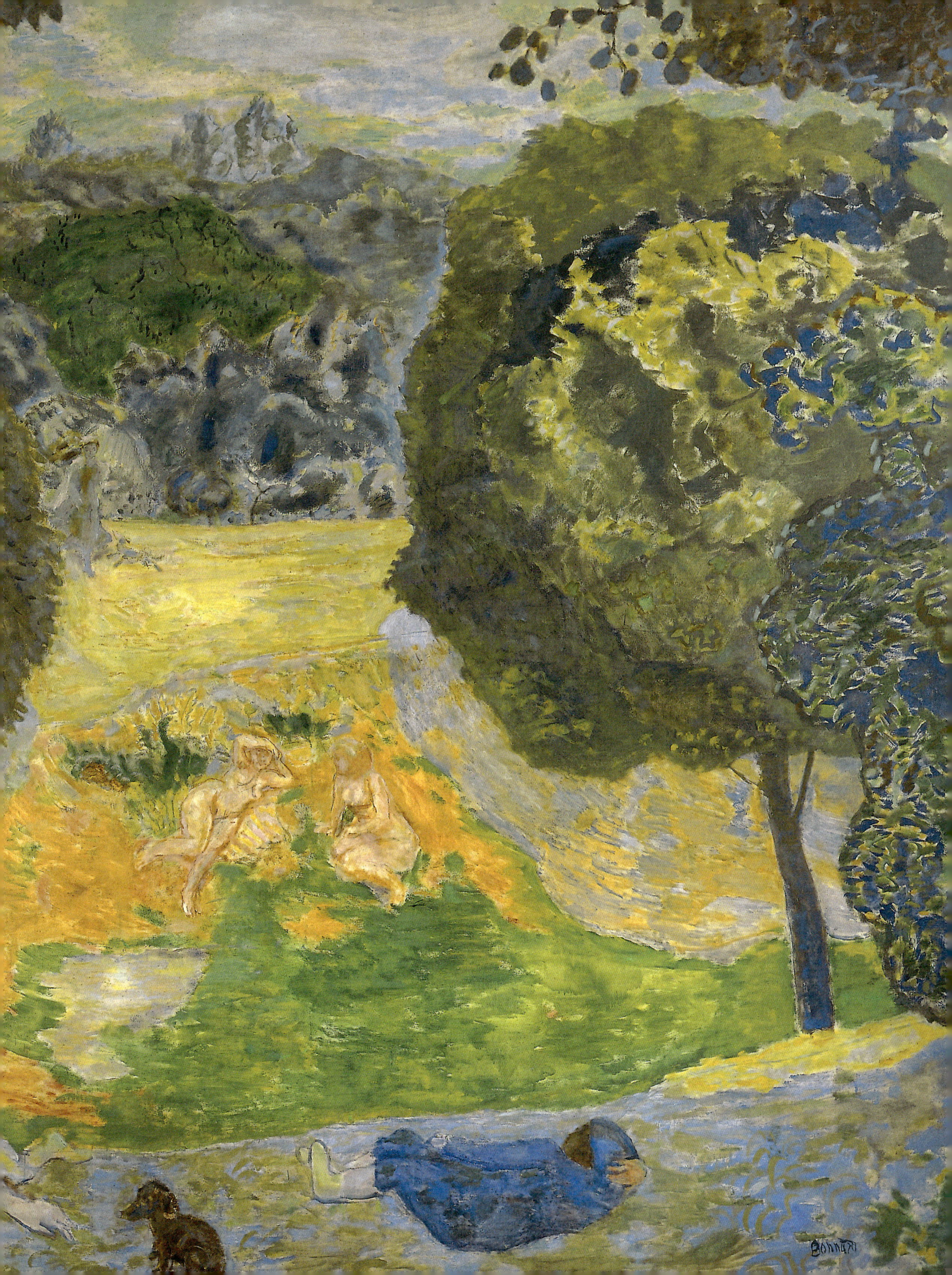
Bonnard

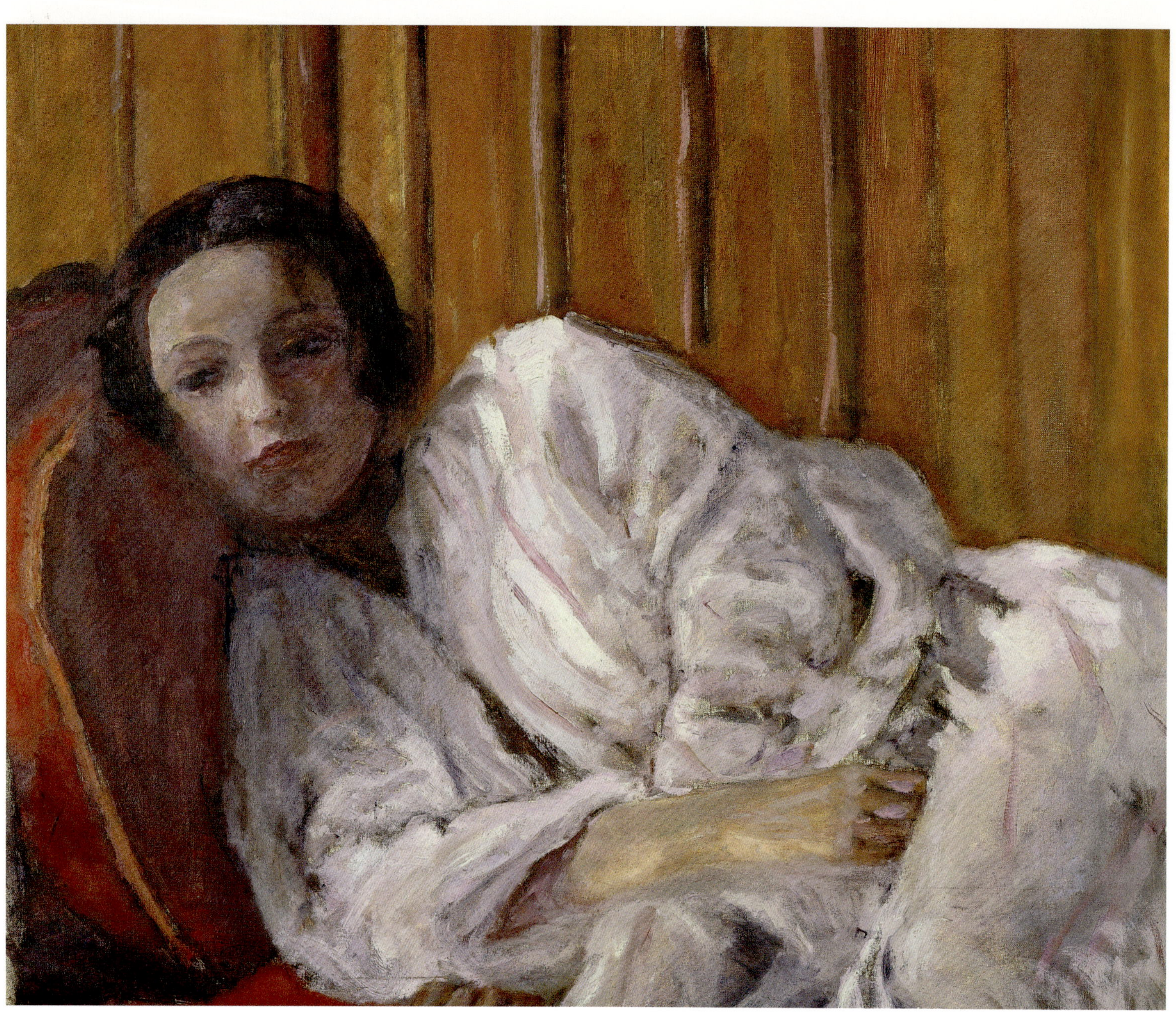

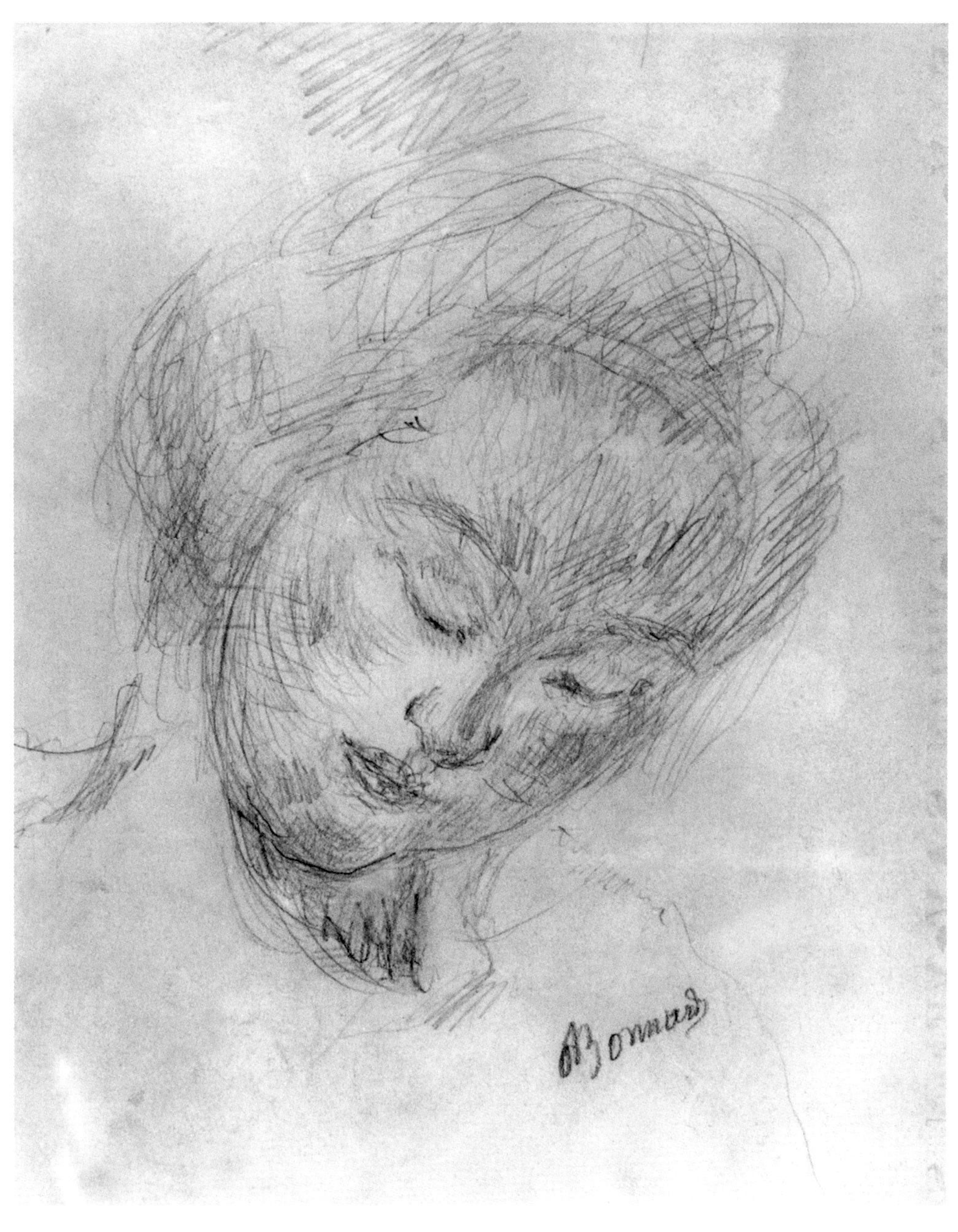

CAT. 2
Pierre Bonnard (1867–1947)
Young Girl Reclining (Jeune fille étendue), 1921
Oil on canvas, 56 x 61 cm

CAT. 3
Pierre Bonnard (1867–1947)
Head of a Woman, Portrait of Marguerite Maeght
(*Tête de femme, portrait de Marguerite Maeght*),
late 1930s
Pencil on paper, 30 x 23 cm

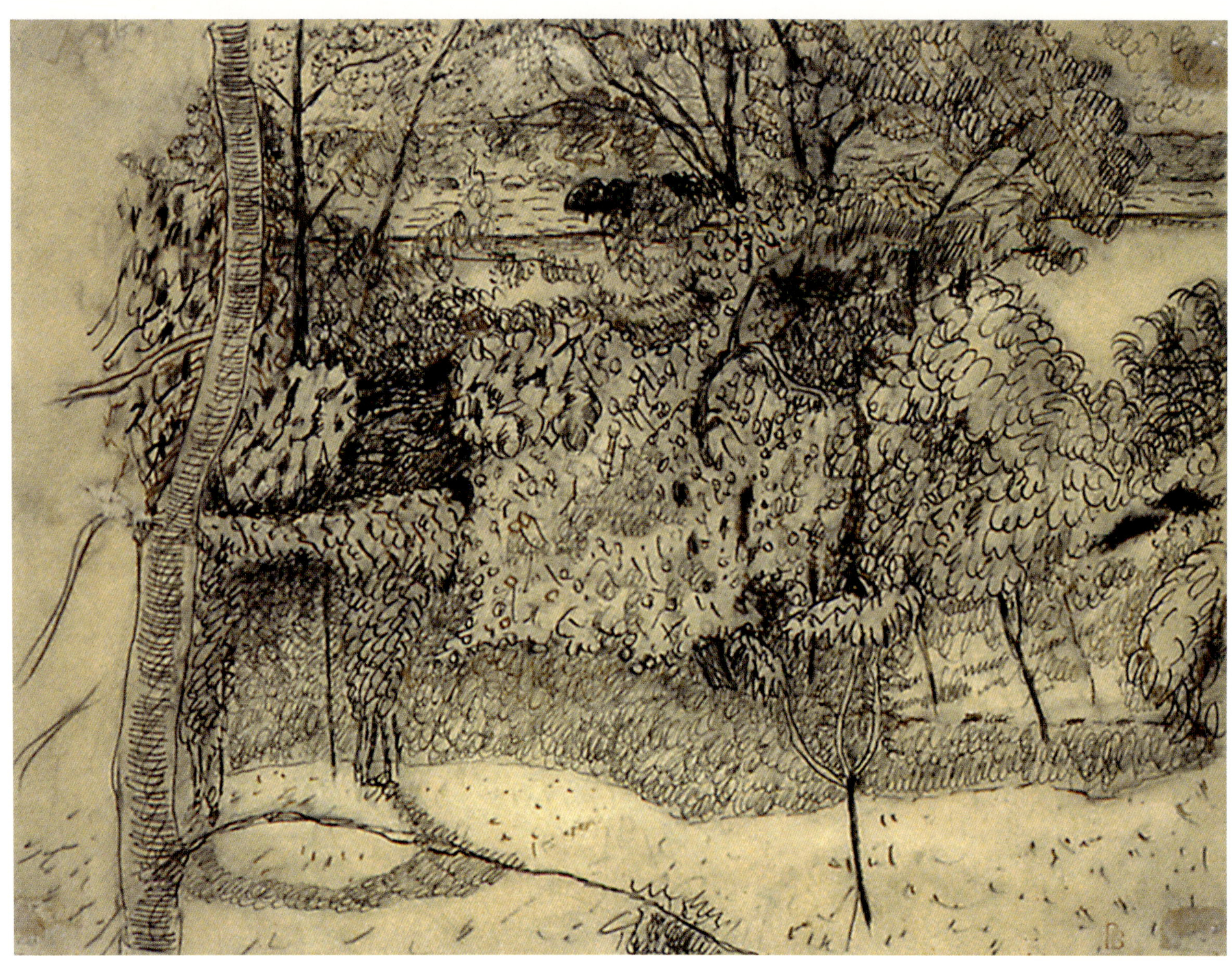

CAT. 4
Pierre Bonnard (1867–1947)
Garden at Vernon (Jardin de Vernon), 1930
Ink on paper, 25 x 32 cm

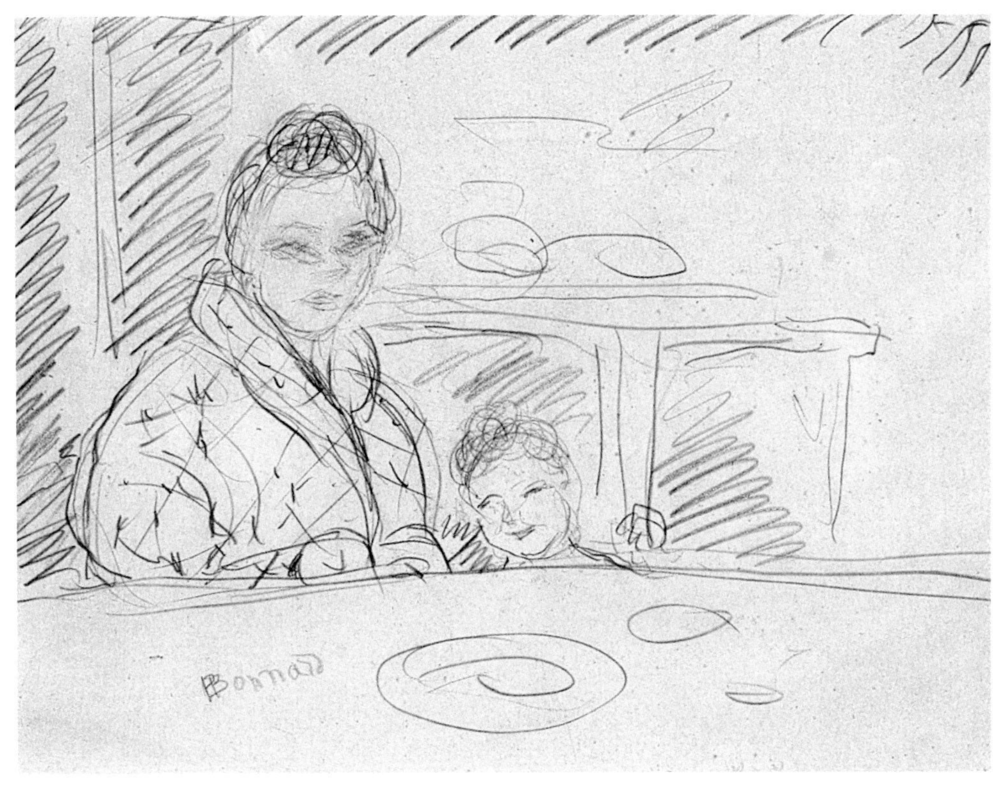

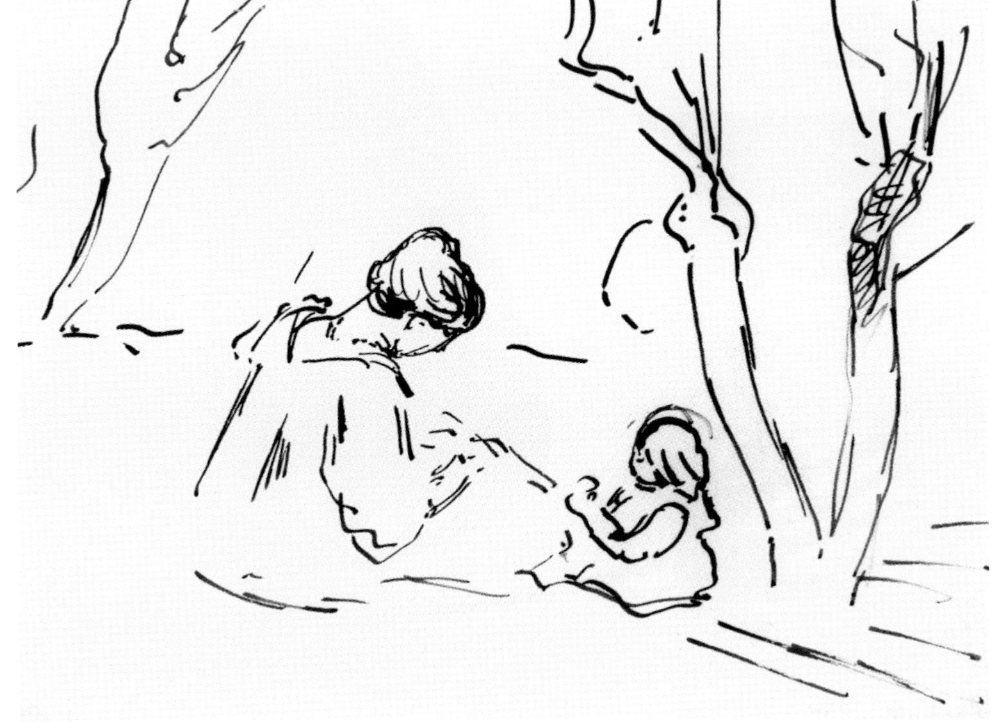

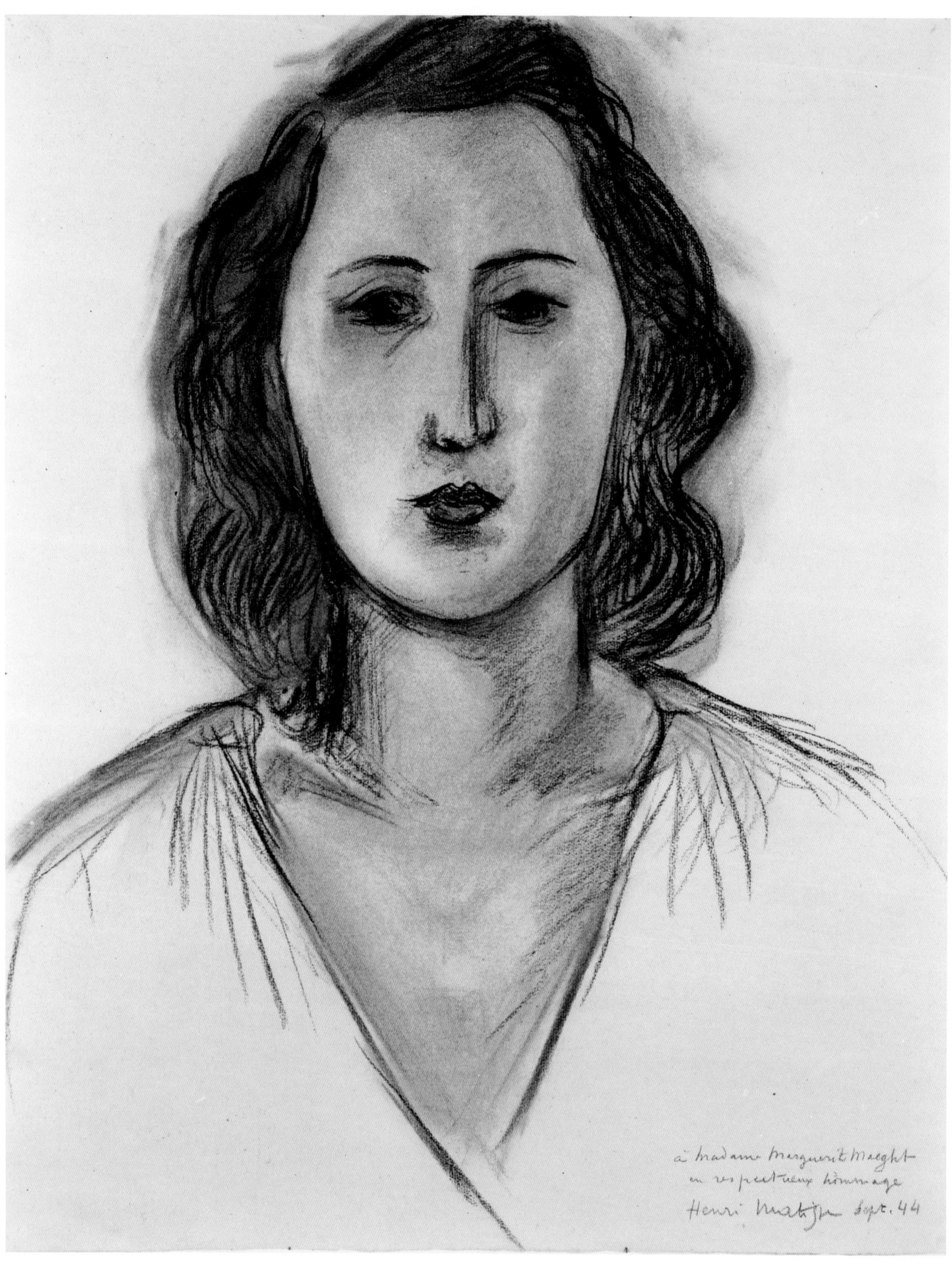

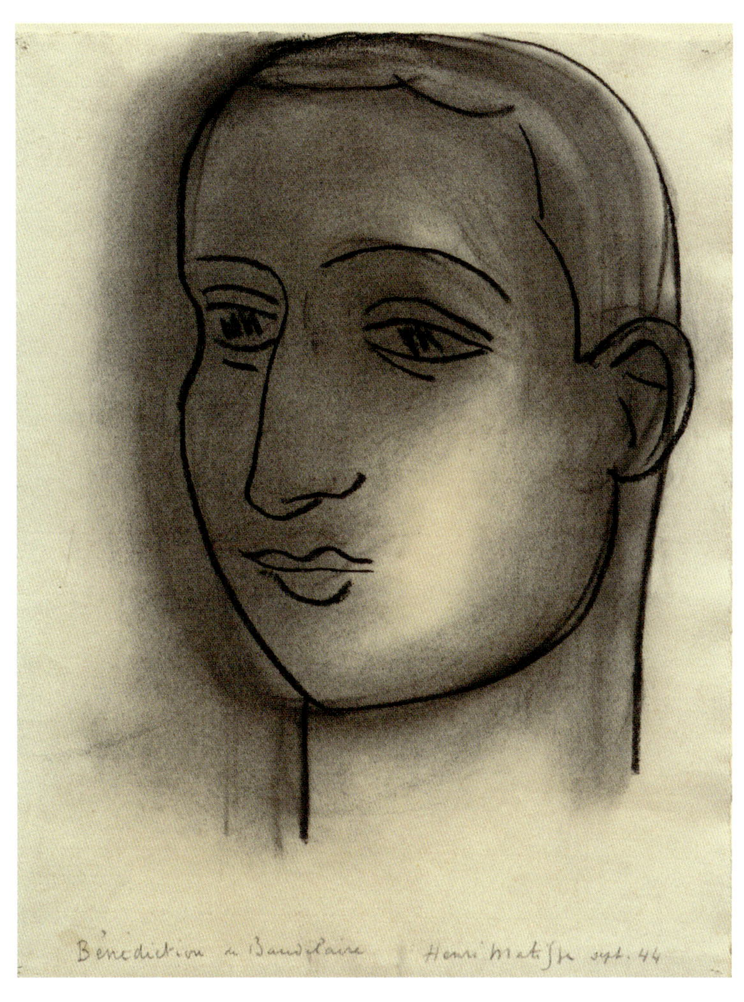

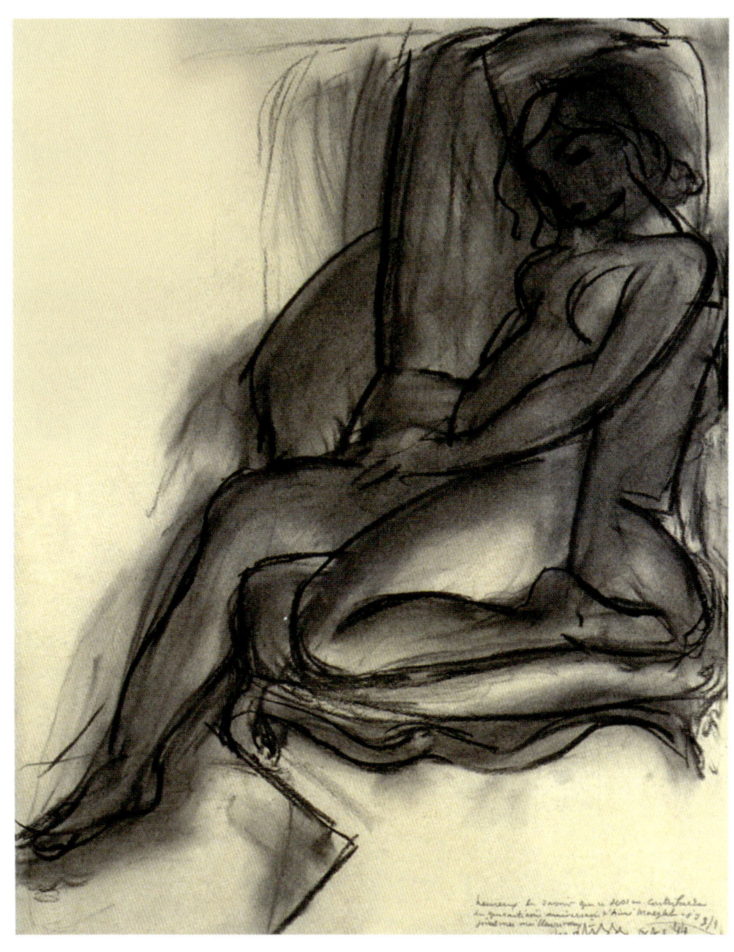

CAT. 7
Henri Matisse (1869–1954)
Portrait of Marguerite Maeght, 1944
Charcoal on paper, 61 x 47 cm

CAT. 8
Henri Matisse (1869–1954)
Blessing to Baudelaire (Bénédiction à Baudelaire), 1944
Charcoal on paper, 40 x 30 cm

CAT. 9
Henri Matisse (1869–1954)
Seated Nude (Nu assis), 1944
Charcoal on paper, 62.5 x 48 cm

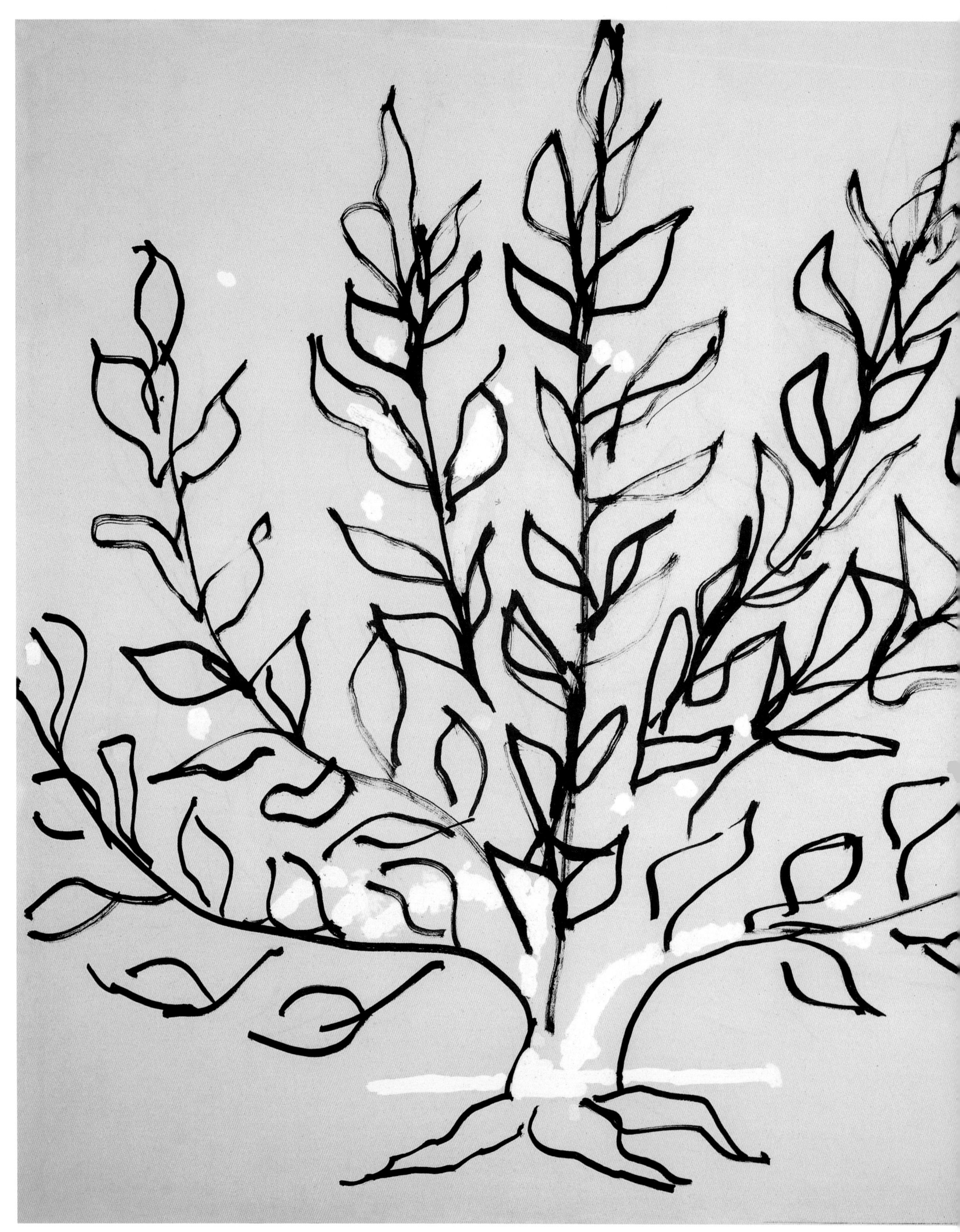

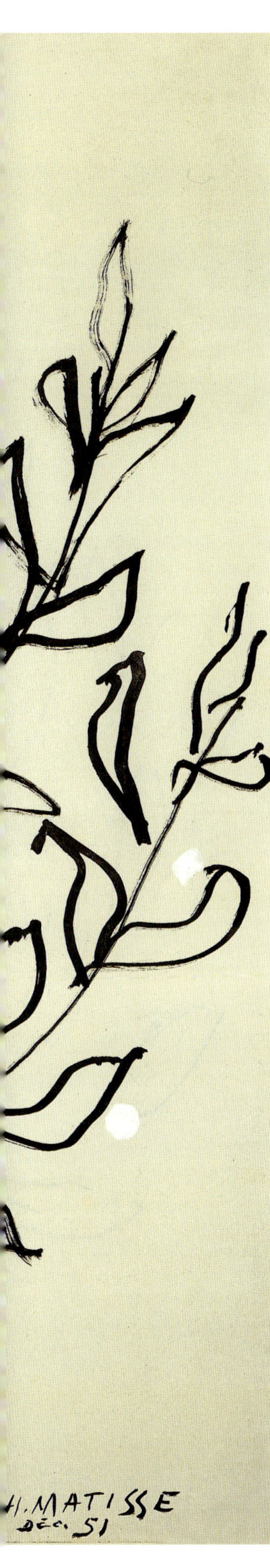

CAT. 10
Henri Matisse (1869–1954)
The Bush (*Le Buisson*), 1951
Ink and gouache on paper, 149 x 149 cm

61

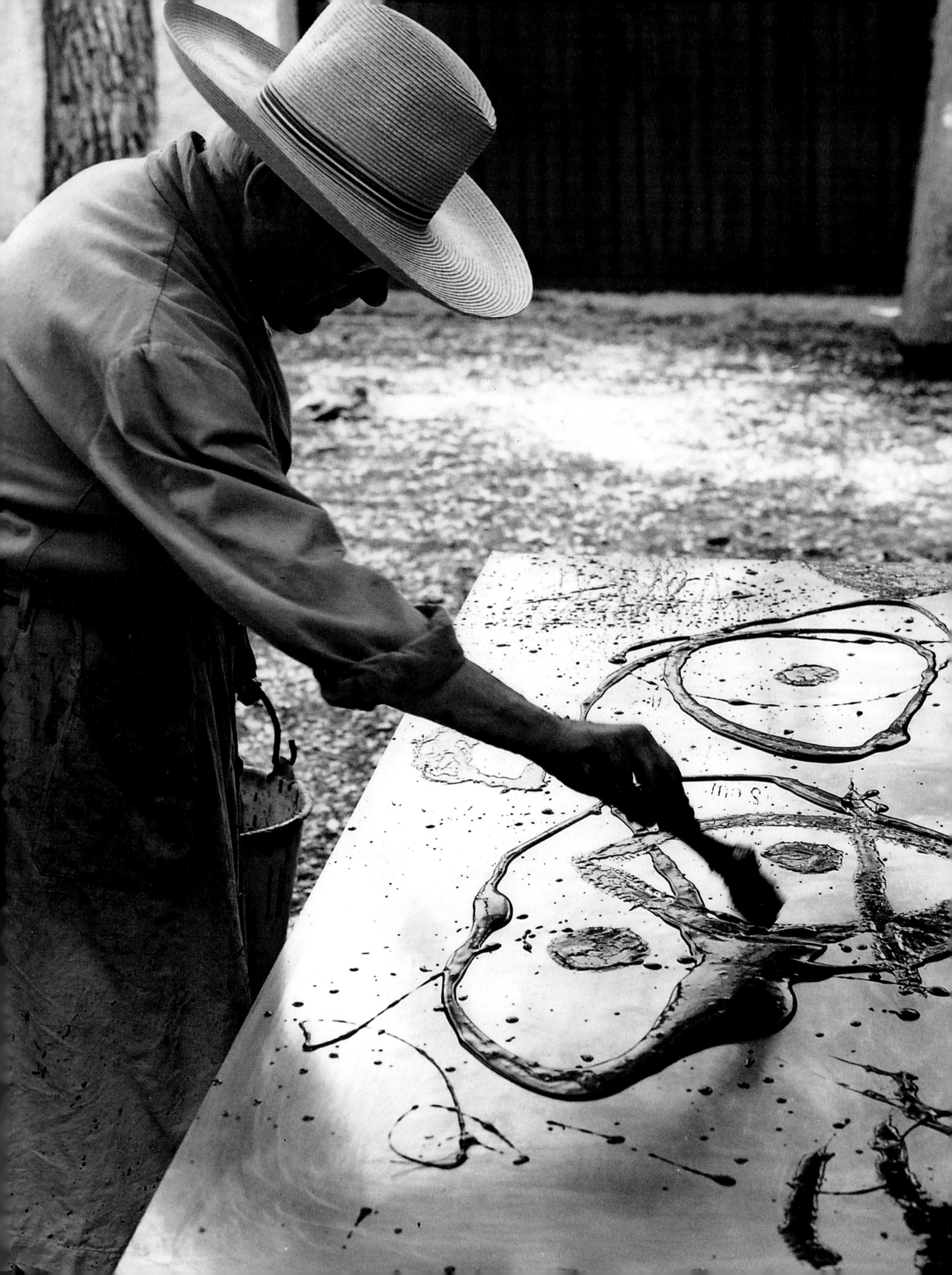

MIRÓ AND CALDER

MIRÓ AND CALDER

From the time of their first meeting at the Galerie Maeght's 'Exposition internationale du surréalisme en 1947', featuring his crazy *Superstition* (1947; cat. 18) unwinding on an imaginary journey across the wall, Joan Miró (1893–1983) and the Maeghts, in a spirit of post-war renewal, moved beyond traditional easel painting and sculpture into ceramics, site-specific public art and graphics. Miró made extensive use of the Maeght facilities and technicians in Paris and at Saint-Paul. His wax crayon drawing '*Pour Adrien Maeght, en hommage à son travail*' (1965; cat. 37) pays testimony to their close collaboration on around 1,500 etchings and lithographs. The Maeghts' extensive holdings of Miró's work include a key early painting, *North–South* (*Nord–Sud*) (1917; cat. 11) – the title of Pierre Reverdy's avant-garde review. With its typically Spanish still-life elements – a *porron* for wine and caged goldfinch – encircled by Delaunayesque concentric rings of colour, it illustrates how closely Miró tracked recent developments in Paris from Barcelona. Paris was the magnet that drew him away from his roots in the Catalan countryside to develop an art of the imagination, inspired by the Surrealist poets, in which his previous themes are universalised and set in simplified, elemental landscapes or in a cosmic dream space that he literally titled *Blue* (*Bleu*) (1925; cat. 12).

A dichotomy opened up in Miró's art. Split between the earth and the sky, he wanted, on the one hand, a new form of realism, based on a hallucinatory scrutiny of everyday matter, and, on the other, to push painting beyond the limits of the medium and achieve the imaginative freedom of Surrealist poetry. The resolution to this crisis came with his increasingly elemental conception of a universe fashioned through the interaction of earth, fire, air and water. Working with his old childhood friend, the master potter Josep Lloréns Artigas, he literally fired base earth into precious matter – a simulacrum of an alchemical act of creation. On everyday vases and plates, treated like found objects, glazes ooze and flow like lava, forms are suggested, cosmic signs are incised. Miró's 'Working Notes 1941–42' outline the process:

> Take a jar with a varnished yellow ground, add a green
> spot and then really sharp drawing in sienna ....When
> Lloréns-Artigas sprays the jars with a fixative and clear
> varnish he gets a lovely quality. Before firing put some
> deep lines in the clay which suggest shapes. Starting from
> these shapes, do some sharp drawings before the varnish
> dries and then paint them, leaving the background
> unpainted.[1] (see cats 15 and 24)

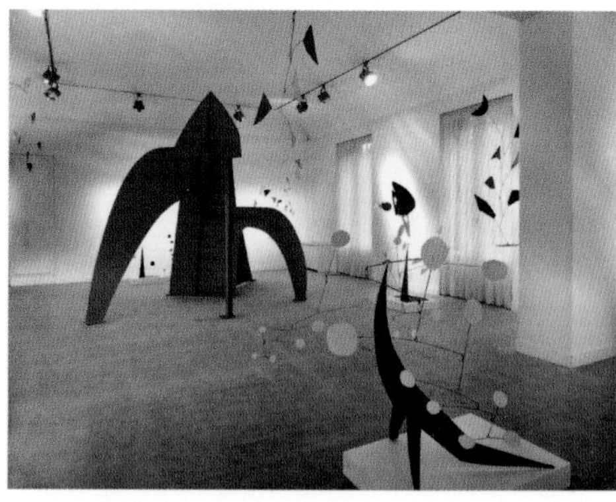

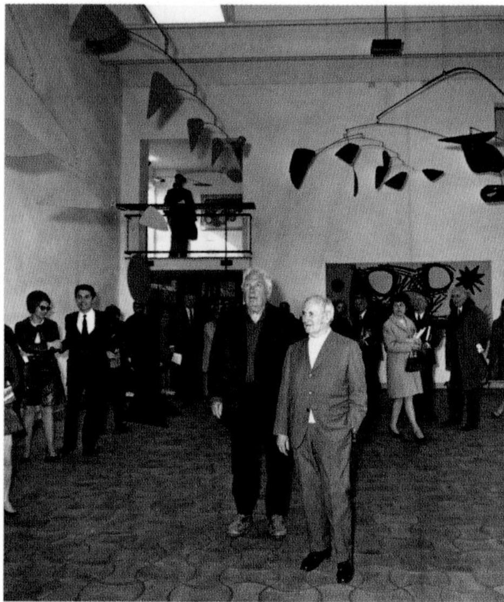

FIG. 39
View of Calder exhibition at Galerie Maeght,
Paris, 1954 (cat. 126)

FIG. 40
Alexander Calder and Joan Miró at the
opening reception of a Calder retrospective,
Fondation Maeght, 1969

Page 62: Joan Miró making an original etching
in the garden behind the Galerie Maeght,
Paris, 1973

The brown centre of a plate takes on the form of a mask's cavernous mouth (cat. 27); cut out of a yellow plate, the sun is encircled by graffiti figures and cosmic signs (cat. 25); painted blue with black signs, the island of Mallorca is surrounded by sea creatures encrusted in salt-like sand.

After the anxieties of the Spanish Civil War and World War II, financial insecurity and the ever-present threat of arrest or harassment by Franco's Guardia Civil, Mallorca meant for Miró an island of calm in a sea of troubles where the elements of air and water merged in a translucent airiness, the substance of the cosmos at the dawn of creation. A young girl looks on in wonderment at the sun rising through the planetary turbulence of the universe (cat. 28). The flight of a bird celebrates an explosive act of generation from gas to squiggly sperm writhing in ecstasy in an airy firmament (cat. 29). The blackened, smoky path of vagina–woman and sperm–bird coinciding in the cosmos is commemorated in *Woman and Bird* (*Femme et oiseau*) (1964). The cosmological beginnings of the world are writ down on velum in an abbreviated linear sign language, a modern Mappa Mundi, a generation myth uniting the palaeolithic with the contemporary (cat. 44). While working with Lloréns Artigas and his son Joan at Gallifa, a hamlet in the mountains above Barcelona, Miró would begin the day by painting directly on to the surrounding rocks, and he brought this feeling of working with the very elements of creation to his painting and sculpture.[2] The bronze *Constellation* (1972; cat. 46) looks like a meteorite excavated from volcanic rock.

Alexander Calder's *Constellations* (1944; cat. 16), begun in 1943, were a direct homage to Miró's similarly titled series in which, moved by the night sky, the Catalan artist dreamt of physical and spiritual freedom. From their first meeting in Paris in December 1928, Miró and Calder's careers followed parallel paths, and the two shared dealers, patrons, commissions and, above all, common sources of inspiration in nature and the universe. Calder (1898–1976) described his appropriate exchange gift to Miró as 'a sort of mechanized volcano, made of ebony'.[3] His quirky *Bird with Balls* (*Oiseau aux roubignolles*) (1954; cat. 13), with genitals suspended like a lorgnette from its belly, looks as though it has hopped out of the famous mechanical toy *Circus* (1926–31, Whitney Museum of American Art, New York) with which he made his name in Paris, where he later performed at the Maeght family's house. In *Bird with Spectacles* (*Oiseau aux lunettes*) (*c*. 1930; cat. 14), the bird, like a myopic matron, picks up and peers through the lorgnette. *Spider* (*Araignée*) (1947; cat. 31) comprises a bulbous black body balanced on three delicate wire legs. *Cat Snake* (*Le Chat serpent*) (1968; cat. 40) slithers across the ground like a red ink blob that has all but digested the black, despairing head of the cat.

This playful, humorous side to Calder's art aligned him with Miró and the biomorphism of Jean Arp. At the same time, it distanced him from

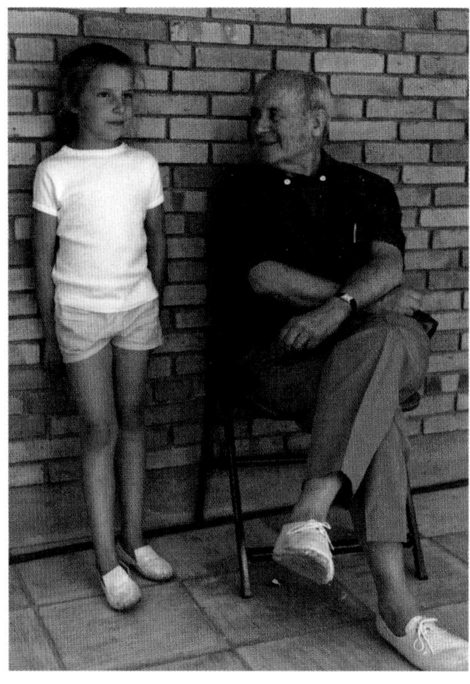

Yoyo Maeght and Joan Miró at the Fondation Maeght, July 1966

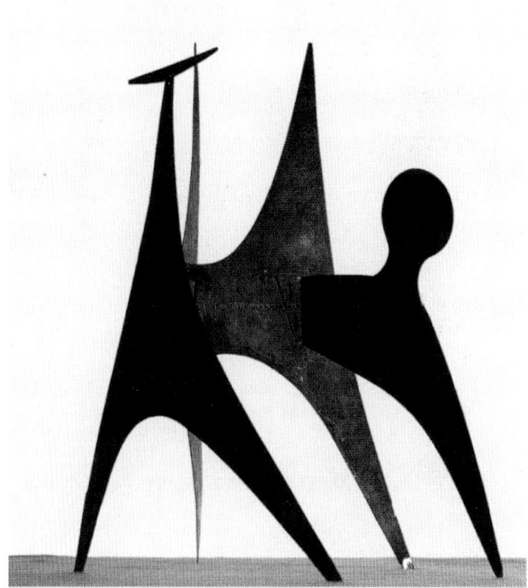

Alexander Calder (1898–1976), *Reinforcements* (*Les Renforts*), 1963. Steel, 630 x 500 cm. Fondation Marguerite et Aimé Maeght, Saint-Paul

the messianic fervour of Piet Mondrian and the machinist purity of
Naum Gabo, who together stimulated his transition to a highly original
constructed, abstract art, christened by Marcel Duchamp the 'mobile' – a
word that in French implies both movement and motive. Arp named the
stationary version the 'stabile'. Hybrid combinations such as *Feathers*
(*L'Empennage*) (1953; cat. 22) were described by Jacques Prévert in
Derrière Le Miroir:

> Mobile en haut
> stabile en bas
> telle est la tour Eiffel
> Calder est comme elle
> Oiseleur du fer
> horologer du vent … [4]

As a trained mechanical engineer, Calder employed the abstract
language of science to evoke a parallel, deeply poetic universe of forms
activated by gravity and the winds' currents. Beginning with the smallest
unit, he would construct a *mobile* through a process of weights and
balances. In Jean-Paul Sartre's words, 'A general destiny of movement is
sketched for them, and then they are left to work it out for themselves'.[5]
The titles confirm their association with the natural world: for example,
Sumac V (1953; cat. 23), a wedding present from Calder to Adrien and
Paule Maeght, suggests the reddened autumnal leaves of the sumac tree.
But there was a serious side to Calder. The scythe-like cutting edges and
tapering sharp points of the looming black constructions seen together
at the Galerie Maeght's 'Stabiles' exhibition in 1959 spoke of anxiety,
malignant giant spiders, flesh-devouring dinosaurs and the Horsemen of
the Apocalypse. Calder was politically committed and ever alive to the dark
side of human existence, whether it be McCarthyite persecution of liberals,
the threat of nuclear destruction or the Vietnam War. *Reinforcements* (*Les
Renforts*) (1963; fig. 42) on the lawn of the Fondation Maeght is a salutary
reminder that even this earthly paradise is not immune.

NW

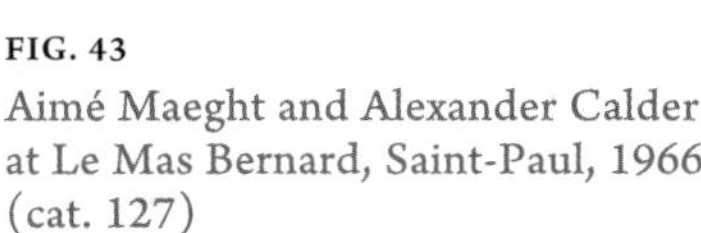

FIG. 43
Aimé Maeght and Alexander Calder
at Le Mas Bernard, Saint-Paul, 1966
(cat. 127)

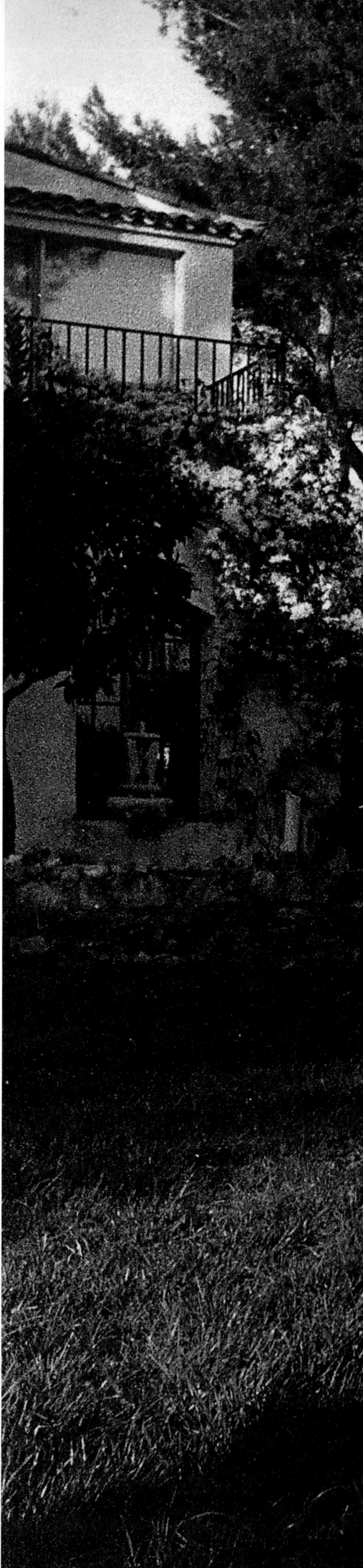

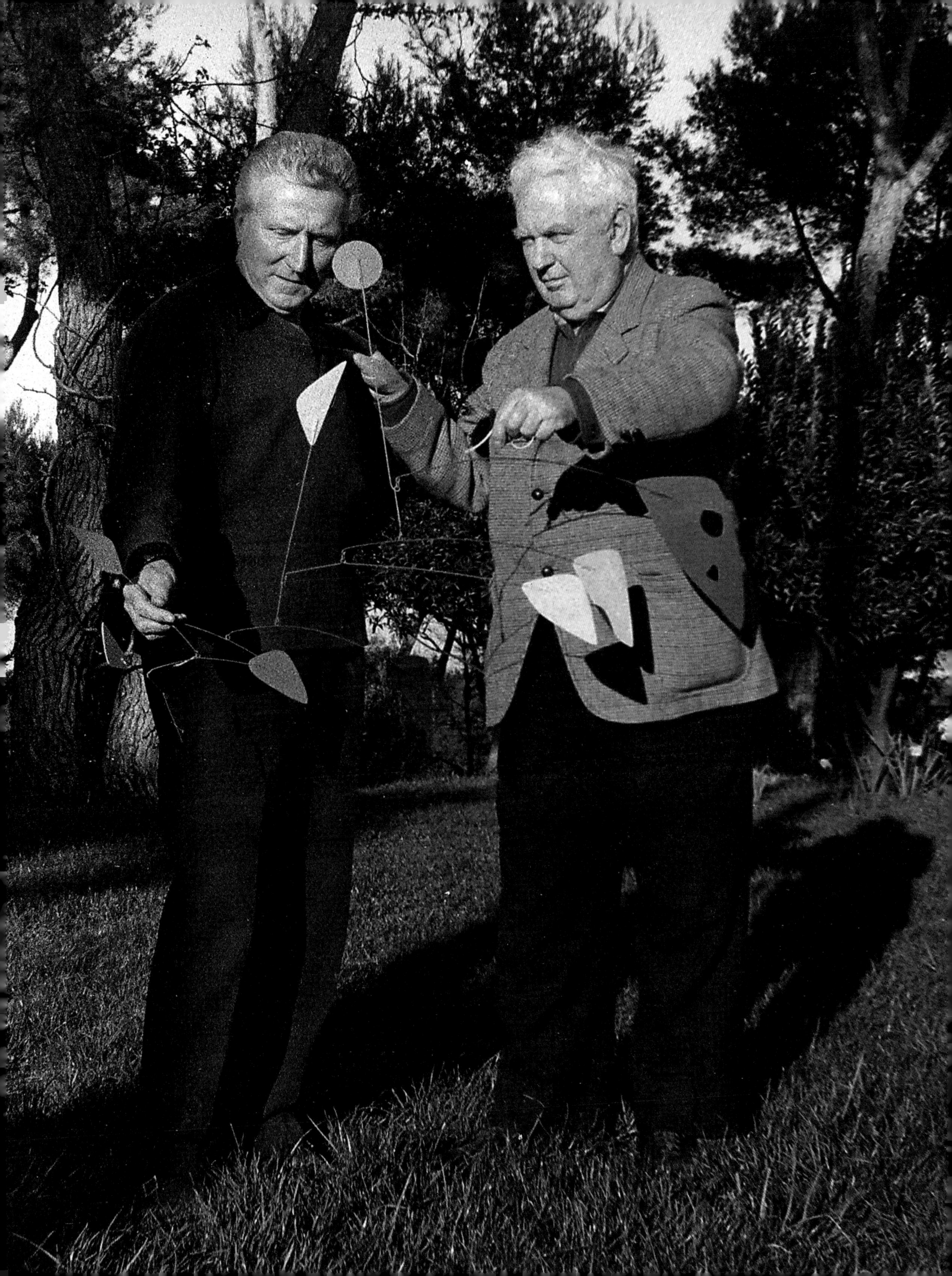

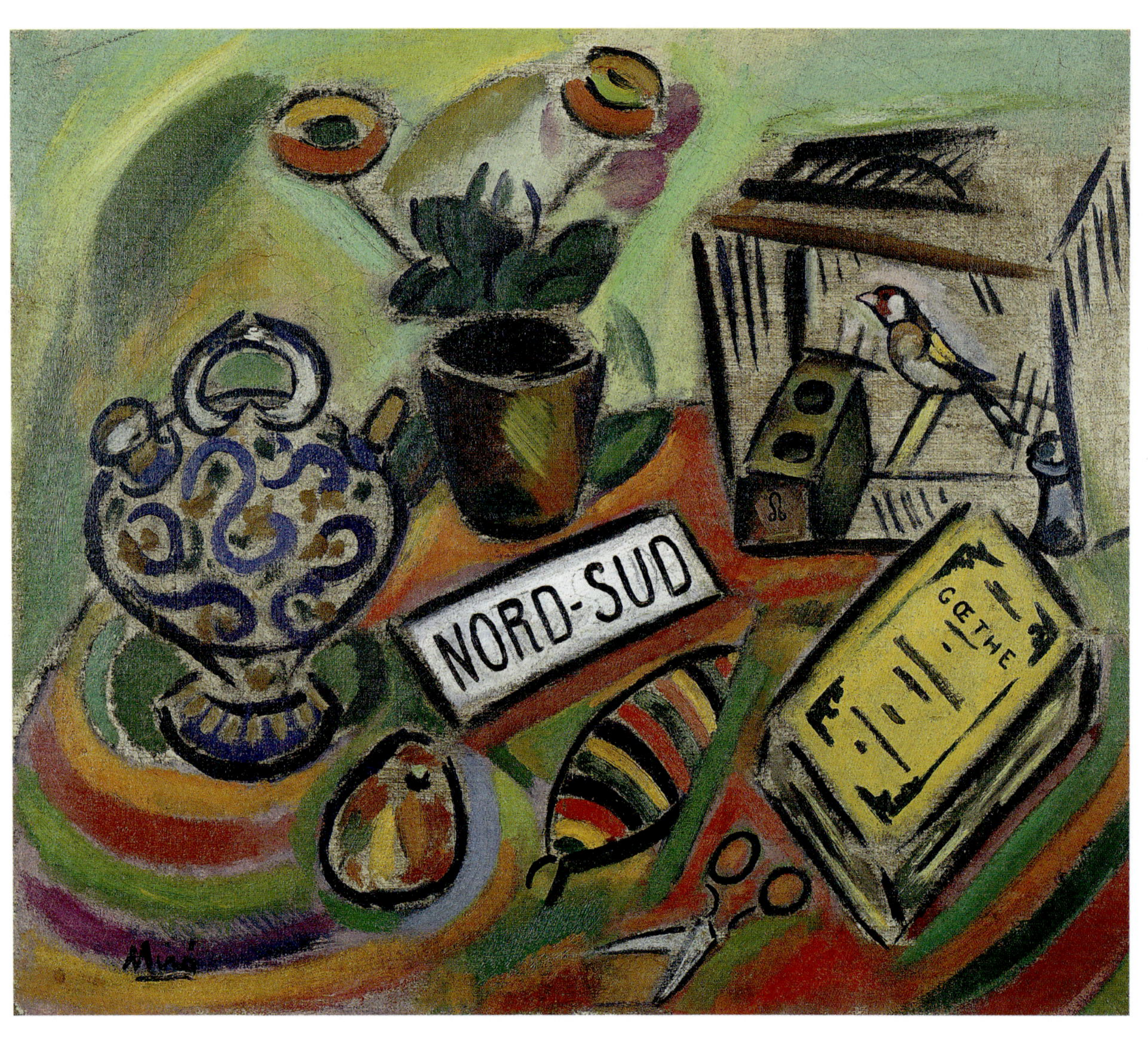

CAT. 11
Joan Miró (1893–1983)
North–South (*Nord–Sud*), 1917
Oil on canvas, 62 x 70 cm

Joan Miró (1893–1983)
Blue (*Bleu*), 1925
Oil on canvas, 64.5 x 91 cm

CAT. 13
Alexander Calder (1898–1976)
Bird with Balls (Oiseau aux roubignolles), 1954
Iron wire, 25 x 27 x 18 cm

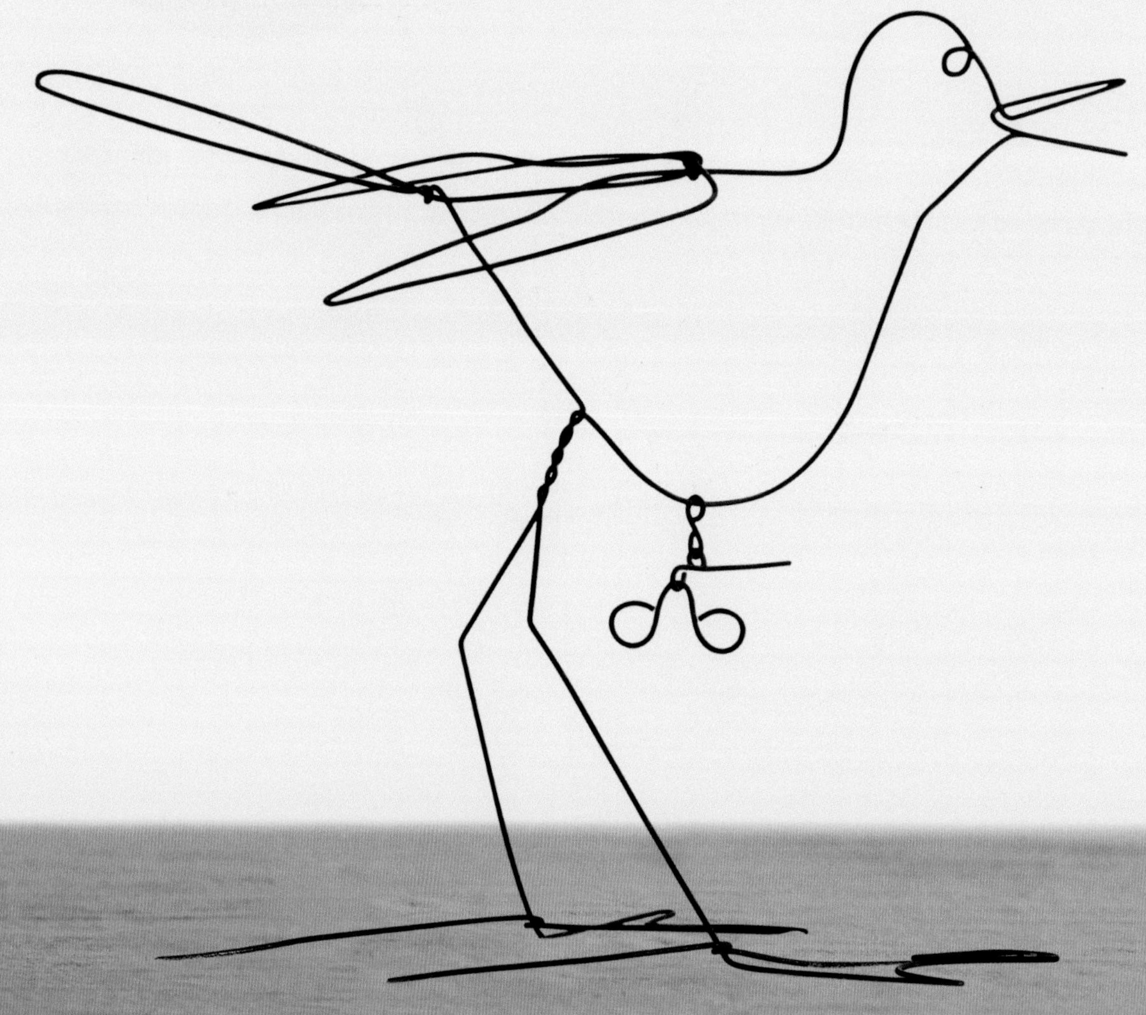

CAT. 14
Alexander Calder (1898–1976)
Bird with Spectacles (Oiseau aux lunettes),
c. 1930
Iron wire, 35 x 32 x 18 cm

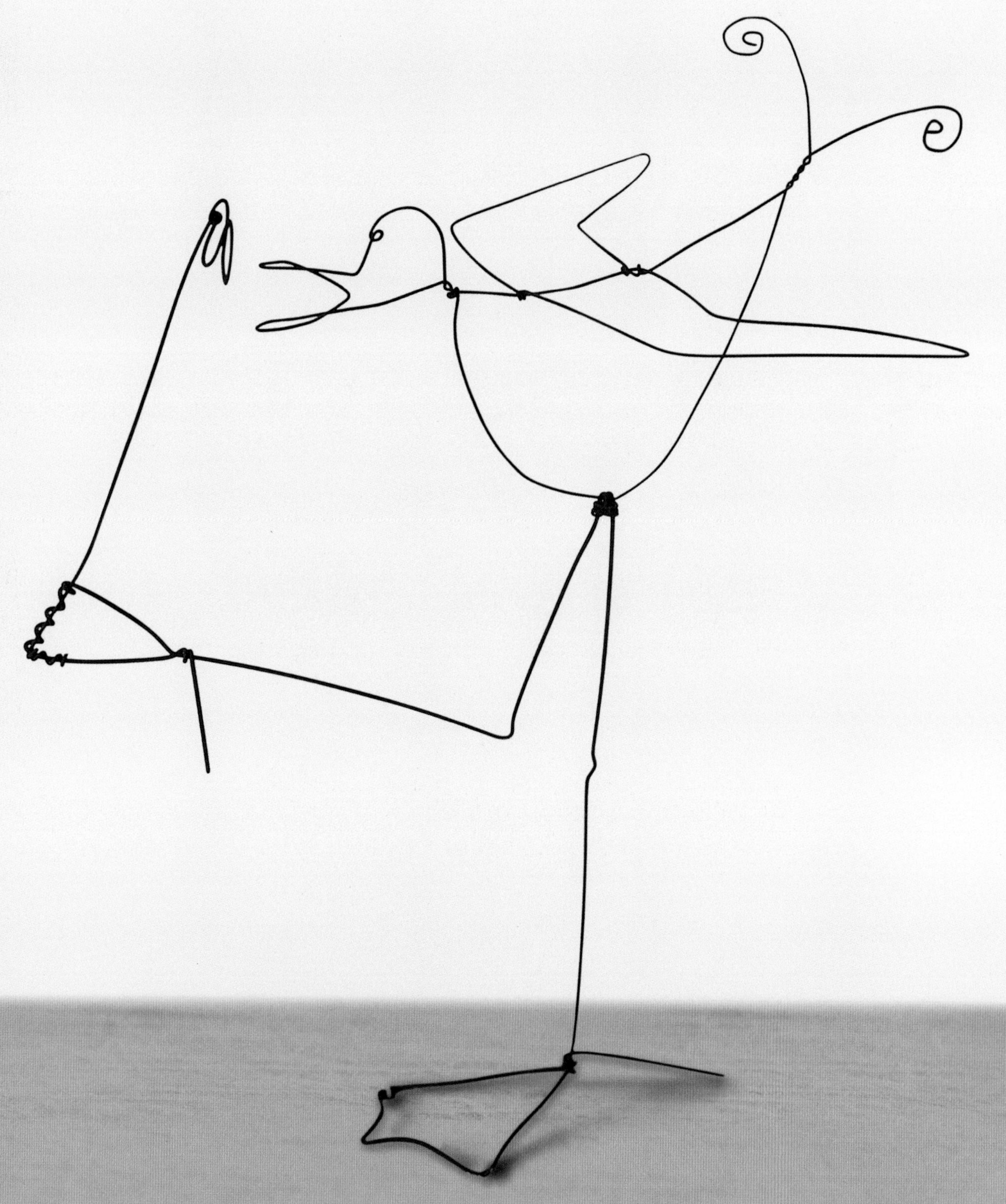

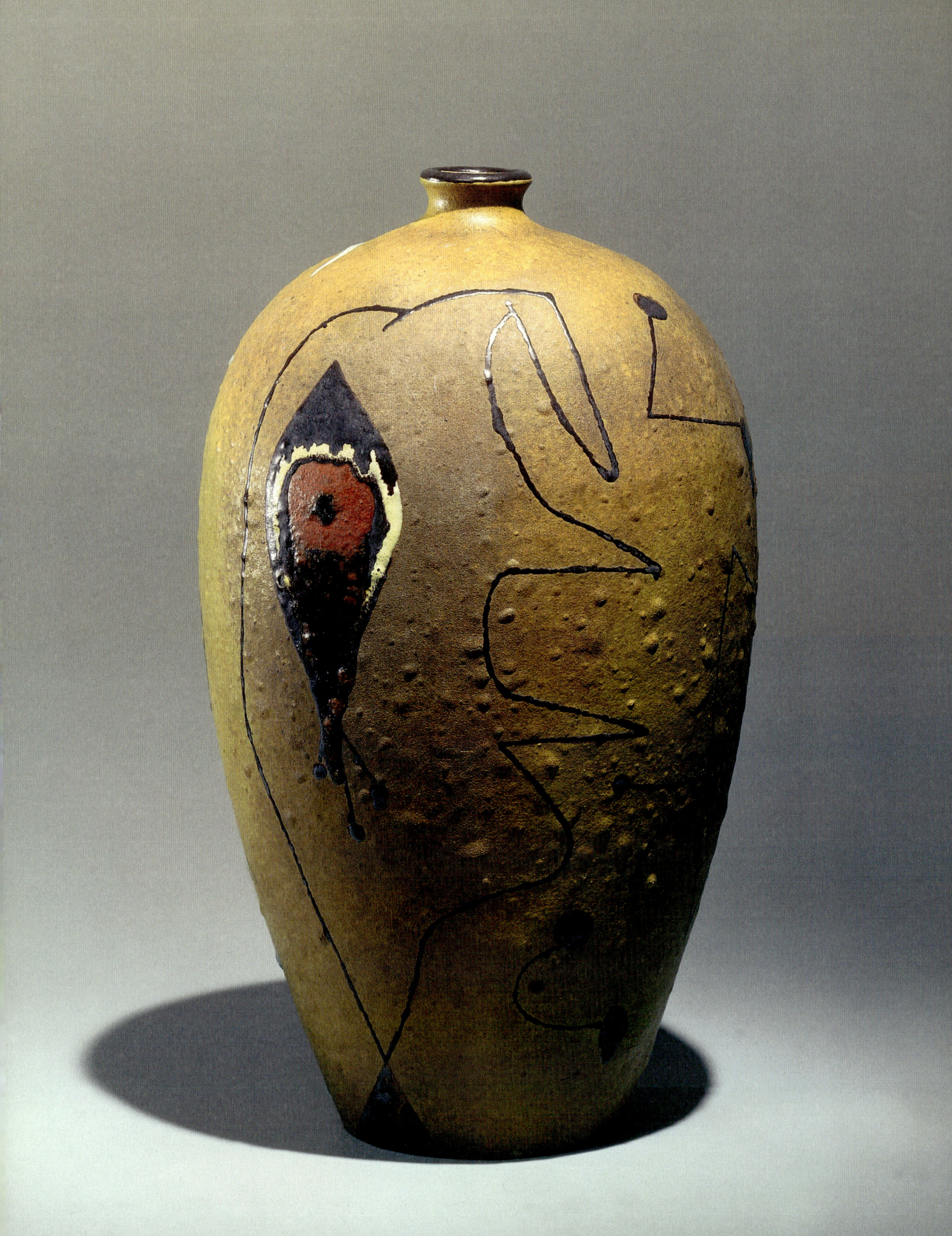

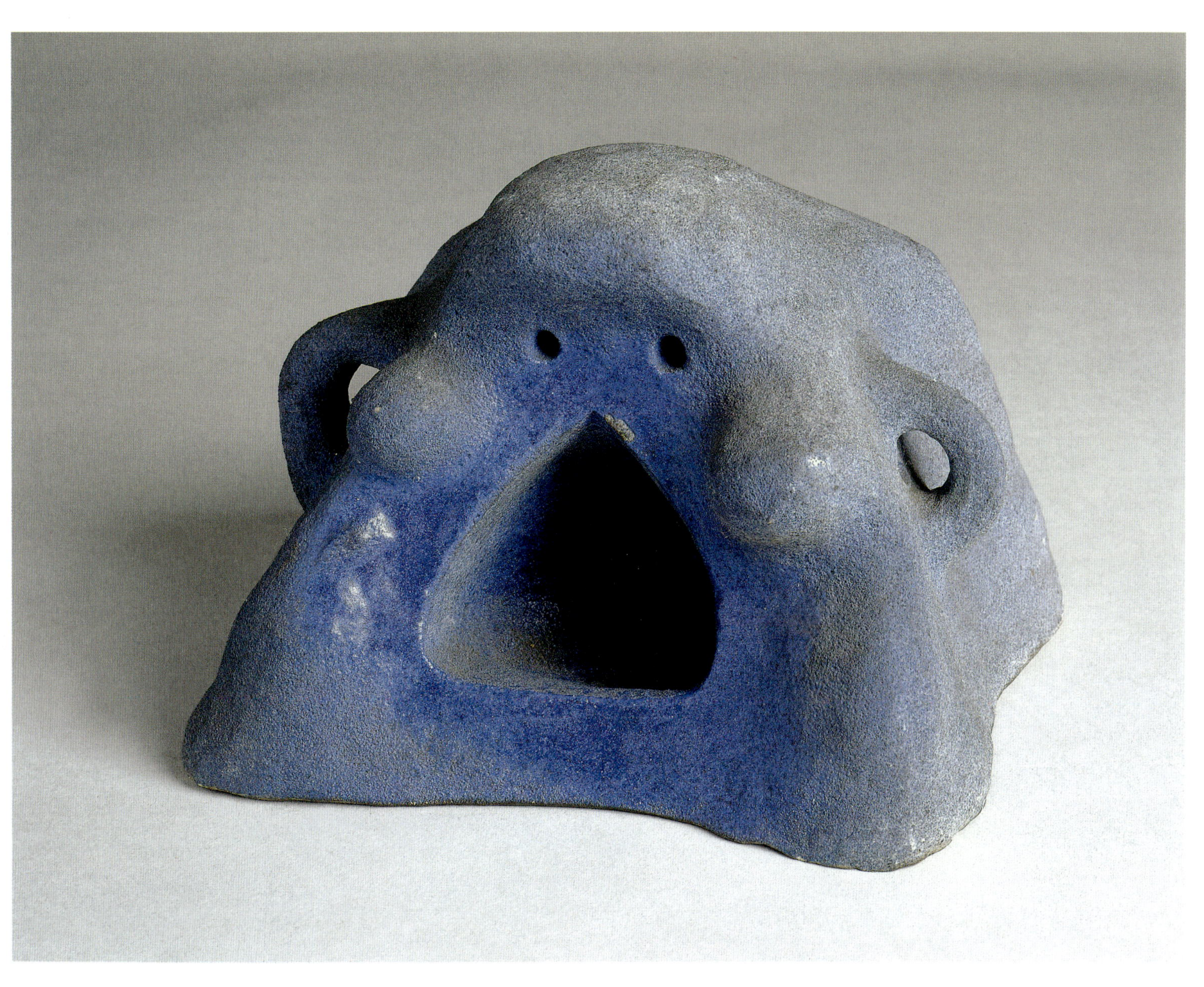

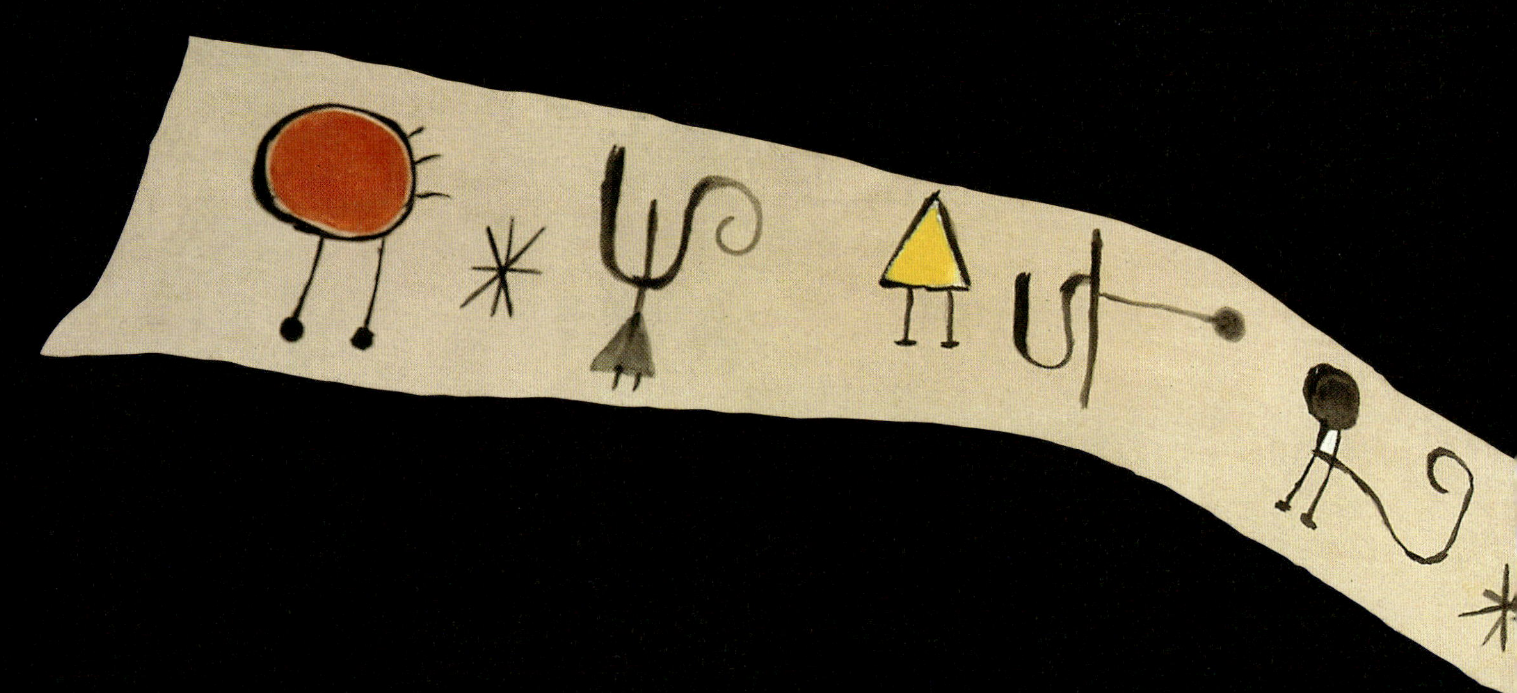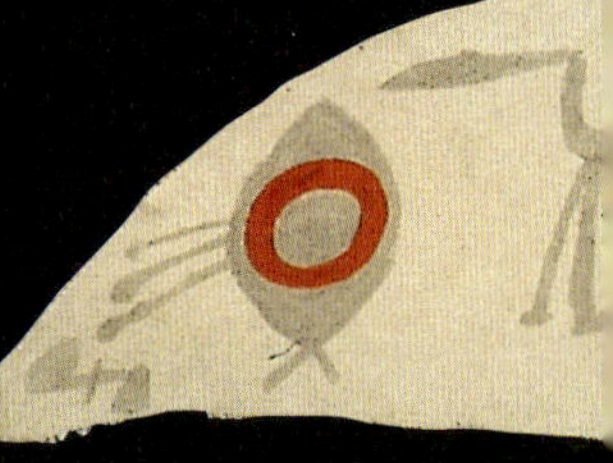

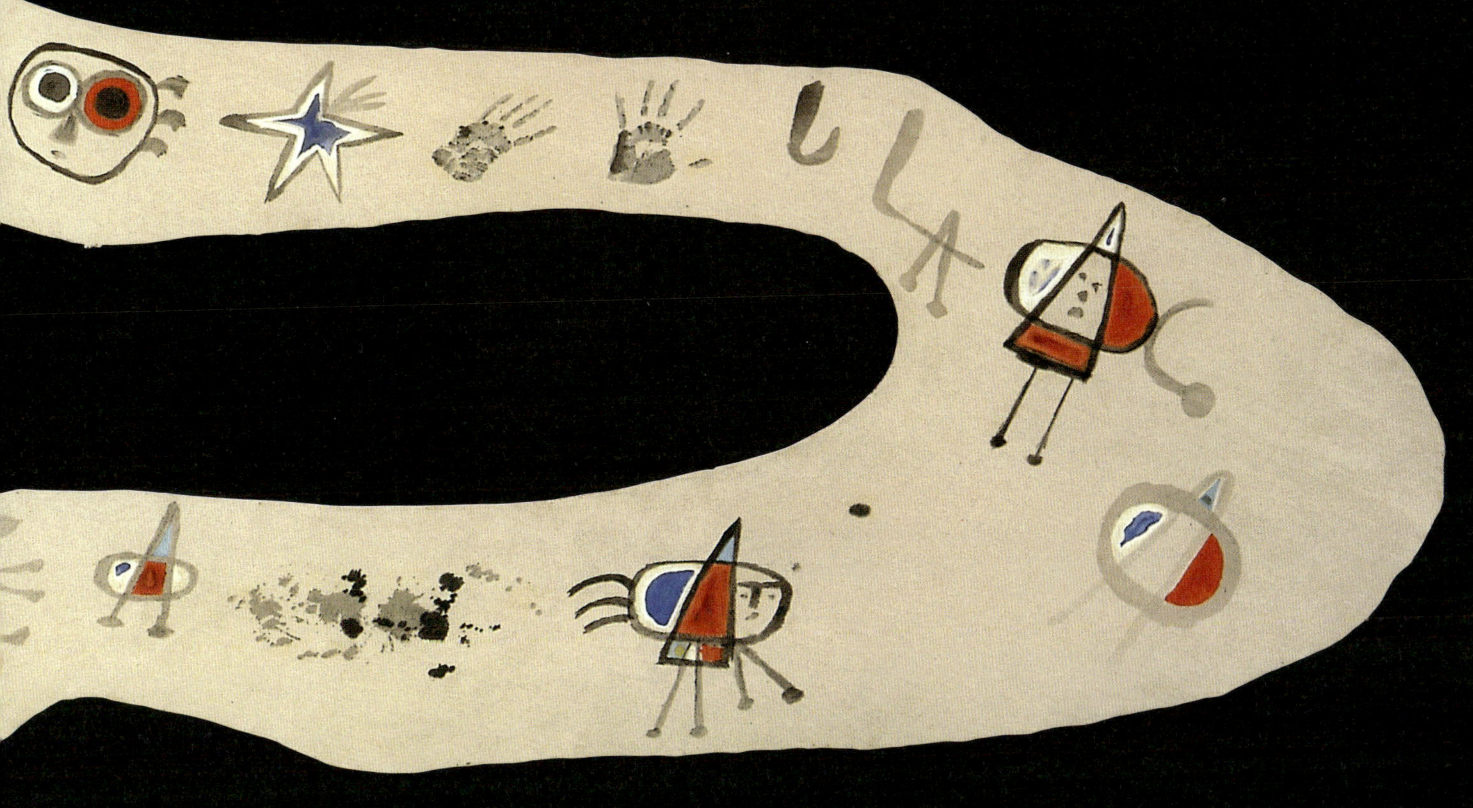

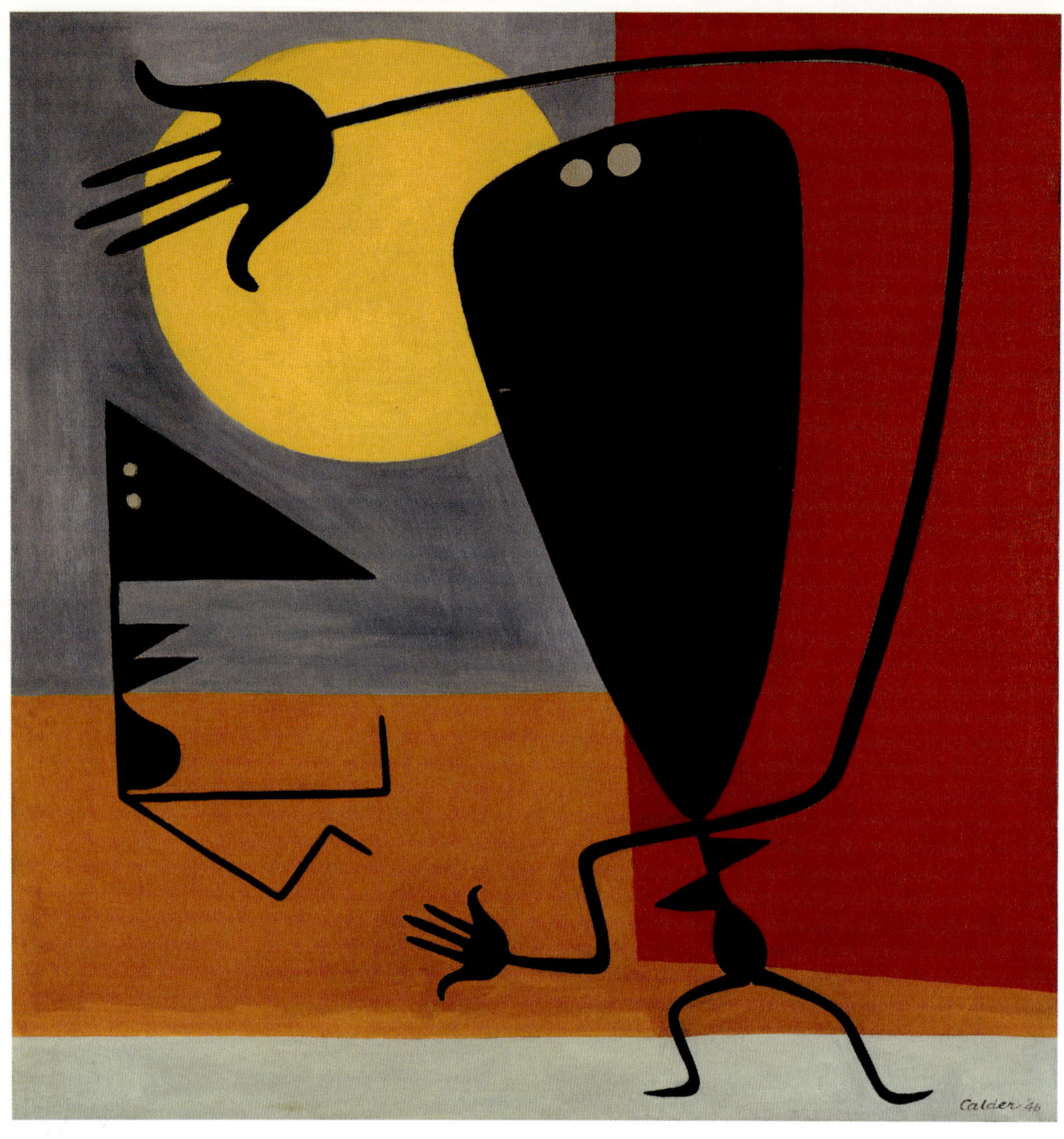

CAT. 19
Alexander Calder (1898–1976)
Personage, 1946
Oil on canvas, 123 x 114 cm

CAT. 20
Joan Miró (1893–1983)
Drawing dedicated to Paul Elúard, 1948
Ink on paper, 27.5 x 20 cm

CAT. 21
Joan Miró (1893–1983)
Blue Totem (Totem bleu), 1953
Oil on canvas, 300 x 20 cm

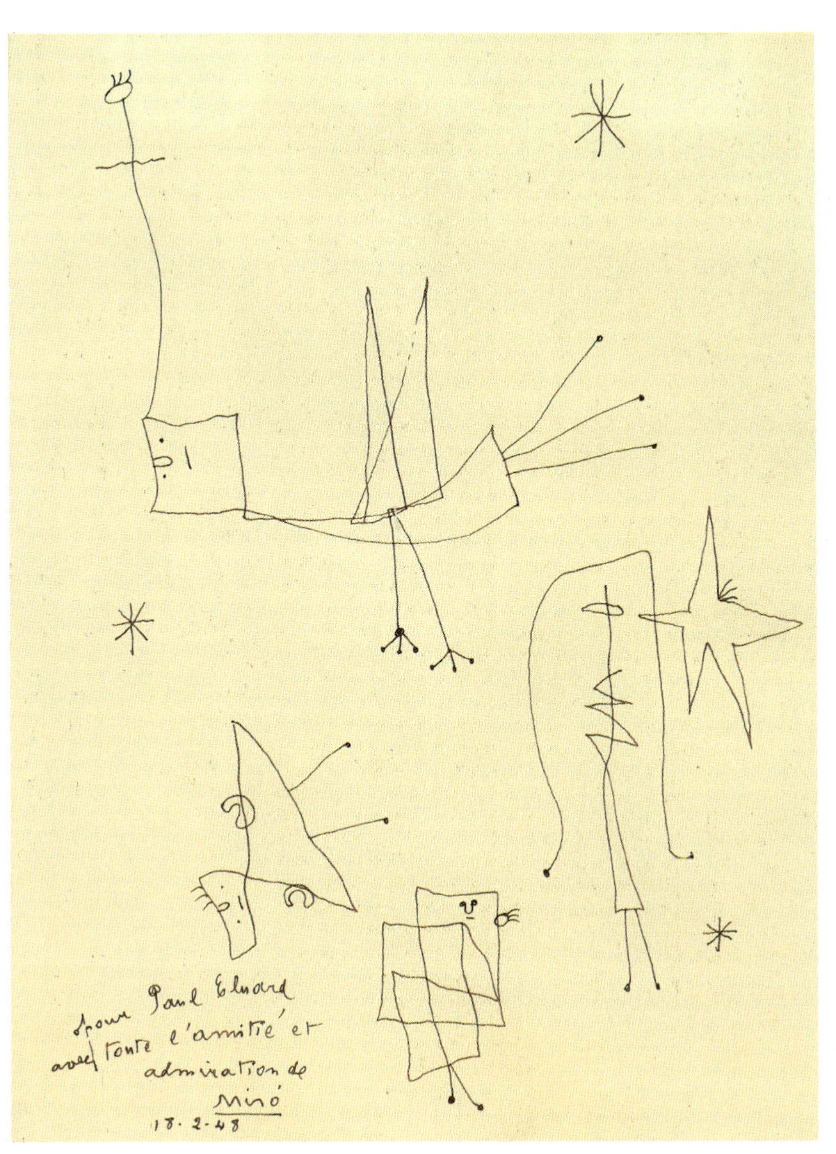

pour Paul Eluard
avec toute l'amitié et
admiration de
Miró
18.2.48

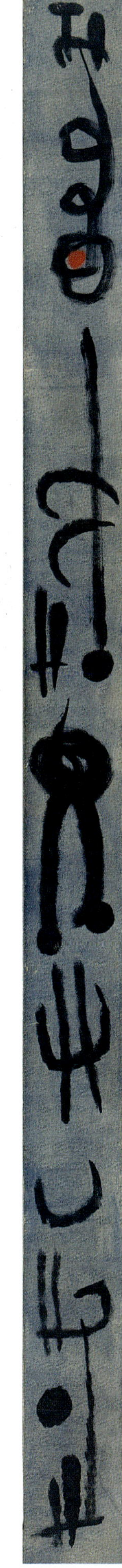

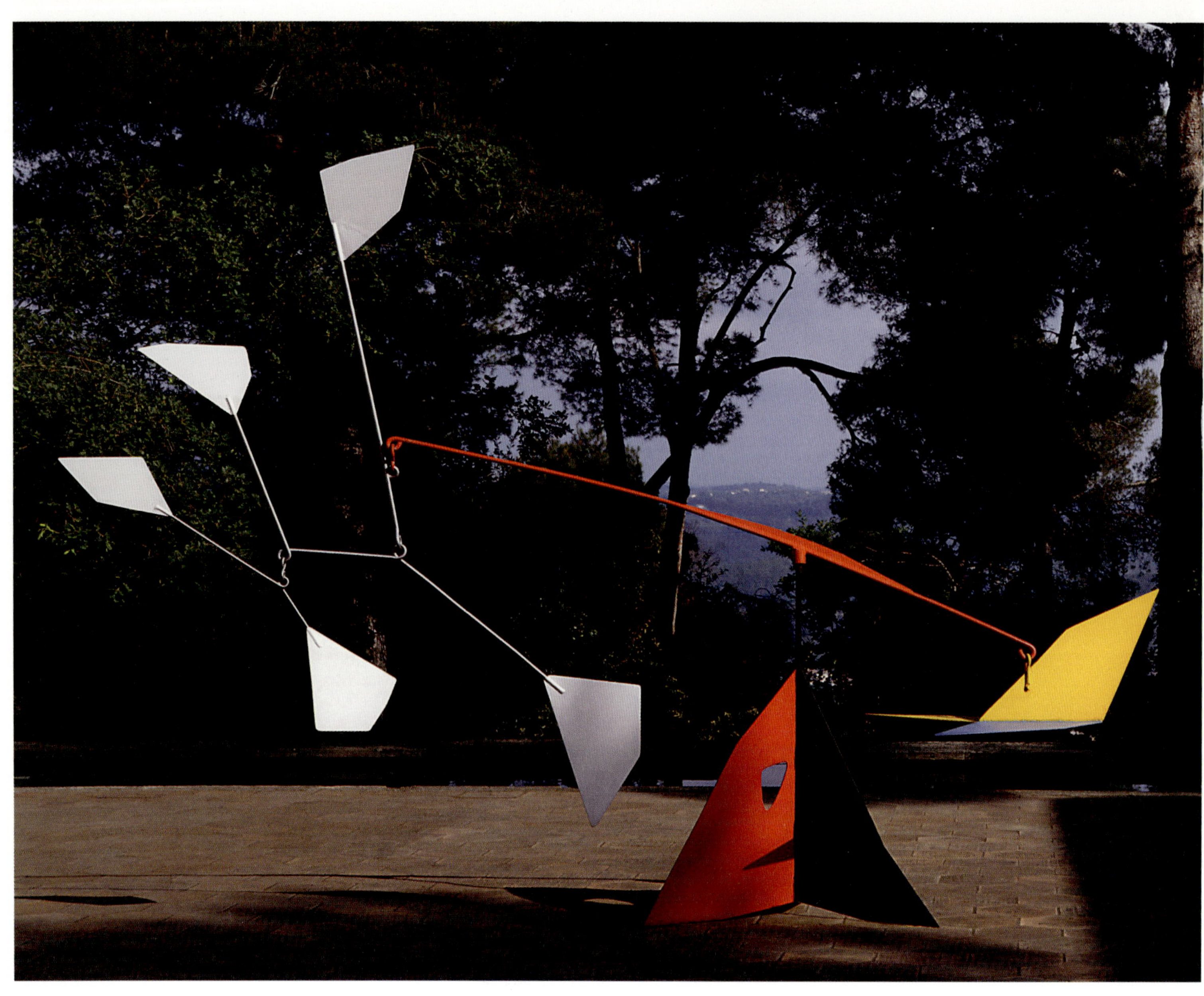

CAT. 22
Alexander Calder (1898–1976)
Feathers (L'Empennage), 1953
Stabile mobile, painted metal, 150 x 284 cm

CAT. 23
Alexander Calder (1898–1976)
Sumac V, 1953
Mobile, painted metal, 125 x 140 cm

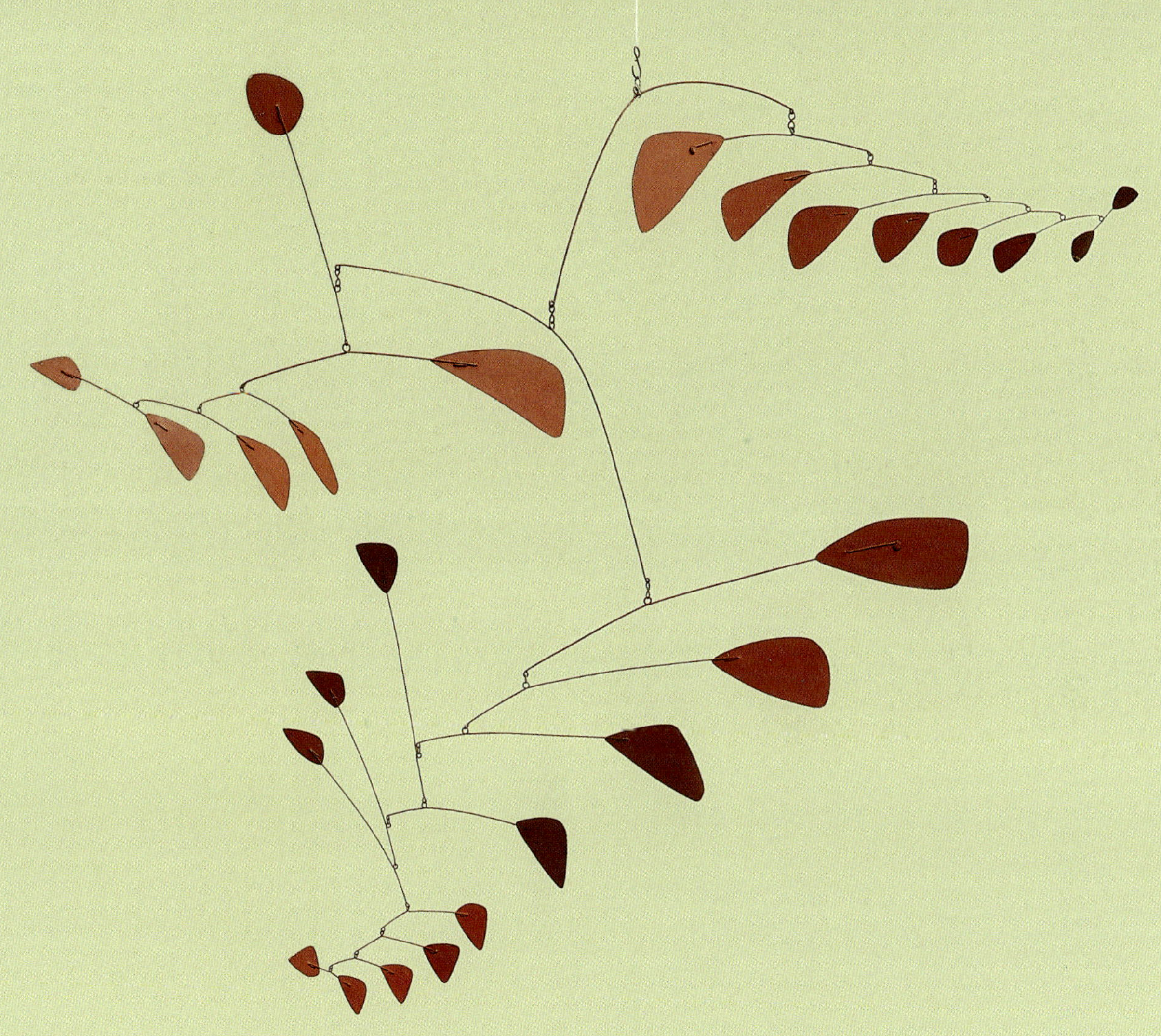

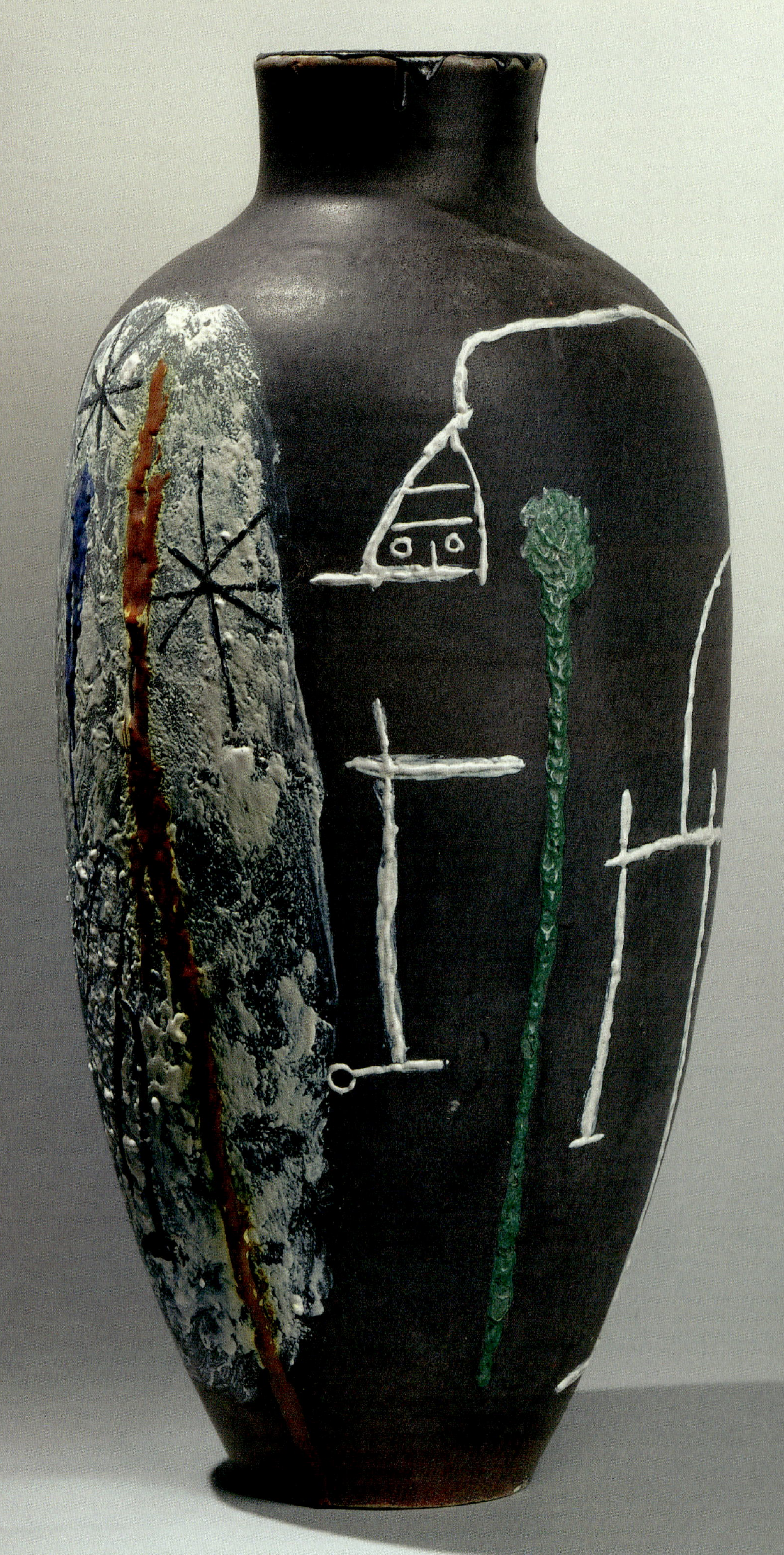

CLOCKWISE FROM LEFT:

CAT. 24
Joan Miró (1893–1983)
Black Vase, 1956
Ceramic, 51 x 27 cm

CAT. 25
Joan Miró (1893–1983)
Large Double-sided Disc
(*Grand disque double face*), 1956
Ceramic, diameter: 59 cm

CAT. 27
Joan Miró (1893–1983)
Red Sun Plate with White Enamels
(*Plat soleil rouge émaux blancs*), 1956
Ceramic, diameter: 37 cm

CAT. 26
Joan Miró (1893–1983)
Catalan Bowl (Coupe Catalane), 1956
Ceramic, 28 x 23.5 x 13.5 cm

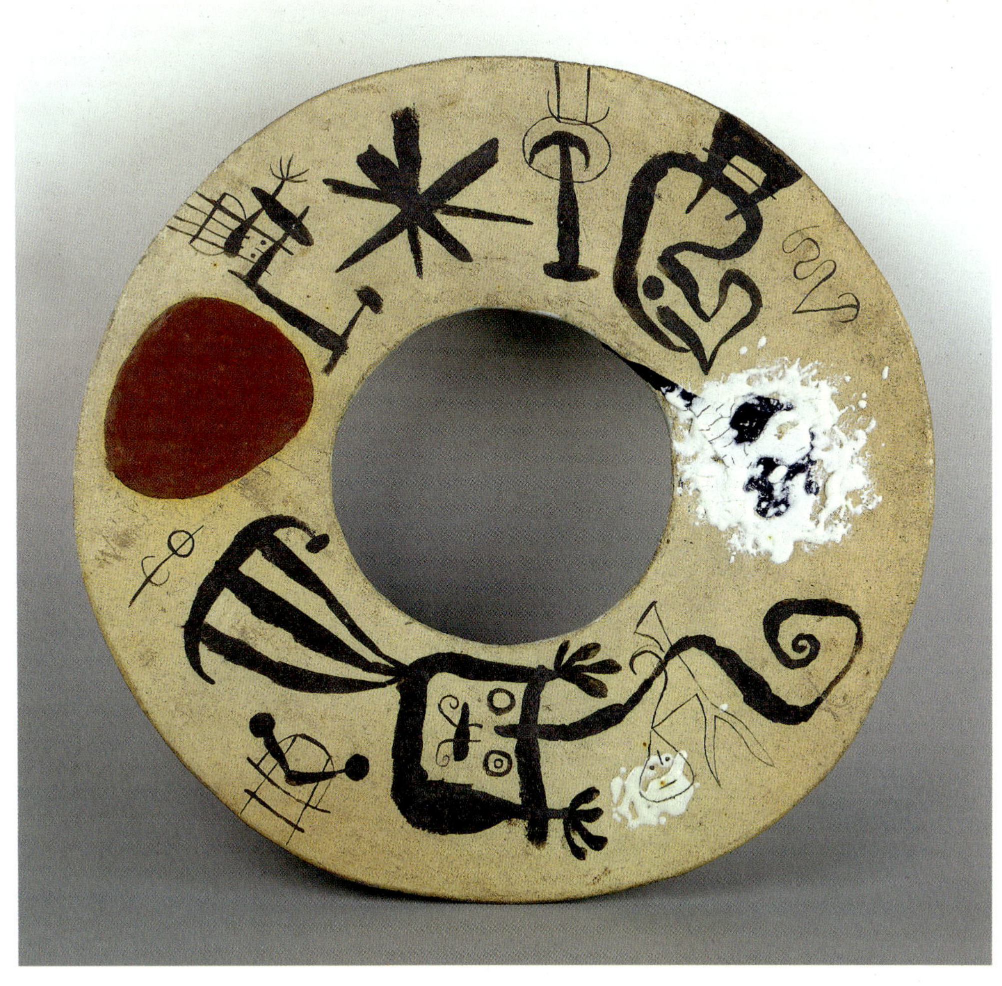

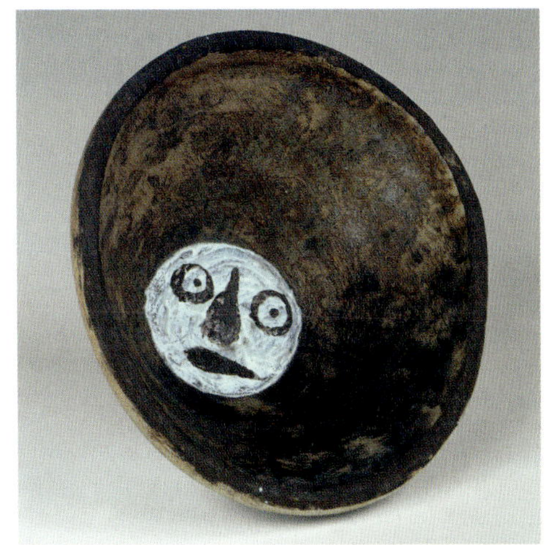

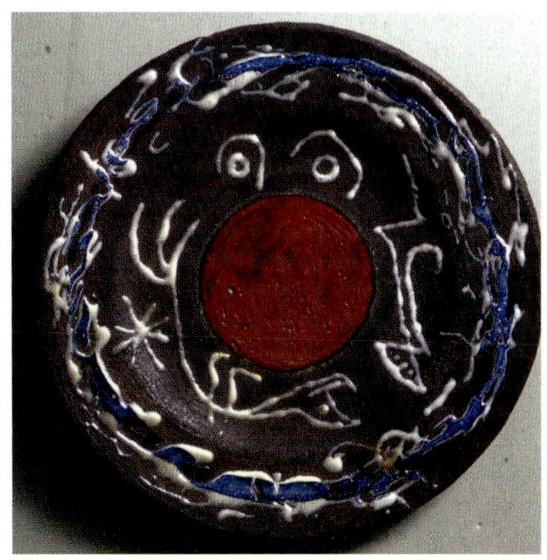

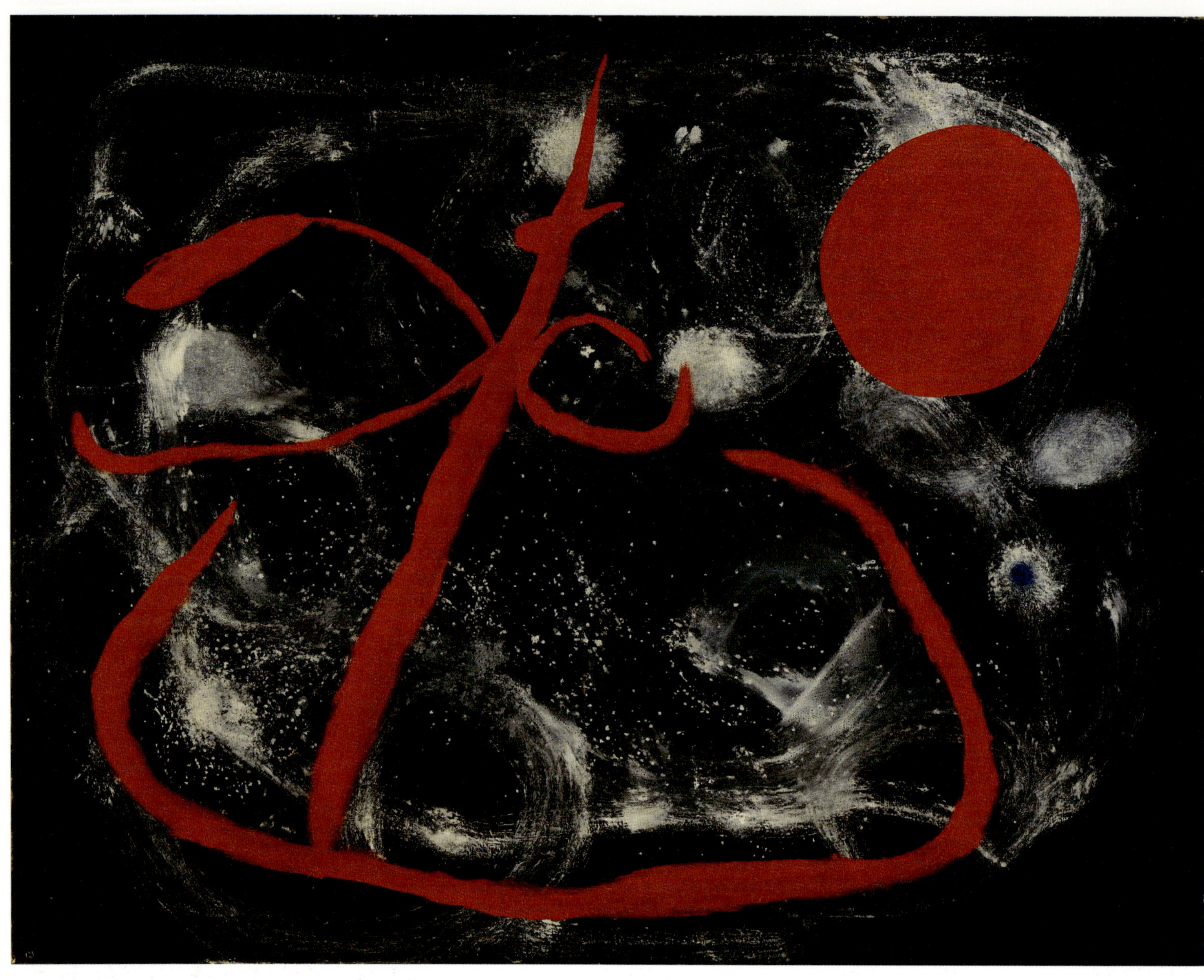

CAT. 28

Joan Miró (1893–1983)
Joy of a Little Girl in Front of the Sun
(*Joie d'une fillete devant le soleil*), 1960
Oil on canvas, 130 x 162 cm

CAT. 29

Joan Miró (1893–1983)
Birds' Flight at the First Spark of Dawn
(*Vol d'oiseaux à la première étincelle de l'aube*), 1964
Oil on canvas, 162 x 130 cm

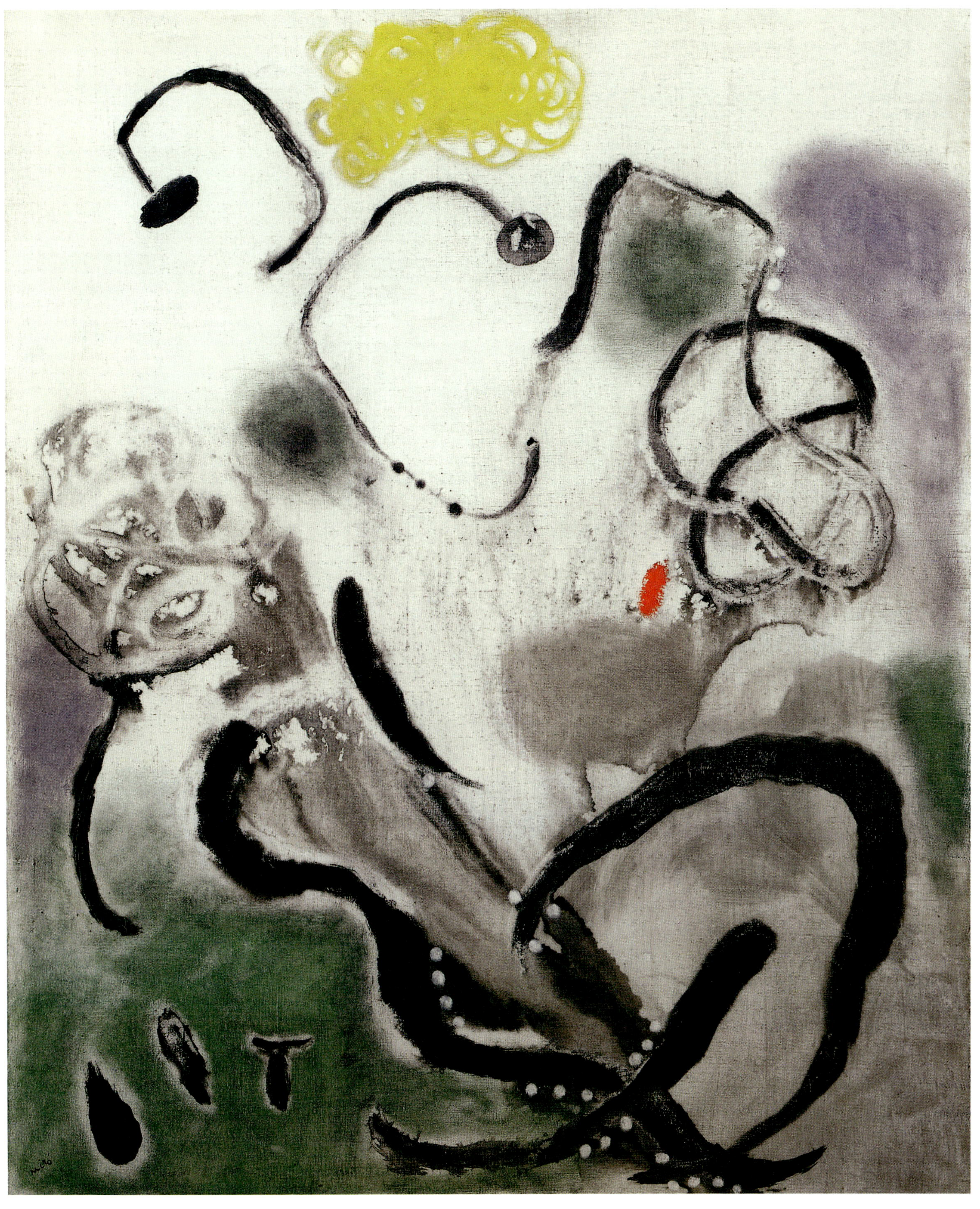

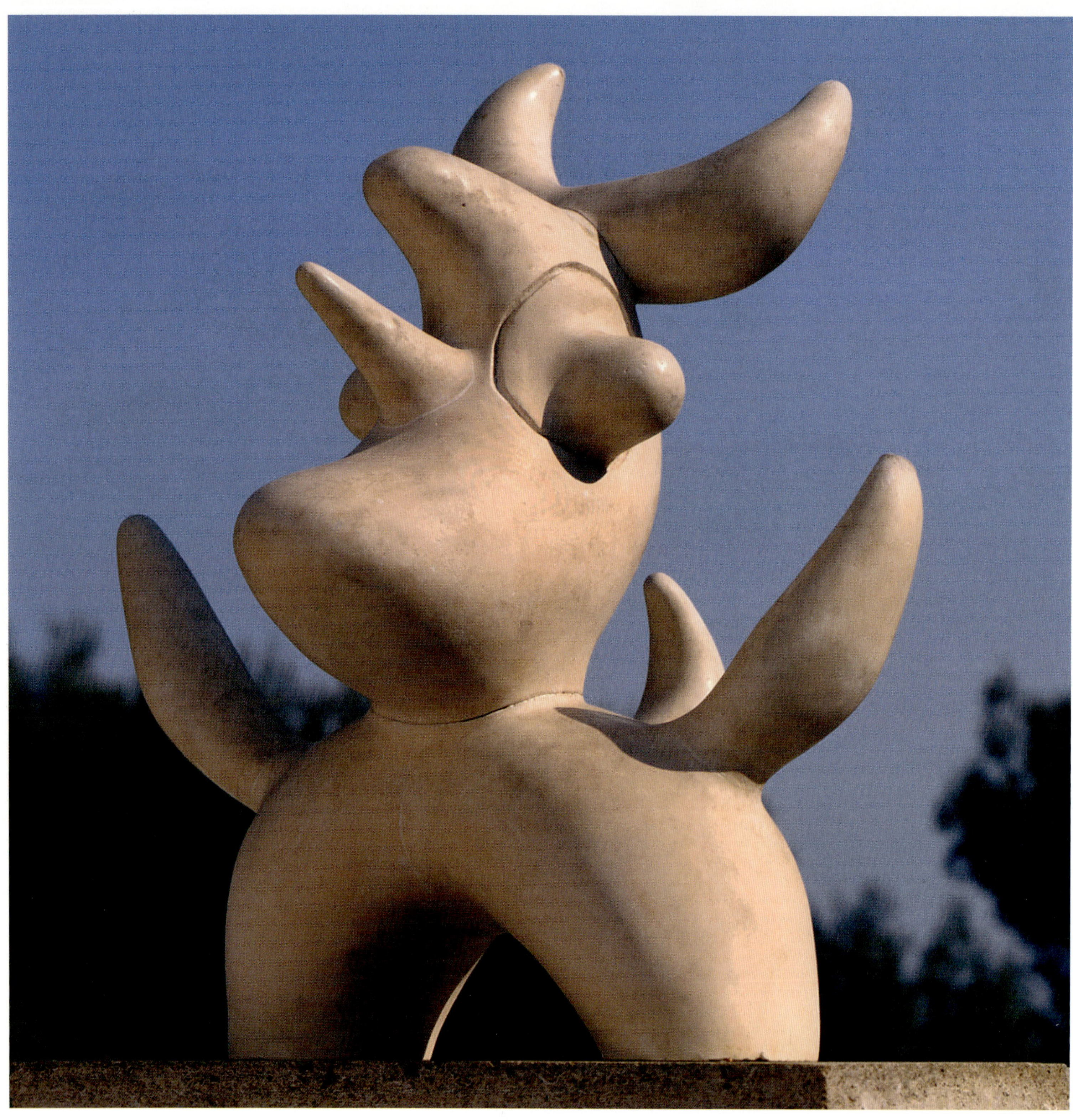

CAT. 32
Joan Miró (1893–1983)
Maquette for *Moon Bird*
(*L'Oiseau lunaire*), *c.* 1963
Plaster, 77 x 69.5 x 69 cm

CAT. 33
Joan Miró (1893–1983)
Maquette for *Arch* (*L'Arc*), 1963
Ceramic, 53 x 65 x 22 cm

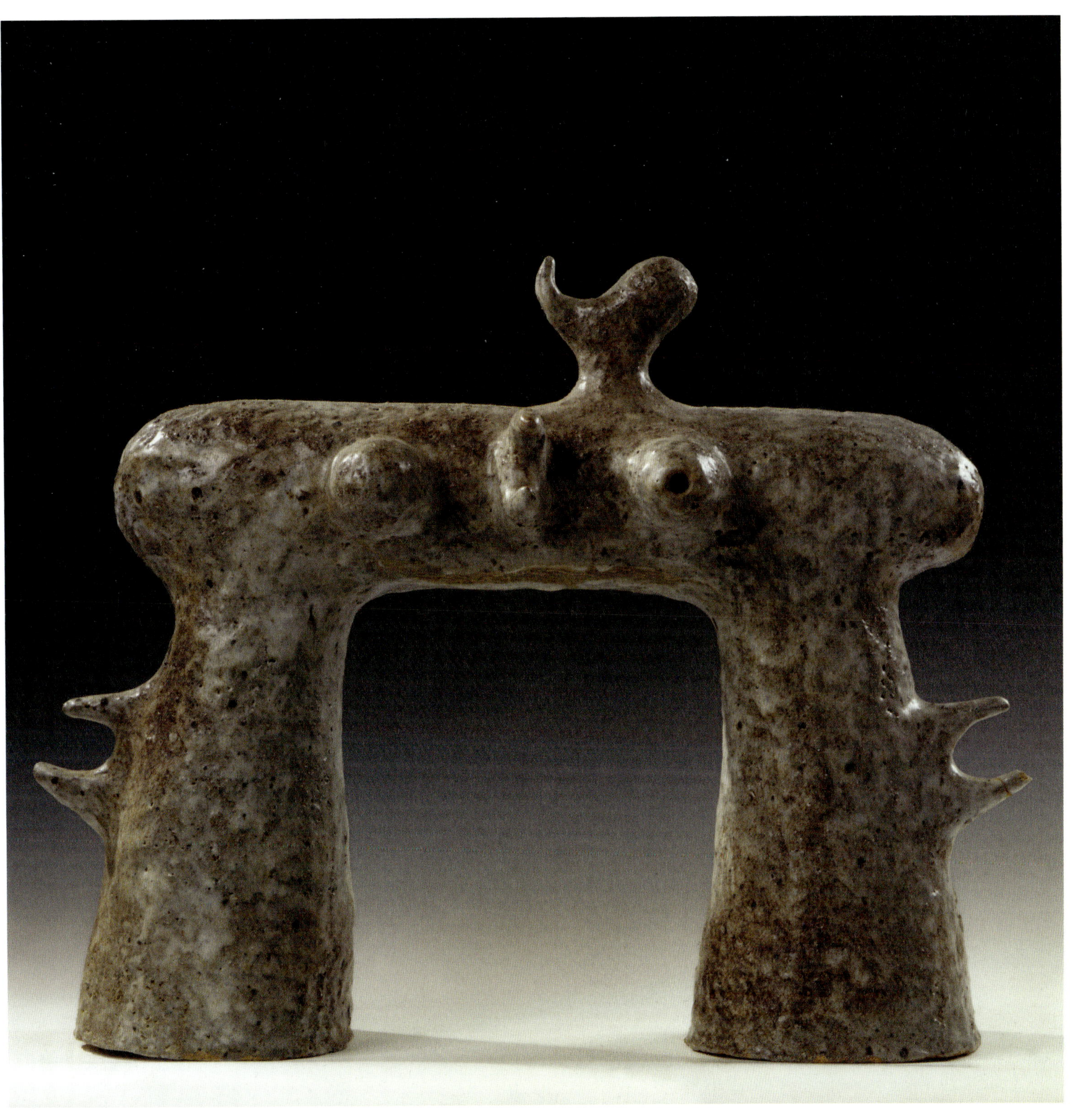

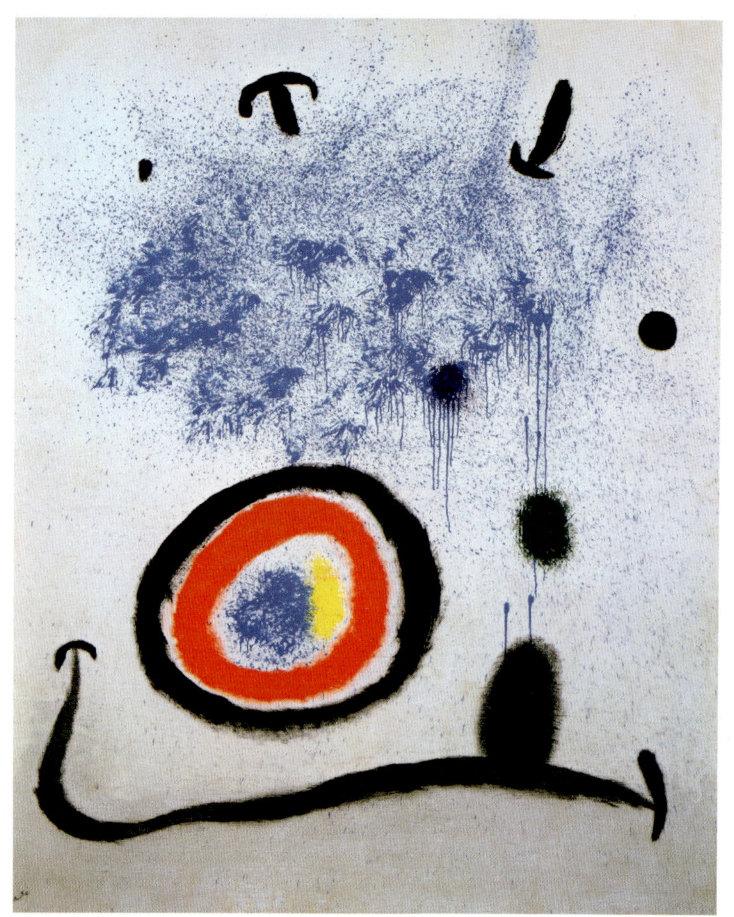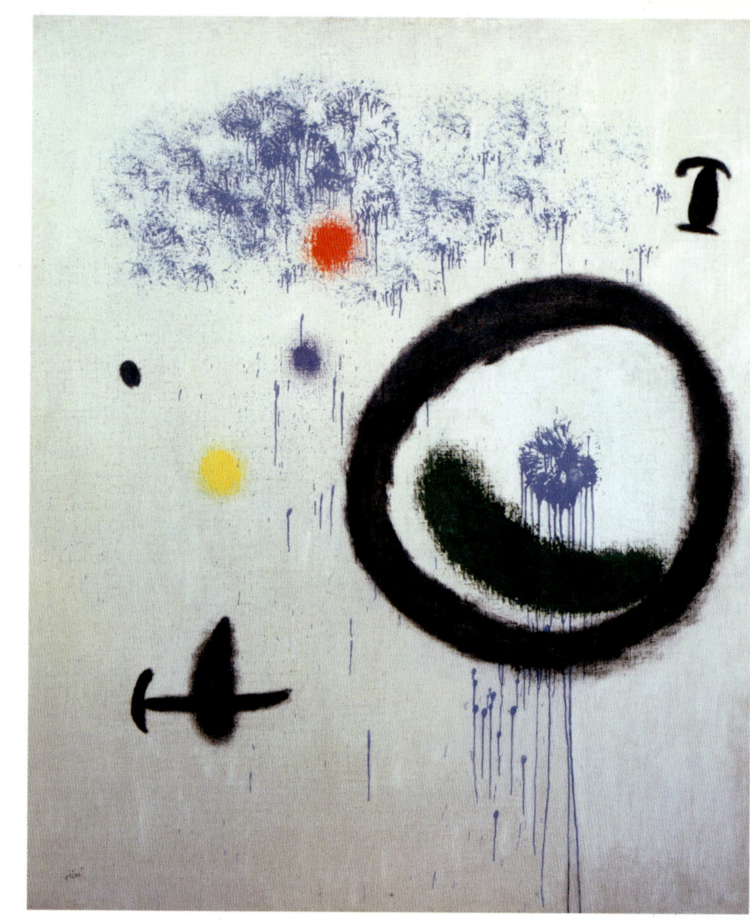

CAT. 34

Joan Miró (1893–1983)
The Birth of Day I (Naissance du jour I), 1964
Oil on canvas, 146 x 113.5 cm

CAT. 35

Joan Miró (1893–1983)
The Birth of Day II (Naissance du jour II), 1964
Oil on canvas, 162 x 130 cm

CAT. 36

Joan Miró (1893–1983)
The Birth of Day III (Naissance du jour III), 1964
Oil on canvas, 162 x 130 cm

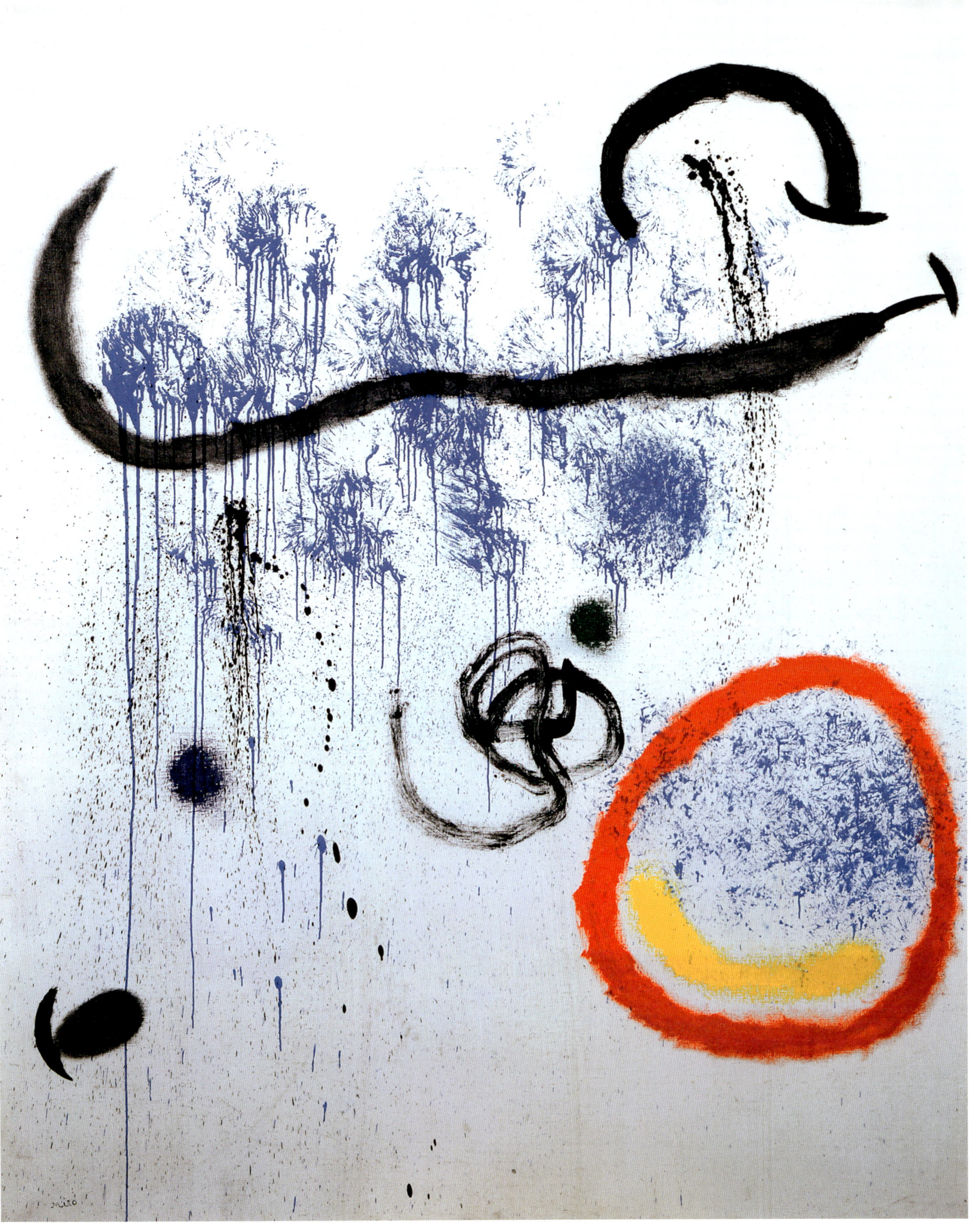

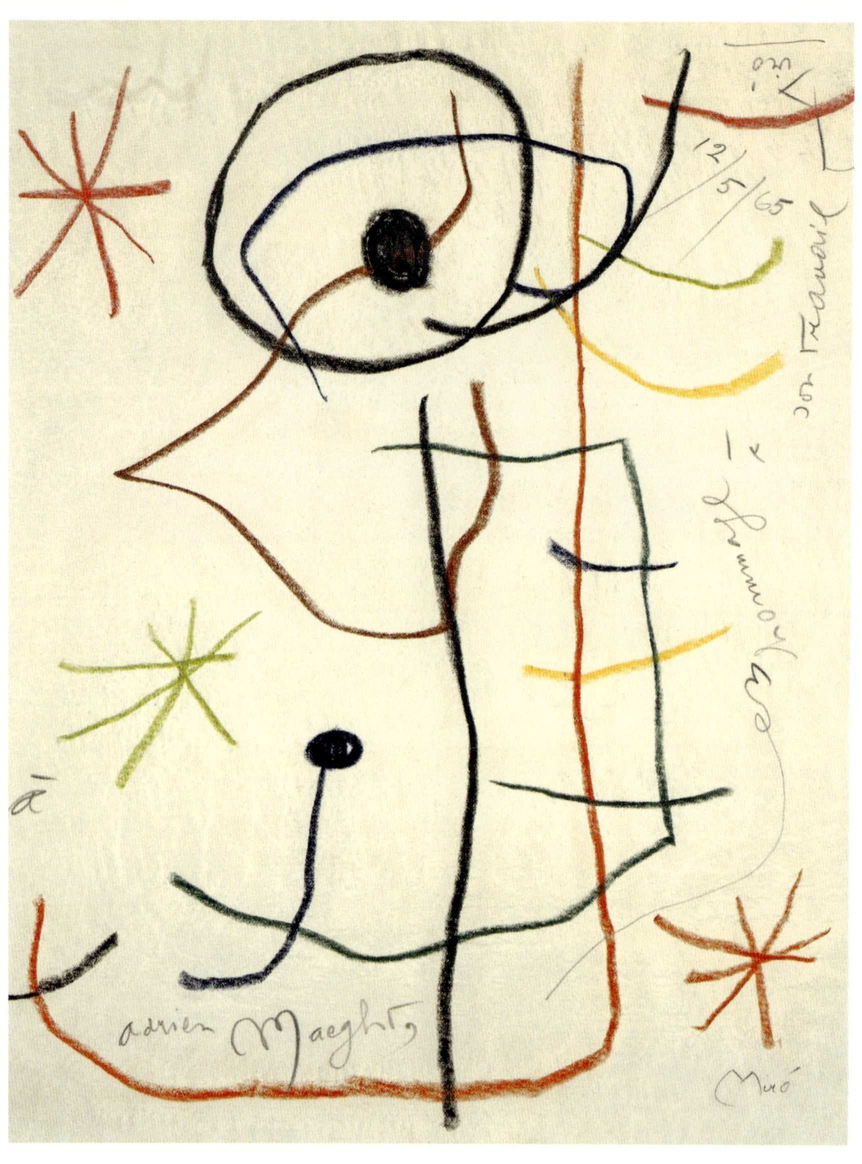

CAT. 37
Joan Miró (1893–1983)
'Pour Adrien Maeght, en hommage à son travail,
12 mai 1965' (*'For Adrien Maeght, in*
Recognition of His Work, 12 May 1965'), 1965
Wax crayon on paper, 37 x 28.5 cm

CAT. 38
Joan Miró (1893–1983)
Poem (Poème), 1966
Oil on canvas, 260 x 175 cm

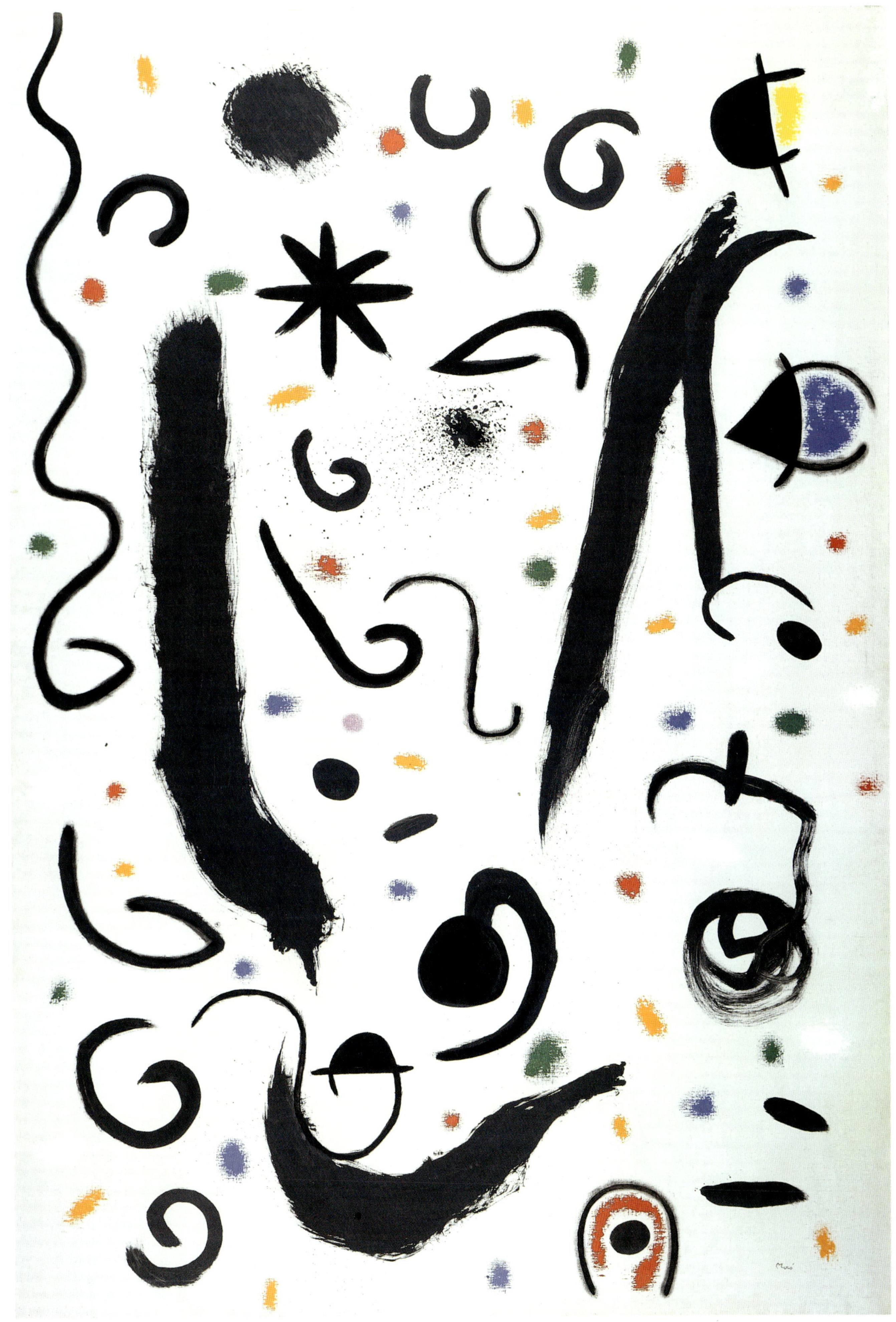

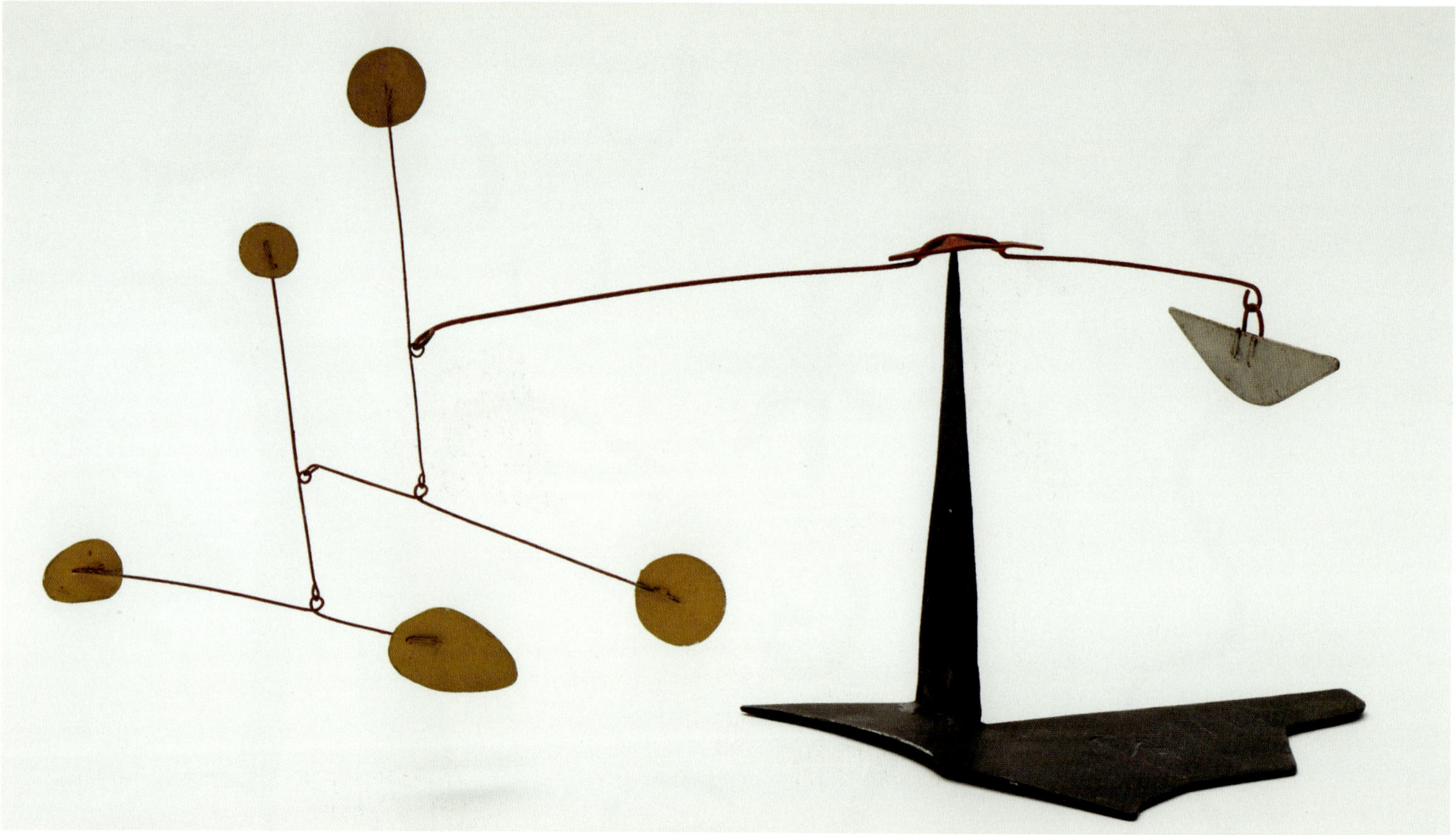

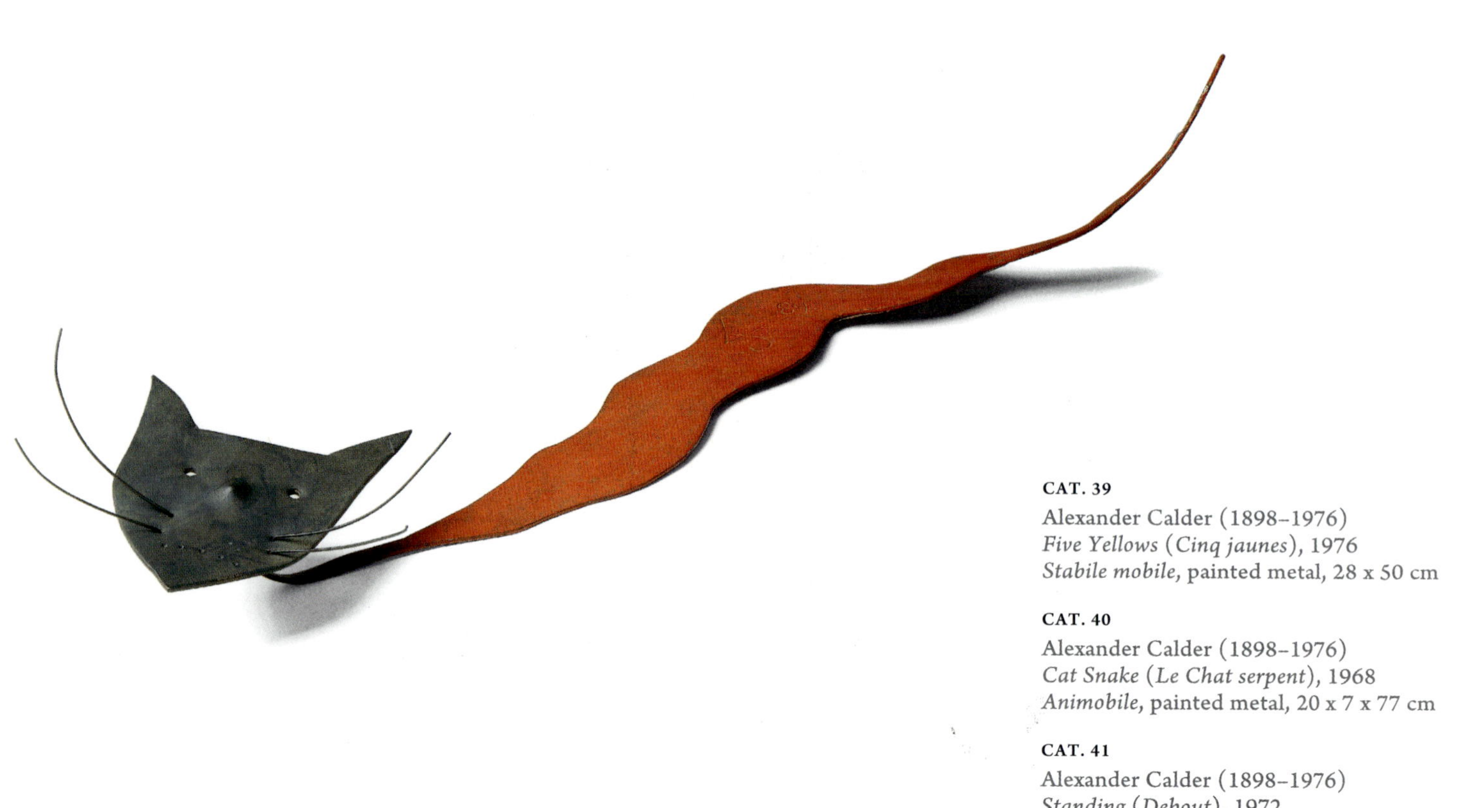

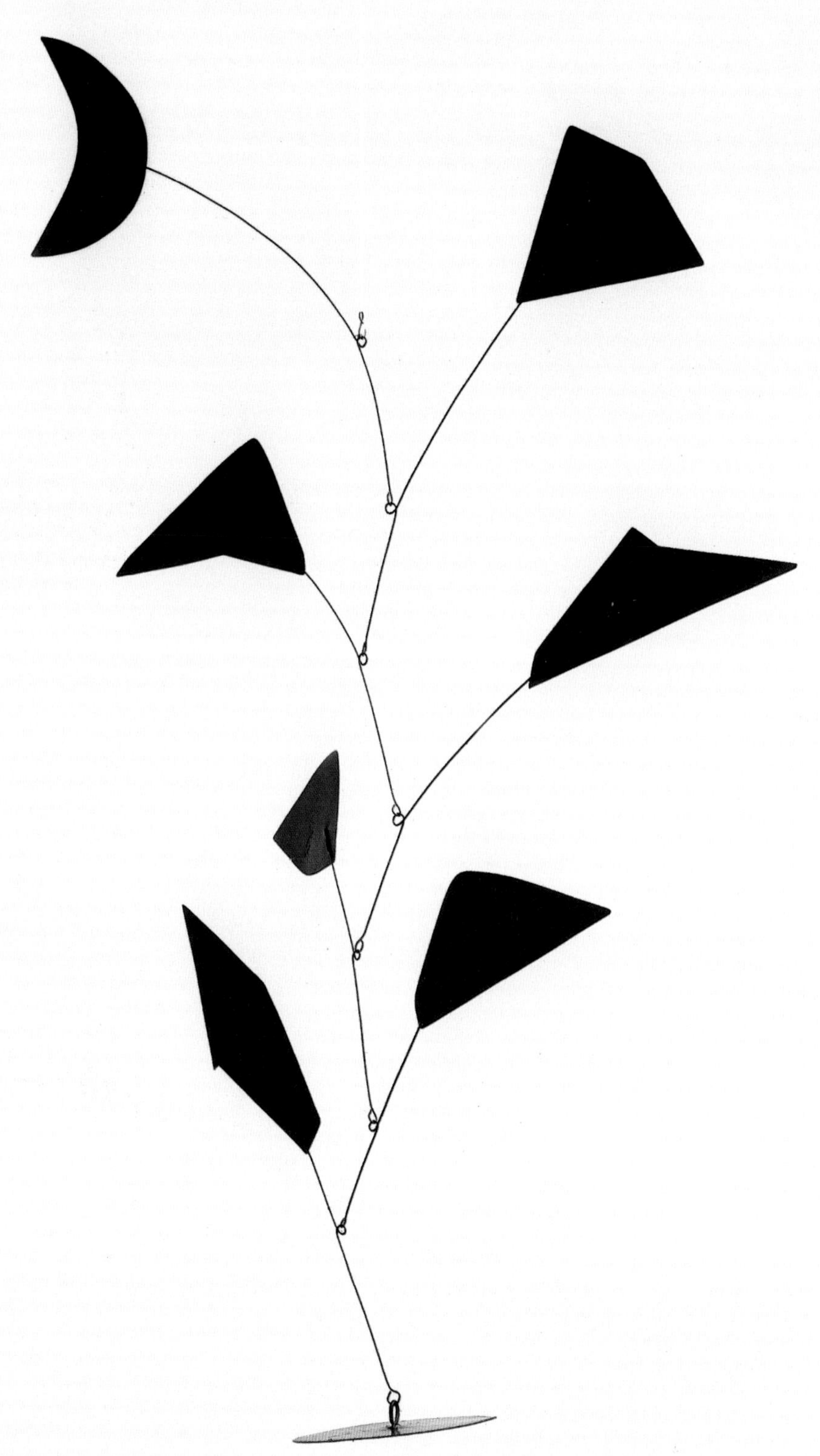

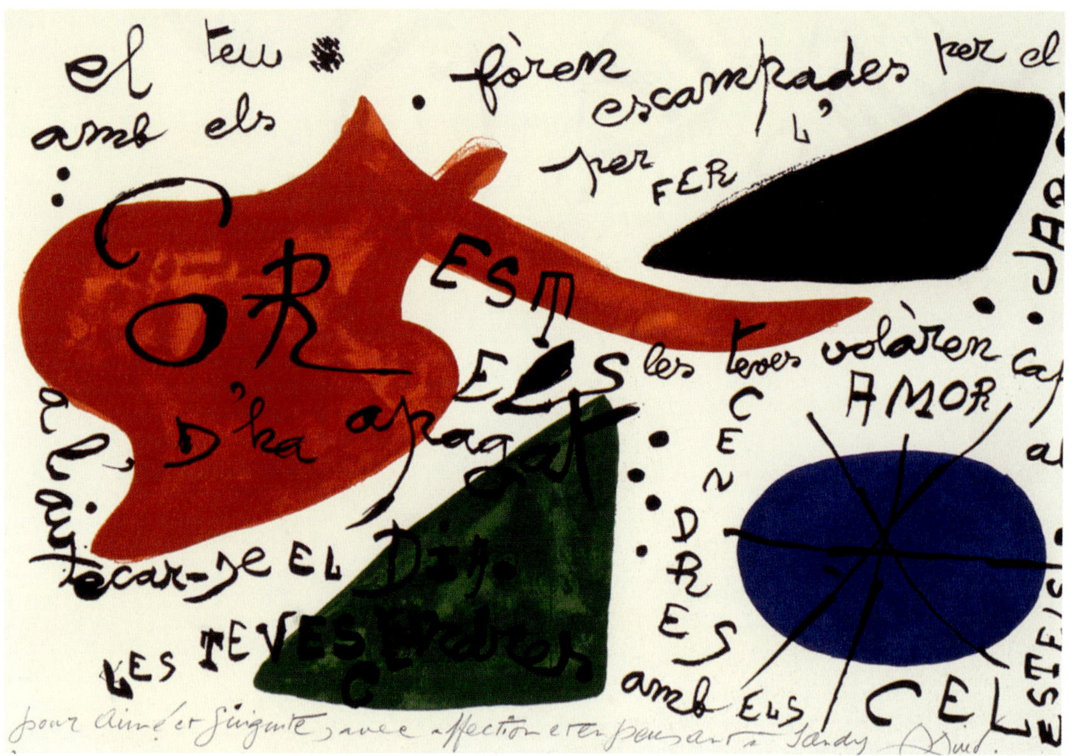

ABOVE:
CAT. 42
Joan Miró (1893–1983)
Thinking about Sandy, Sandy, 1973
Gouache on paper, 36 x 79 cm

BELOW:
CAT. 43
Joan Miró (1893–1983)
Painting on Table Mat
(*Peinture sur napperon*), 1972
Oil on table mat, 32.5 x 48 cm

RIGHT:
CAT. 44
Joan Miró (1893–1983)
The Birds of Prey Swoop Down on Our Shadows
(*Les Oiseaux de proie foncent sur nos ombres*), 1970
Oil on cowskin, 250 x 200 cm

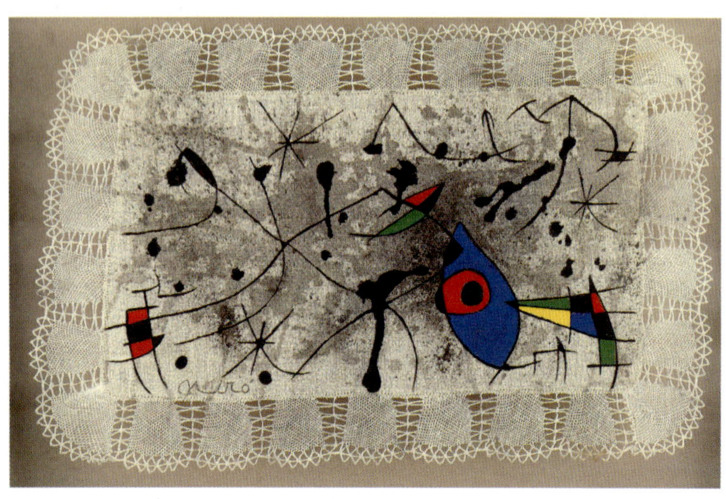

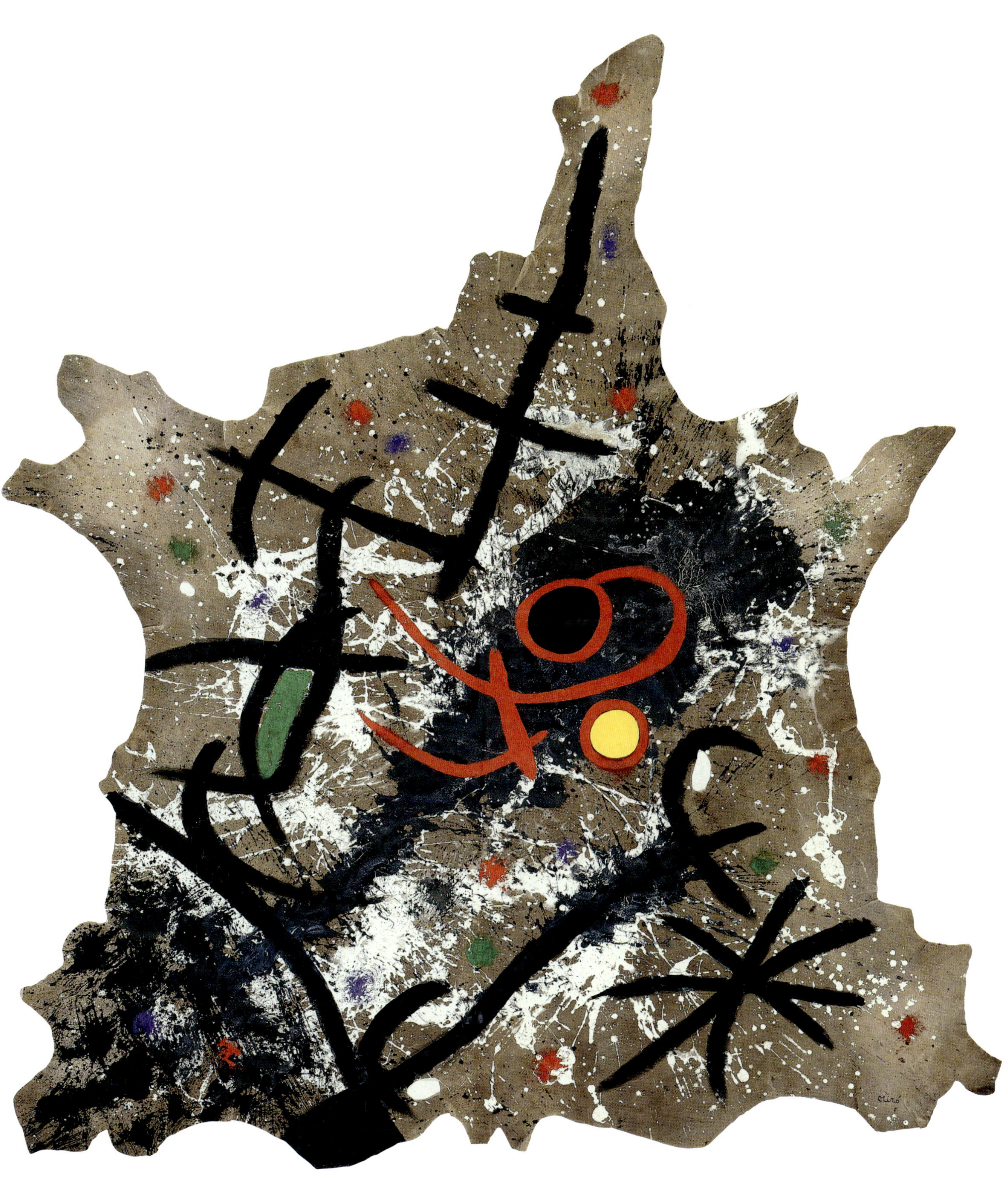

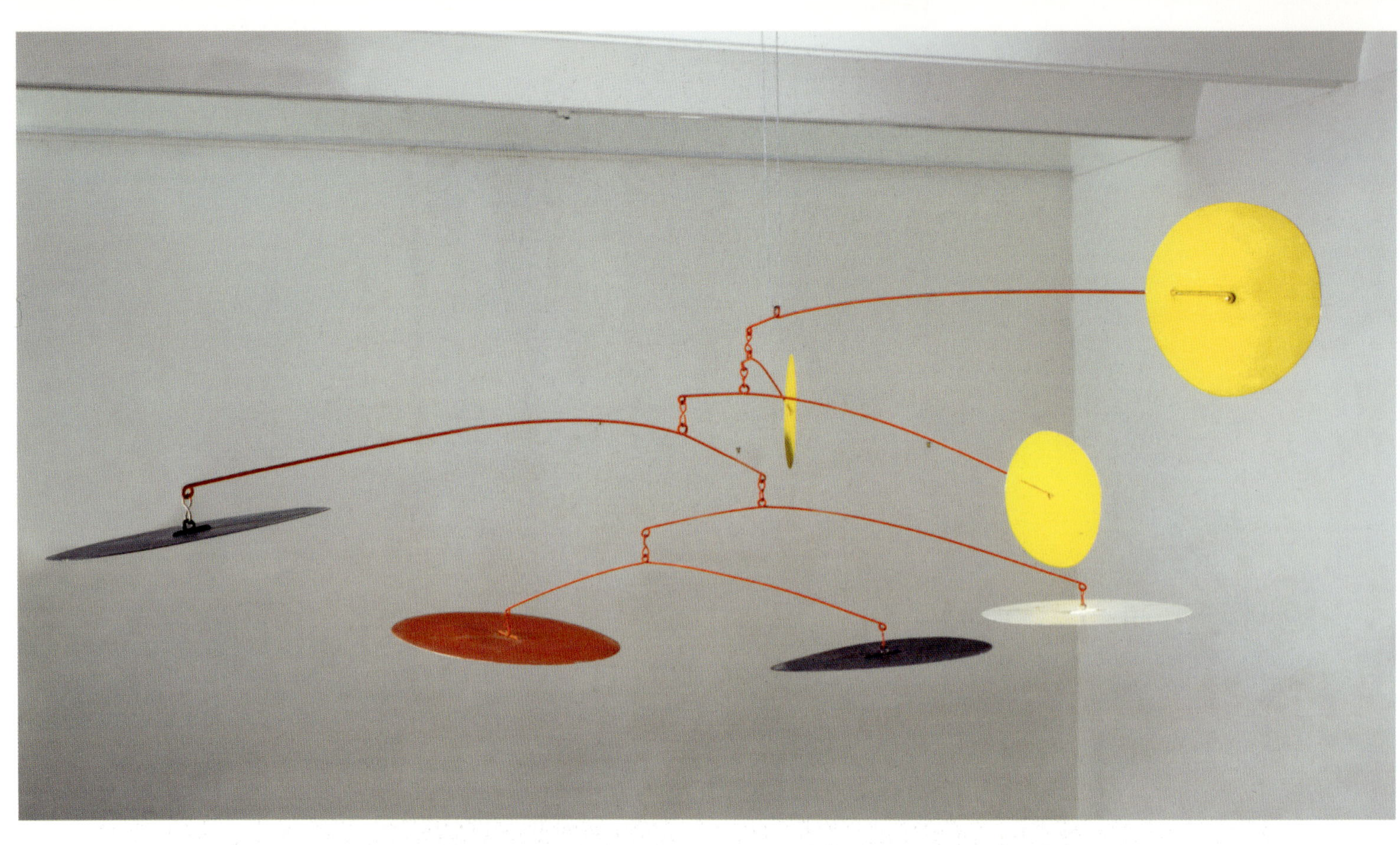

CAT. 45
Alexander Calder (1898–1976)
Three Yellow Suns (Trois soleils jaunes), 1965
Mobile, painted metal, 150 x 400 cm

CAT. 46
Joan Miró (1893–1983)
Constellation, 1972
Bronze, 142 x 130 x 44 cm

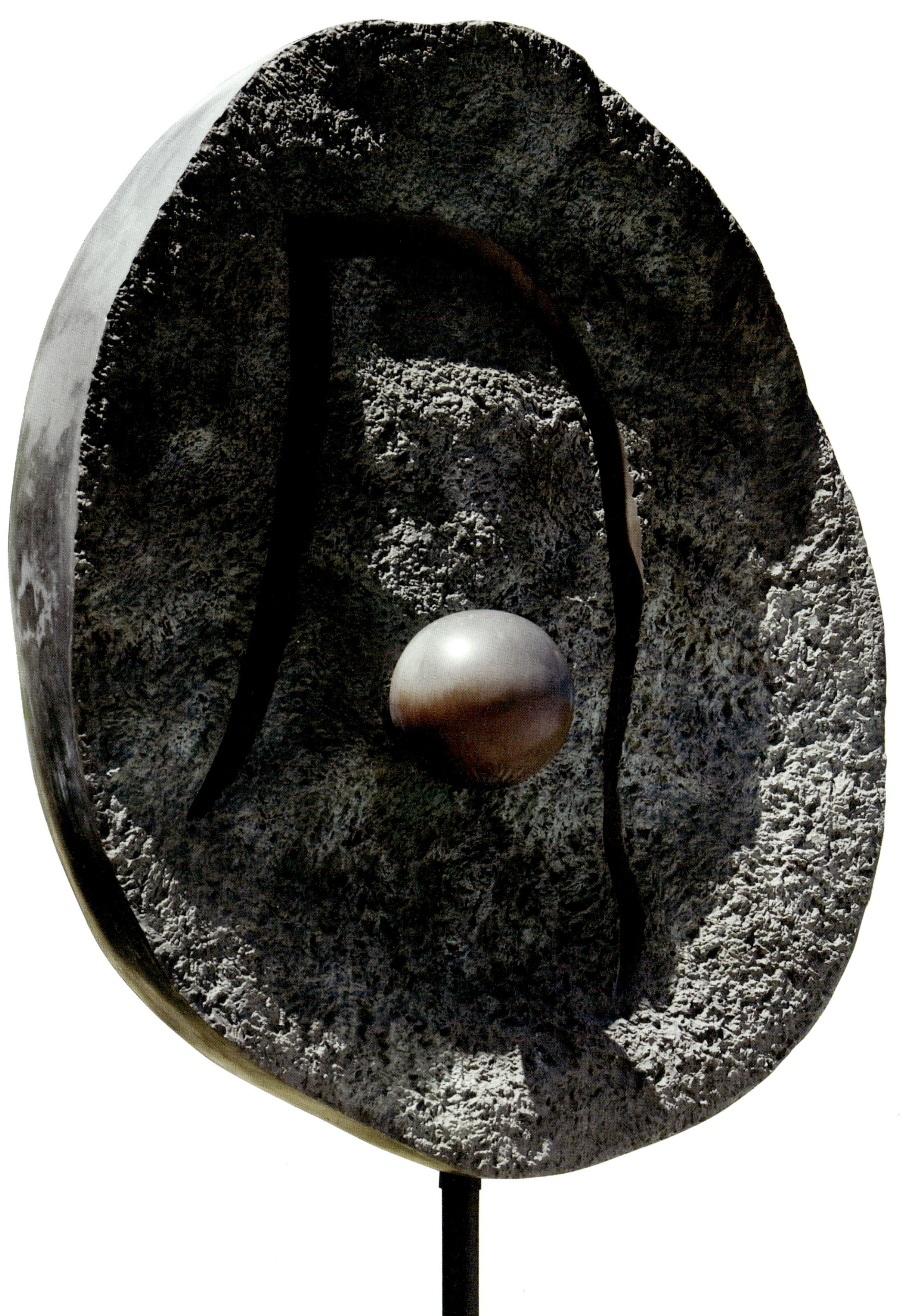

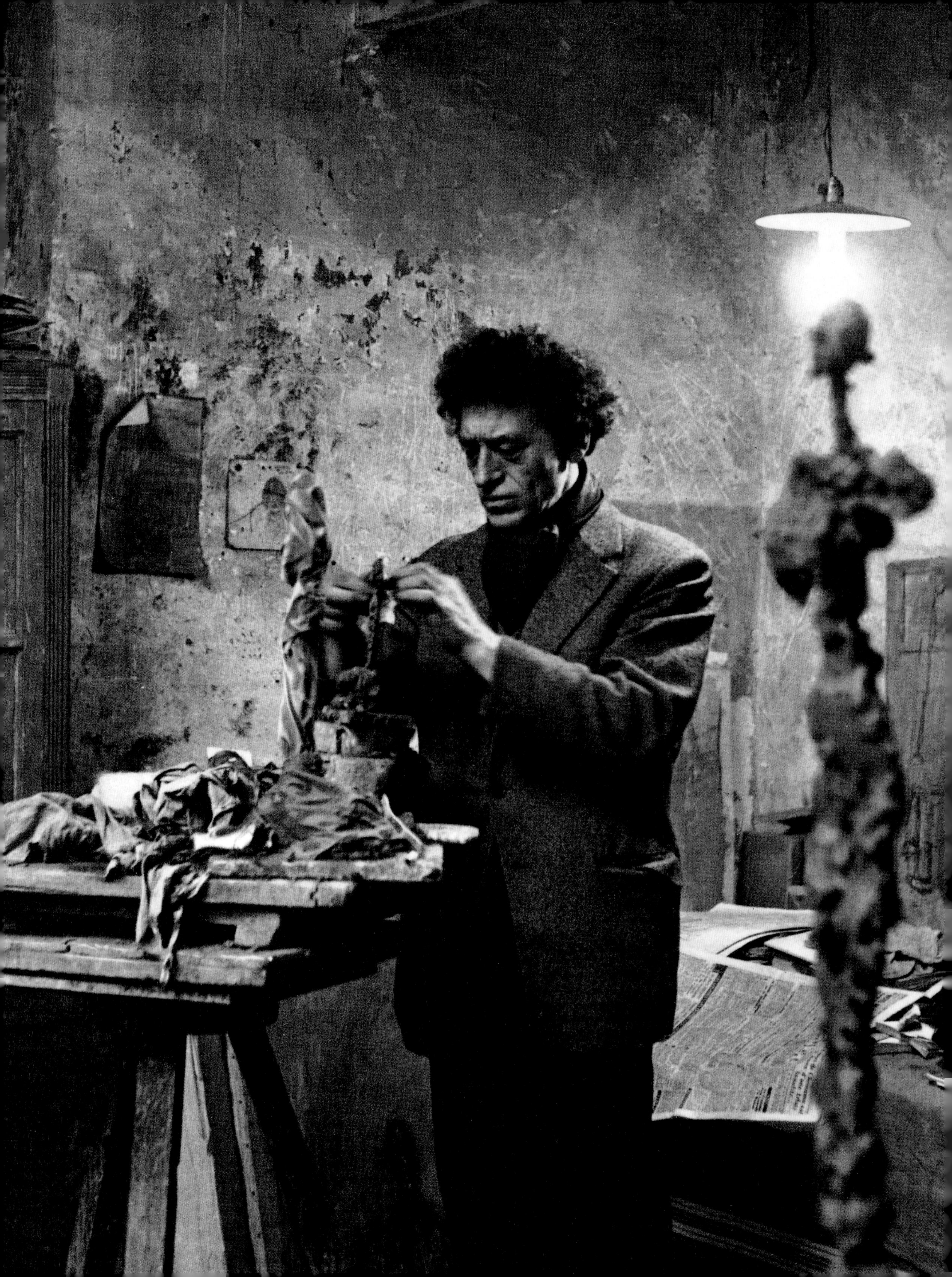

BRAQUE AND GIACOMETTI

BRAQUE AND GIACOMETTI

Georges Braque (1882–1963) and Alberto Giacometti (1901–1966)
were linked by a shared distrust of all labels, all systems and all utopias,
and, in meditating on the processes of perception and creation, they both
arrived at ways of working far removed from the styles that made their
initial reputations. Who would have thought that Ambroise Vollard's
commission in 1930 to illustrate the little-known, archaic Greek eighth-
century BC poet Hesiod's *Theogony* would enable Braque to distance
himself from his co-invention of Cubism, opening up a range of subject
matter, media and techniques that would inform his late work? Braque's
looping lines releasing from their plaster ground the immortal figures of
Heracles and *Zao* (both 1931; cats 53 and 71) provided him with the
means to take on the subjects of the classical nude and the reclining
female figure, which Henri Matisse and Pablo Picasso had made their own.
Matisse's and Picasso's lines, though different, suggest form and feeling by
encapsulating contours in a few quick strokes. Braque, by contrast, weaves
the figure allusively out of chaos, as in Hesiod's description of the creation
of the immortals: *Heracles* emerges proud and dominant from his mortal
coils; *Zao*, the water nymph, on her horse, rises and falls within the lilting
lines of the ocean's currents.[1] Braque worked without a female model.
Woman Lying Down (Femme couchée) (1930–56; cat. 50) denies sensuality.
With bulbous body, puny arms and small protruding insect head, the nude,
like Hesiod's woman after the Fall, is an anguished creature condemned to
suffer, portrayed in a style that anticipated the subject matter and body
language of European art in the 1950s.

At the same time, the sheer fluidity of the linear style provoked
in Braque a reaction – a wish to re-establish contact with solid matter
without departing from the themes that Hesiod had opened up to him.
In fact, Dora Vallier has suggested, the classic demanded sculpture.[2]
Hesperus – Theogony (Hespéris – Théogonie) (1939; cat. 58), like some
classical fragment, cuts a crisp silhouette, with her forehead indented in
the shape of a crescent moon. In *Hymen* (1939–57; cat. 57), the god of
marriage, the concept of union is conveyed by two silhouetted heads
joined together, the intervening negative space forming a nuptial chalice.
*Work and Days – Fragment from Hesiod (Les Travaux et les jours – fragment
d'Hésiode)* (1939–55; cat. 59) ushers in another theme: Hesiod, who
evidently felt cheated, wrote *Theogony* as a homily addressed to his
errant brother Perses, prescribing dedicated work on the land, according
to the seasons, as the only way for Perses to clear his debts and avoid
famine. Following Hesiod closely, Braque focuses on the essential
plough, drawn by a horse rather than two oxen, which he renders
with archaic simplicity.

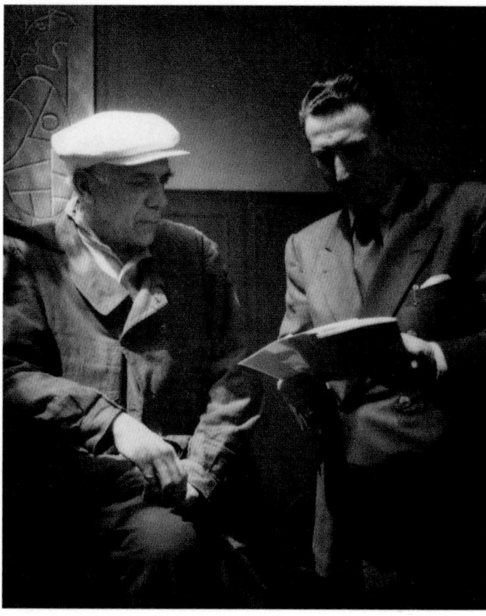

FIG. 44
Aimé Maeght and Georges Braque, 1948
(cat. 129)

Page 96: Alberto Giacometti in his studio,
Paris, 1963 (cat. 128)

The complexity of Braque's late work is illustrated by his treatment of two subjects: birds and landscapes. Neither realist nor visionary, his art floated between the naturalistic aspirations of the landscape painting of his childhood in Argenteuil and Le Havre – the birthplace of Impressionism – and his deeply felt need to perpetuate in a hostile atmosphere classical culture, Western civilisation, through the employment of symbolic forms sanctioned by antiquity. Hesiod advocated divination through the study of birds: 'Take heed when you hear the voice of the crane from high in the clouds … it brings the signal for ploughing.'[3] Braque's *Black Birds* (*Les Oiseaux noirs*) (1956–57; cat. 67) float through the firmament like birds of ill omen. The image of the birds occurs in numerous guises. The crows and seagulls tossed up like rags in the wind above the Normandy landscape near Braque's home at Varengeville conjured up for him Vincent van Gogh's *Wheatfield with Crows* (1890, Van Gogh Museum, Amsterdam) and the Auvers-sur-Oise landscapes painted shortly before the Dutch artist's suicide.[4] In a sense, they are a meditation on mortality, the end of a culture. The isolated black plough in *Landscape with Plough* (*Paysage à la charrue*) (1955; cat. 72) has tilled its last furrow.

At the same time, Braque's last landscapes, seascapes and flower paintings are very much about his pleasure both in painting his native Normandy landscape and in remaking contact with a tradition of landscape and still-life painting that he had enjoyed since his youth, stemming from Corot, Courbet and Impressionism. In his touching tribute to these last landscapes and flower pieces, Giacometti describes how Braque in turn opened up for him ways of representing his observations – ways that he could not escape (cat 136, not illustrated). Far from being limited in ambition, these paintings represented for Giacometti 'a quite different kind of audacity, indeed a much greater audacity than that of the distant years: this is painting that for me occupies the highest peak in the art of today, with all its conflict'.[5] A series of ceramics encapsulated Braque's favourite images: an archaic profile of a woman (1960; cat. 90); a mysterious white bird trapped for eternity within the blue of a dish (1961; cat. 89); and his final metamorphosis of a spoon and plate into a waltz-playing mandolin (1960; cat. 88).

Giacometti went through Paul Cézanne and Cubism to distance himself both from traditional styles of representation and from classicism, and he soon achieved a reputation as an avant-garde sculptor in the Surrealist group. His totemic *Spoon-woman* (*La Femme-cuillère*) (1926; cat. 47), inspired by a ceremonial spoon with anthropomorphic handle made by the Dan tribe from West Africa, encapsulated a number of Surrealist concerns: metamorphosis; the coming together of two alien elements to form a third 'surreal' image; and an interest in tribal art as a repository of instinct and feeling. According to James Lord, who sat for

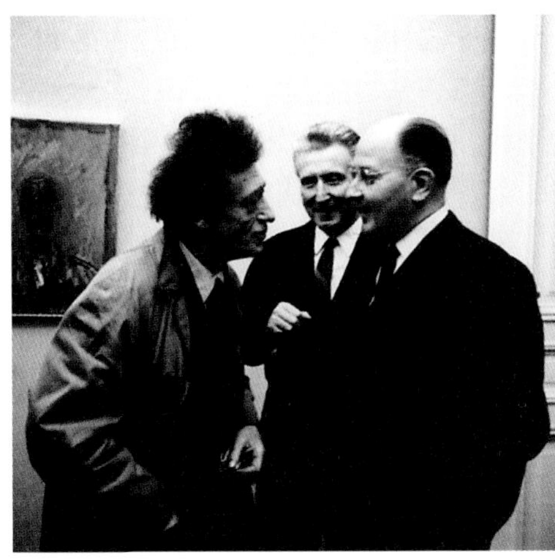

FIG. 45
Alberto Giacometti, Aimé Maeght and Louis Clayeux at the opening of the Galerie Maeght's Giacometti exhibition, Paris, 1951

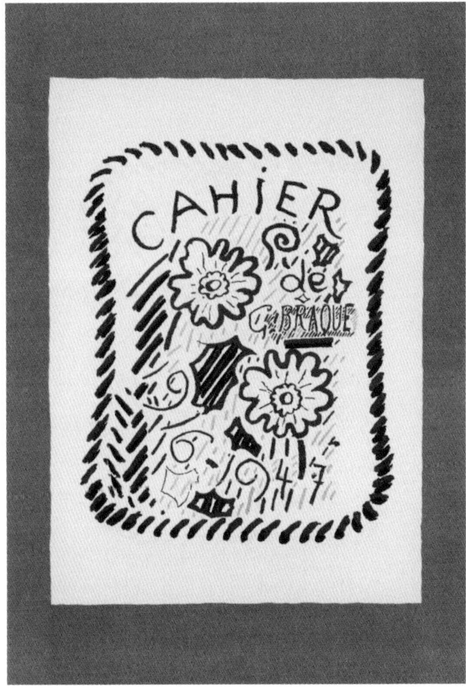

FIG. 46
Georges Braque (1882–1963), Sketchbook, 1916–47. Book, 50 x 33 cm (cat. 130)

him, Giacometti liked to reiterate Cézanne's dictum that everything is a
'square, a cone or a cylinder'.[6] In its construction out of these fundamental
shapes, *Cubist Head* (*Tête Cubiste*) (1934–35; cat. 54) is, on one level,
Giacometti's homage to Cézanne and Braque. But, more tellingly, in its
approximation of Mexican heads made out of rock crystal in the Musée
d'Ethnographie du Trocadéro, it concurs with the interest shown by the
dissident Surrealist Georges Bataille, and the contributors to his review
Documents (1929–30), in the human sacrifices of Central America,
shrunken heads and trophy skulls.[7]

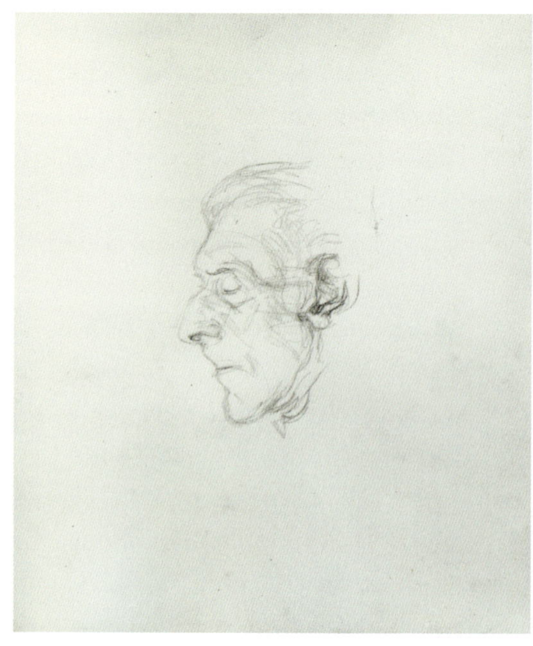

Following Giacometti's expulsion from the official Surrealist
group in 1934 for returning to work from the live model, the hieratic
standing female figure and the human head became his obsessive subjects.
Prostitutes standing for inspection in his favourite brothel set in motion his
central interest in the paradoxical relationship between physical proximity
and psychological distance, and he went on to produce classic images of
human alienation. For Jean Genet, 'The beauty of Giacometti's sculptures
resides in the incessant, uninterrupted attention between the furthest
distance and the closest familiarity: this coming and going never ends,
and it is in this sense that they can be said to be in movement.'[8]

From a solid grounding on an immense foot firmly attached to a
wedge-shaped base, Giacometti's *Standing Woman with Arms by Her Side*
(*Femme debout bras le long du corps*) (1952; cat. 83) is attenuated into a
hieratic presence, like the long shaft of a spoon ending in a female figure.
Giacometti came to appreciate that representational accuracy did not
necessarily convey psychological truth. The language of realism had to be
re-invented. From totemic figure to totemic figure, he changed the scale
and varied the contours. Limbs were truncated or fused with the body (cat.
84), features were withdrawn and restored to a face (cat. 85), forms were
whittled away to the point of destruction or built up and accentuated. Jean-
Paul Sartre commented on 'these moving outlines, always between nothing
and being, always modified, for good, destroyed and begun once more …
Never was matter less eternal, more fragile, nearer to being human.'[9]

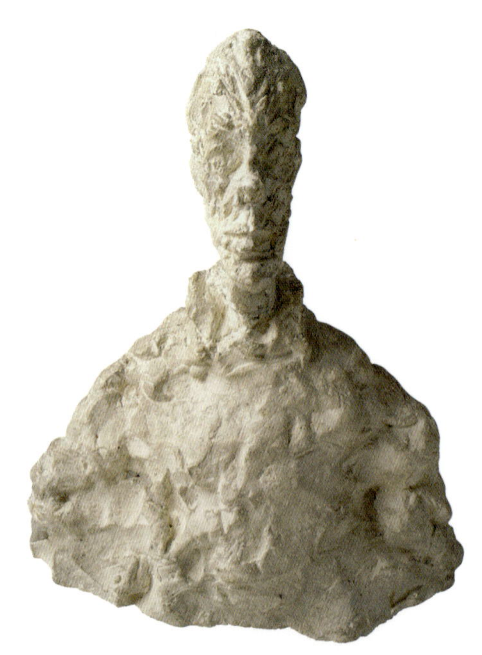

The sight of his figures when they had been cleared off a work
table and placed at random on the floor, forming what appeared to be
two groups, sparked off *The Glade* (*La Clairière*) (1950, Alberto Giacometti
Foundation, Zurich) and *The Forest* (*La Forêt*) (1950; cat. 61). Giacometti
became fascinated by the ways in which the grouped figures interrelated
to create their own self-contained world. *The Forest* reminded him of a
childhood experience 'in which the trees … always seemed to me to be
like people who have stopped still while walking, talking to one another'.[10]

The unsettling intrusion of the male bust may well have originated
in Giacometti's experiences on entering brothels. The archetype of the
passive female called for the male archetypes of voyeur and action man.

He intended *Walking Man I* (*L'Homme qui marche I*) (1960; cat. 87) to be placed near *Standing Woman I* (*Femme debout I*) (1960; cat. 86). The Paris of Montparnasse became his habitat and he cast himself in the role of a dilapidated old dog (cat. 74) patrolling its territory in competition with its archetypal rival, the cat (cat. 62). His paintings and lithographs in a more relaxed, picturesque key document his haunts in Paris (cat. 77) and at his native home in Switzerland.

After World War II, portraiture became Giacometti's principal preoccupation. His challenge was how to re-invent the representation of the human head and yet still communicate a particular living presence in space without falling back on either caricature or classicism. He elongated the head and deeply scoured the eyes of his bust of Diane Bataille (cat. 60). The silhouette and the sightless gaze became the hallmarks of his portraits. He portrayed Aimé Maeght (cat. 81) as a slightly detached, imperious silhouette. The gaze of a bust of his brother, Diego (fig. 48), his main sitter, both draws us in and repels us. Yves Bonnefoy pointed to a parallel between Giacometti's and Samuel Beckett's constant preoccupation with absence and instants of presence.[11] Marguerite Maeght (cat. 82) is portrayed as a solid presence and yet placed back in space, psychologically withdrawn. 'The sense of depth begets silence,' Giacometti observed, 'drowns objects in silence.'[12] There was, for him, a felt correlation between personality – a living presence – and scale. In 1946 he recalled his waking nightmare of seeing the living in terms of his dead neighbour, 'T': 'What I was looking at was no longer a living head, but an object like any other, no, different, not like any object, but like something which was alive and dead at the same time.'[13] His portrait drawing of Braque on his deathbed in 1963 (fig. 47) was his way of coming to terms with the diminished presence, the shockingly small-scale object quality, of an immense personality who had meant so much to him.

NW

FIG. 47
Alberto Giacometti (1901–1966), *Braque on His Deathbed* (*Braque sur son lit de mort*), 1 August 1963. Pencil on paper, 29.5 x 29 cm (cat. 131)

FIG. 48
Alberto Giacometti (1901–1966), *Bust of Diego* (*Buste de Diego*), 1955. Plaster, 27.5 x 11 x 20.5 cm (cat. 132)

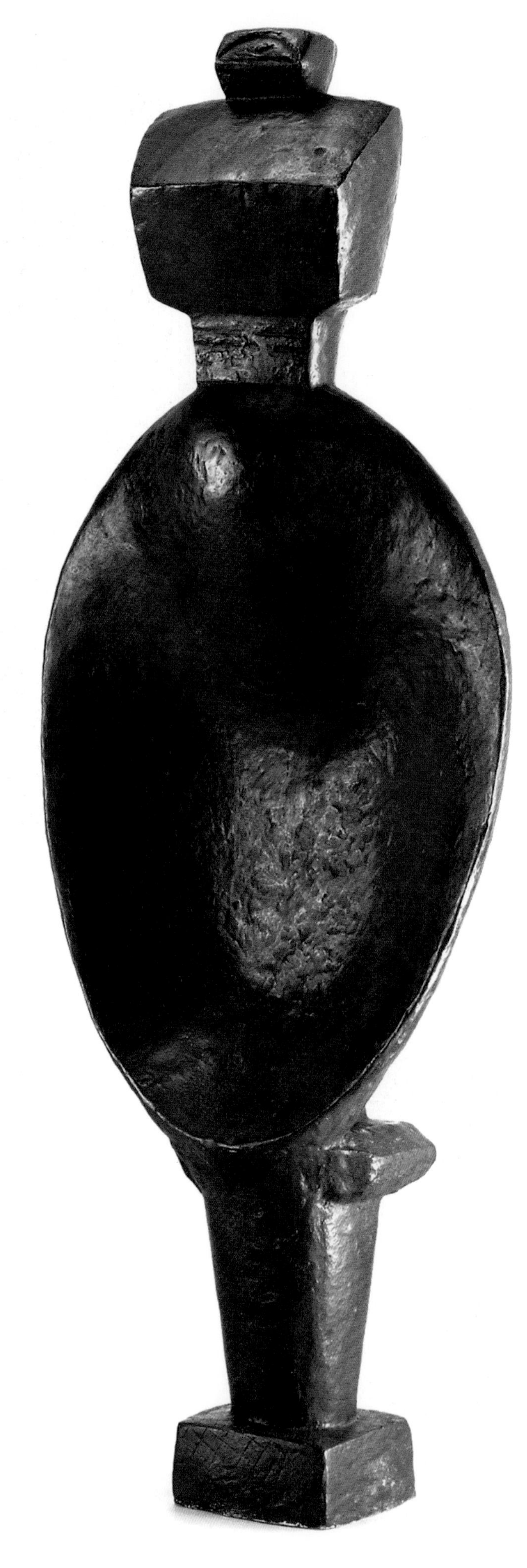

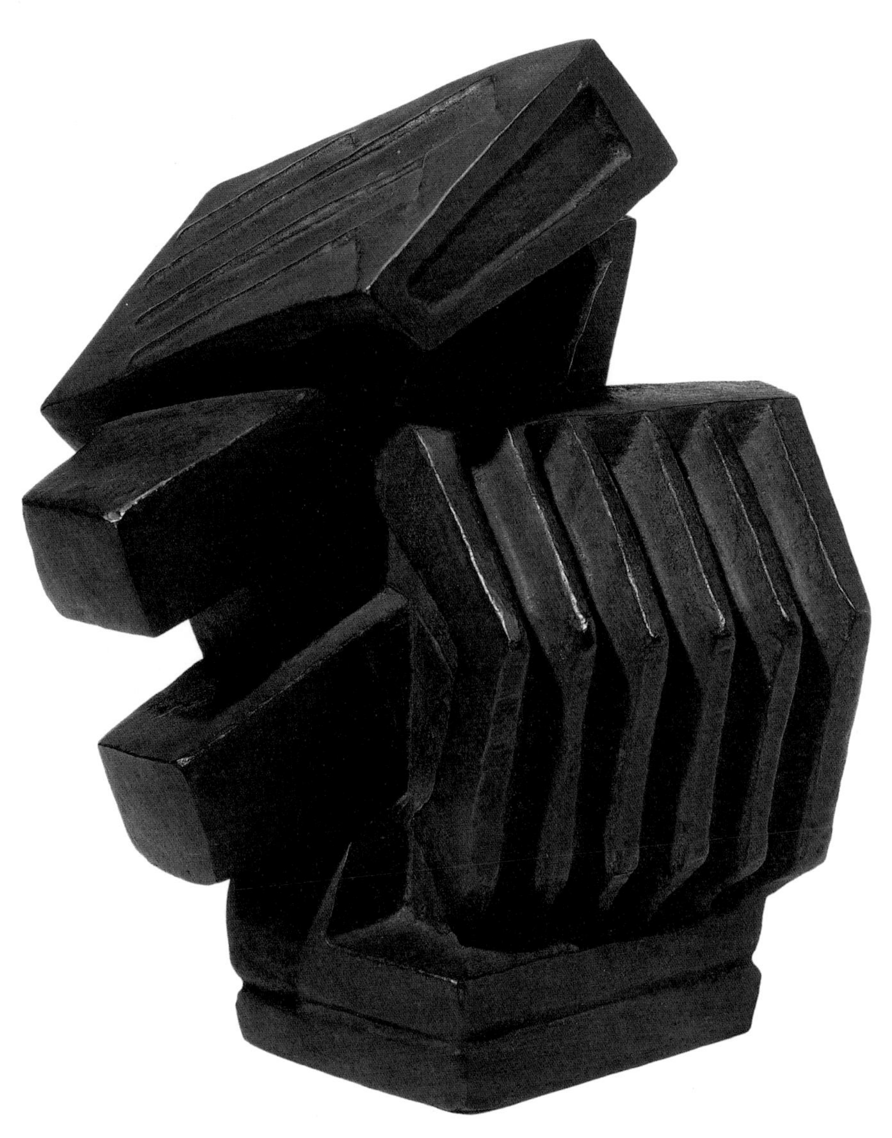

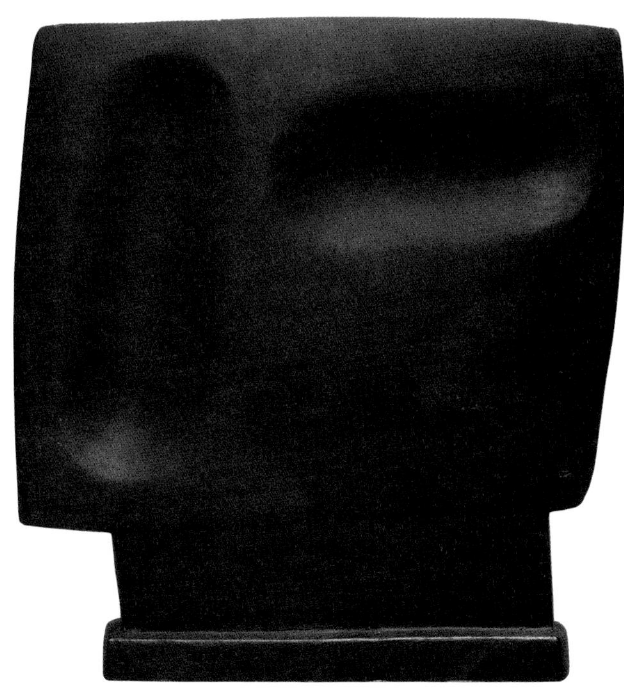

CAT. 47
Alberto Giacometti (1901–1966)
Spoon-woman (*La Femme-cuillère*), 1926
Bronze, 145 x 51 x 21 cm

CAT. 48
Alberto Giacometti (1901–1966)
Bust with a Sharp Head
(*Buste tête tranchante*), 1927
Bronze, 40 x 35.5 x 7 cm

CAT. 49
Alberto Giacometti (1901–1966)
Composition, 1927
Bronze, 38 x 27 x 25 cm

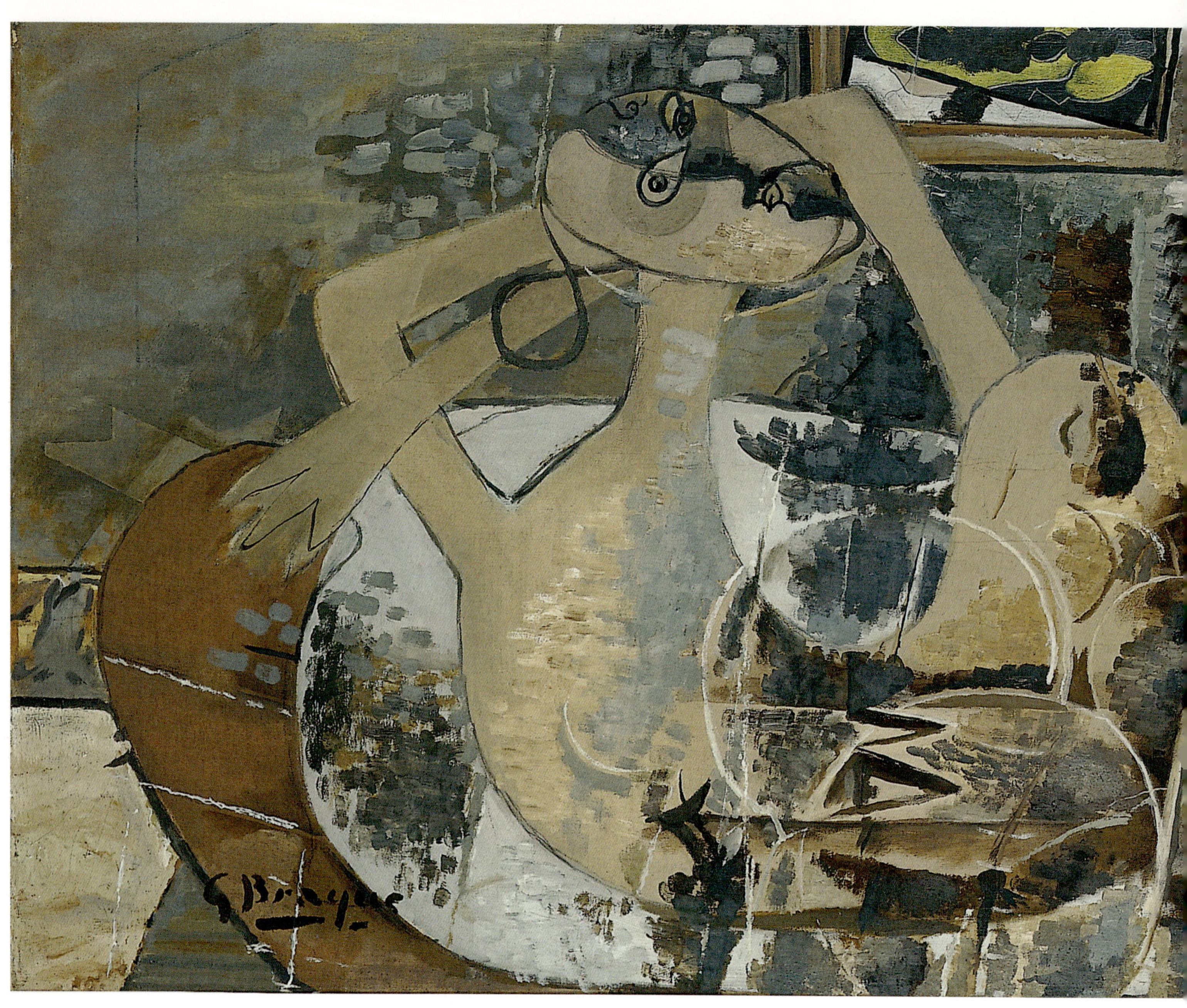

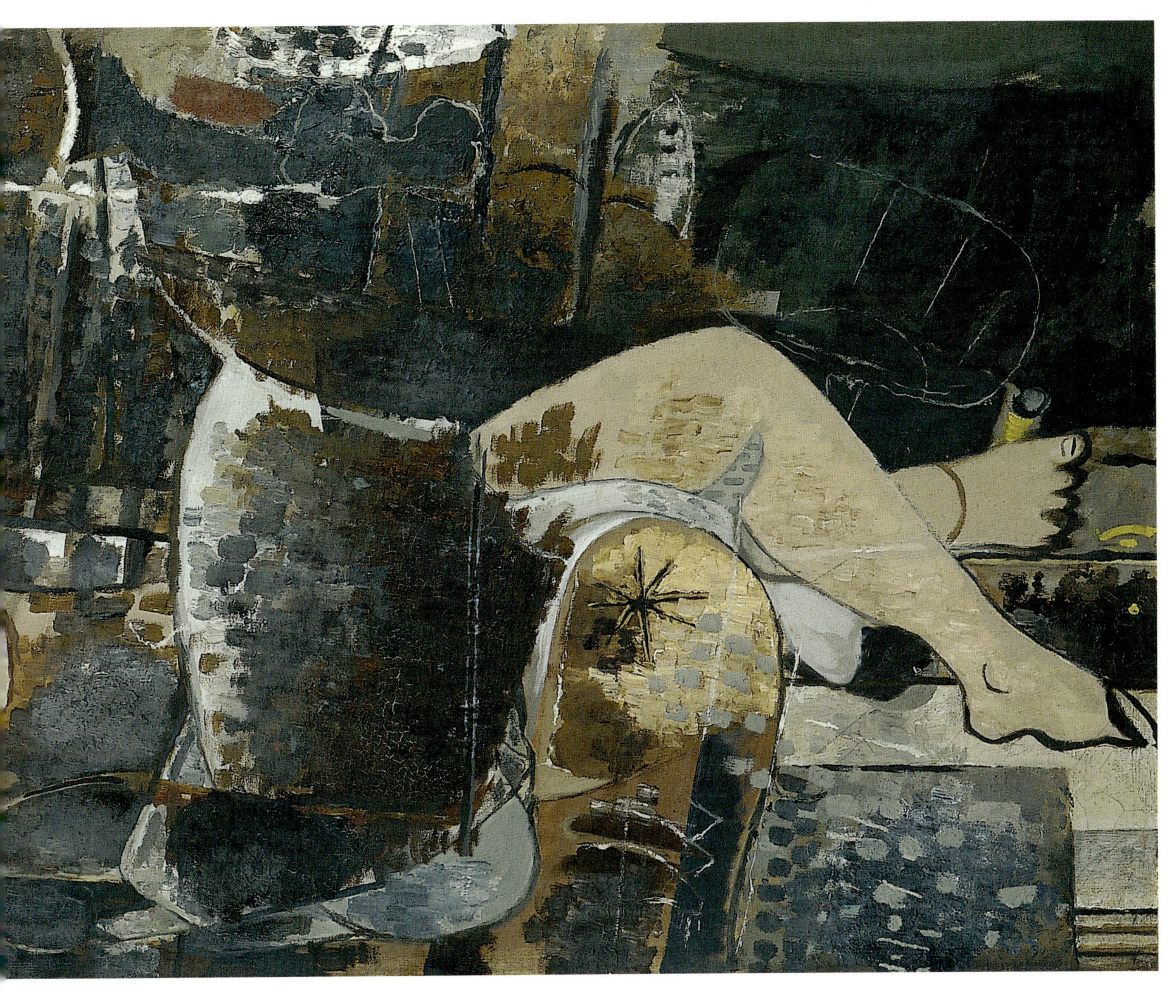

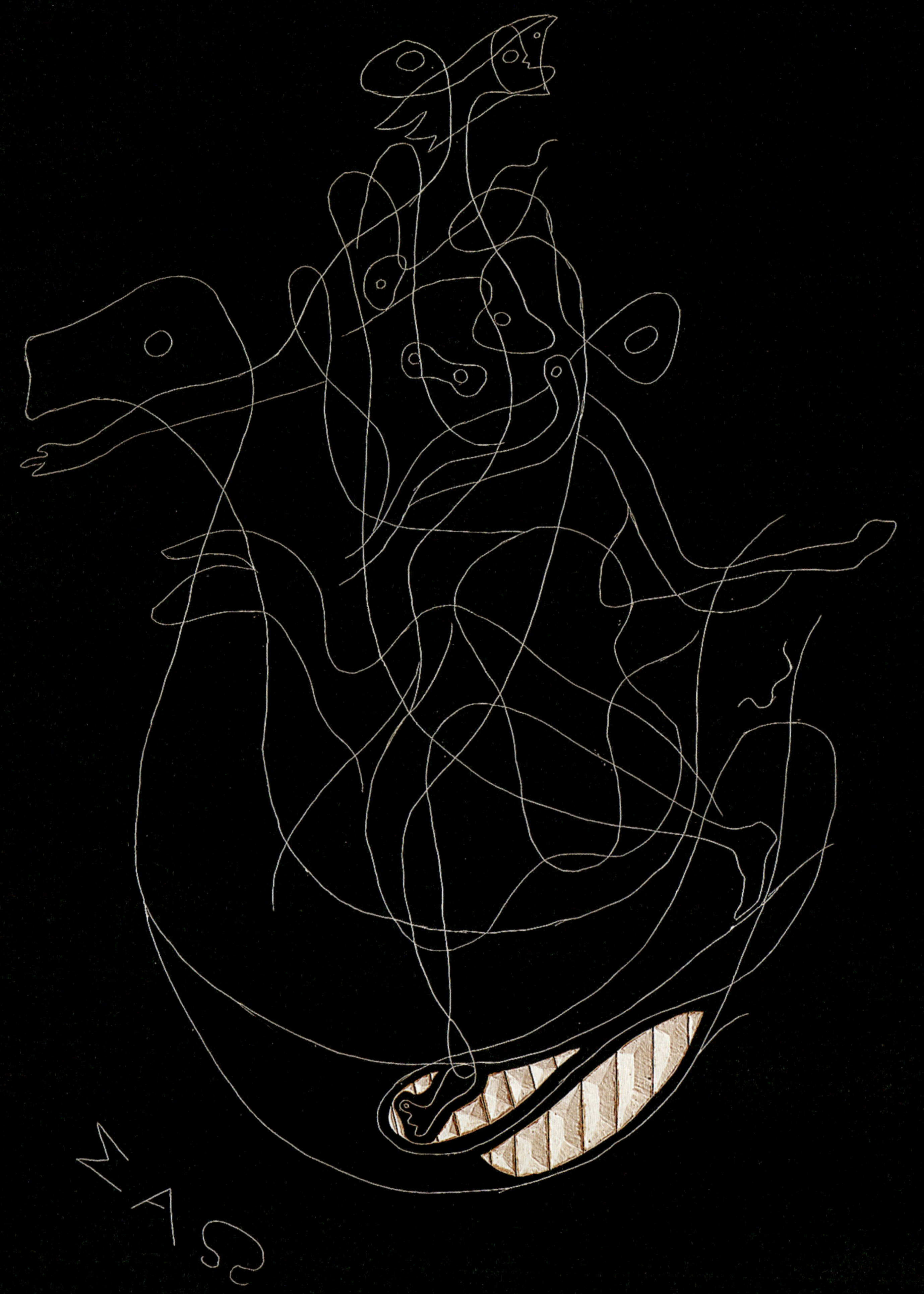

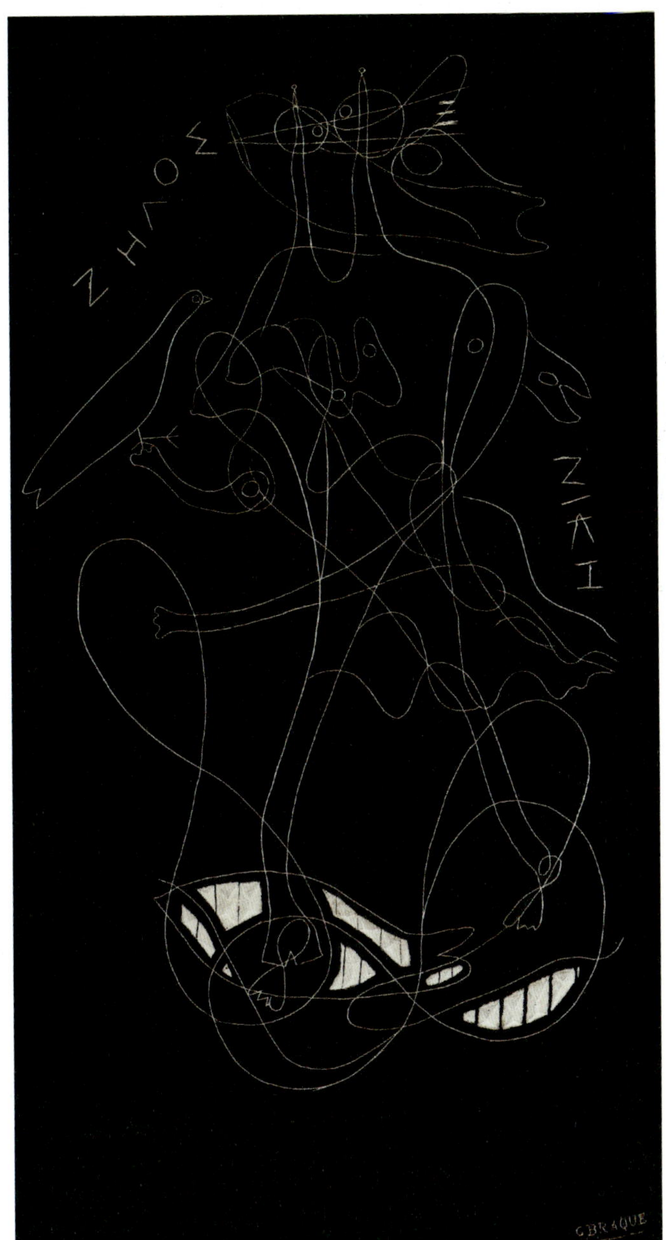 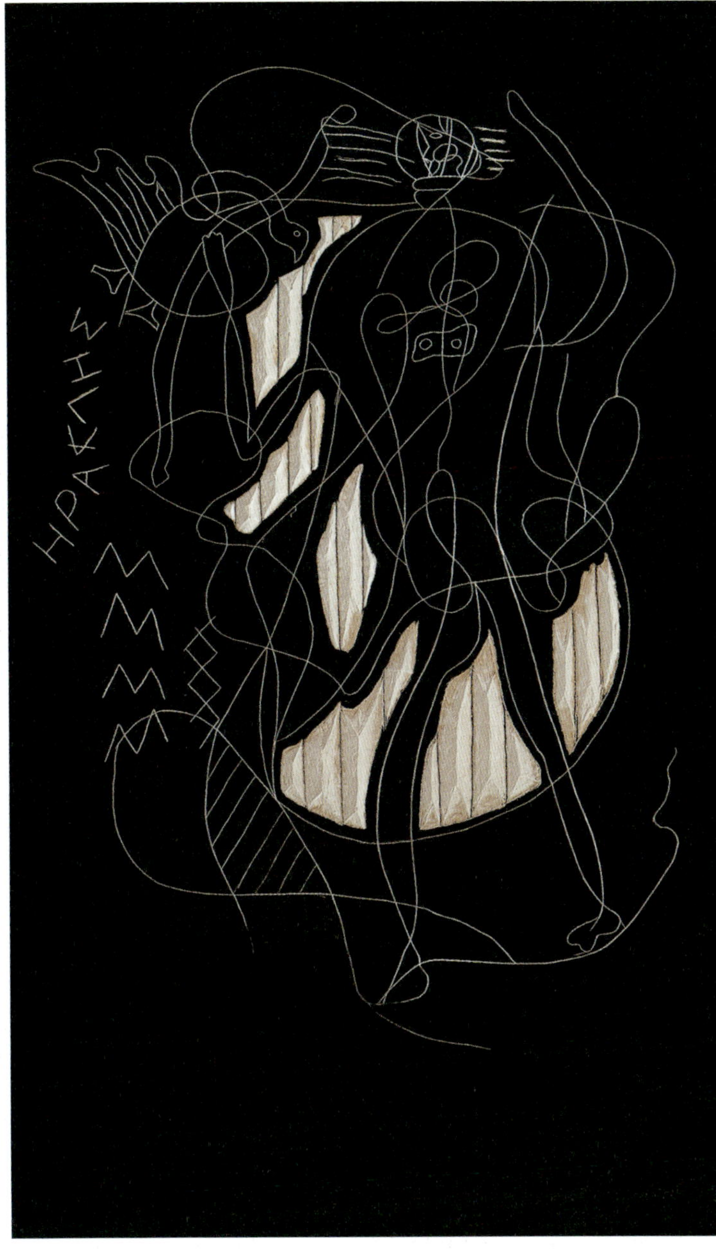

CAT. 51

Georges Braque (1882–1963)
Zao, for Hesiod's *Theogony*, 1931
Engraved plaster, 187.5 x 129.5 cm

CAT. 52

Georges Braque (1882–1963)
Zelos, for Hesiod's *Theogony*, 1931
Engraved plaster, 185 x 98 cm

CAT. 53

Georges Braque (1882–1963)
Heracles, for Hesiod's *Theogony*, 1931
Engraved plaster, 187 x 105.5 cm

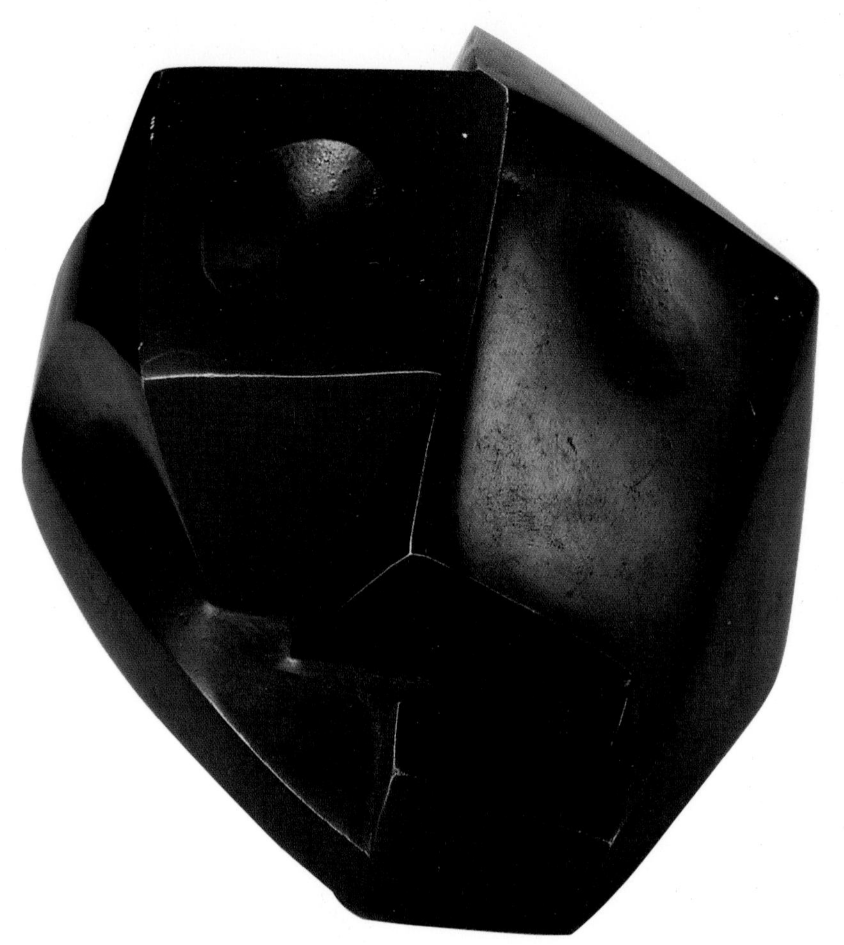

CLOCKWISE FROM LEFT:

CAT. 54
Alberto Giacometti (1901–1966)
Cubist Head (*Tête Cubiste*), 1934–35
Bronze, 18 x 25 x 20 cm

CAT. 55
Georges Braque (1882–1963)
Ibis, 1945
Bronze, 18 x 11 x 6 cm

CAT. 56
Georges Braque (1882–1963)
Bone and Ovoid Form
(*Os et forme ovoide*), 1949
Bone and plaster, 18.5 x 18.5 x 16 cm

CAT. 57
Georges Braque (1882–1963)
Hymen, 1939–57
Bronze, 76 x 50 x 35 cm

CAT. 58
Georges Braque (1882–1963)
Hesperus – Theogony
(*Hespéris – Théogonie*), 1939
Bronze, 41 x 23 x 10 cm

CAT. 59
Georges Braque (1882–1963)
Work and Days – Fragment from Hesiod
(*Les Travaux et les jours – fragment d'Hésiode*),
1939–55
Bronze, 25 x 47 x 22 cm

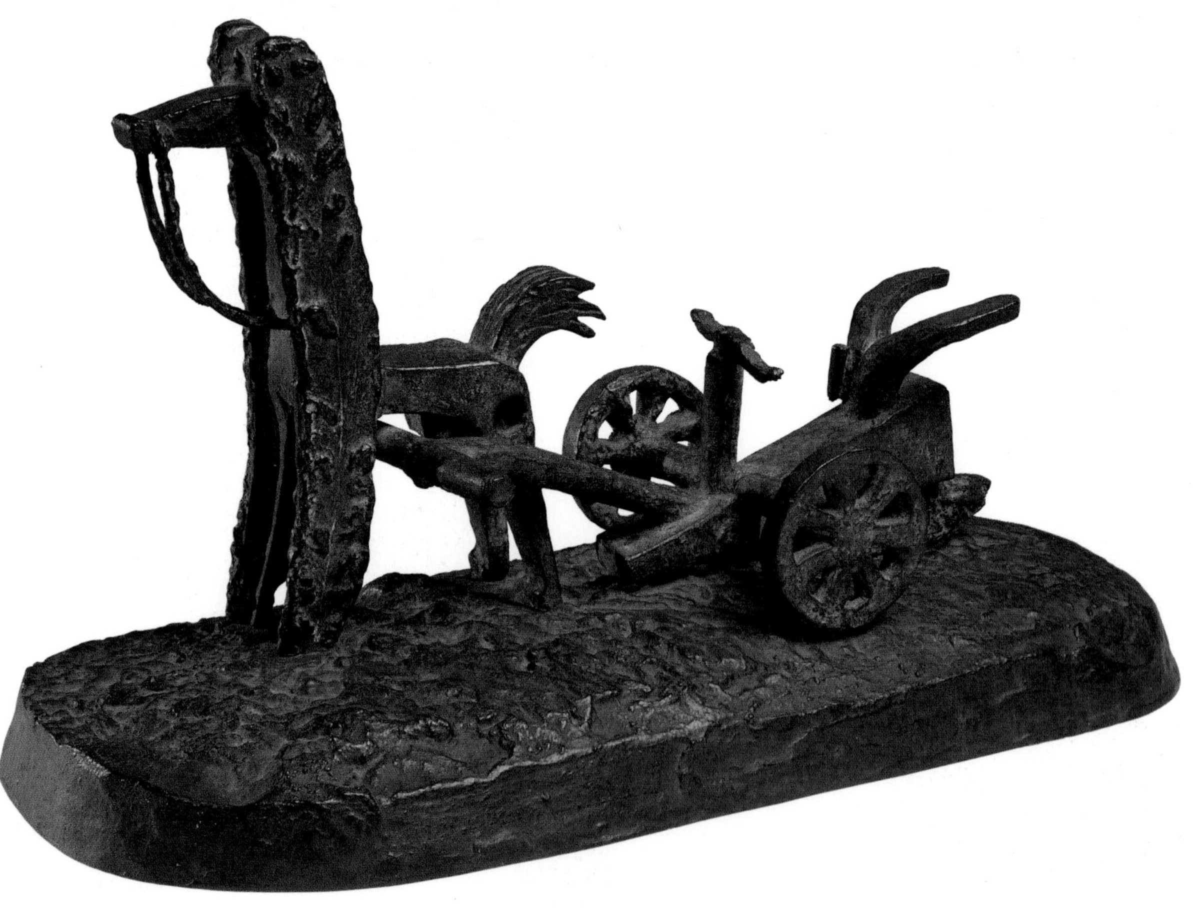

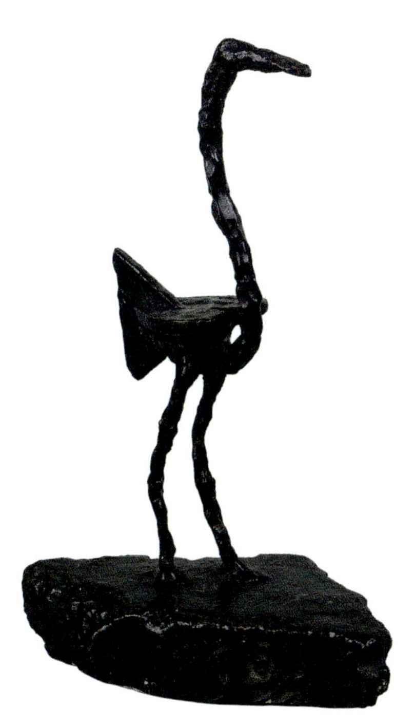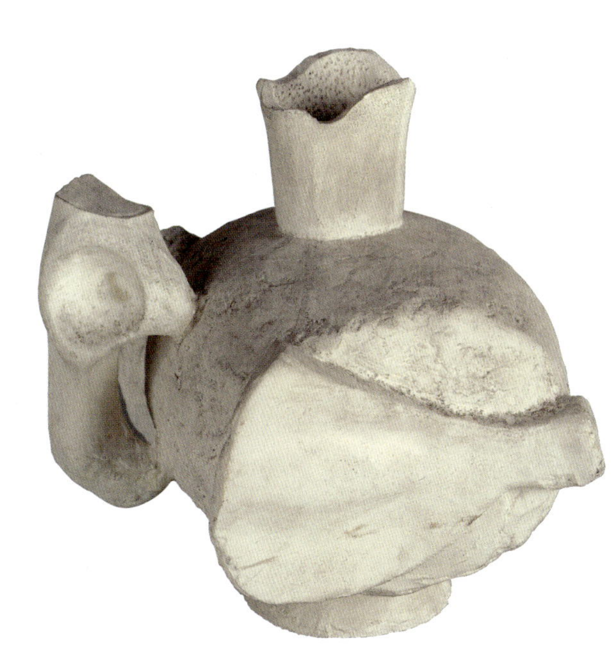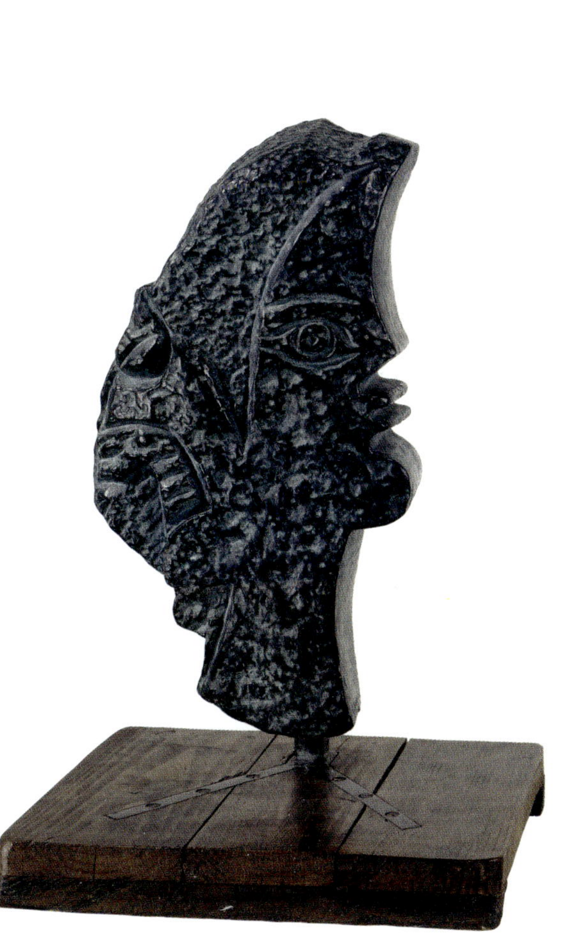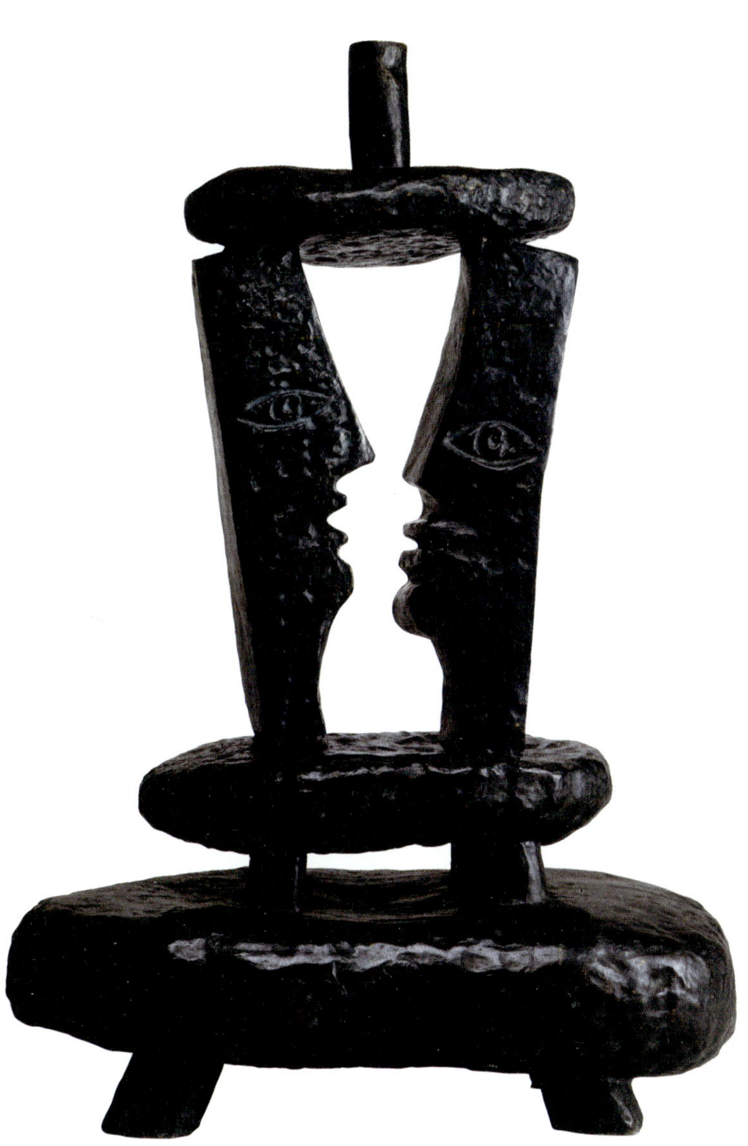

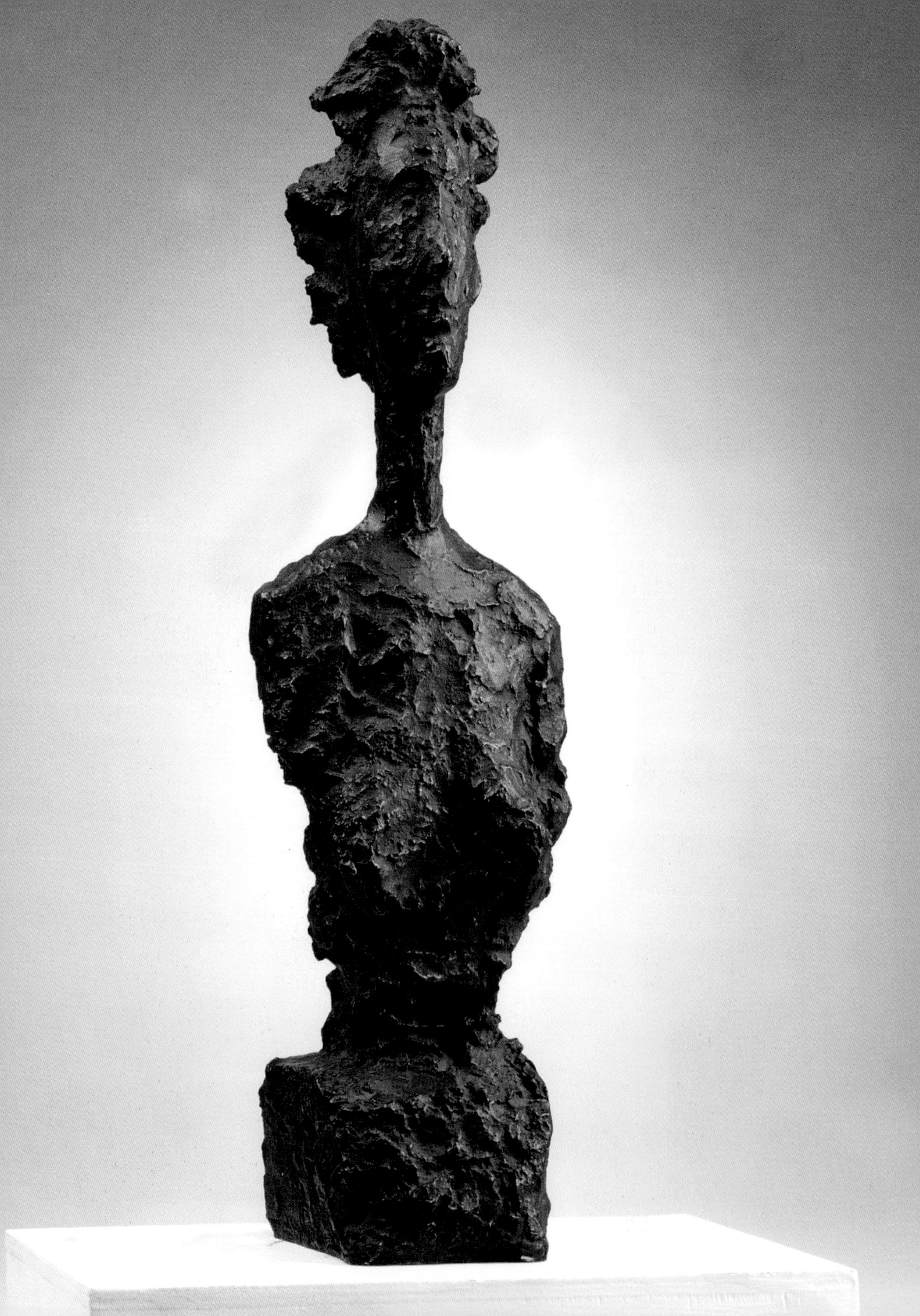

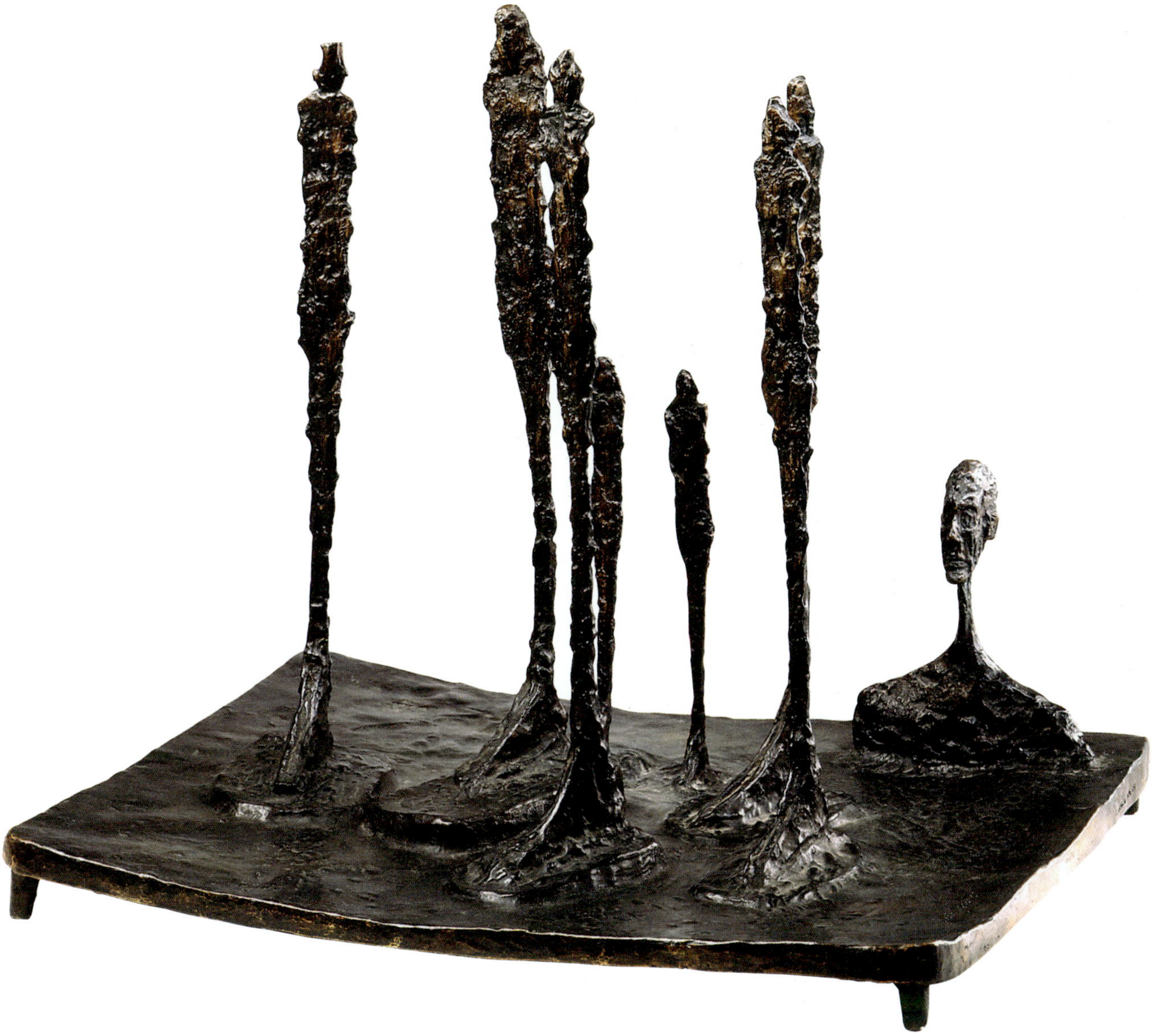

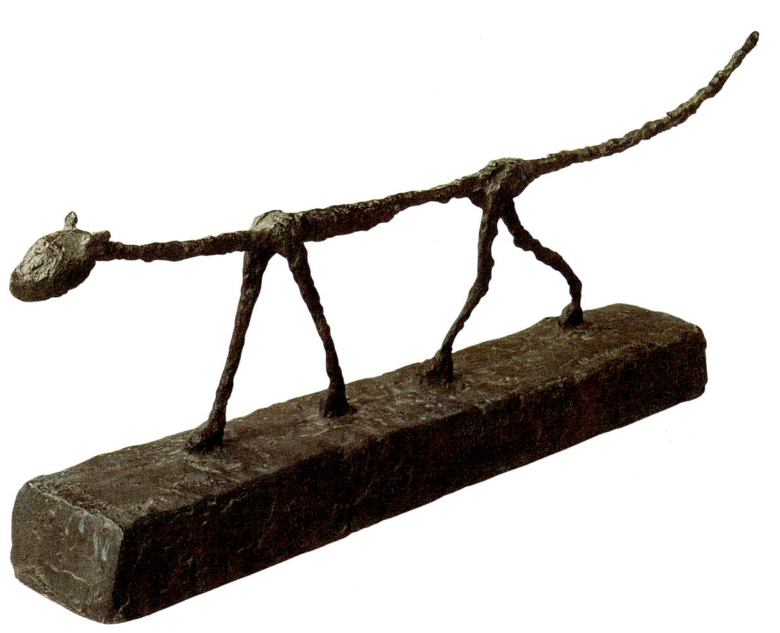

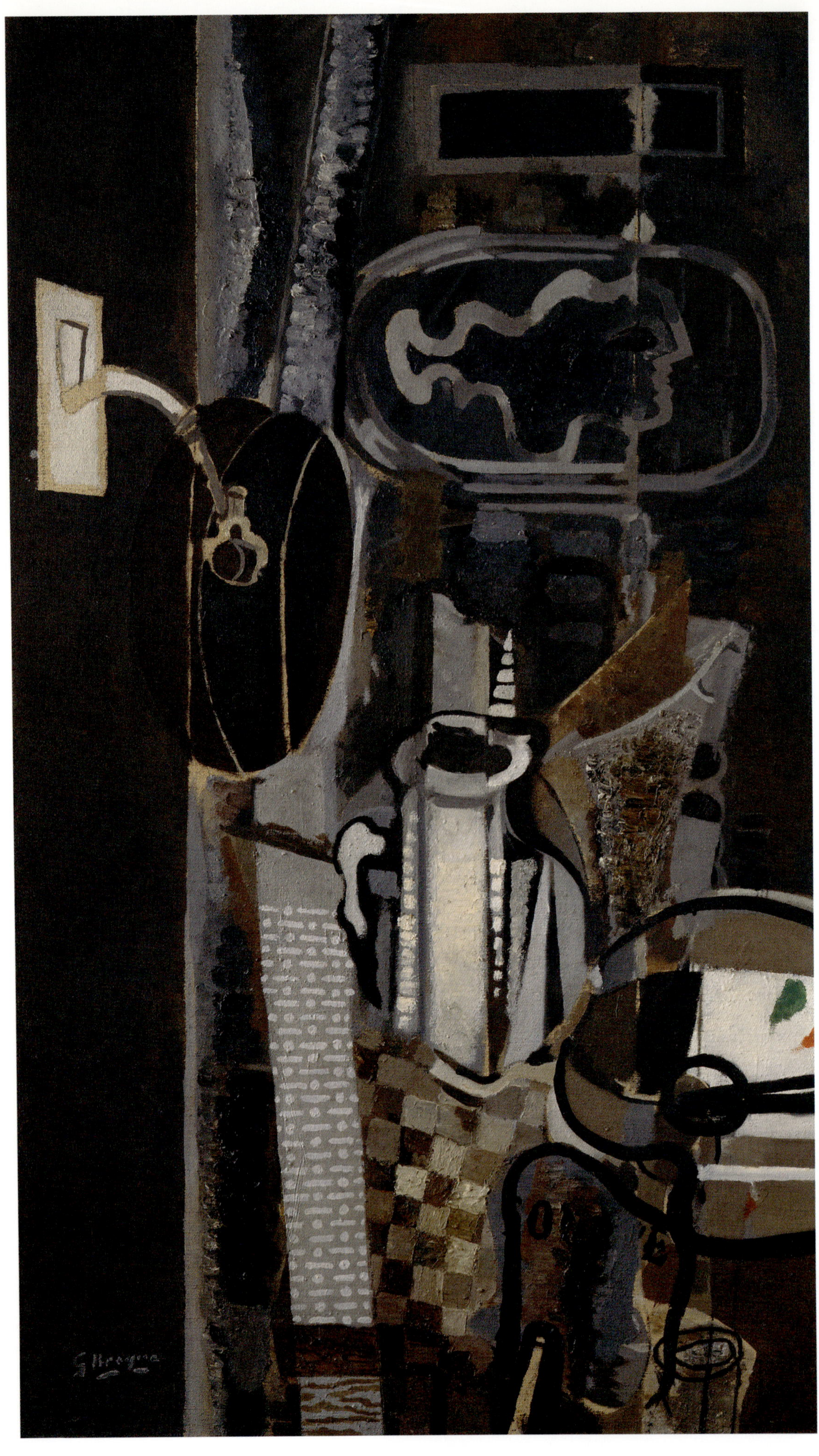

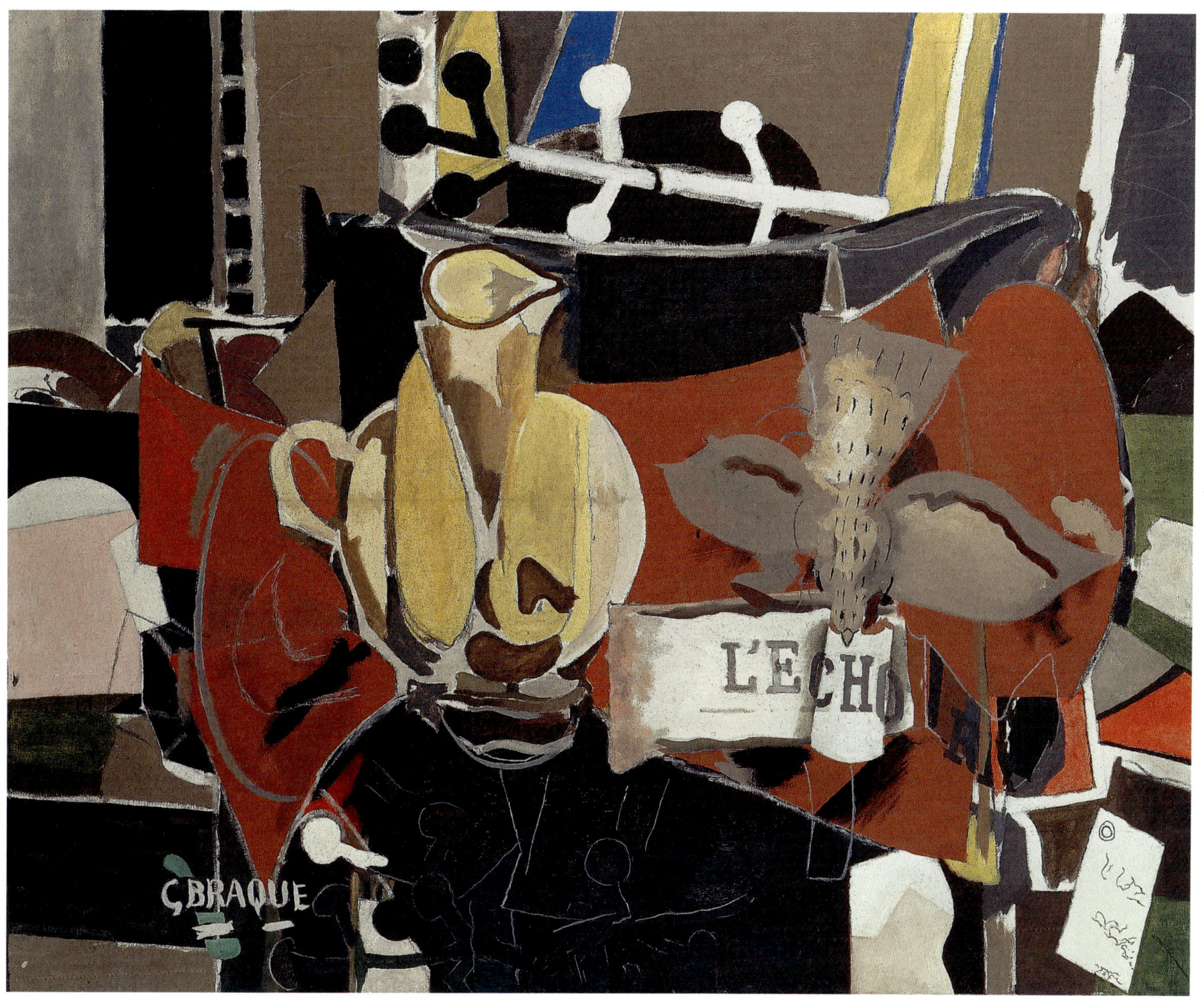

CAT. 63

Georges Braque (1882–1963)
The Studio (L'Atelier), 1949
Oil on canvas, 130.8 x 74 cm
The Metropolitan Museum of Art, New York.
Bequest of Florene M. Schoenborn, 1995
(1996.403.13a, b)

CAT. 64

Georges Braque (1882–1963)
The Echo (L'Echo), c. 1953–56
Oil on canvas, 130.2 x 161.9 cm
Nahmad Collection, Switzerland

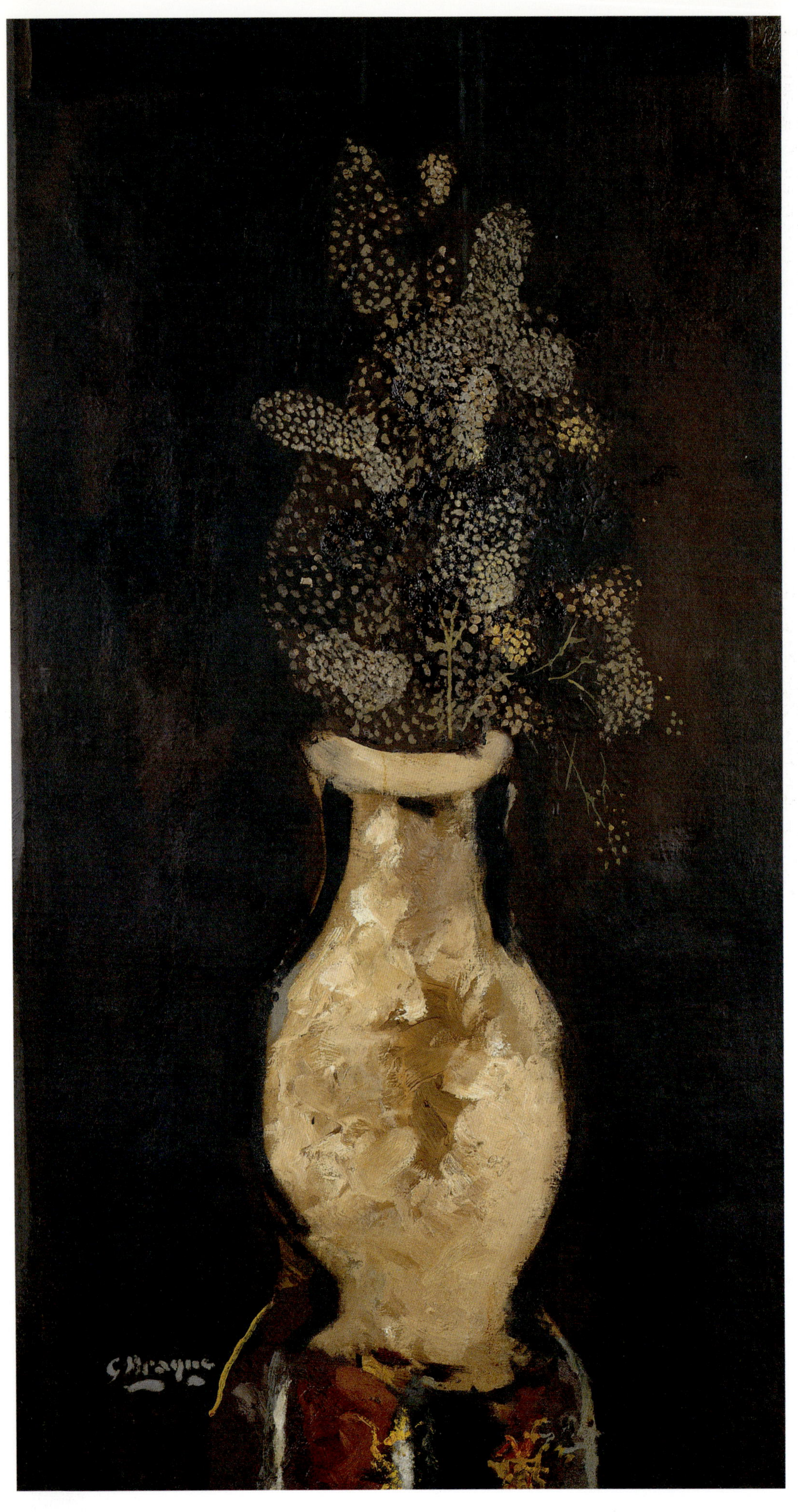

CAT. 65
Georges Braque (1882–1963)
Vase of Flowers (*Vase des fleurs*), 1954
Oil on canvas, 116 x 60 cm

CAT. 66
Georges Braque (1882–1963)
Hyacinths (*Les Jacinthes*), 1959
Oil on canvas, 33 x 41 cm

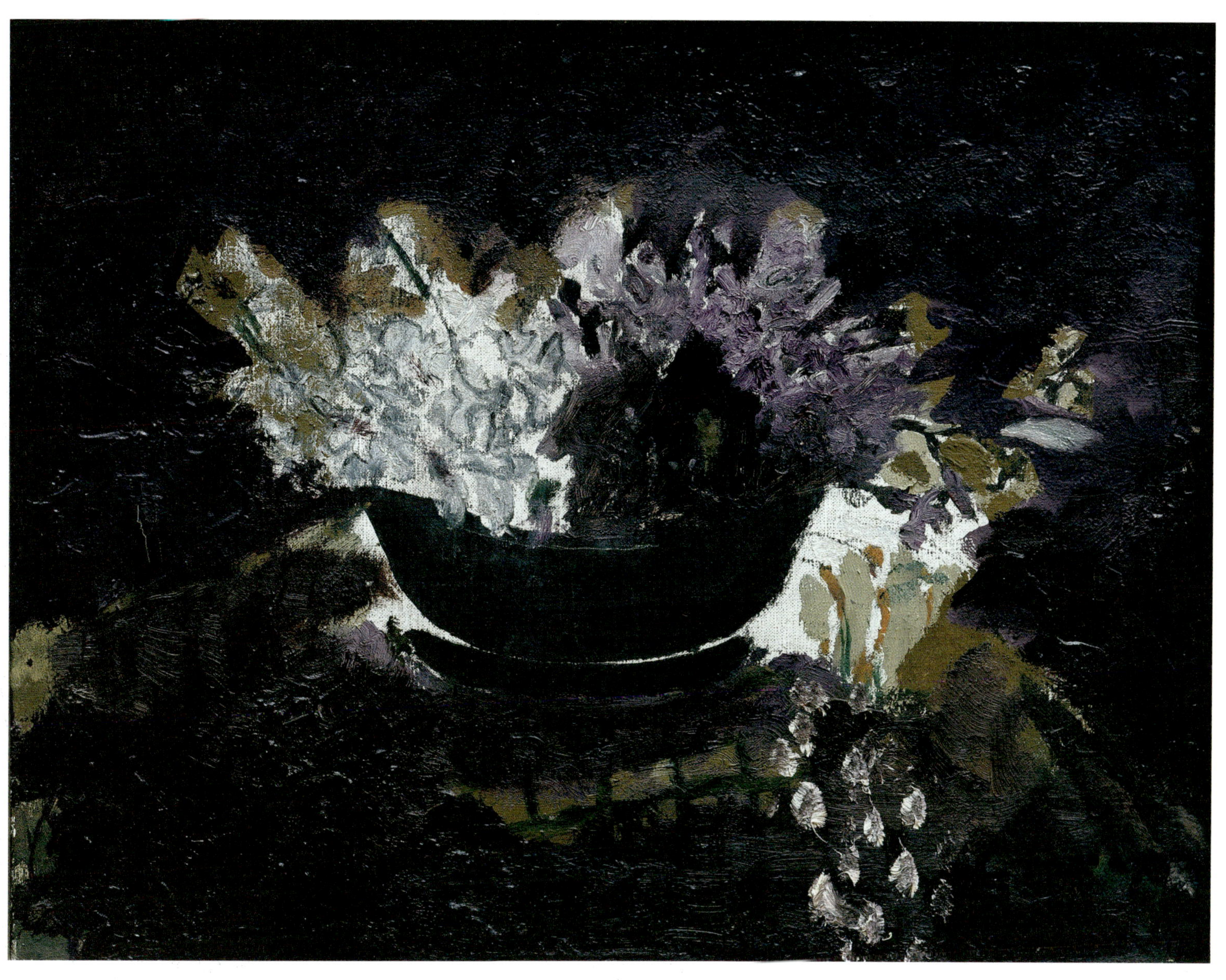

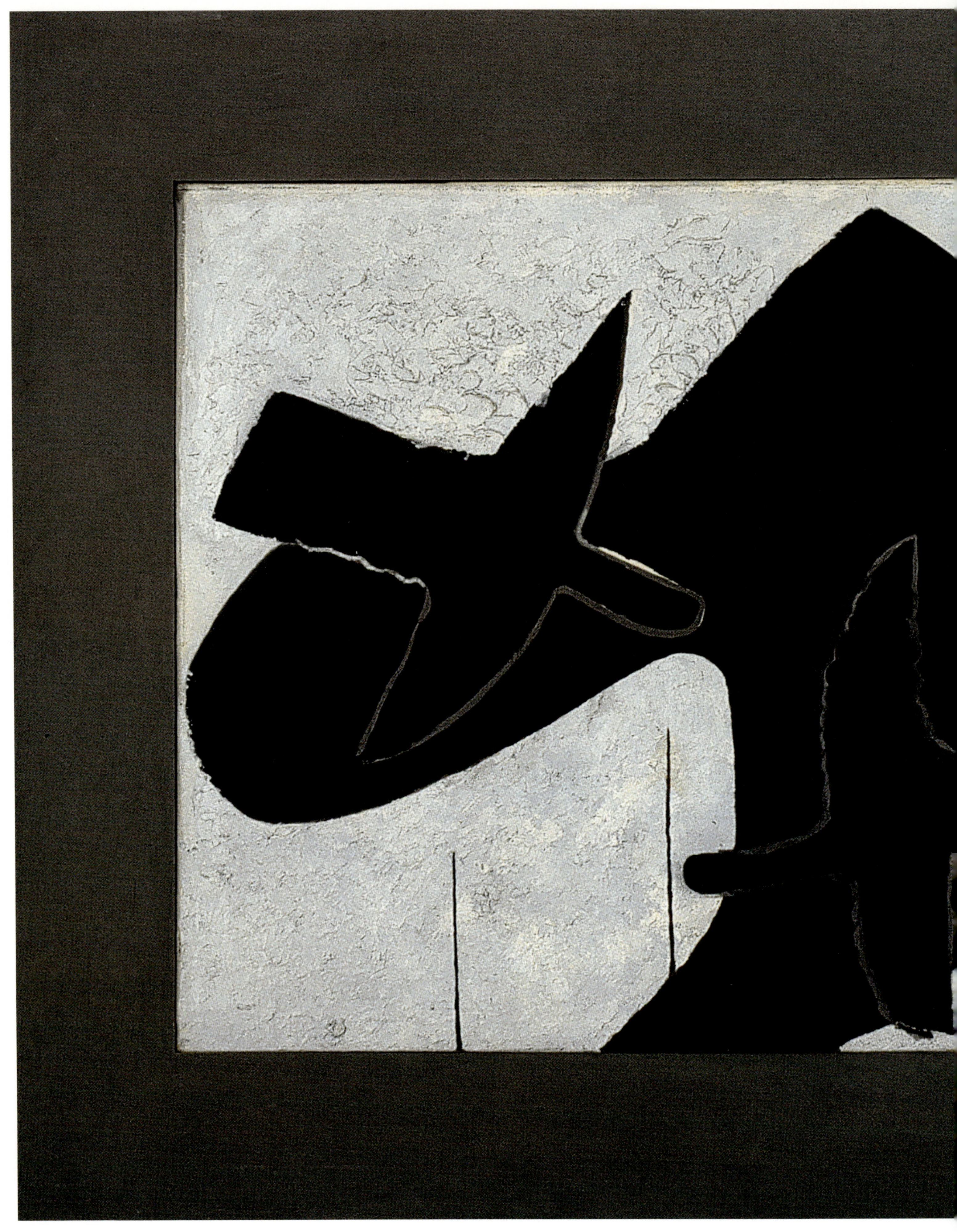

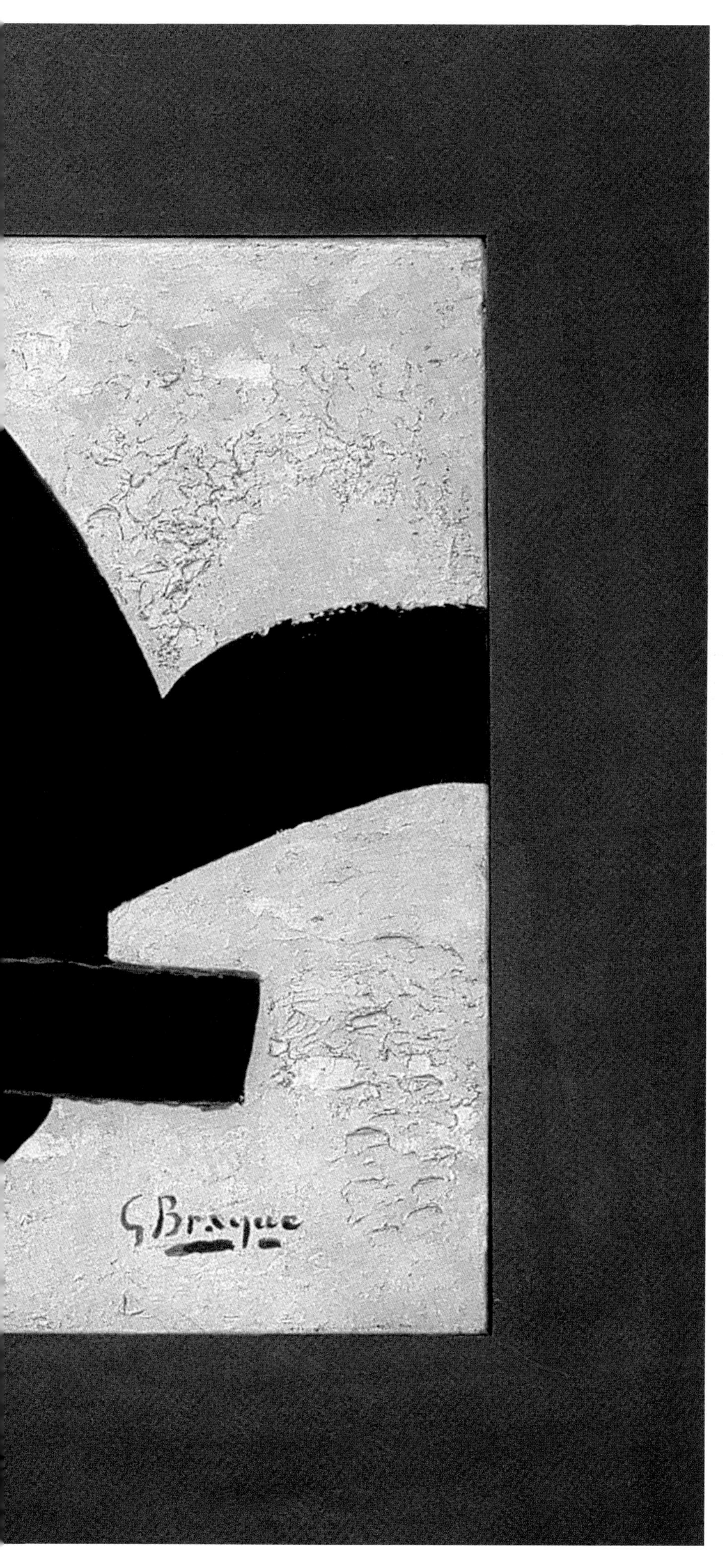

CAT. 67
Georges Braque (1882–1963)
Black Birds (*Les Oiseaux noirs*),
1956–57
Oil on canvas, 181 x 229 cm

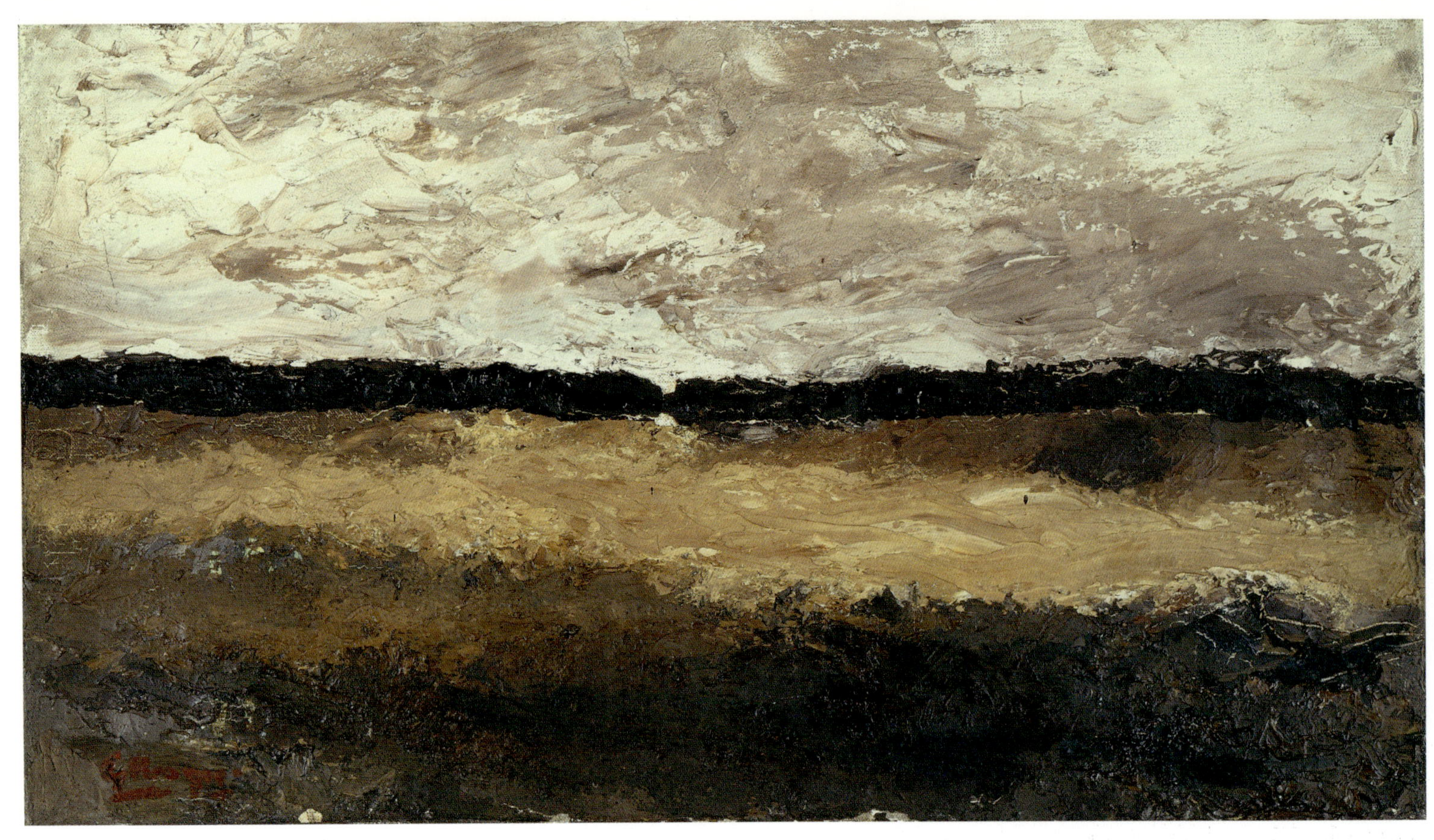

CAT. 68

Georges Braque (1882–1963)
Landscape – Fields with Overcast Sky
(*Paysage – les champs ciel bas*), 1956–57
Oil on canvas, 27 x 44.5 cm

CAT. 69

Georges Braque (1882–1963)
Storm, Boat on the Pebbles
(*Marine l'orage barque sur les galets*), 1959
Oil on canvas, 24 x 42 cm

CAT. 70

Georges Braque (1882–1963)
Plain I (*La Plaine I*), 1955–56
Oil on canvas, 21 x 73 cm

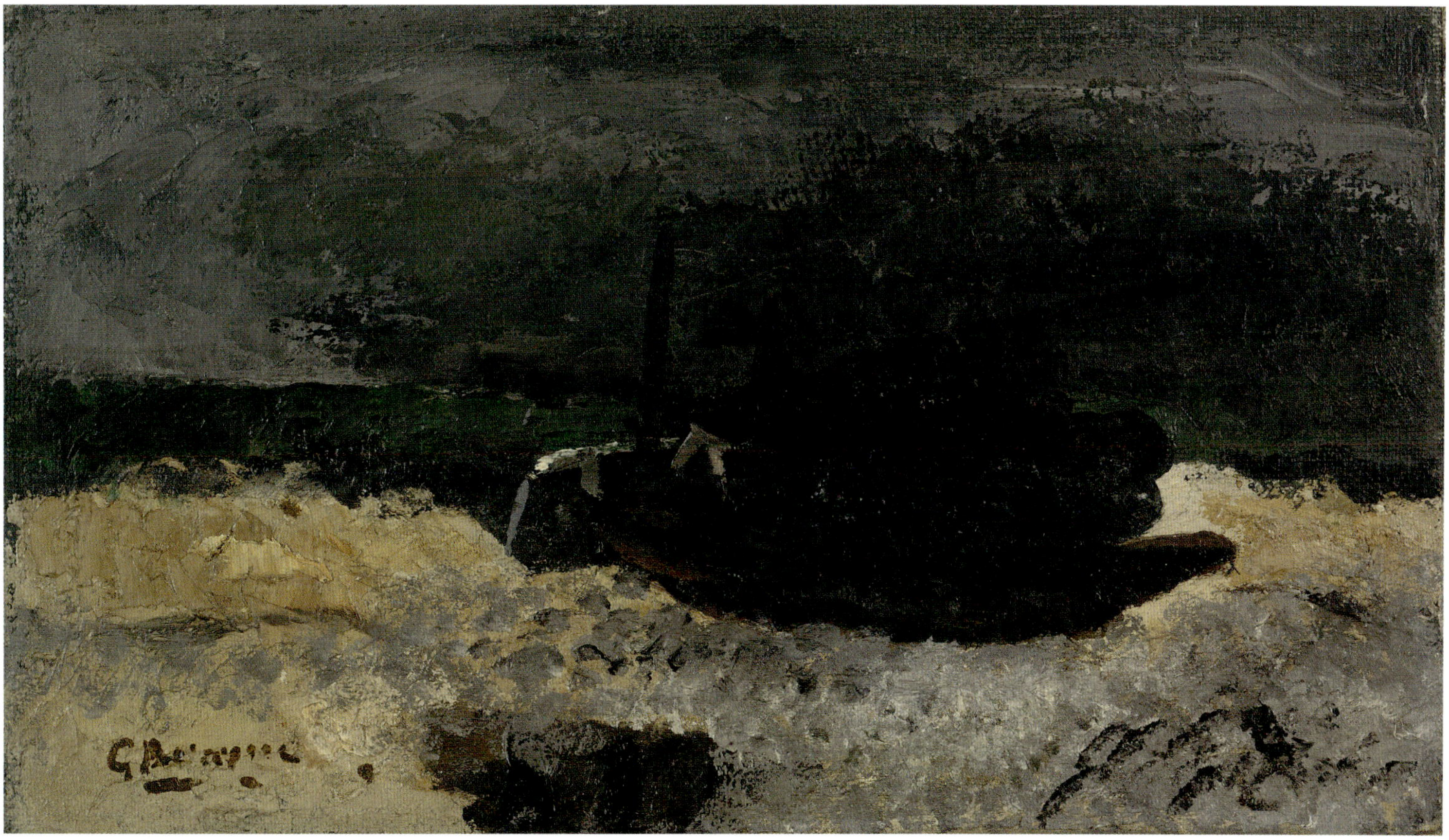

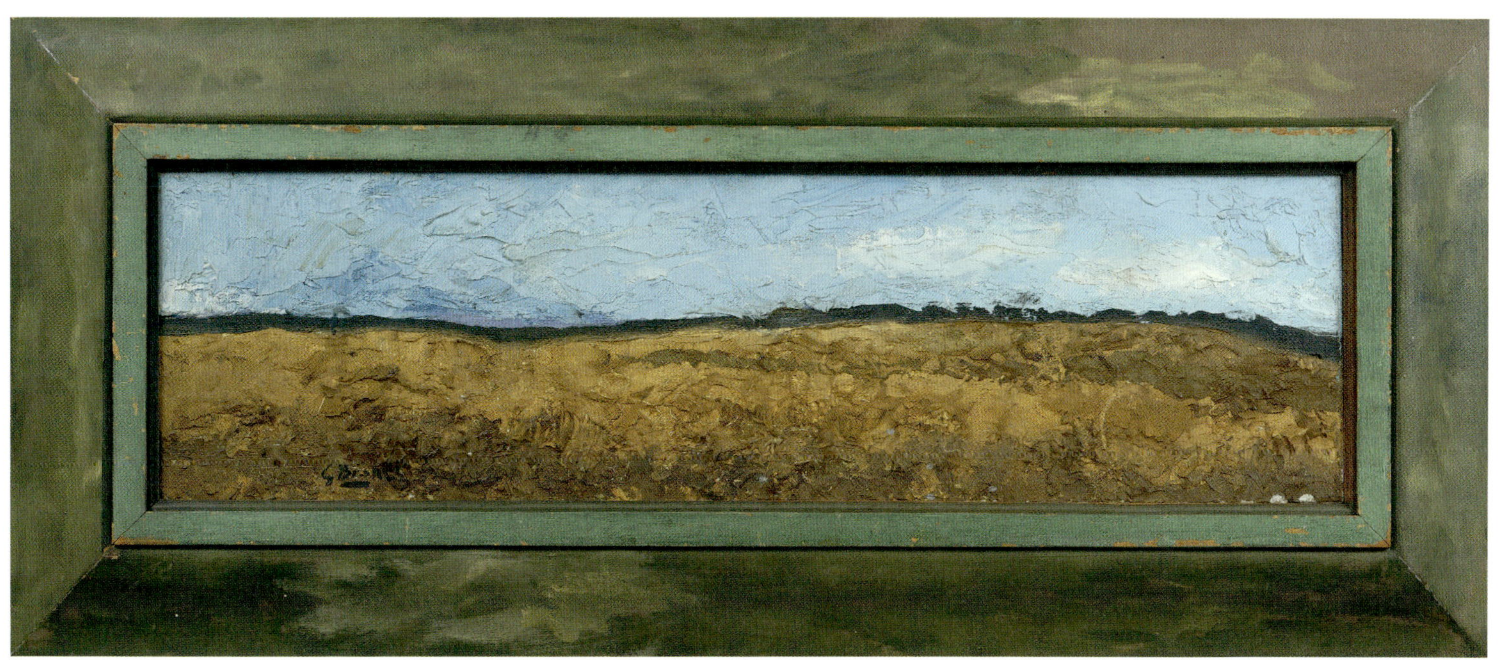

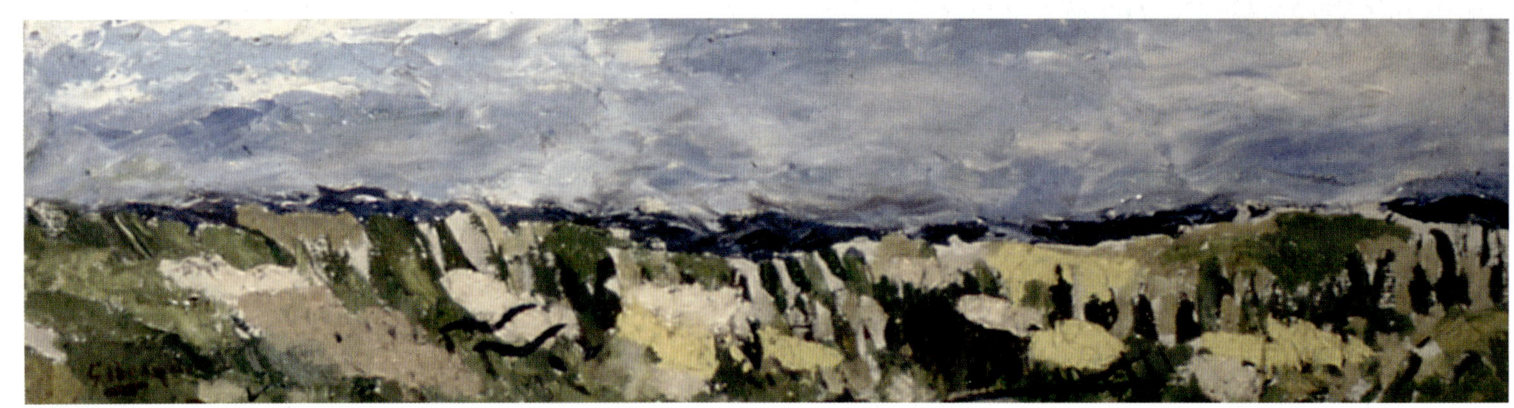

CAT. 71
Georges Braque (1882–1963)
Landscape (Paysage), 1959
Oil on canvas, 21 x 73 cm

CAT. 72
Georges Braque (1882–1963)
*Landscape with Plough
(Paysage à la charrue)*, 1955
Oil on canvas, 34 x 64 cm

CAT. 73
Georges Braque (1882–1963)
Plough (Charrue), 1959
Oil on canvas, 22 x 33 cm

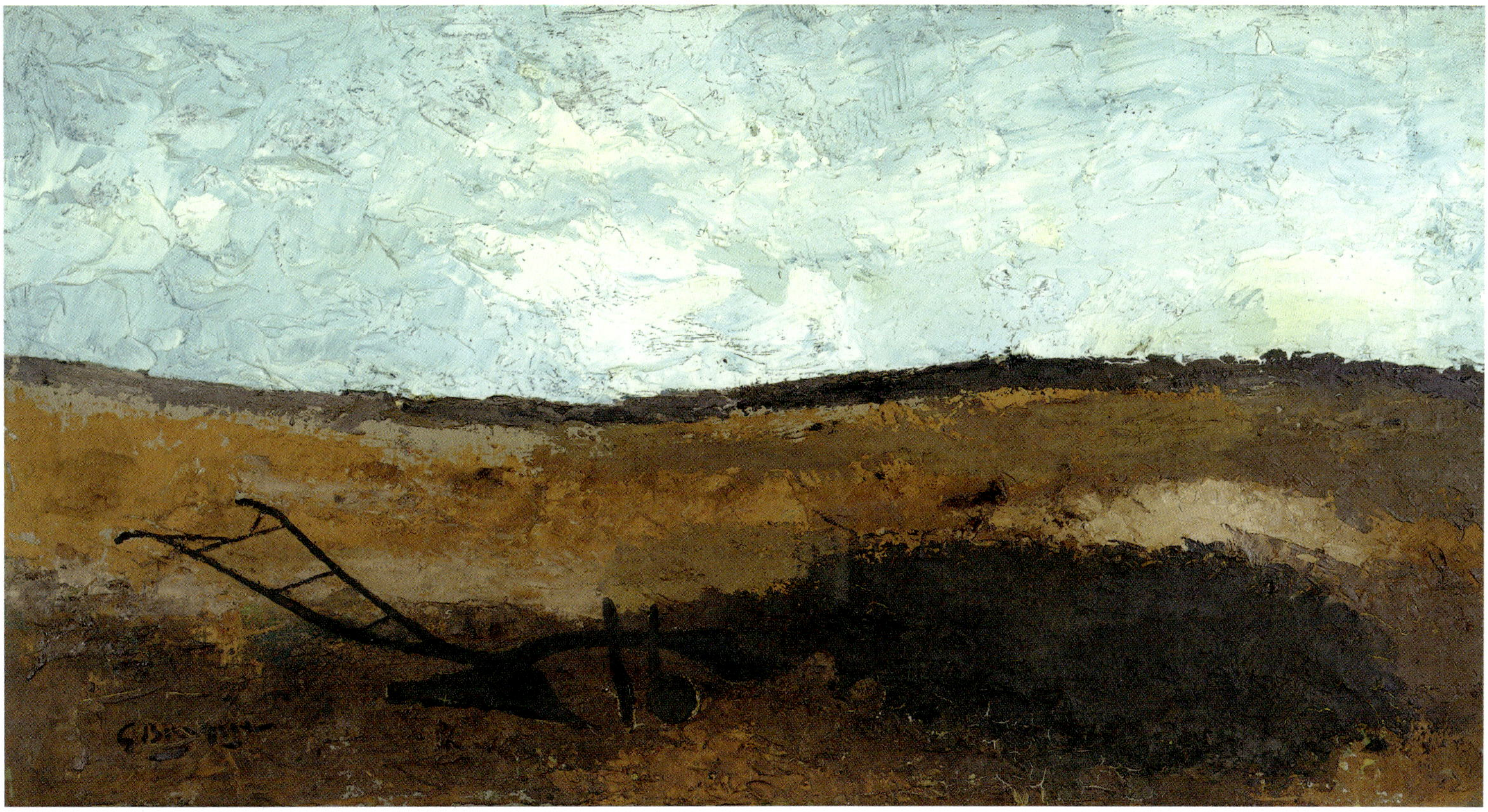

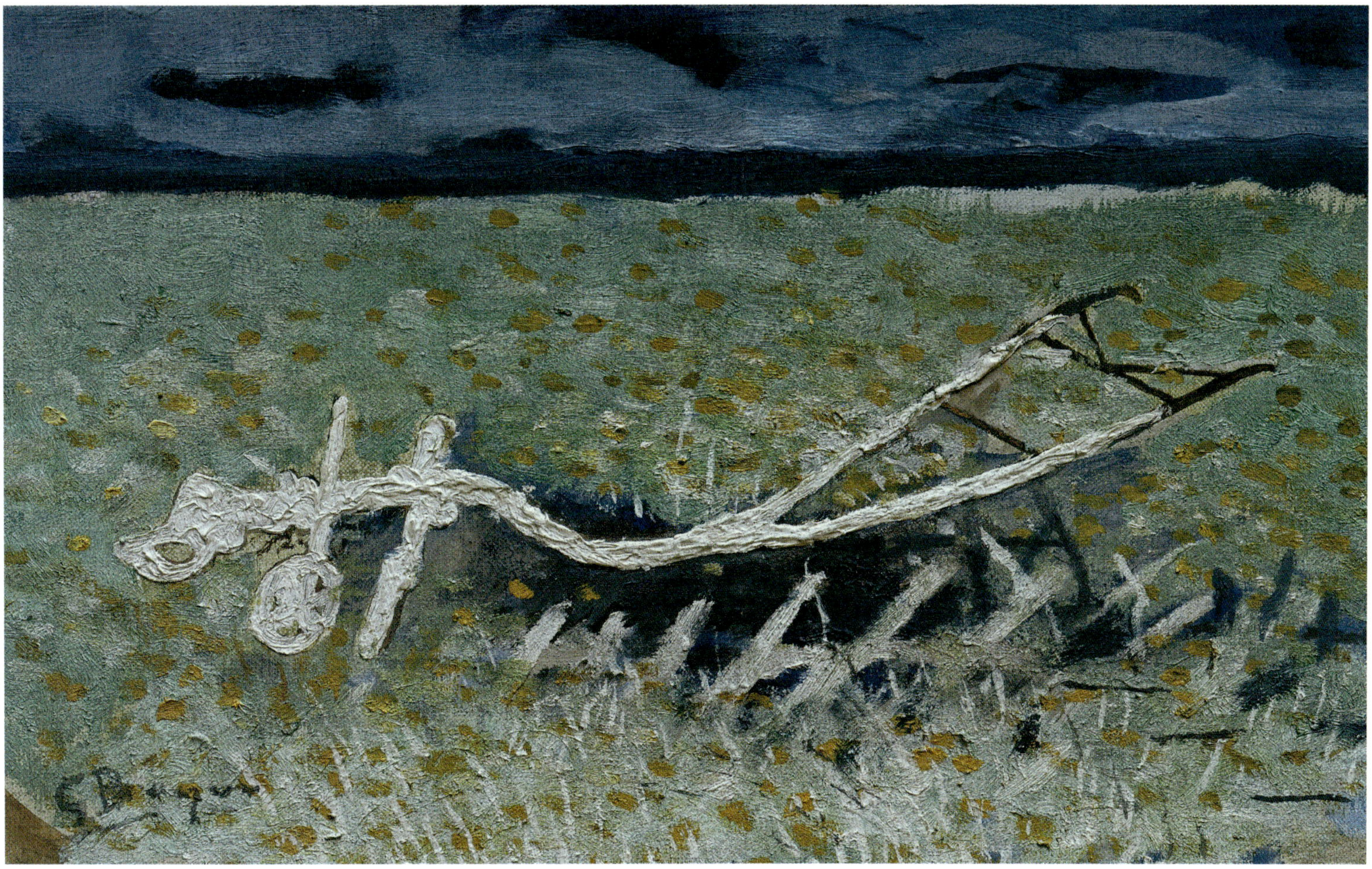

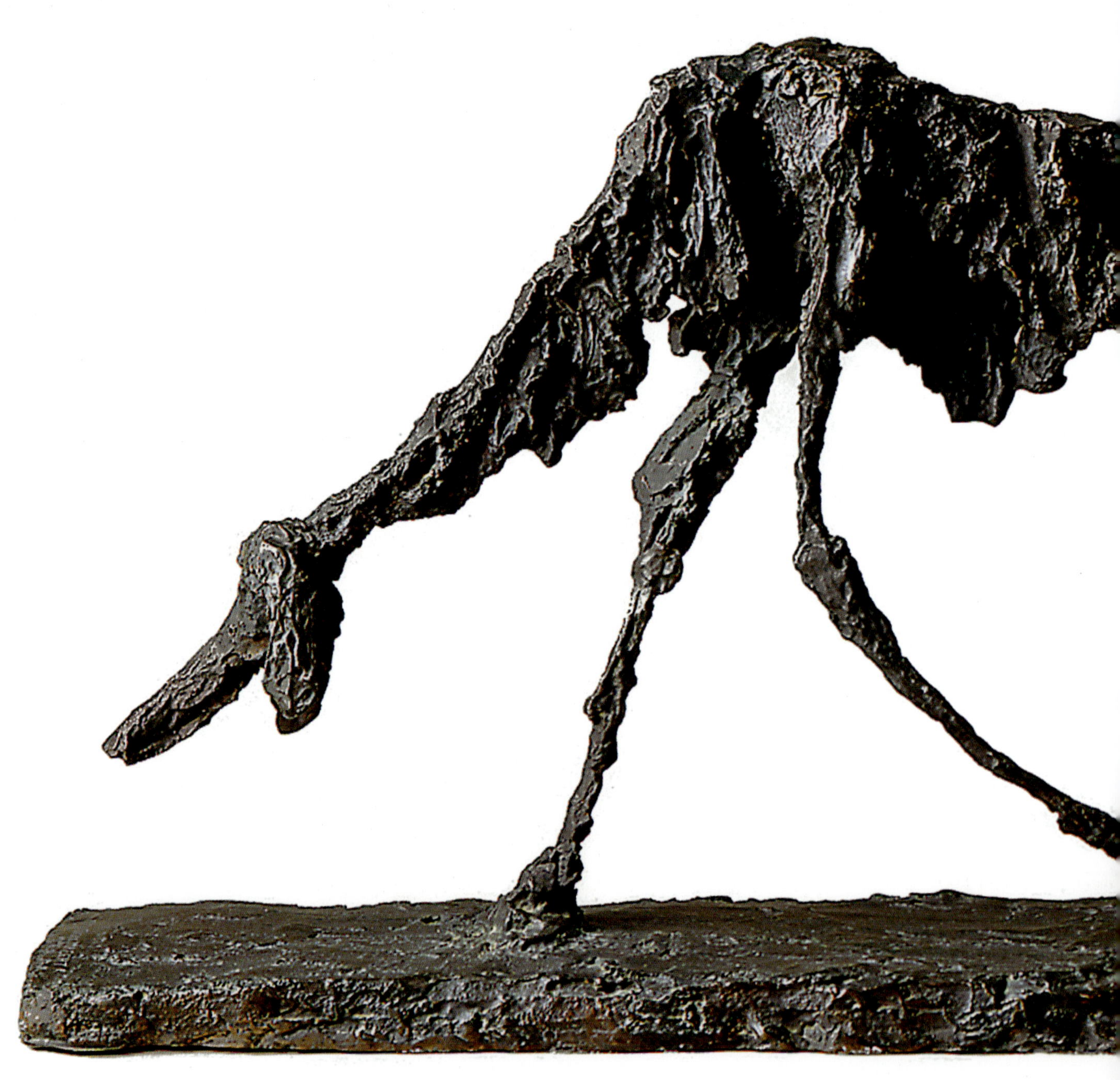

Alberto Giacometti (1901–1966)
Dog (Le Chien), 1957
Bronze, 47 x 100 x 15 cm

Georges Braque (1882–1963)
Thoroughbred (Pur-sang), 1955–56
Bronze on stone, 25 x 47 x 22 cm

Georges Braque (1882–1963)
Little Horse (Petit cheval), 1955–56
Bronze, 22 x 19 x 5 cm

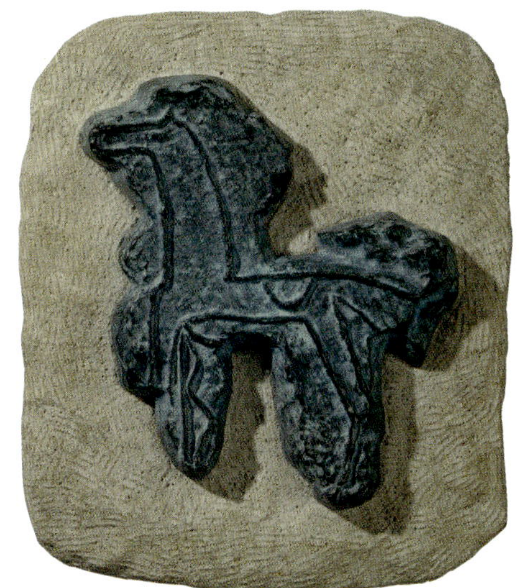

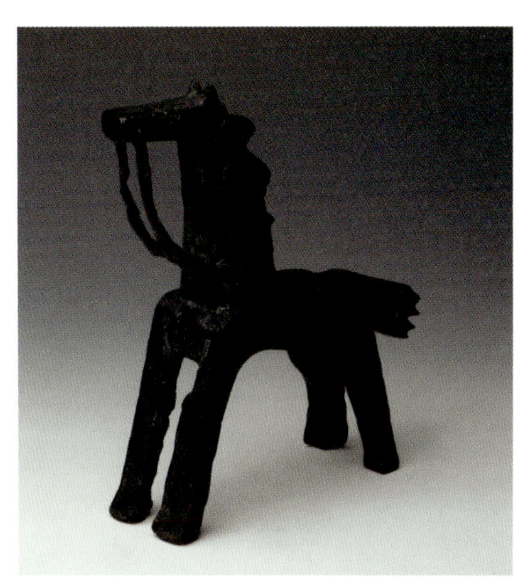

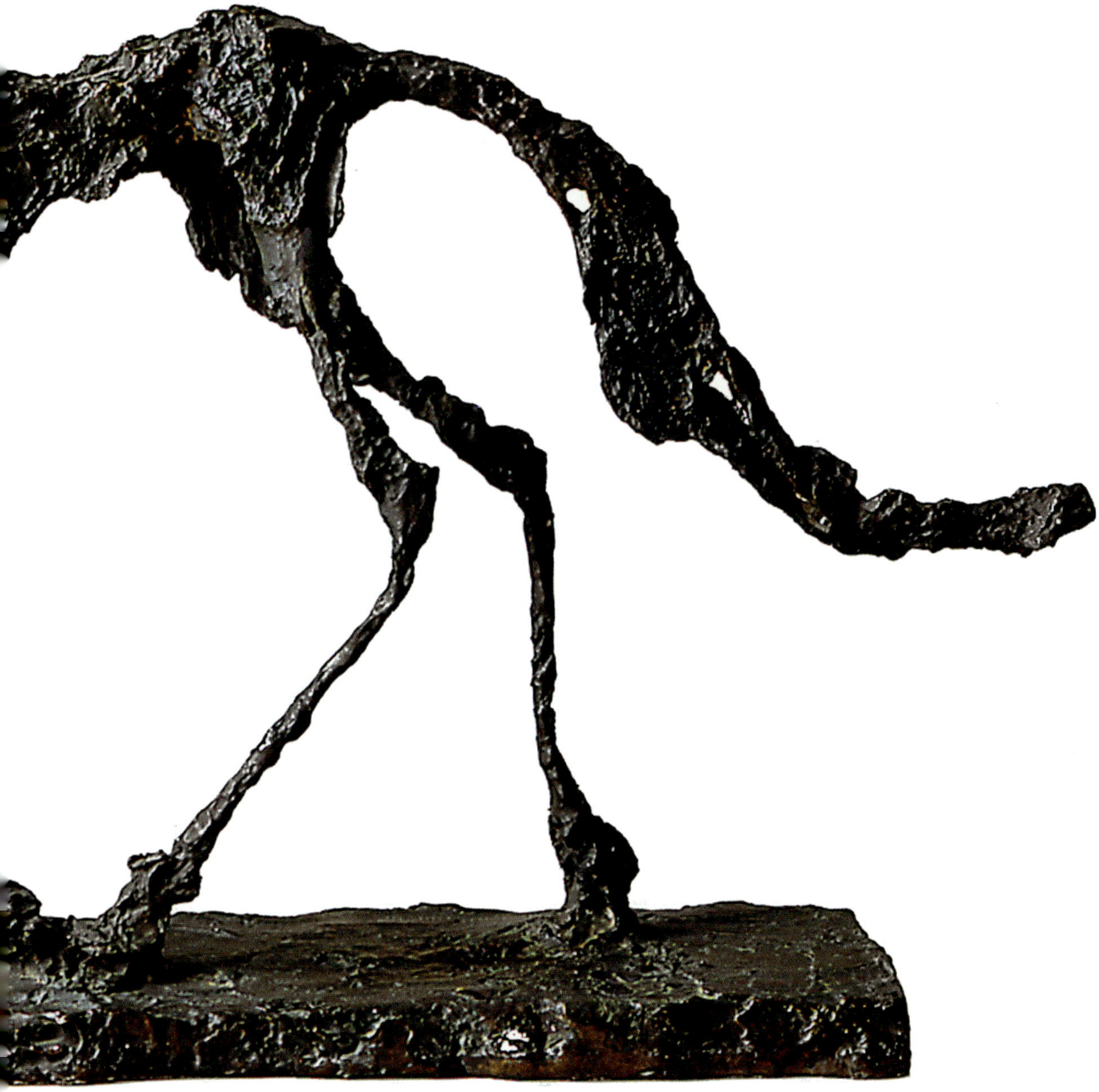

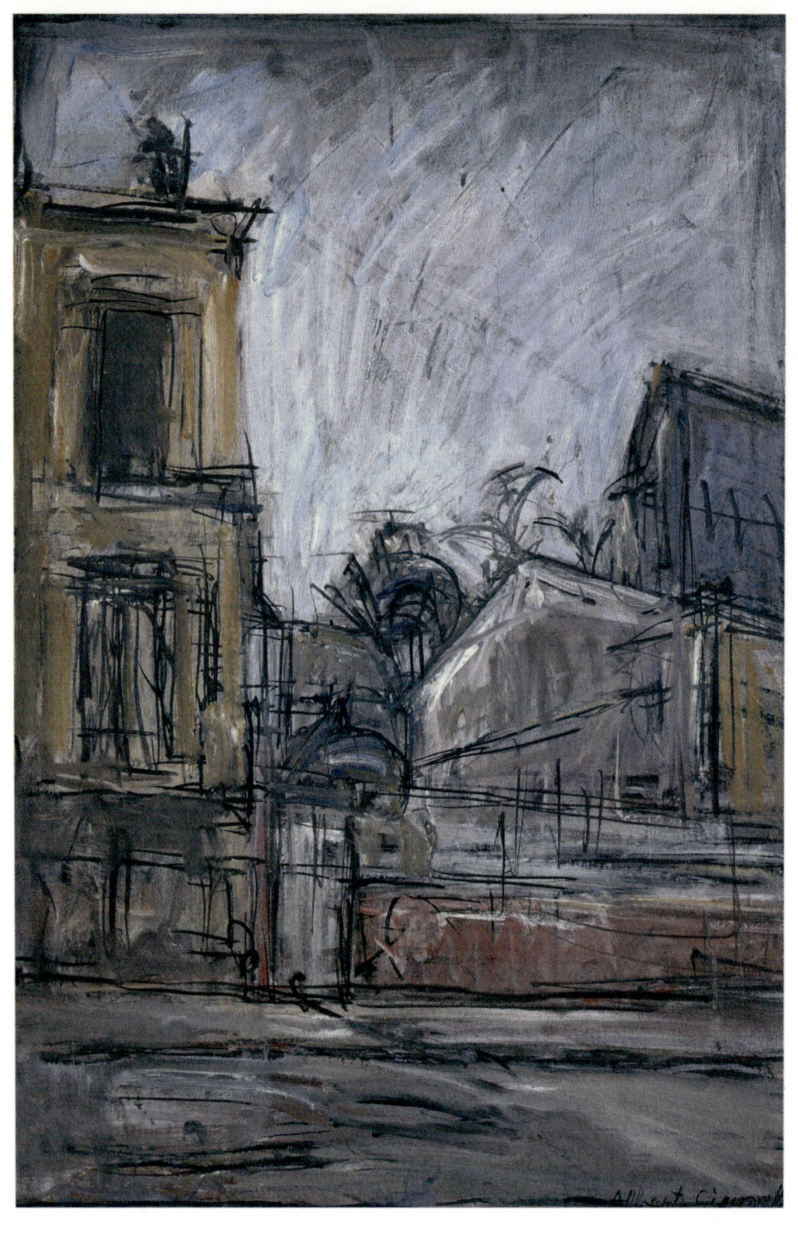

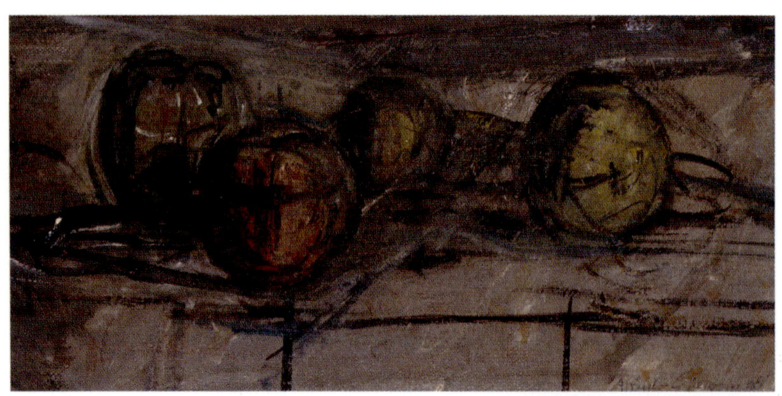

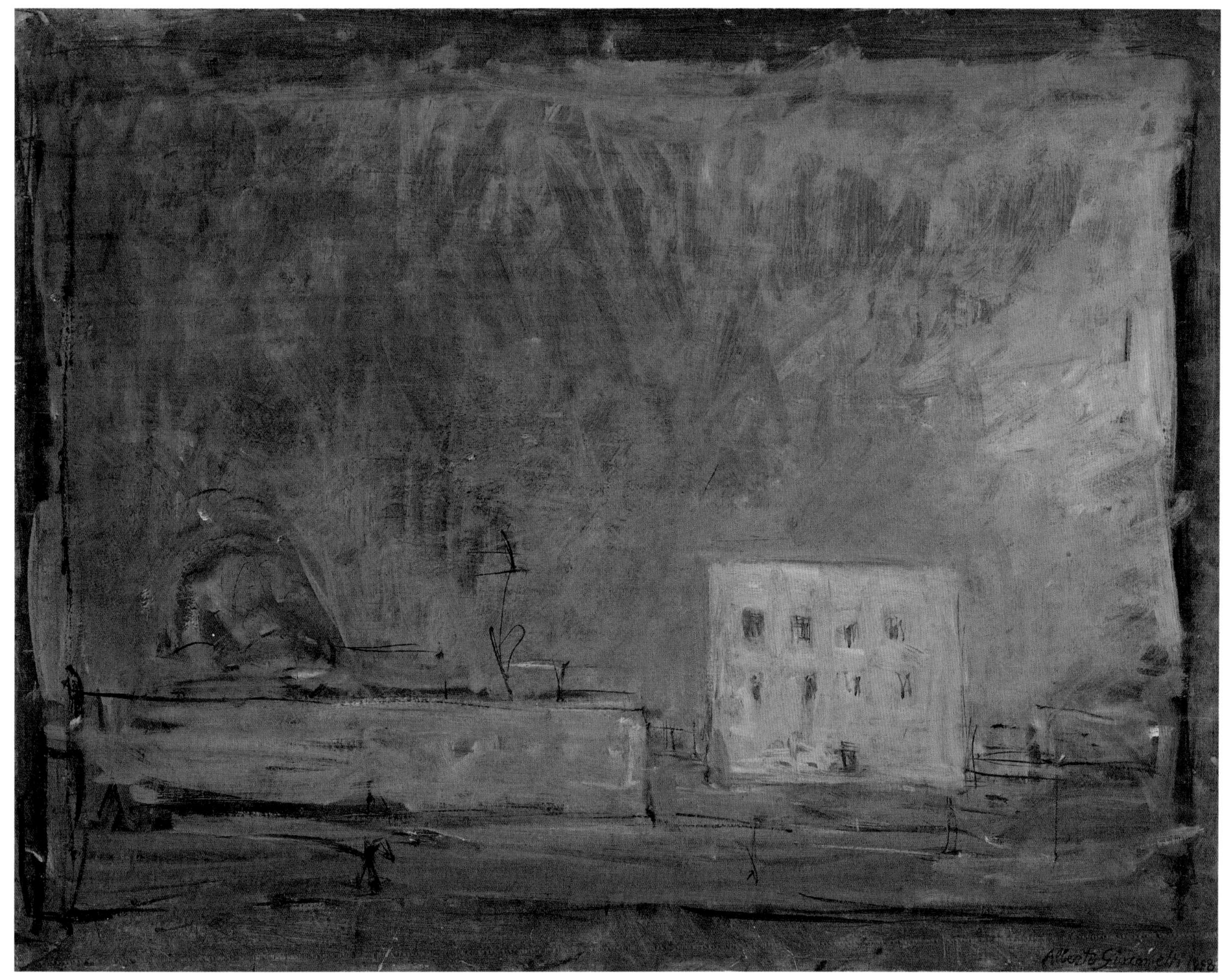

CLOCKWISE FROM LEFT:

CAT. 77
Alberto Giacometti (1901–1966)
The House Opposite (Maison d'en face), 1952
Oil on canvas, 69 x 45 cm

CAT. 78
Alberto Giacometti (1901–1966)
White House (La Maison blanche), 1958
Oil on canvas, 81 x 65 cm

CAT. 79
Alberto Giacometti (1901–1966)
Apples (Les Pommes), 1960
Oil on canvas, 16 x 33 cm

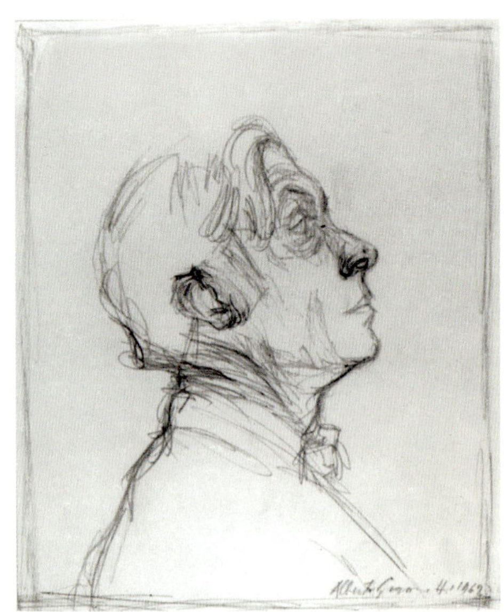

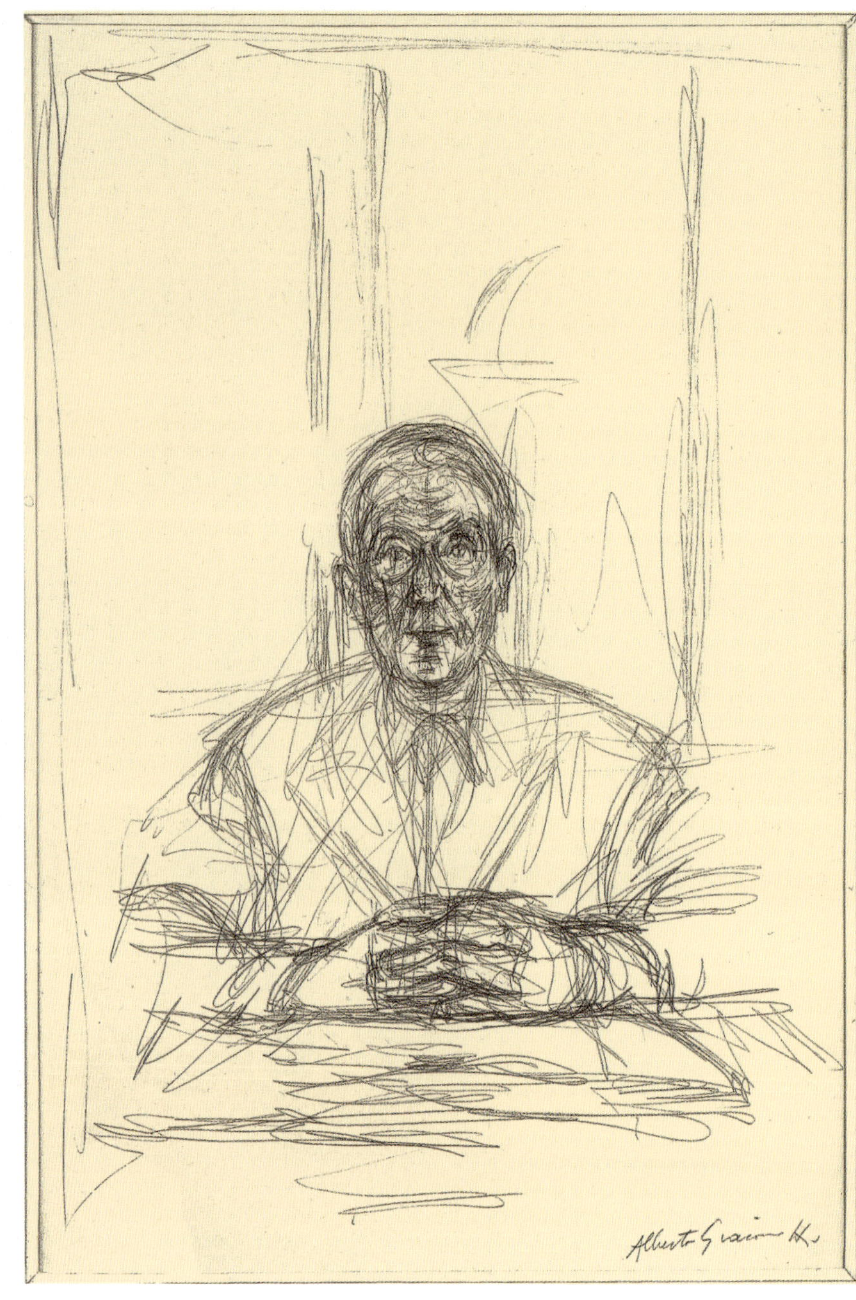

CAT. 80
Alberto Giacometti (1901–1966)
Portrait of Reverdy, c. 1960
Pencil on paper, 24 x 19 cm

CAT. 81
Alberto Giacometti (1901–1966)
Portrait of Aimé Maeght, 1960
Pencil on paper, 48.5 x 31.5 cm

CAT. 82
Alberto Giacometti (1901–1966)
Portrait of Marguerite Maeght, 1961
Oil on canvas, 145 x 95 cm

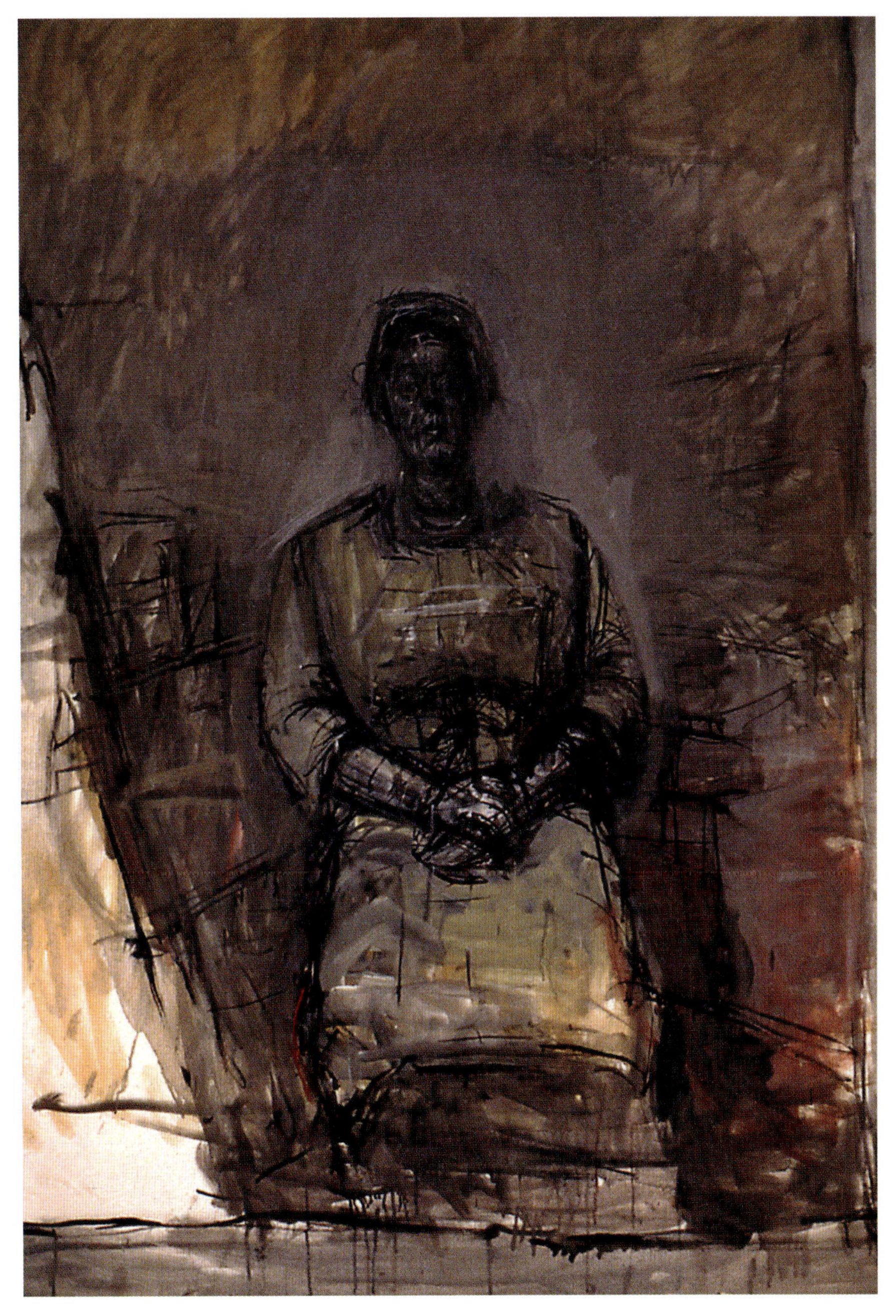

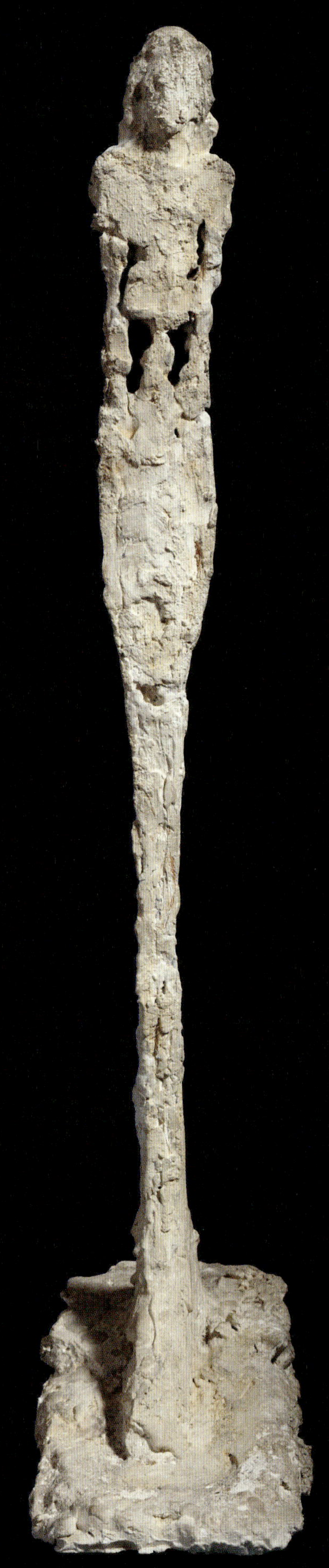

Alberto Giacometti (1901–1966)
Standing Woman with Arms by Her Side
(*Femme debout bras le long du corps*), 1952
Plaster, 51 x 17 x 9 cm

Alberto Giacometti (1901–1966)
Standing Woman (*Femme debout*), 1960
Plaster, 24 x 10 x 6 cm

Alberto Giacometti (1901–1966)
Standing Woman with Arms by Her Side
(*Femme debout bras le long du corps*), 1952
Plaster, 23 x 8 x 5.5 cm

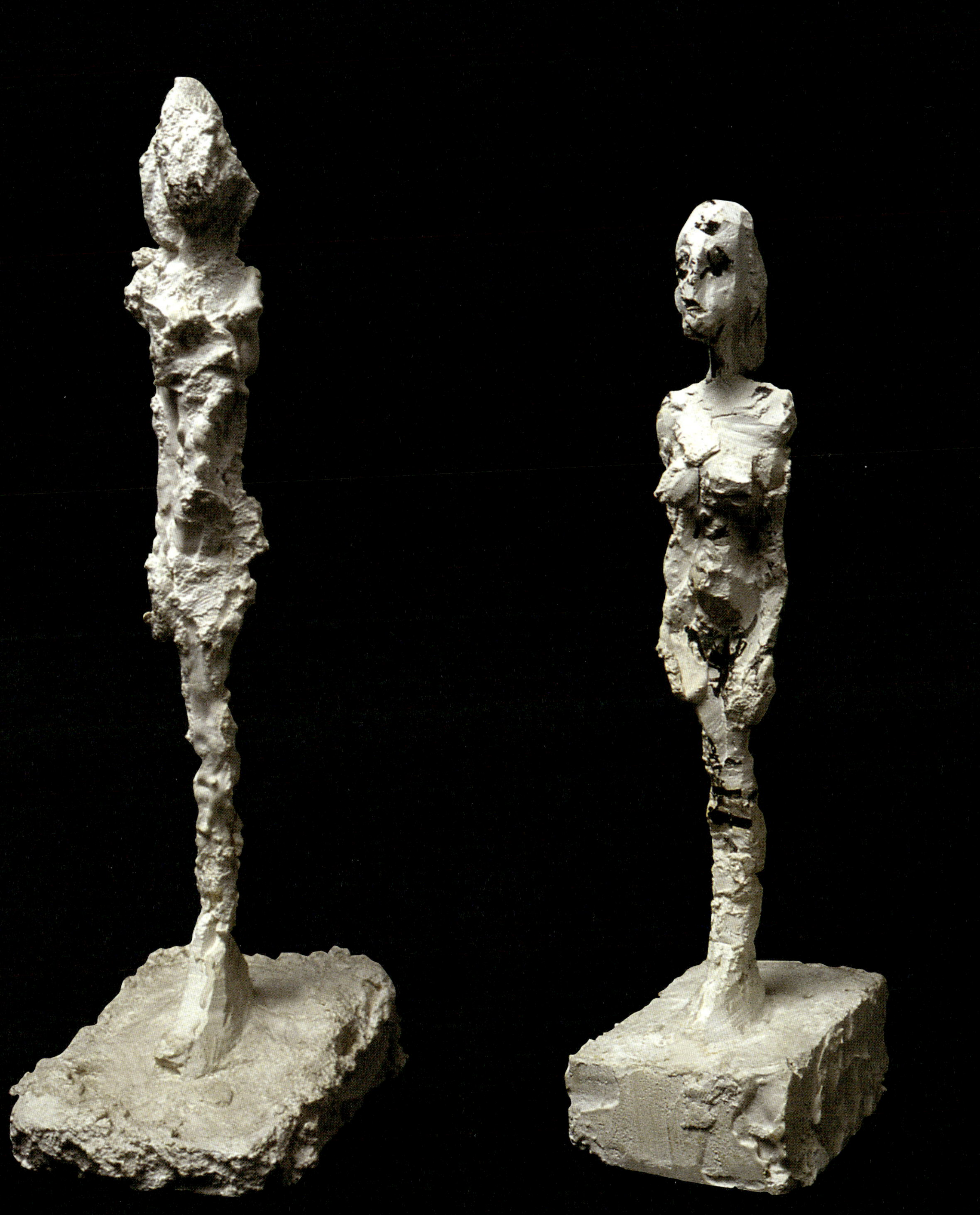

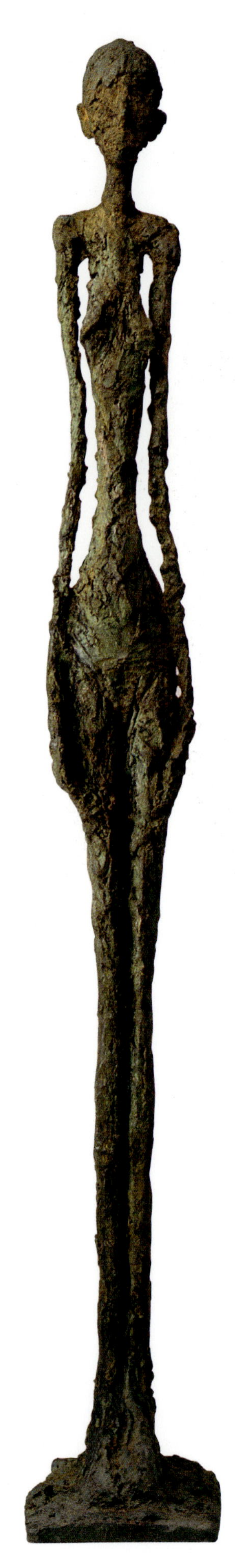

CAT. 86
Alberto Giacometti (1901–1966)
Standing Woman I (Femme debout I), 1960
Bronze, 270 x 54 x 36 cm

CAT. 87
Alberto Giacometti (1901–1966)
Walking Man I (L'Homme qui marche I), 1960
Bronze, 183 x 26 x 95.5 cm

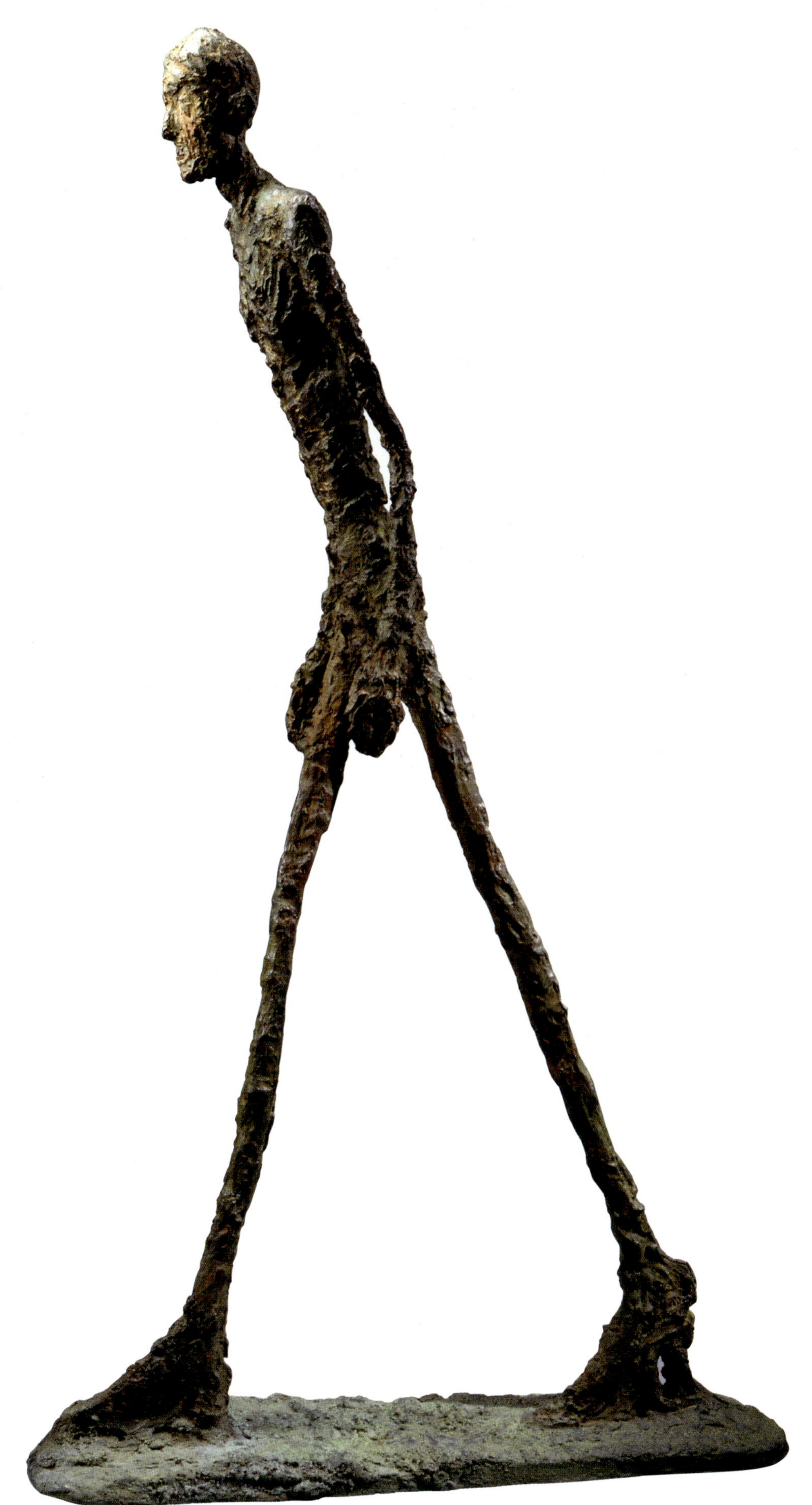

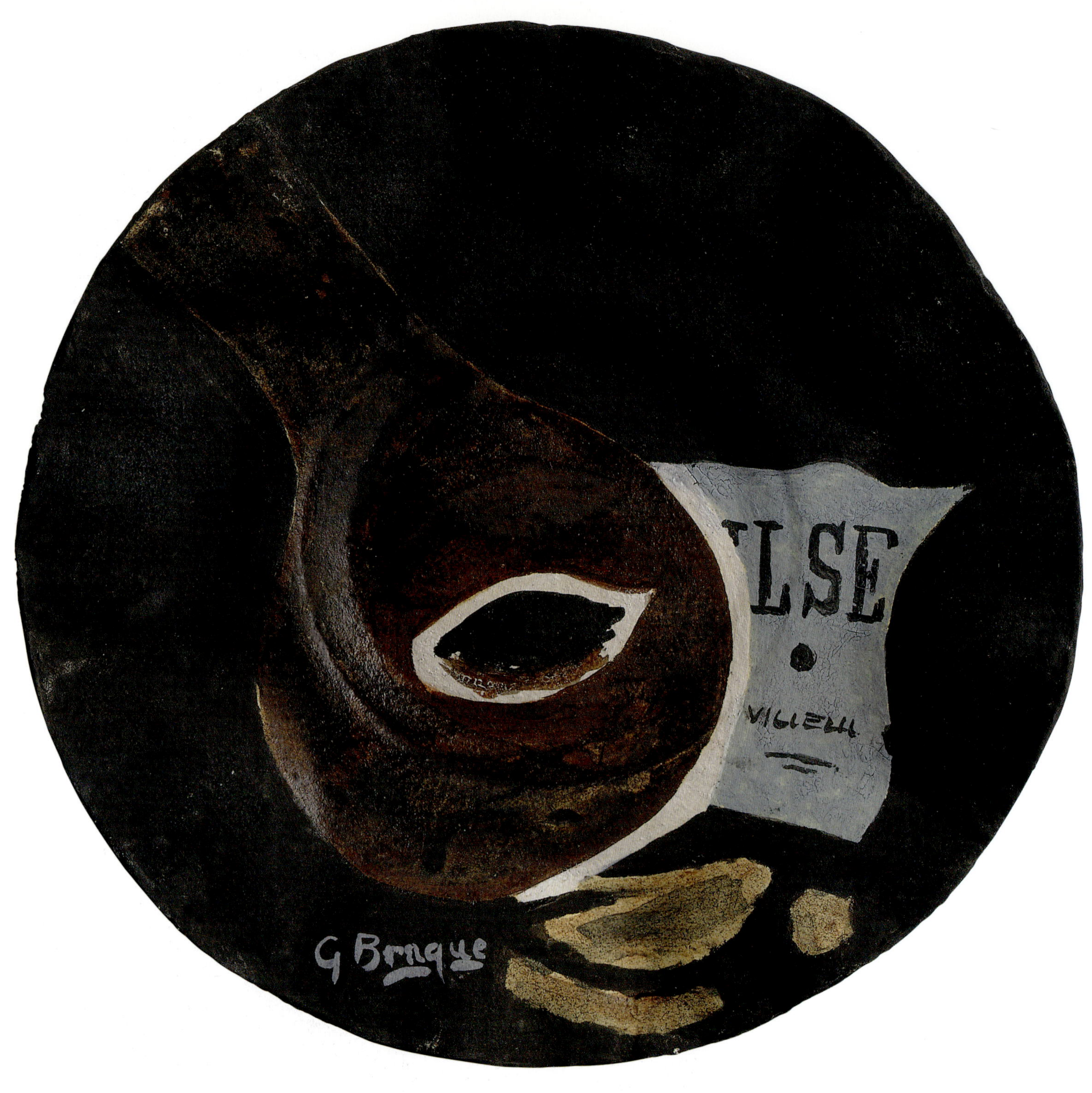

CLOCKWISE FROM LEFT:

CAT. 88
Georges Braque (1882–1963)
Waltz (Valse), 1960
Ceramic, diameter: 27 cm

CAT. 89
Georges Braque (1882–1963)
White Bird (Oiseau blanc), 1961
Ceramic, diameter: 24 cm

CAT. 90
Georges Braque (1882–1963)
Profile (Profil), 1960
Ceramic, diameter: 28 cm

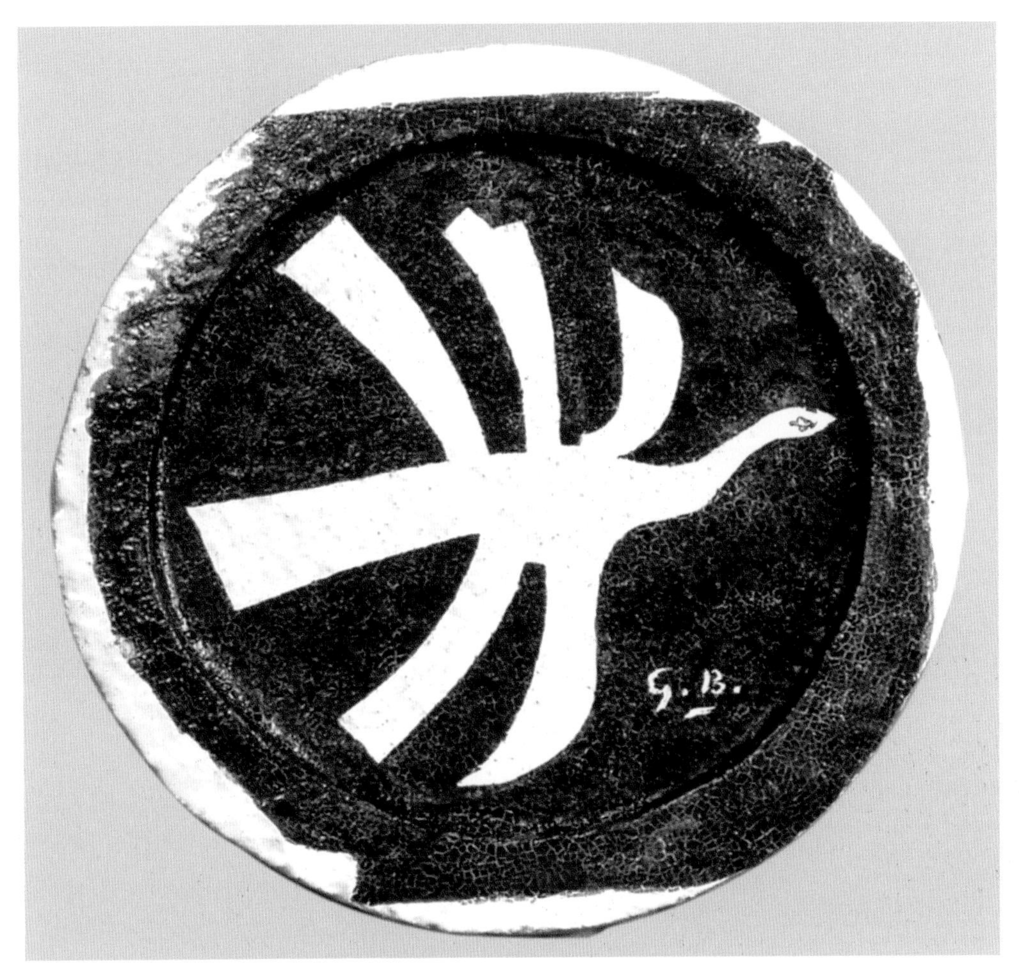

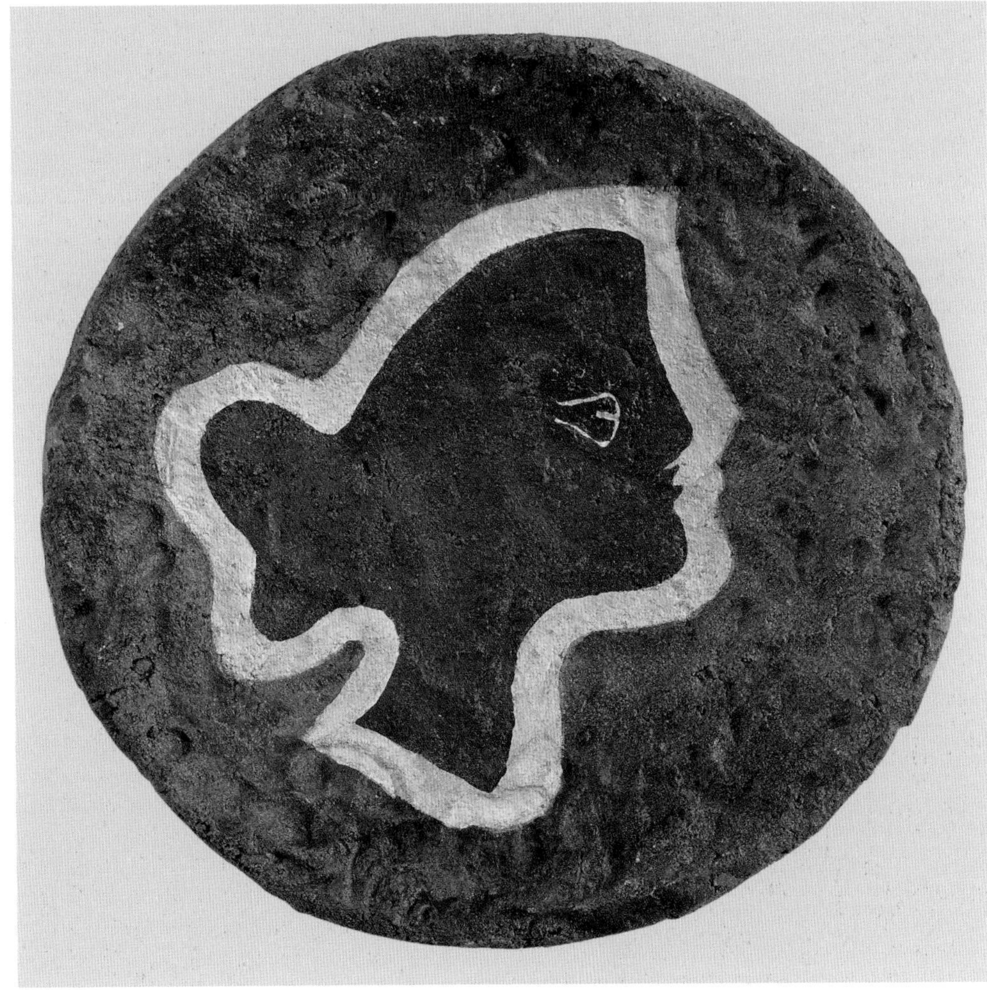

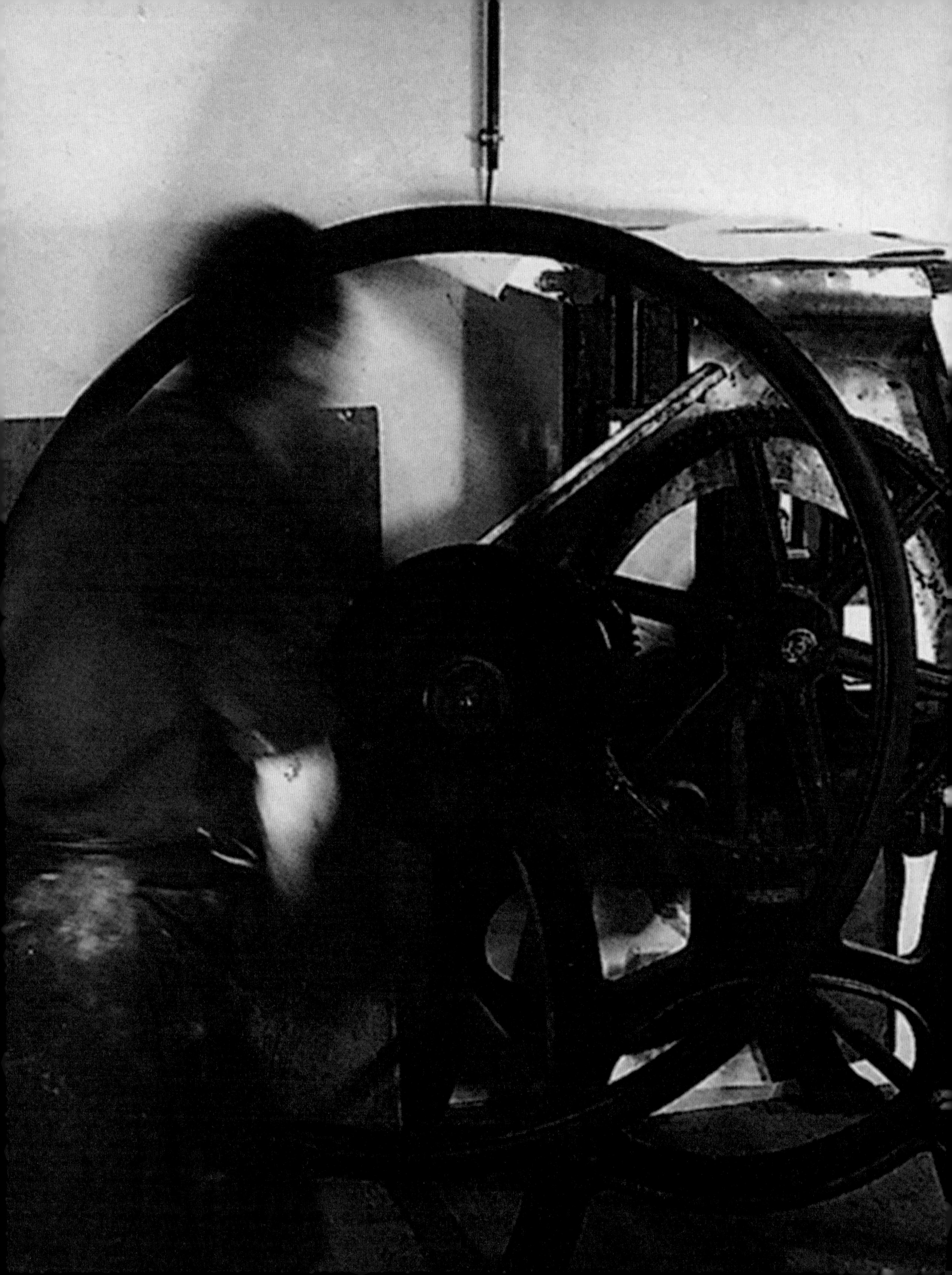

EDITIONS MAEGHT

From the very outset, Aimé Maeght looked upon publishing as an integral part of his family business. The 253 issues of the Maeghts' in-house periodical, *Derrière Le Miroir*, give a good impression of the sheer scale of their enterprise. As a way of promoting the artists and making their work available at a modest price, each issue of *Derrière Le Miroir* accompanying an exhibition at the Galerie Maeght had a cover specially designed by the artist and usually included original lithographs. The first issue (December 1946 to January 1947), included six original lithographs by the young artist Geer van Velde. The fourth (June 1947), commemorating Georges Braque's first exhibition at the gallery, contained one original lithograph and three facsimile reproductions of his drawings. There was no house style and no single artist came to dominate. Both Aimé and his son Adrien were highly skilled professional lithographers and liked nothing better than to collaborate with their artists on graphic editions and very beautiful illustrated books. They used the lithographers Mourlot Imprimeurs and other specialist graphic workshops before developing their own facilities. For the Maeghts, it was the ideal way to draw on all their talents. For their artists, it provided a stimulating opportunity to escape the solitary studio-bound routine and work as a creative team. Rather than impose a single technique or genre, the Maeghts responded to each artist's particular needs and took great pains to team them up with the appropriate technicians.

Although Braque tended to treat graphic editions as a way of reproducing subjects rehearsed in his paintings, he discovered through working with the lithographic colour specialist Henri Deschamps at Mourlot Imprimeurs that the enforced reduction of colour range, coupled with his acute sensitivity to the slightest variation in tint or shade, could lead to restrained effects of near Oriental simplicity. In *Teapot and Lemons* (*Théière et citrons*) (1949; cat. 99), for instance, the suggestively spouted black teapot is set off by two deliciously fragrant lemons against a grey background.[1] Black, for Braque, was definitely a colour. *Leaves, Colour, Light* (*Les Feuilles couleurs lumière*) (1953; cat. 100) is framed in black to silhouette the leaves against the light released by the pale cream ground. There is also humour in Braque's prints, a love of visual and verbal puns. *Bird in Foliage* (*L'Oiseau dans le feuillage*) (1961; cat. 105) is a witty compilation of several themes. The background, as in Braque's pioneering Cubist days, is formed from collaged newspapers. The black bird – half swift with swept-back wings, half flamingo from the Camargue with long neck thrust forward to balance its heavy body – glides over the printed furrows as over fields seen from the air. The word *feuilles* implies both the sheets of newspaper and the green leaves on which the bird is served up on a plate. *The Chariot II* (*Le Char II*) (1953; cat. 101) looks as though it is glimpsed galloping out of the pages of Braque's edition of Hesiod's *Theogony* (1955; cat. 92) across the grey-framed porthole of a wooden ship. Touches of aqueous blue hint at a watery domain.

There was a mutual dialogue between the Maeght artists. According to Isabelle Maeght, it was Adrien Maeght who taught Alberto Giacometti how to turn his drawings into prints by literally employing a transfer process. They are like pallid pencil sketches, wispy memories of his habitual subject matter. It was as though, to be provoked into making prints at all, Giacometti had to fall back on the familiar. They are, perhaps, his final meditations on mortality as the once finite images fade away: *The Dog* (*Le Chien*) (1954; cat. 102), the tacky old mongrel, his canine alter ego; *Self-portrait* (1965; cat. 103) with the face scrunched by time into a poignant mask. *Walking Man* (*L'Homme qui marche*) (1957; cat. 104) looks as though it has been freeze-framed from the barely visible last copy of a favourite old film. Never has humanity looked more vulnerable. 'Ce ne sont pas les fleurs, c'est nous les peintres qui sommes plus fragiles,' Giacometti observed.[2]

Working with Adrien Maeght, Alexander Calder and Joan Miró adopted more experimental attitudes to printmaking. Adrien encouraged Calder, who disliked lithography, to adapt his metalworking procedure to printing for his illustrations for *Fêtes* (1971; cat. 97) by welding the cut-metal shapes on to copper printing plates and then inking them.[3] Calder made no distinction between mechanical abstract shapes and organic form as, for him, form itself and the operations of the universe were determined by mathematical imperatives. There is a remarkable correspondence between Calder's organic conception of a universe realised in abstract form and D'Arcy Wentworth Thompson's celebrated book *On Growth and Form* (1917), which provided artists with an accessible, up-to-date philosophical and scientific rationale, amply illustrated with diagrams and photographs. In volume I, Thompson wrote, 'In our day the philosopher neither minimises nor unduly magnifies the mechanical aspect of the Cosmos.' And he went on to conclude, 'In short it is obvious that the *form* of an organism is determined by its rate of *growth* in various directions … and organic growth is found, mathematically speaking, to be a *function of time*.'[4] Calder transformed his scientific sources and employed forms poetically, playfully reconnecting them with the natural world and with the evolving culture of modern art. In *Saucers in the Dark* (*Soucoupes dans le noir*) (1969; cat. 107), flying saucers drift towards the horizon like lily pads in a painting by Claude Monet. In *Dripping Balloons* (*Ballons dégoulinés*) (1969; cat. 108) Thompson's diagram of ink drops falling into water is inverted into a festive, syncopated pattern of red, black and blue balloons.[5] Thompson's exemplars of the geometric development of organic forms – the nautilus and the ram's horn – were employed by Calder as the dynamic

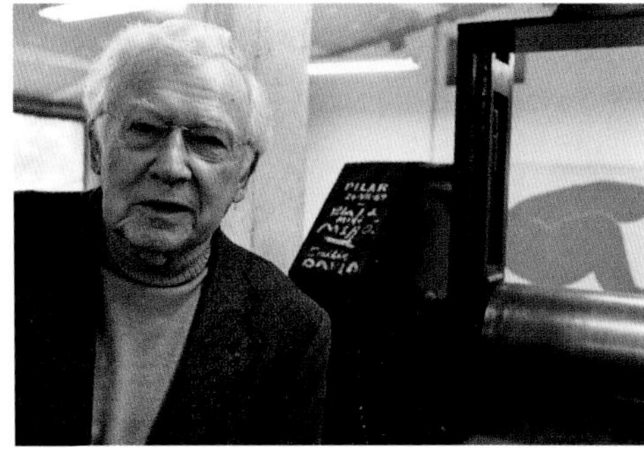

FIG. 49
Adrien Maeght in front of 'La Pilar' press, signed by Joan Miró, in the engraving studio at Saint-Paul, August 2006 (cat. 133)

structuring principle of *Two Spirals* (*Deux spirales*) (1974; cat. 109), one of his most striking compositions.[6]

It was, above all, Miró who took full advantage of the Maeghts' graphic facilities and reinvigorated his art through printmaking. For him, printmaking was not just a means of making his work available but an innovatory art form in its own right. While in New York in 1947, he had learnt copperplate engraving, etching and aquatint at Studio 17 – Stanley William Hayter's famous print workshop. However, Miró's vastly expanded awareness of the expressive potential of printmaking came through making lithographs and etchings with Adrien Maeght, who provided him with immense plates to meet his new-found ambition.

Fired up by the calligraphic freedom of Jackson Pollock's new painting and by the range of novel effects now available in lithography, Miró recaptured the explosive creative energy of his youth to unleash a series of disquieting images on a large scale, cutting back to a highly anarchistic tradition stemming from Alfred Jarry and Dada. As Maurice La Belle noted, Jarry 'was never able to conceive man as anything but a primordial brute struggling for supremacy in the slime of life or a beautiful creature brought to bay and slaughtered by social forces'.[7] He created a monstrous marionette called *Ubu Roi* (1896) who, like a stupid, cruel, vindictive, superannuated child, triumphs through being utterly ruthless.[8] For Spaniards, like Picasso and Miró, Francisco Franco was Ubu. Miró, who went on to create his own version of Ubu for the burlesque satire *Mori el Merma* (1978), depicted *The Hundred-year-old Warrior* (*La Guerrière de cent ans*) (1975; cat. 111) as a manically expansive, toad-eyed, Jarry-esque monster snuffing out the reddened sun. The absurdly pretentious red pepper bird in *Madwoman with Hot-tempered Pepper* (*La Folle au piment rageur*) (1975; cat. 112) struts like a one-eyed pirate king, shell-headed and crowned by a preposterous gauze cocked hat. *Woman Leading the Moon* (*La Meneuse de lune*) (1975; cat. 110) leads us through a whole range of lithographic effects, textures and colours: the chromatic impact of the red-headed bird–fish outlined by a heavy black contour; the delicate perforations of the orange-tinted muslin net; and the pale green crescent moon collapsing over the stars like a Hokusai wave.

Ambitious, beautifully illustrated books in which the artist collaborated with a poet and graphic technicians became a Maeght speciality. Braque's edition of Hesiod's *Theogony* (cat. 92), commissioned by Ambroise Vollard and then printed and published by Aimé after the dealer's untimely death, was followed by an illustrated edition of Pierre Reverdy's *La Liberté des mers* (1959; cat. 93) – a far more sophisticated integration of text and image. Reverdy, who lived close to the abbey at Solesme in western France and died in 1960, had been inspired by Cubism, which he championed. Both poet and artist lived lives through

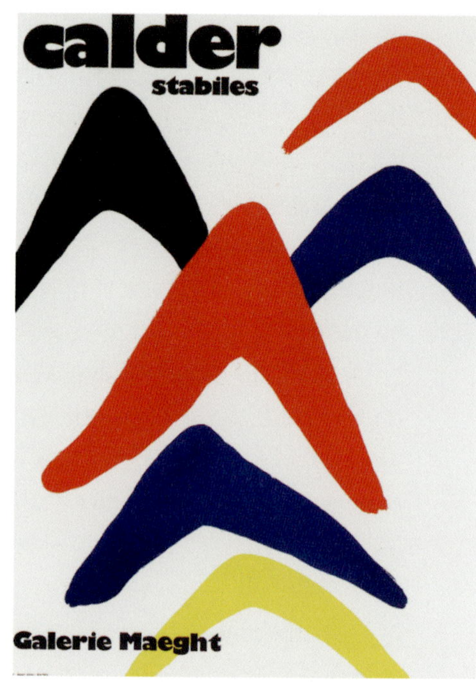

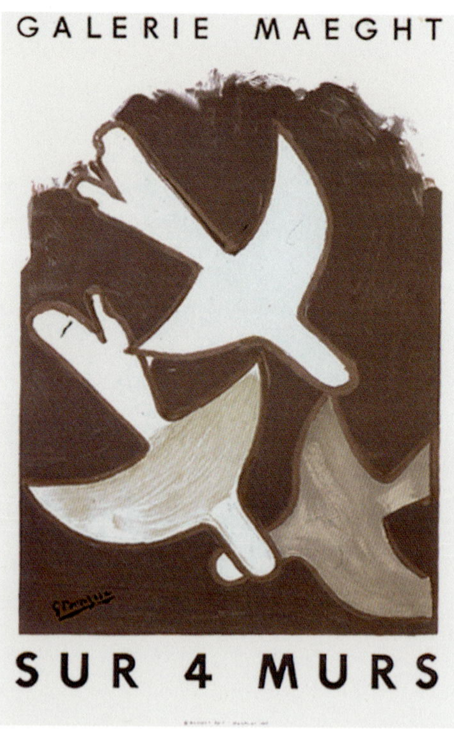

FIG. 50.1–4
Galerie Maeght posters for exhibitions by (clockwise from top left) Calder, Giacometti, Miró and Braque

the contemplation of objects and the everyday, where the familiar ebbs
away leaving gaps, voids, areas of silence, filled by a sense of isolation, often
despair, and a feeling that the only thing to be ultimately trusted is art. As
in Henri Matisse's coloured album, *Jazz* (1943–46), which established a
new benchmark for the balance between highly coloured images and a
handwritten text, Braque wrote the poems out in a languid, looping script
rising and falling in the rhythm of Reverdy's words, tossed up and down as
on the waves of the sea. Full pages are left blank for the words and images
to resonate. Ambiguously shaped leaves or birds or sails drift down the
opening page opposite the title, *La Liberté des mers*, heavy with the dark
watery green of late summer. Past with present is united in a mood of often
bitter nostalgia. Birds take flight at the sound of the words 'Murmures entre
les / quatre murs aux gout- / tes de sang des épines'.[9] Expectancy is not so
much denied as subverted in the correlation between word and image. A
heavy, black bird–hand weighs down the words 'Une main / d'un mouve- /
ment ryth- / mique et / sans pensée, / jetait ses cinq', and then on the next
page 'doights vers / le plafond'.[10] In the poem 'Souffle' ('Breath') – 'Il neige
sur / mon toit et / sur les arbres' – the whiteness of the page obliterates the
scene with silence, leaving just three suggestive black lines.[11]

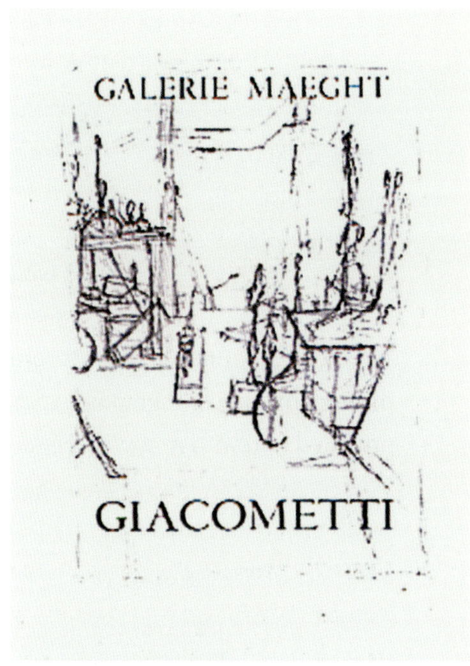

Miró and Calder, though different, both chose poets whose
imagery dazzles, entertains and provokes the imagination. For *Parler seul*
(1948–50; cat. 96), Miró teamed up with Tristan Tzara, the co-founder
of Zurich Dada, his old friend from his first days in Paris in 1920. The title
is scrawled out on a tiny scrap of torn paper to emphasise from the outset
the improvisatory nature of the relationship between poetry and art,
sparking each other off. Both Tzara and Miró invoke chance and irrational
juxtapositions as weapons of assault against nostalgia, the sentimental and
autobiographical revelation. Tzara memorably stated: 'Every page must
explode.'[12] The central image of the title page looks like an inebriated
pound sign printed over a pink newspaper. The agenda has been changed:
poetry and art have taken over. Normal hierarchies are reversed. A bloated
tick plucked from the arse of a grazing bull becomes the enlarged green
head and body of a hybrid humanoid orbiting with the stars. Cosmic
imagery predominates.

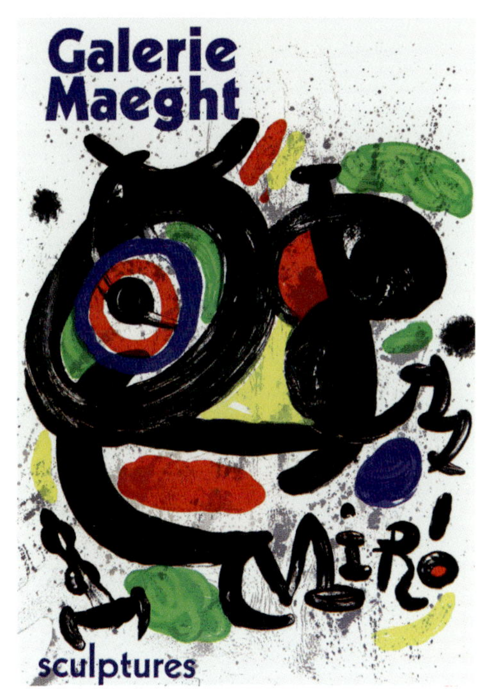

Although not necessarily of the same order as Reverdy as a
poet, Jacques Prévert, the polymath actor, scriptwriter, poet, film-maker
and composer of popular songs, provided the texts for two of the Maeghts'
greatest books: *Fêtes*, illustrated by Calder (1971; cat. 97), and *Adonides*,
illustrated by Miró (1975; cat. 98). Like both Calder and Miró, Prévert
drew on popular culture, children's rhymes and circus imagery to convey
the dreams that entertained and captured the imagination of his
generation. His texts were tailor-made to bring out the best from each
artist. His celebrated opening lines to *Fêtes* – 'Mobile en haut / Stabile

en bas / telle est la tour Eiffel / Calder est comme elle' – are balanced by
Calder's five geometric figures with black circles for heads and red and
yellow triangles for bodies dancing in the deep blue of the cosmos.[13] His
strikingly simple mechanistic images and signs crank up memories of
childhood. A bright red star hovers above just three black, undulating
lines separating sea from sky to complement the children's poem 'Solomon
Grundy / né le lundi / baptisé le mardi / mariée le Mercredi', and presage
a descriptive passage on the precise drawing of boat, sea and quay.[14]

Prévert's text, coupled with the expressive effects opened up by the
printer, inspired Miró's *Adonides*, which undoubtedly remains the ultimate
testament to the Maeghts' collaborative ideal. It is highly inventive but not
over-complicated. The opening double spread employs the Surrealist
automatic drawing technique of free-flowing wandering lines to release
a bestiary of strange beasts, birds, elevated insects and marine creatures.
Allusive double and triple images suggest multiple meanings:
dog–bird–breasts–algae–gaping orifices. The frontispiece exploits a range
of graphic techniques to indicate levels of consciousness on an imaginary
journey, from the central images simply dry-stamped into the thickness
of the page to the scratchily etched handwritten text and, finally, the free-
flowing aquatinted red trajectory of the bird powering into the sky to join
the powdery blue star. On the following page (page 5) the short text, 'Toute /
réflexion faite / par ces temps de malheur / Le miroir s'est brisé', is stepped
up like the ladder helpfully provided below to transport the imagination from
the bestiary pressed into the page to the sun and the stars.[15] Not all is whimsy.
The threatening penis-like head of a green gecko snake (pages 18–19)
pushes up between the text 'et Dieu / surprenant Eve et Adam / leur dit /
continuez je vous en prie / ne vous dérangez pas / pour moi / Faites /
comme si je n'existais pas'.[16]

NW

FIG. 51
Joan Miró in the engraving workshop
at Saint-Paul, 1978

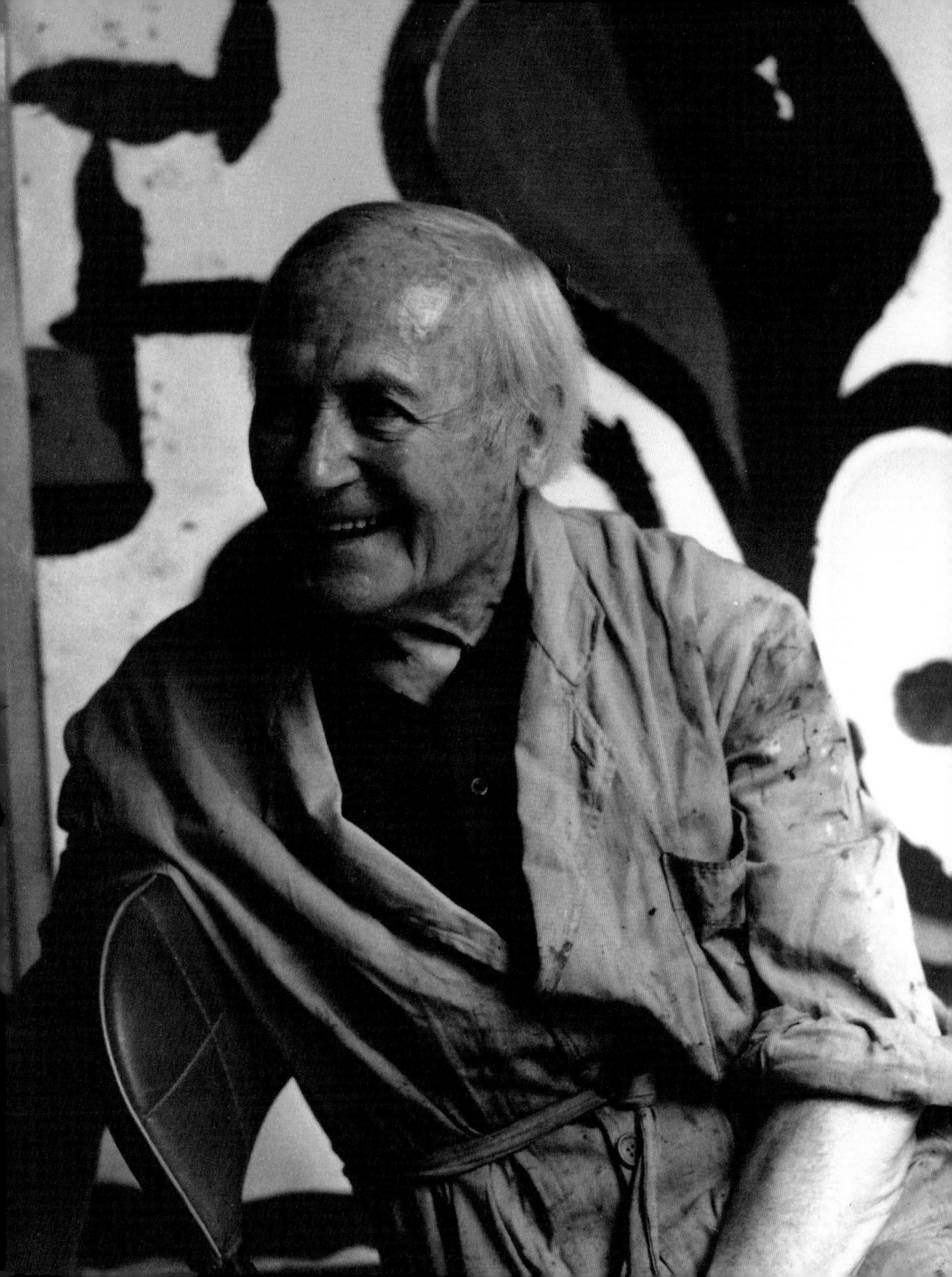

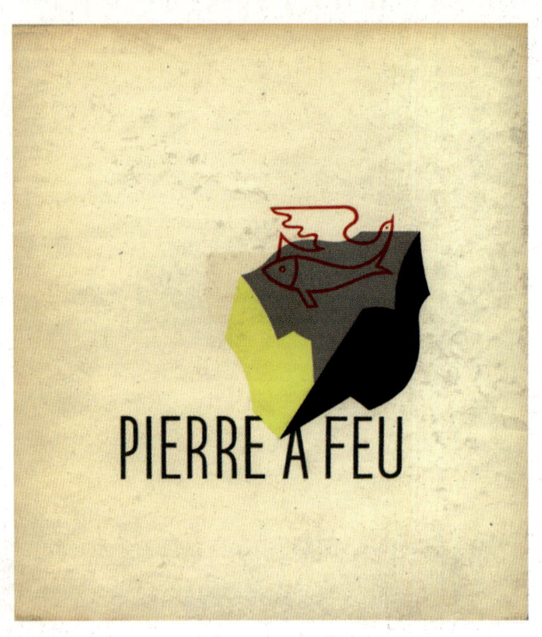

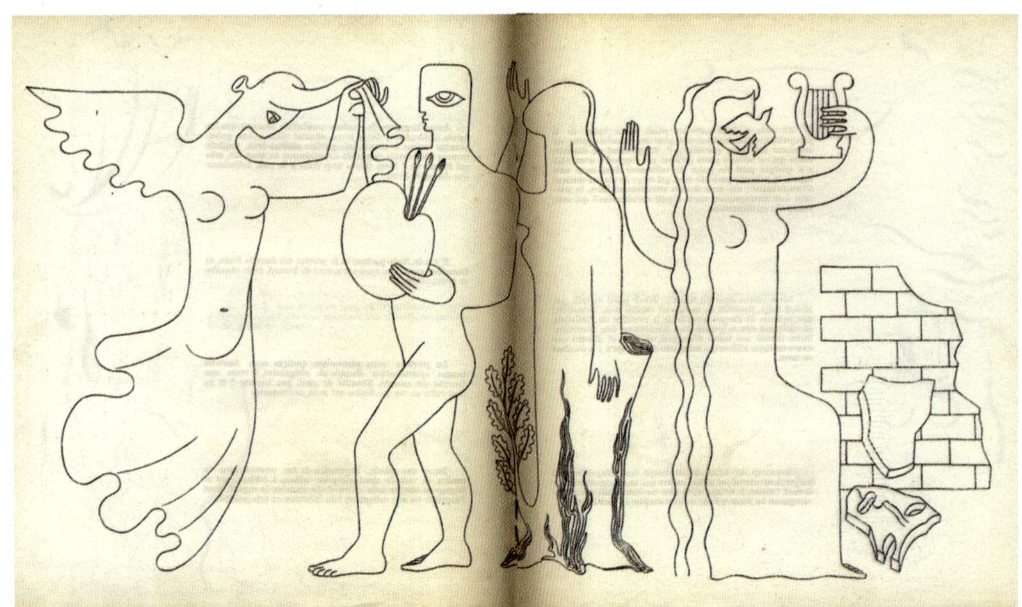

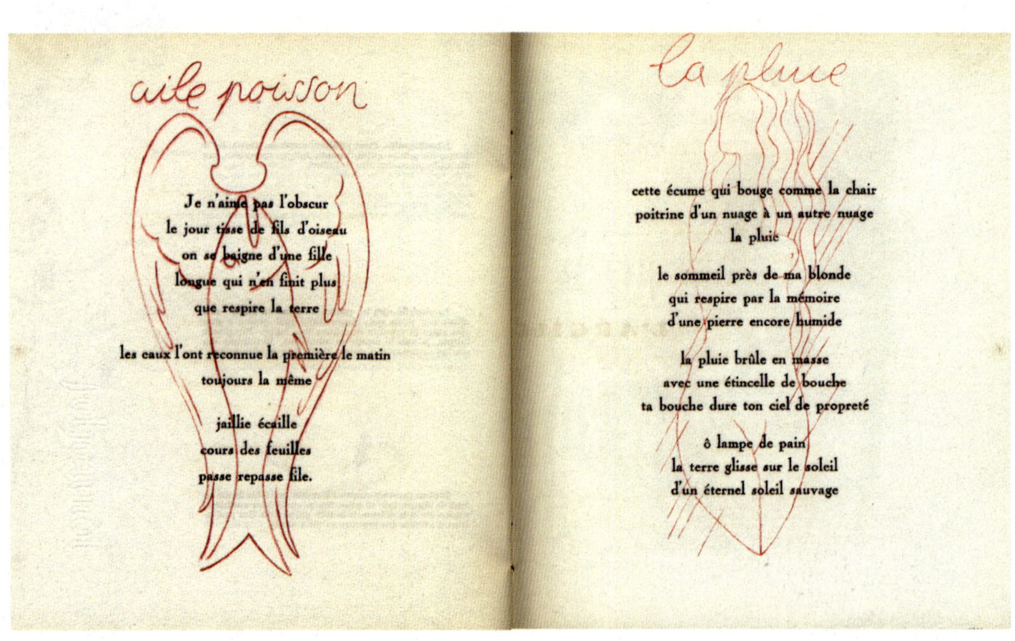

CAT. 91

Jean Cassarini (1910–2004)
Pierre à feu, 1944
Book, 24 x 22 cm

CAT. 92

Georges Braque (1882–1963)
Théogonie, text by Hesiod, 1955
Book, 53 x 38 cm

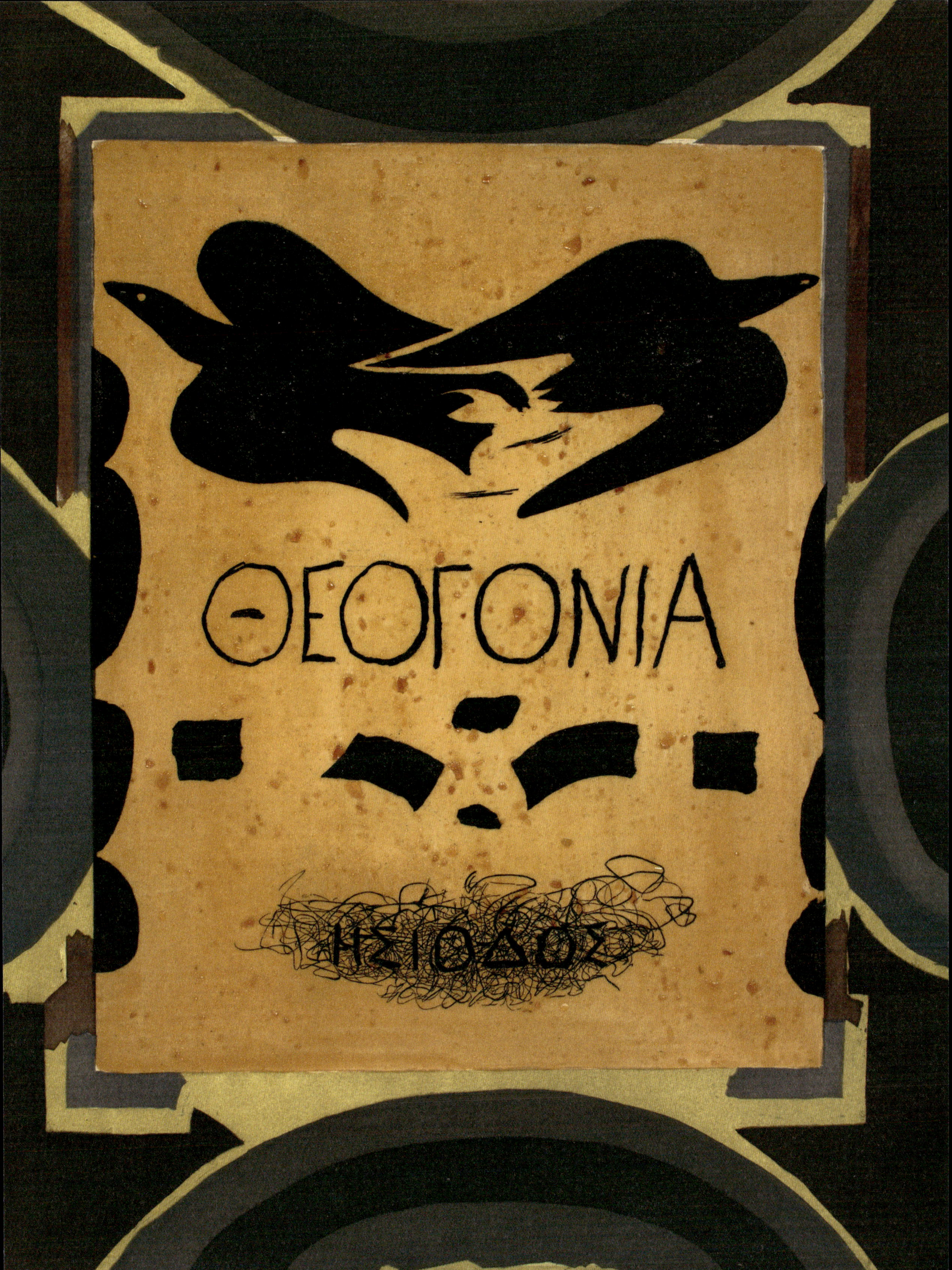

ΘΕΟΓΟΝΙΑ
ΗΣΙΟΔΟΣ

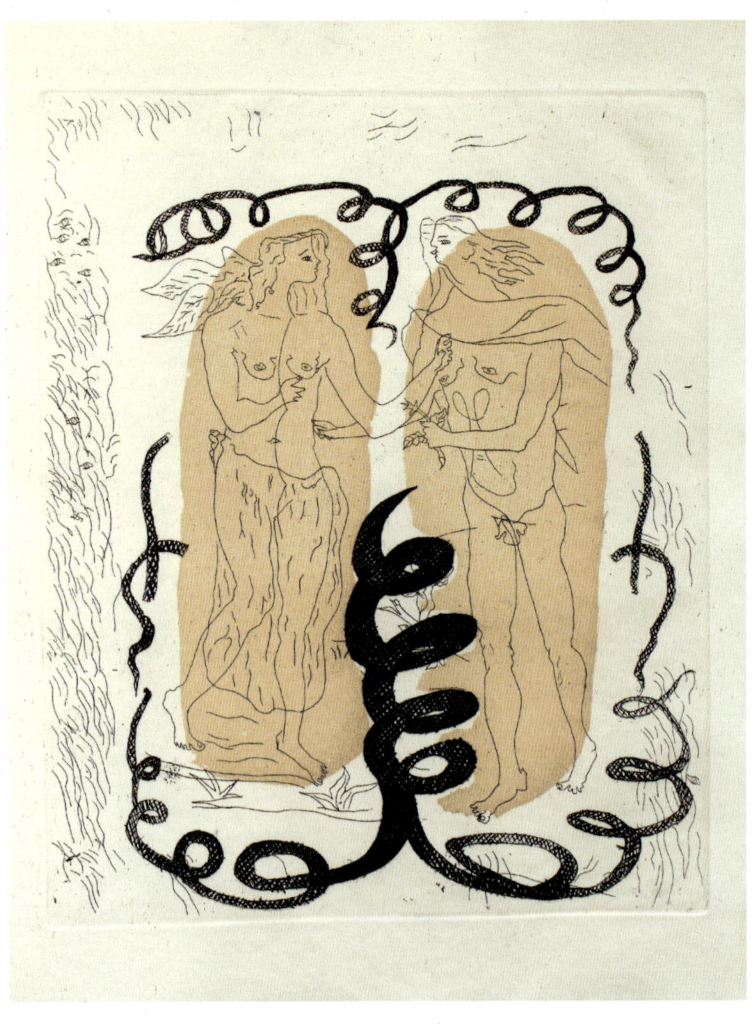

CAT. 92
Georges Braque (1882–1963)
Théogonie, text by Hesiod, 1955
Book, 53 x 38 cm

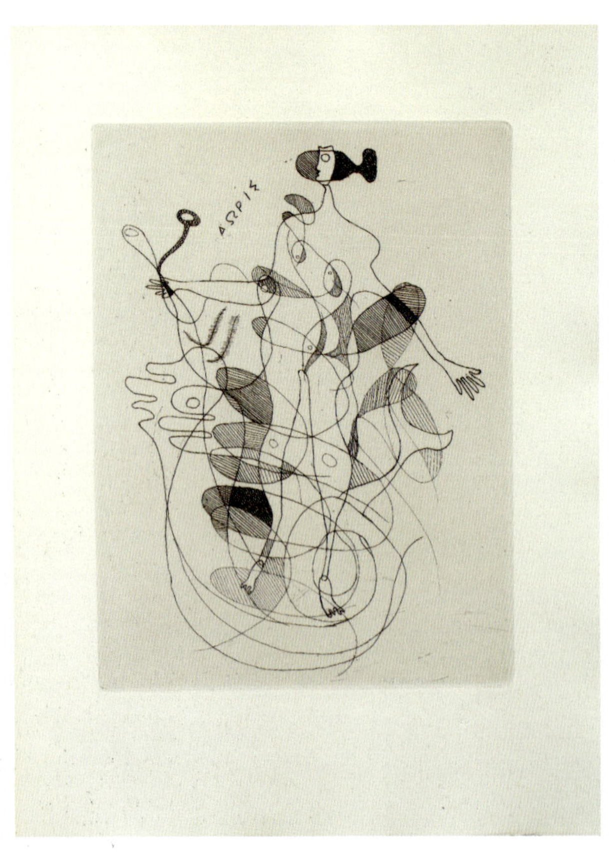

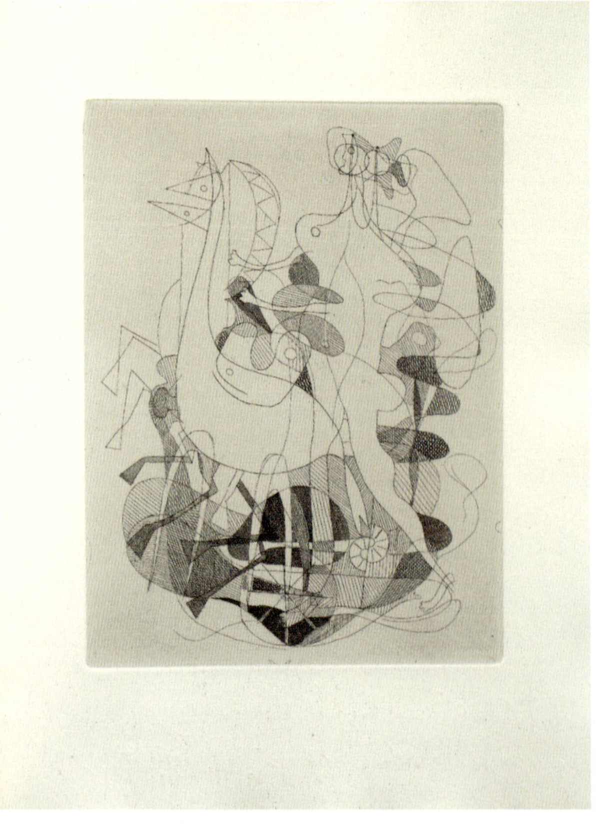

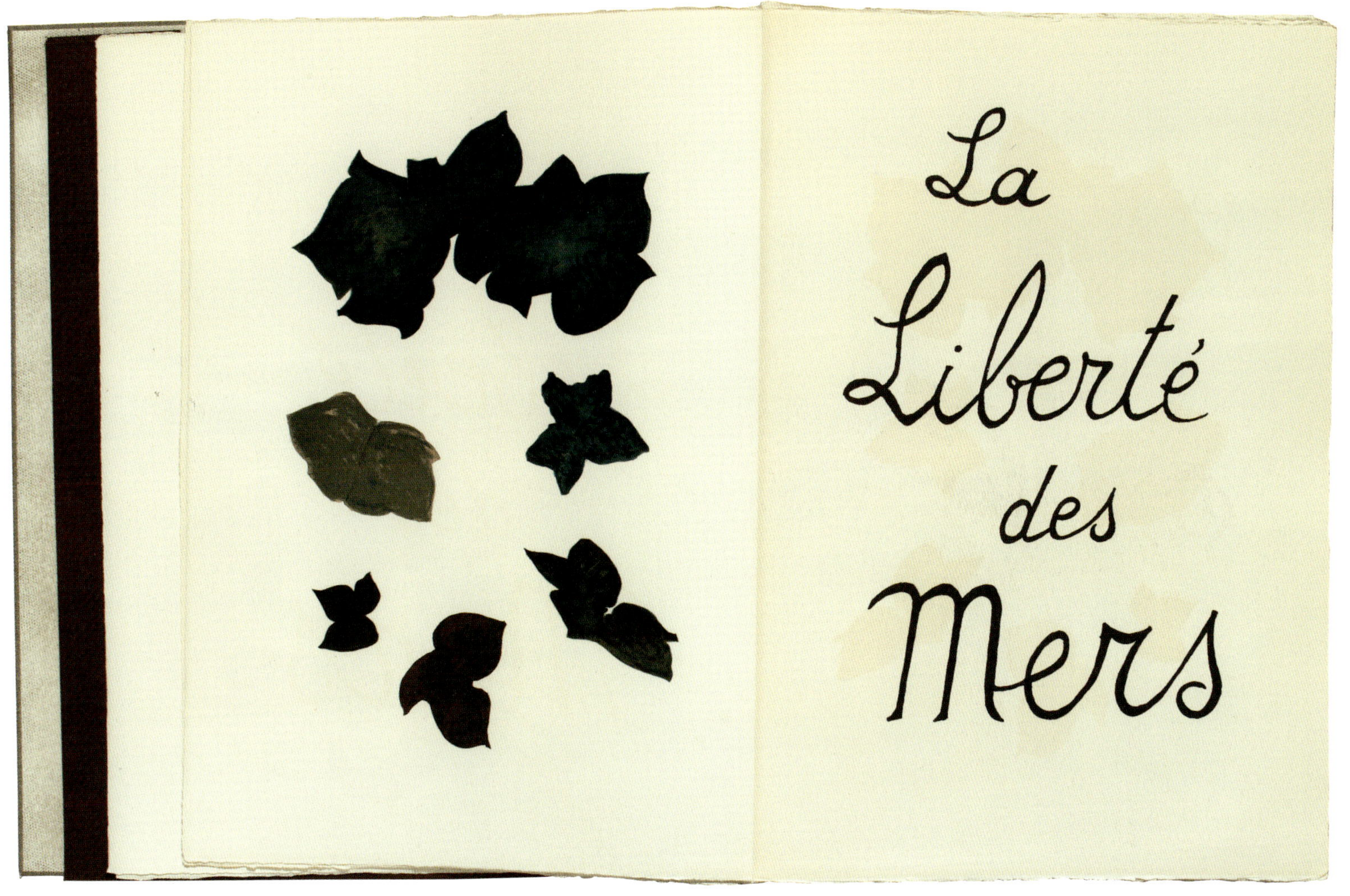

CAT. 93
Georges Braque (1882–1963)
La Liberté des mers, text by Pierre Reverdy, 1959
Book, 57.5 x 39.5 cm

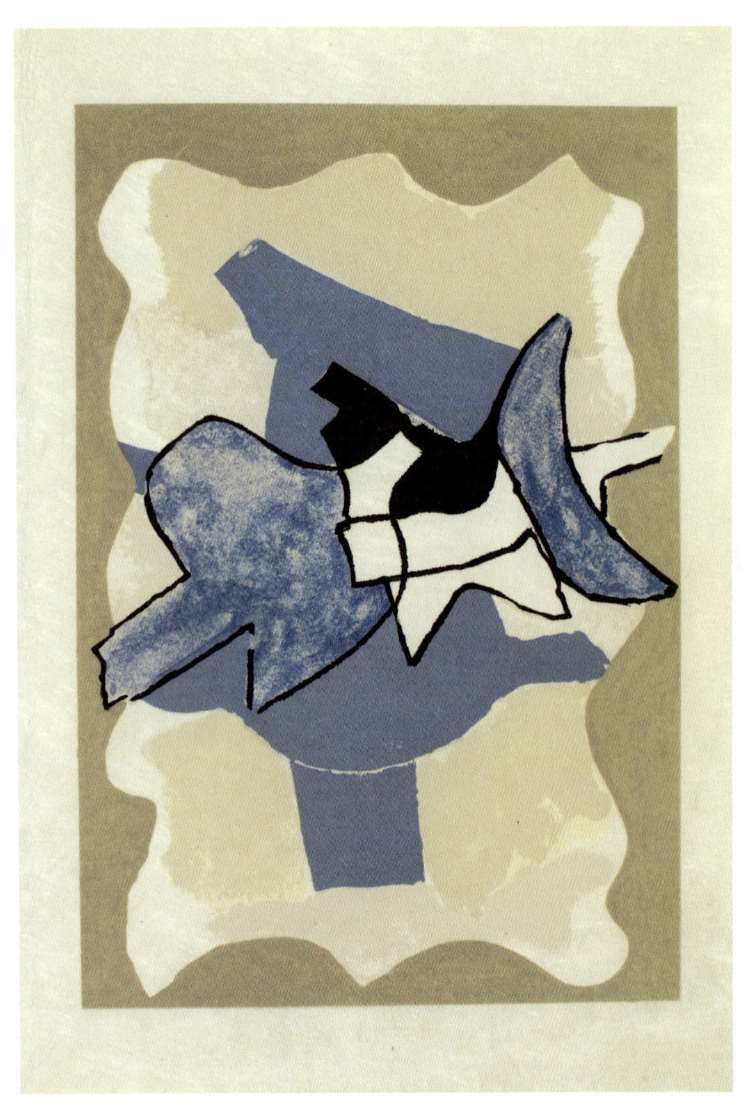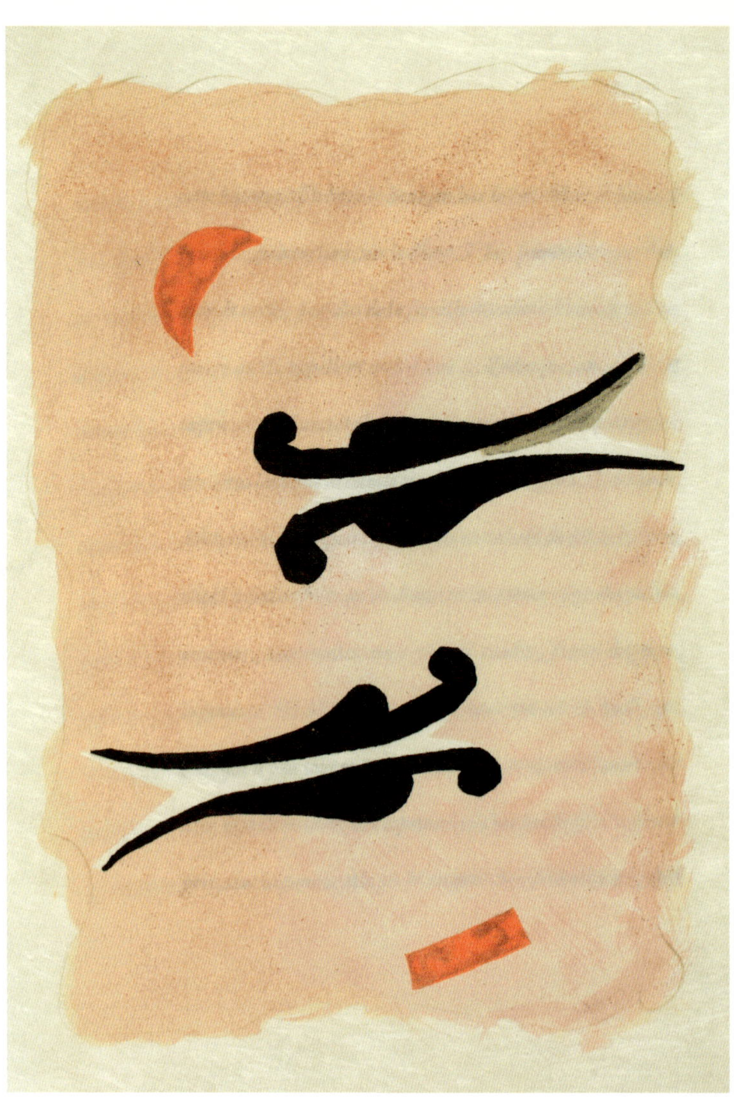

CAT. 94
Georges Braque (1882–1963)
La Nuit, la faim, text by Georges Ribemont-Dessaignes, 1960
Book, 28 x 18.5 cm

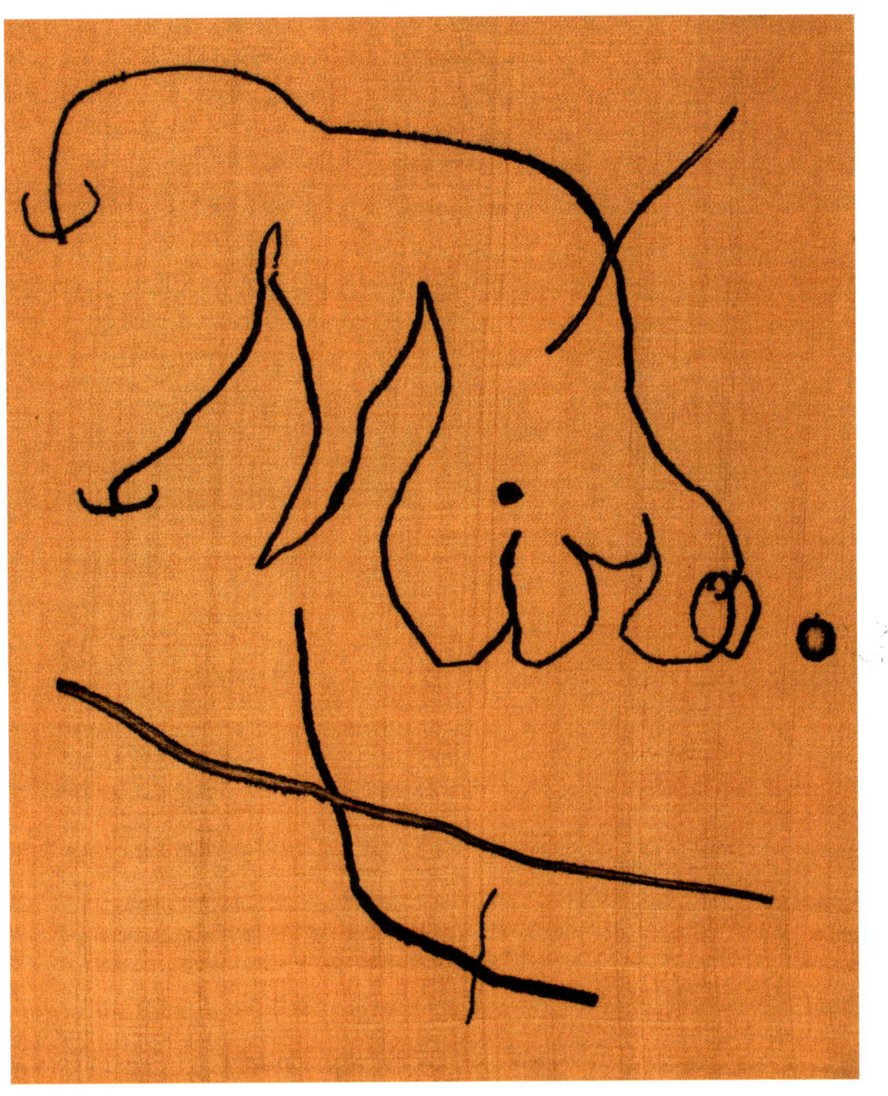

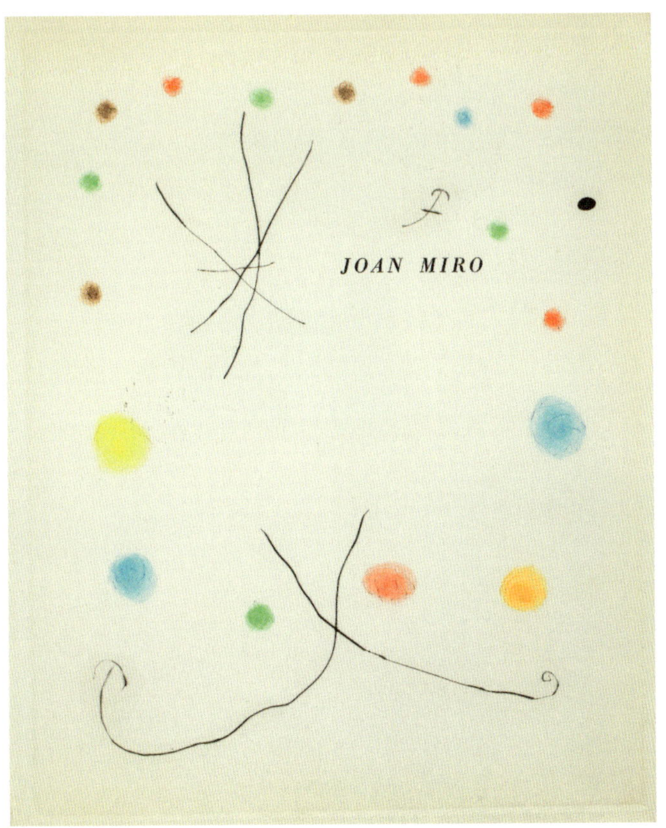

JOAN MIRO

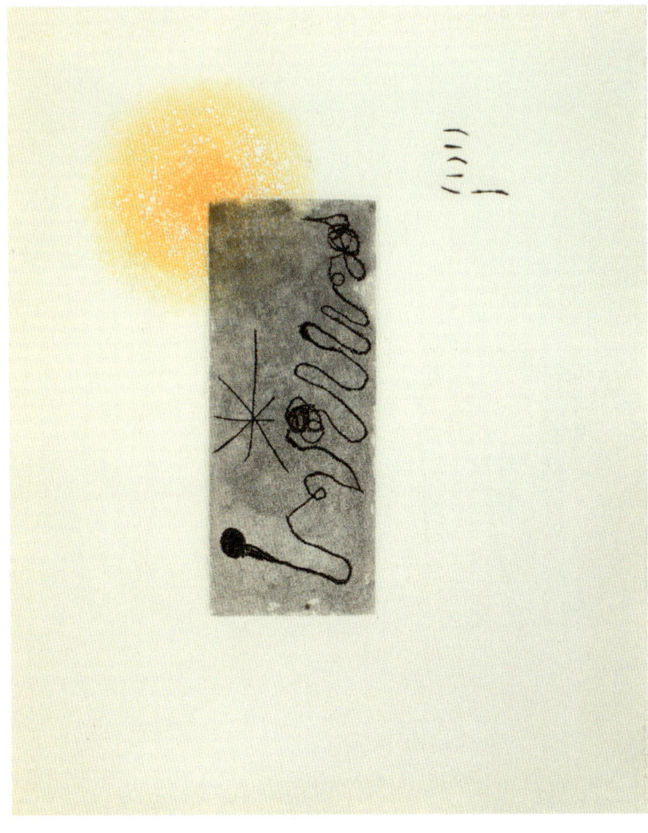

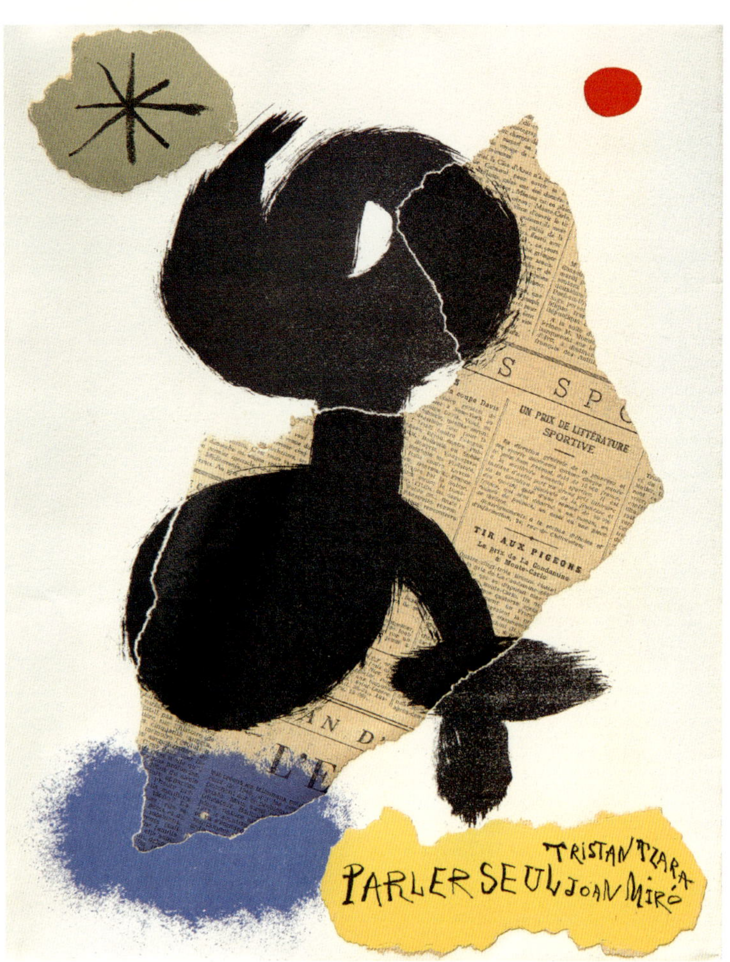

CAT. 96
Joan Miró (1893–1983)
Parler seul, text by Tristan Tzara, 1948–50
Book, 38.5 x 29 cm

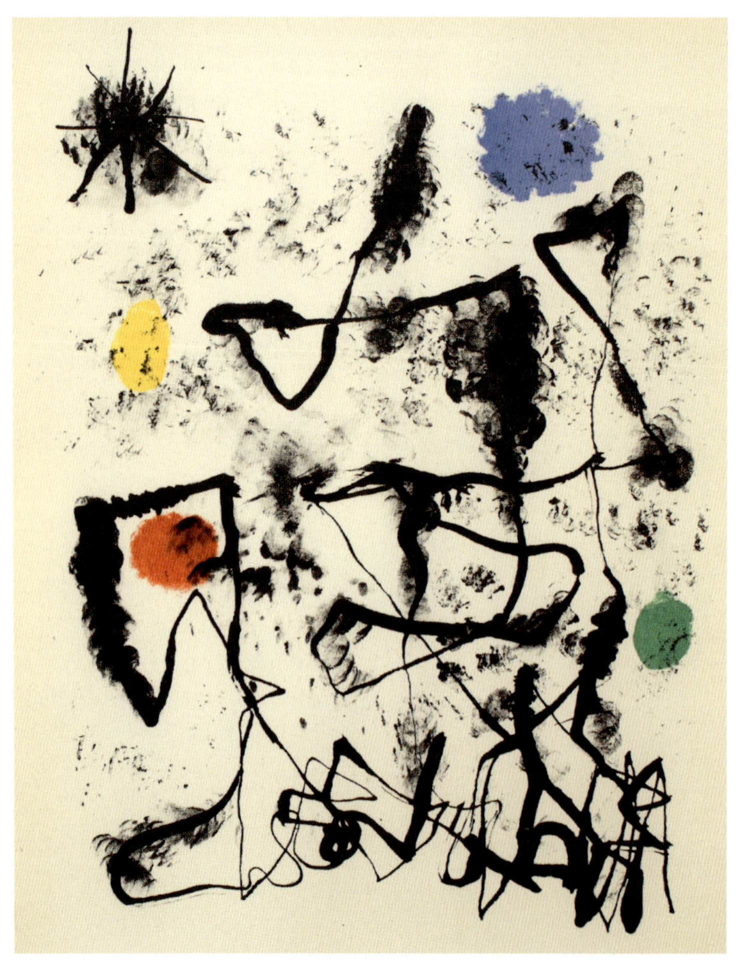

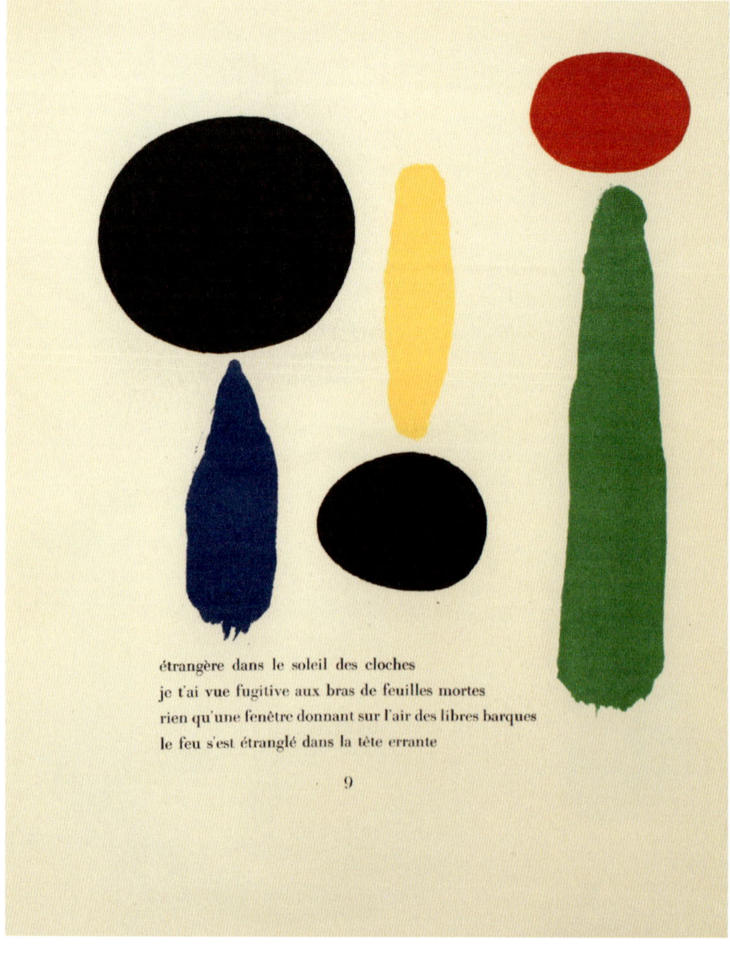

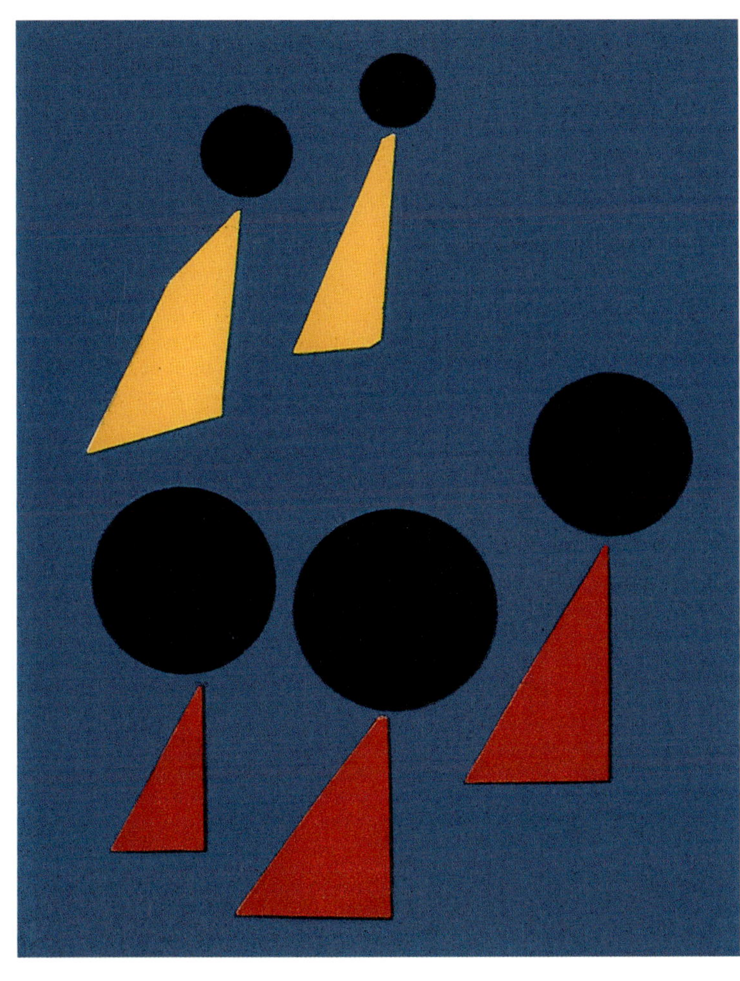

CAT. 97
Alexander Calder (1898–1976)
Fêtes, text by Jacques Prévert, 1971
Book, 46 x 34 cm

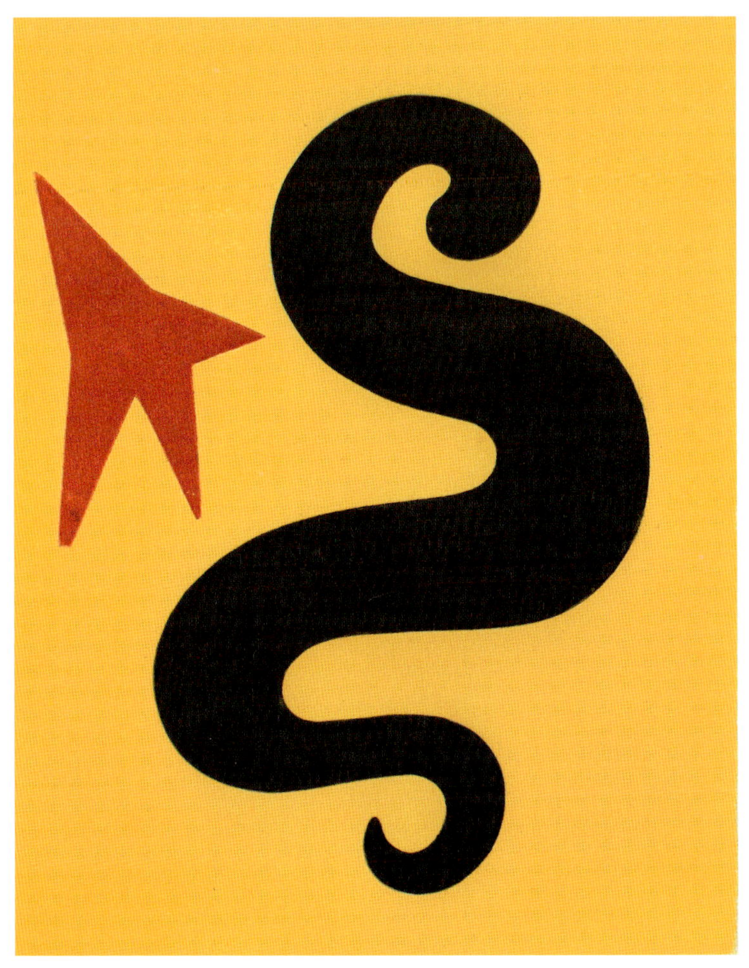

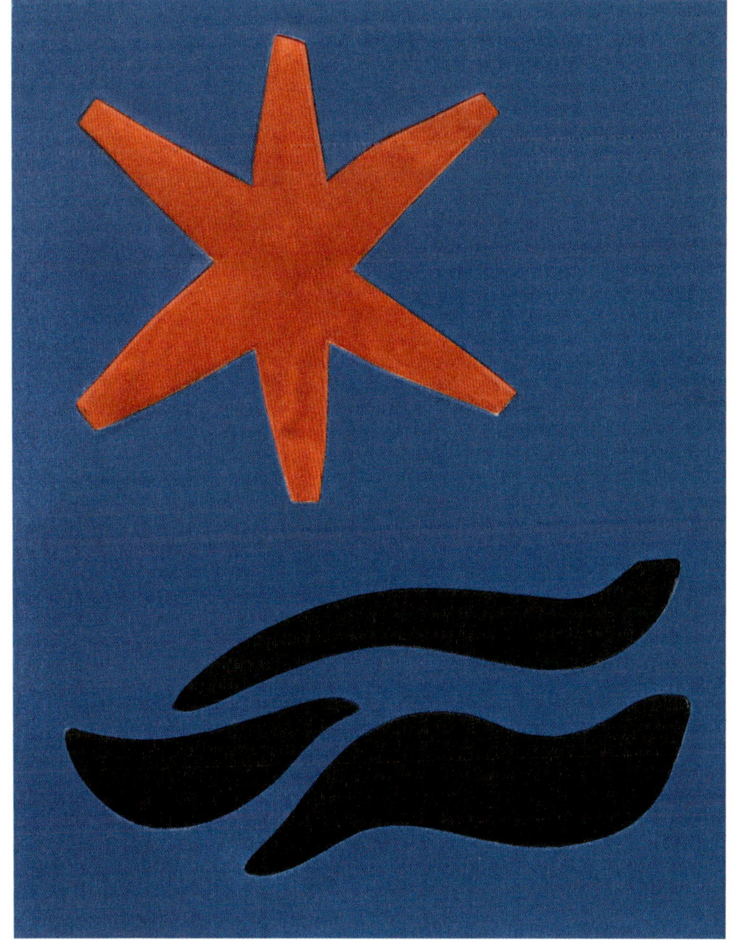

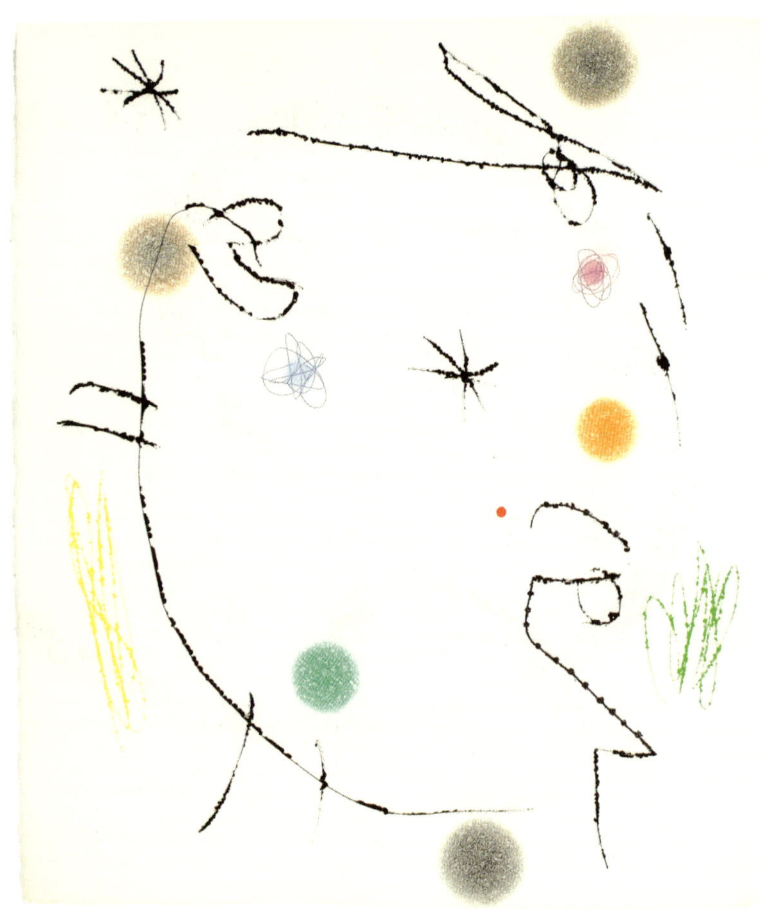

CAT. 98
Joan Miró (1893–1983)
Adonides, text by Jacques Prévert, 1975
Book, 40.5 x 33.5 cm

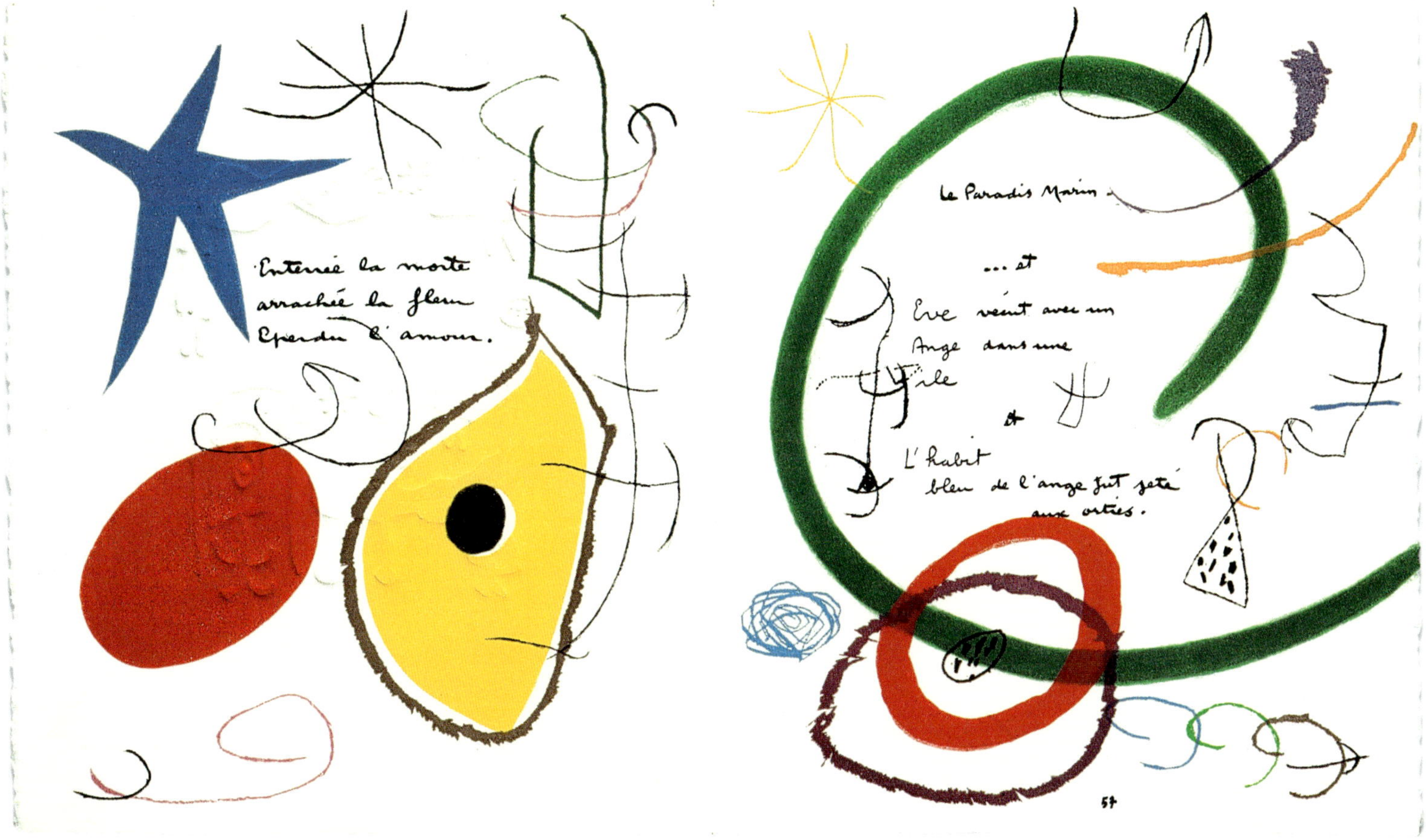

Enterrée la morte
arrachée la fleur
Éperdu l'amour.

Le Paradis Marin

... et

Eve vient avec un
Ange dans une
île
et
L'habit
bleu de l'ange fut jeté
aux orties.

54

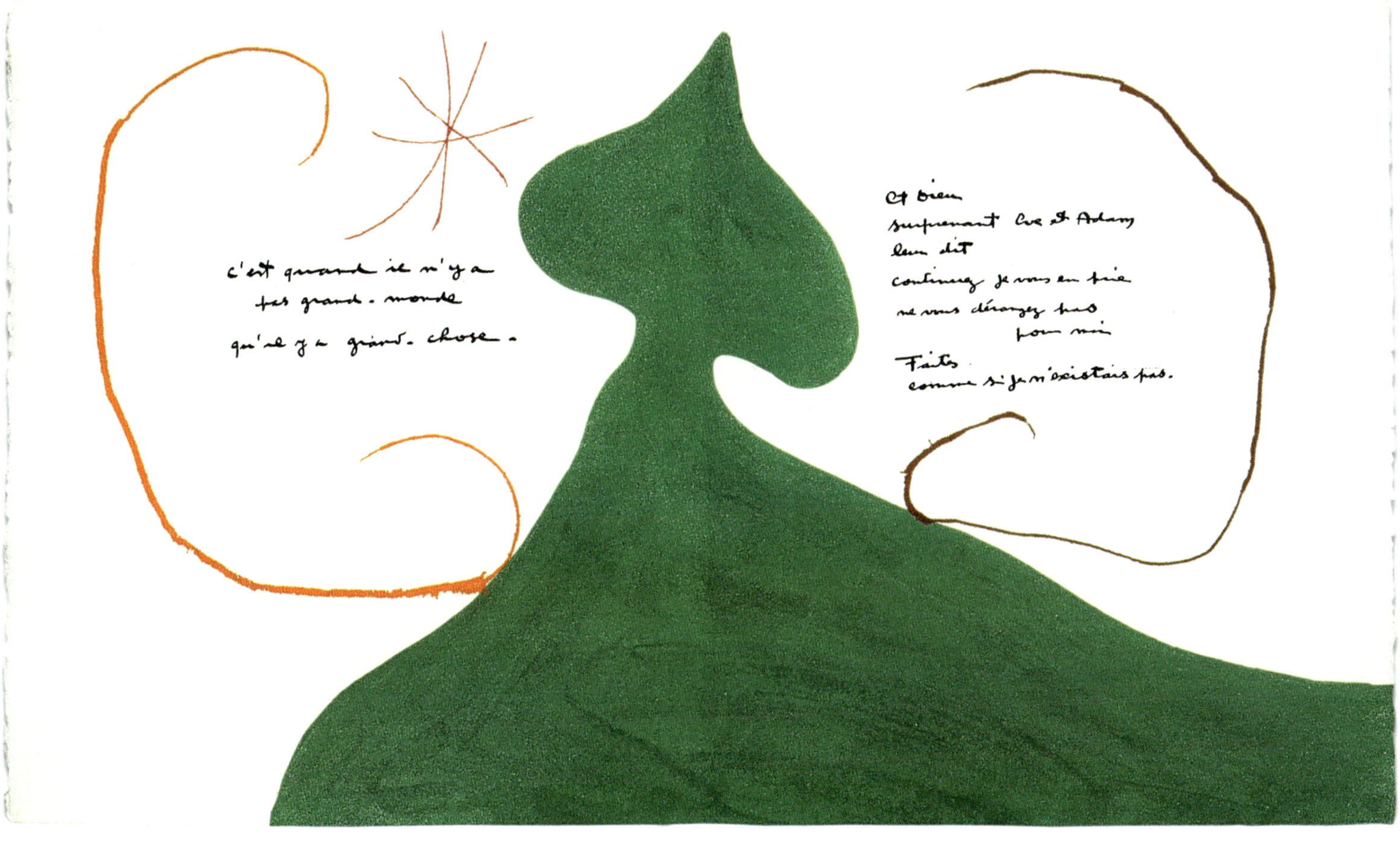

c'est quand il n'y a
pas grand-monde
qu'il y a grand-chose.

Et bien
surprenant Eve et Adam
leur dit
continuez je vous en prie
ne vous dérangez pas
pour moi
Faites
comme si je n'existais pas.

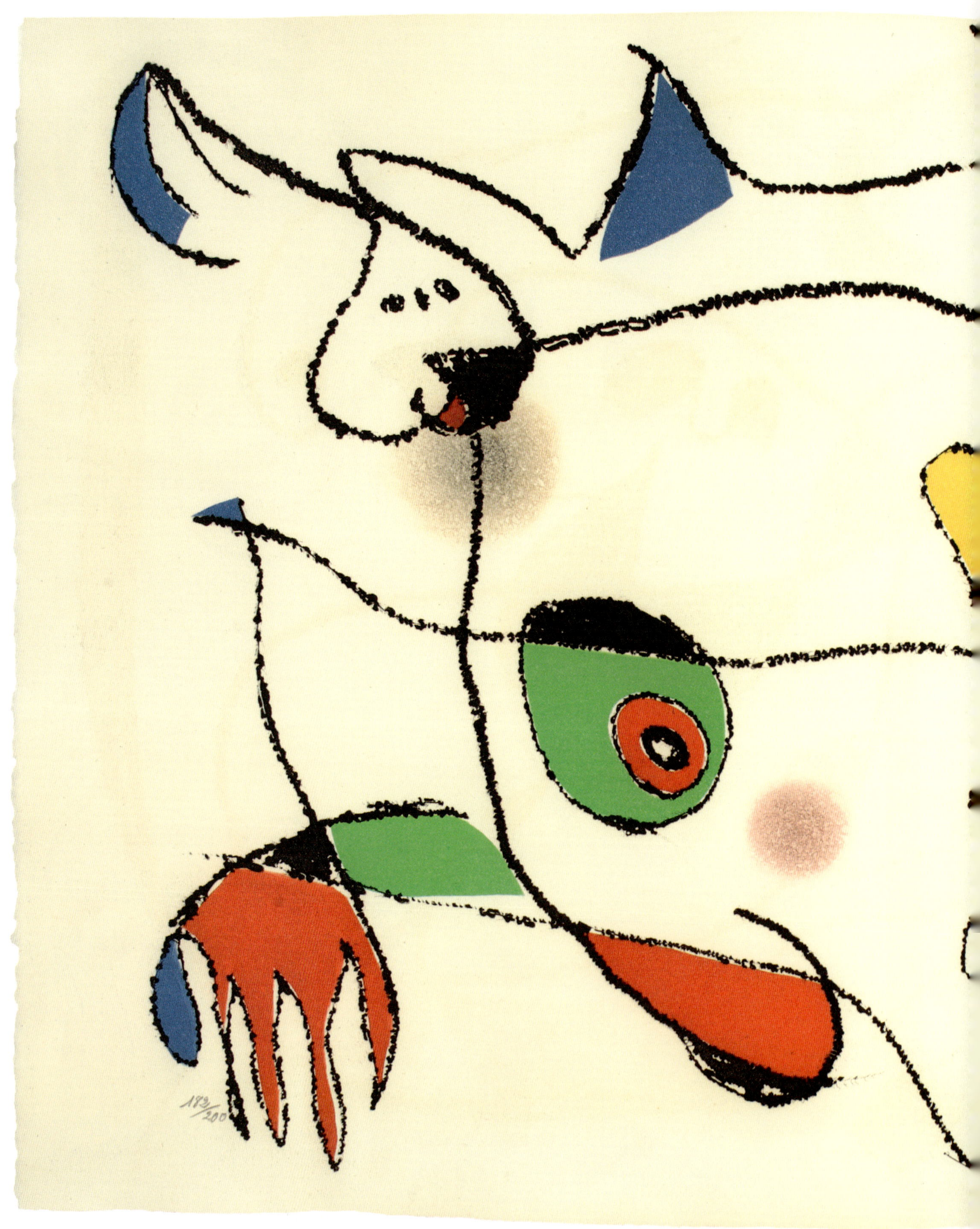

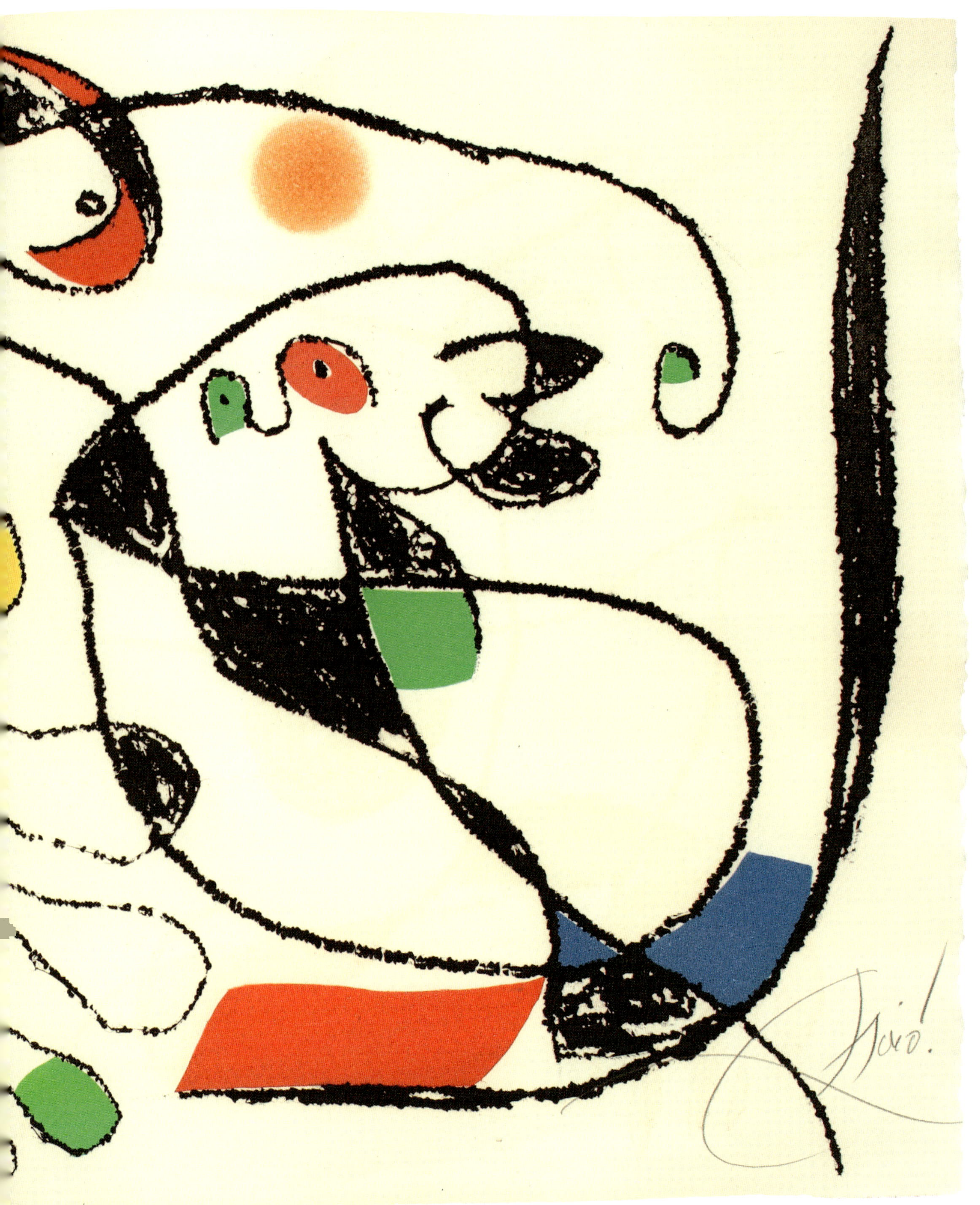

CAT. 98
Joan Miró (1893–1983)
Adonides, text by Jacques Prévert, 1975
Book, 40.5 x 33.5 cm

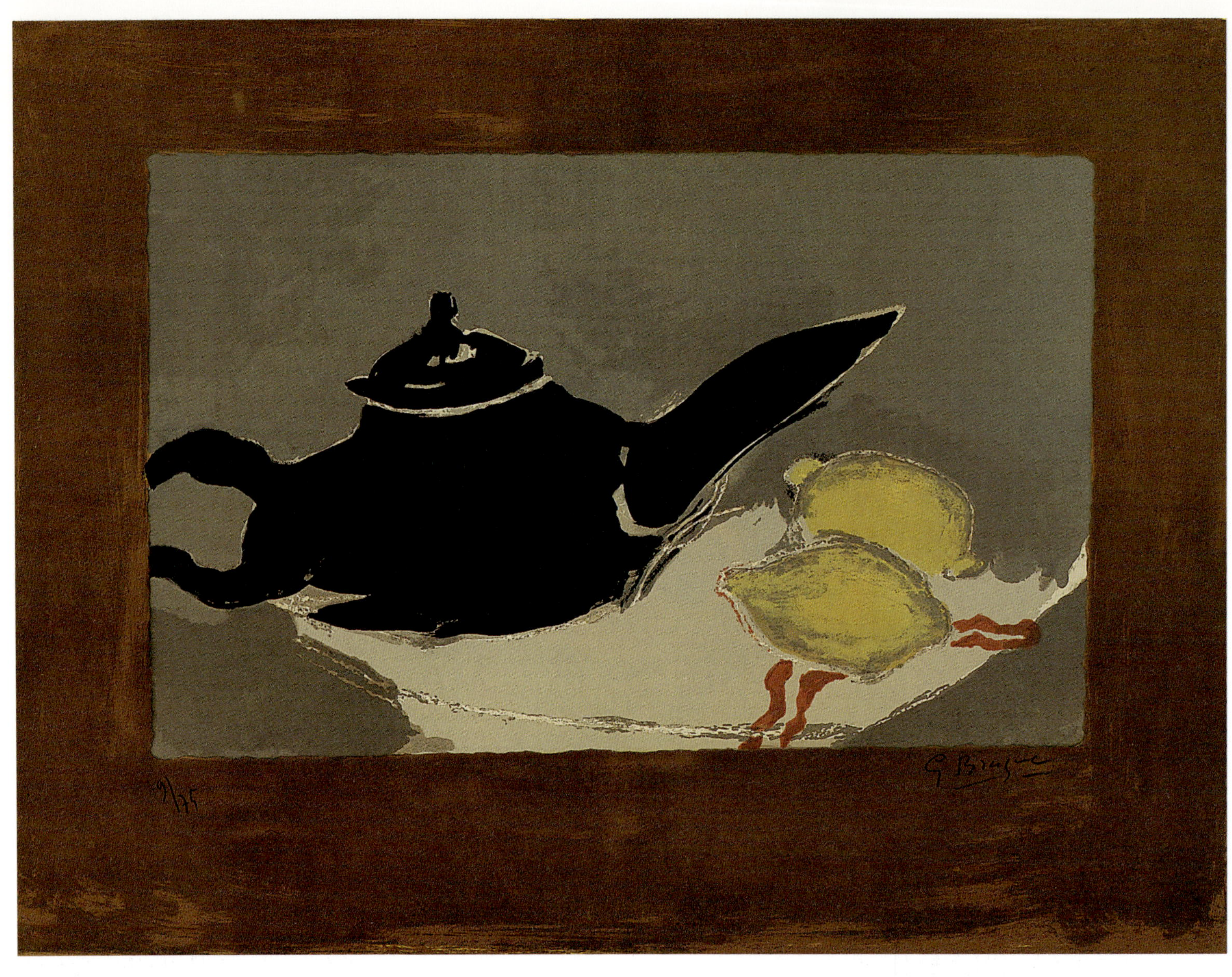

CAT. 99
Georges Braque (1882–1963)
Teapot and Lemons (*Théière et citrons*), 1949
Original lithograph, 50 x 65 cm

CAT. 100
Georges Braque (1882–1963)
Leaves, Colour, Light
(*Les Feuilles couleurs lumière*), 1953
Original lithograph, 97.5 x 60 cm

154

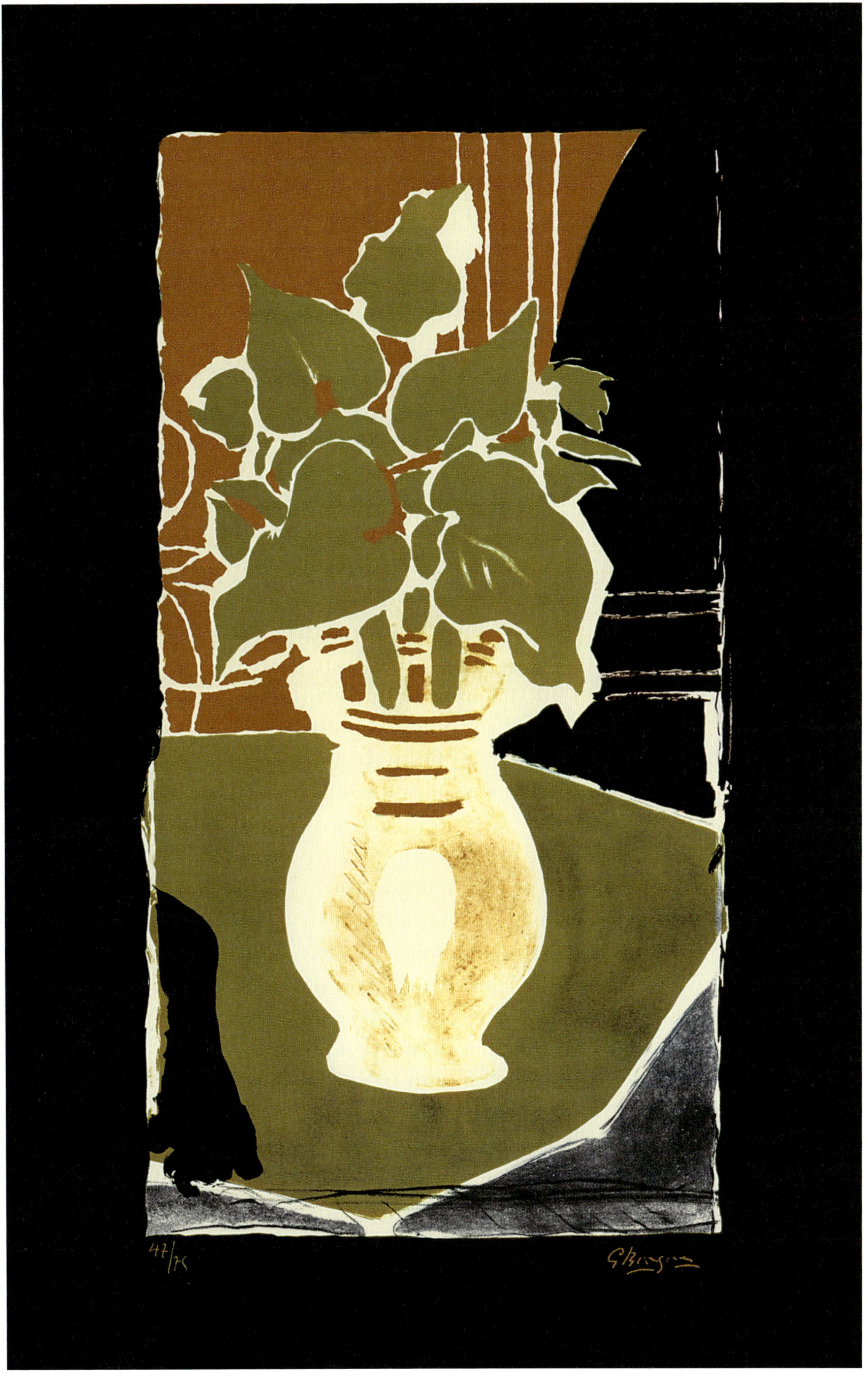
47/75
G Braque

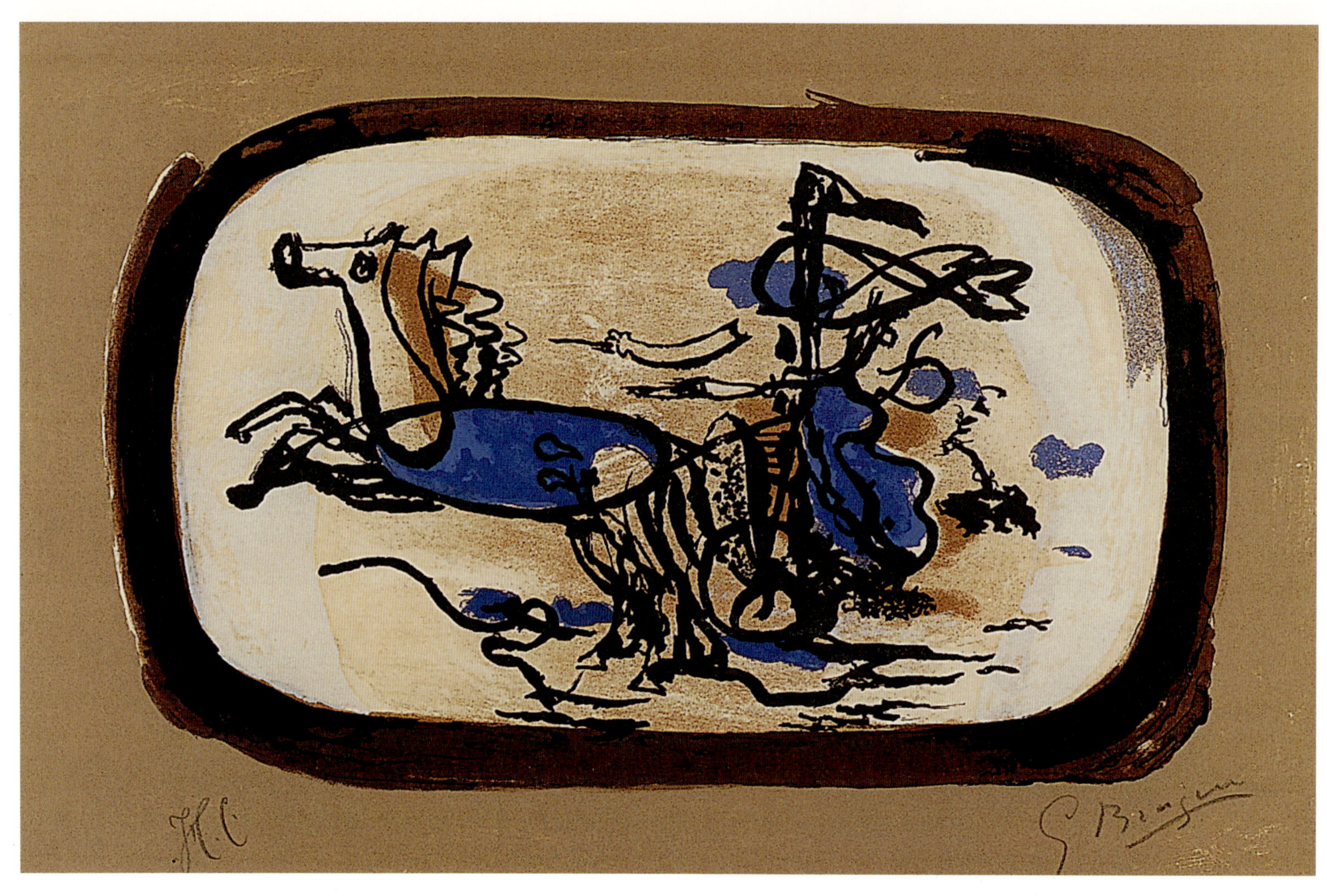

CAT. 101

Georges Braque (1882–1963)
Chariot II (*Le Char II*), 1953
Original lithograph, 50 x 65 cm

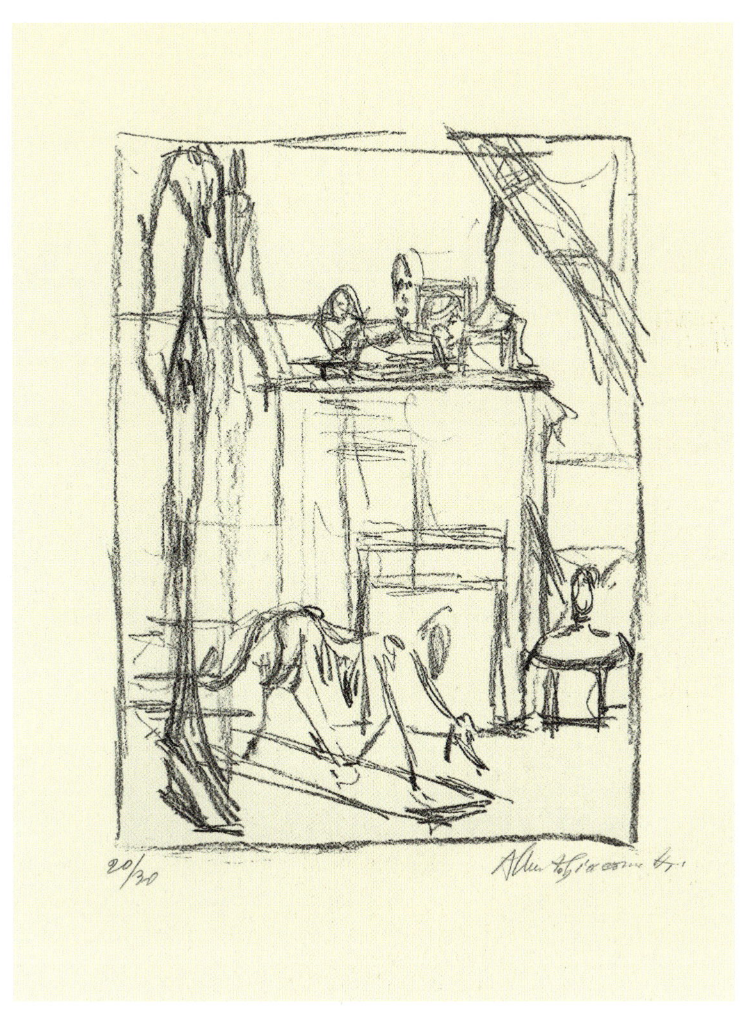

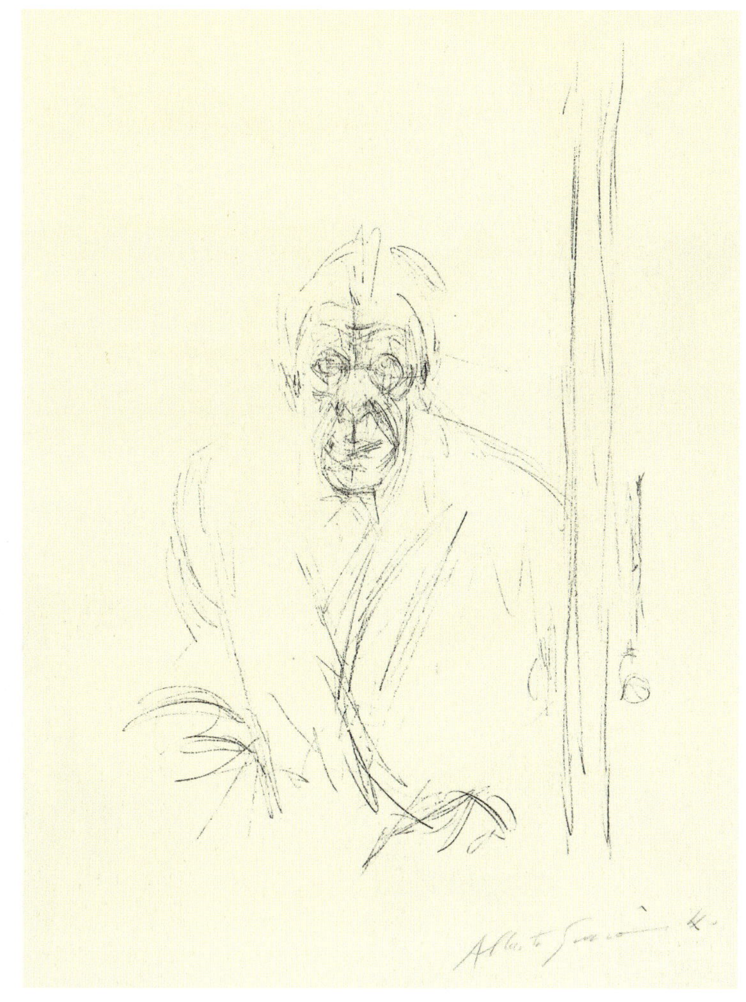

CAT. 102
Alberto Giacometti (1901–1966)
The Dog (*Le Chien*), 1954
Original lithograph, 53.5 x 44 cm

CAT. 103
Alberto Giacometti (1901–1966)
Self-portrait (*Autoportrait*), 1965
Original lithograph, 65.5 x 50.5 cm

CAT. 104
Alberto Giacometti (1901–1966)
Walking Man (*L'Homme qui marche*), 1957
Lithograph, 76.5 x 57 cm

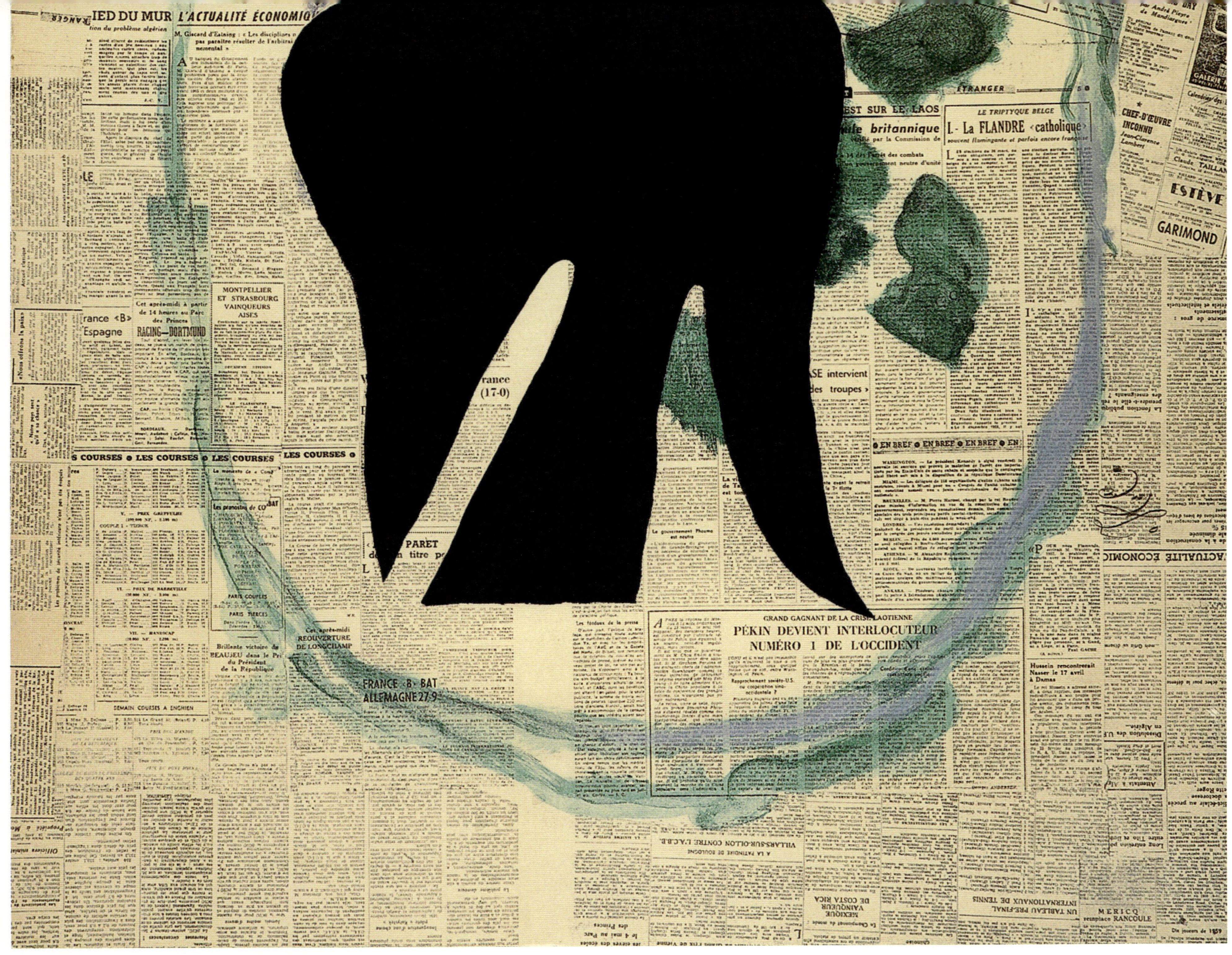

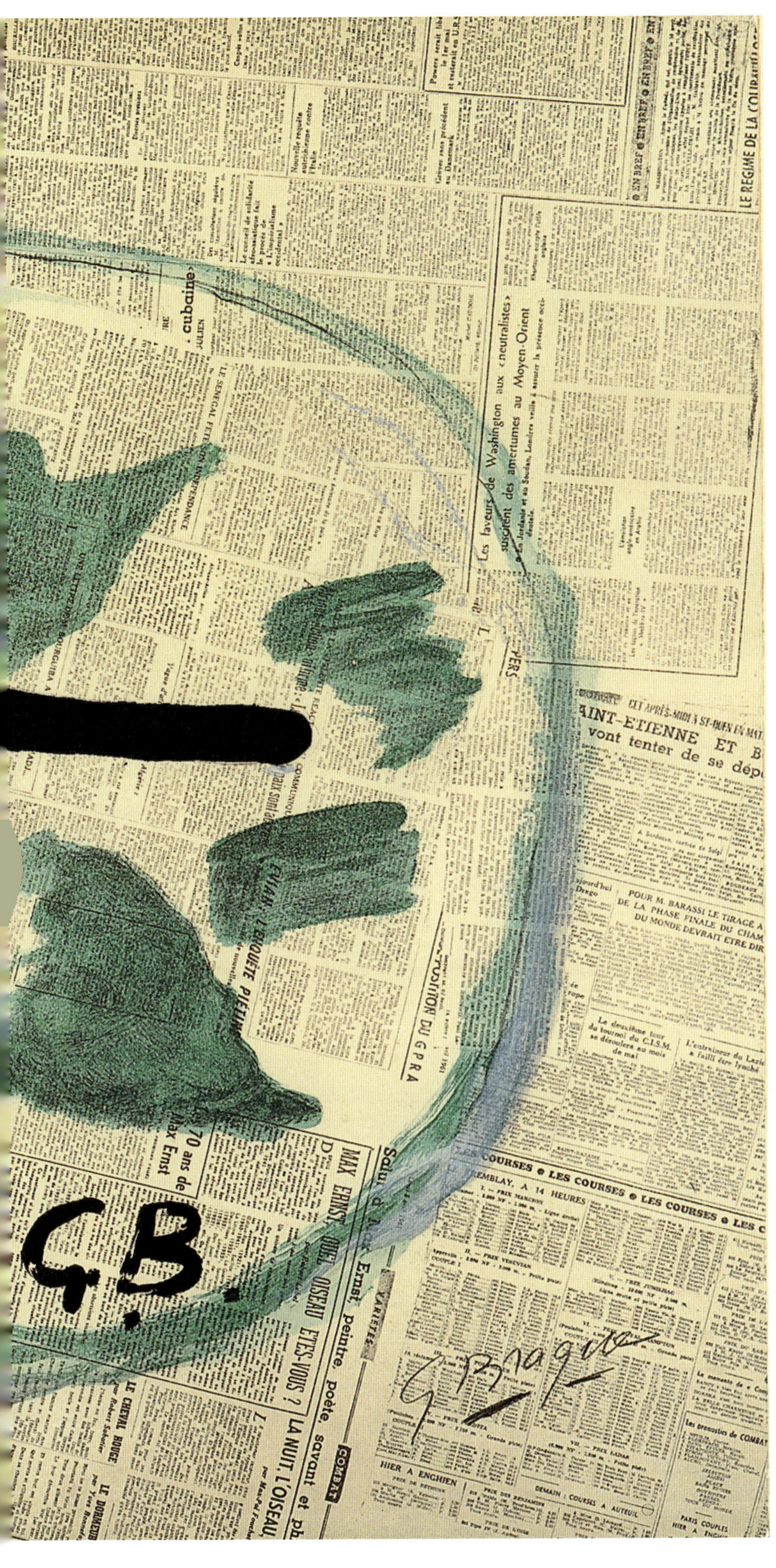

CAT. 105
Georges Braque (1882–1963)
Bird in Foliage (*L'Oiseau dans le feuillage*), 1961
Original lithograph, 80.5 x 105.5 cm

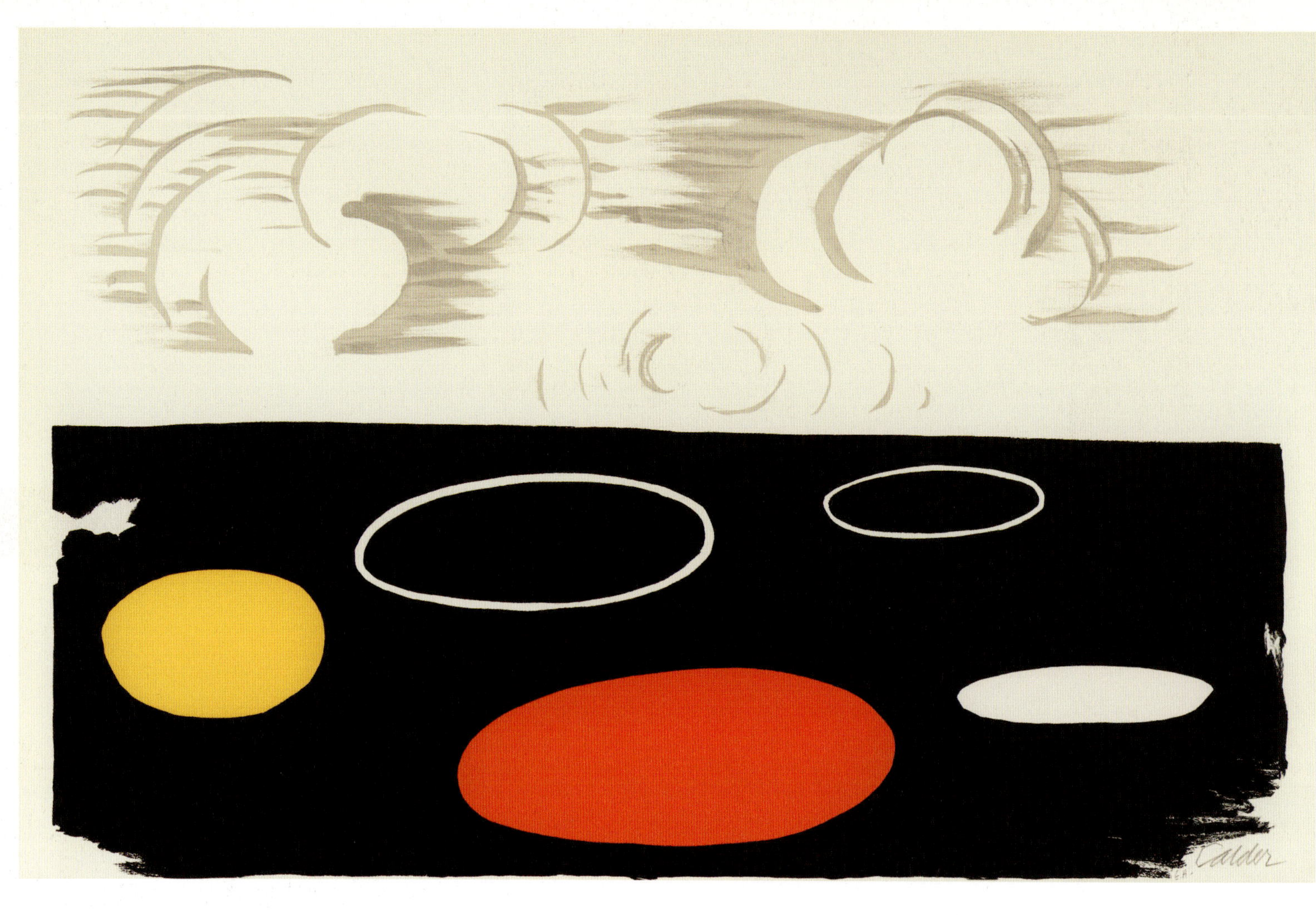

CAT. 106
Alexander Calder (1898–1976)
Low Tide (Marée basse), 1969
Lithograph, 76 x 115 cm

CAT. 107
Alexander Calder (1898–1976)
Saucers in the Dark (Soucoupes dans le noir), 1969
Lithograph, 109.5 x 74 cm

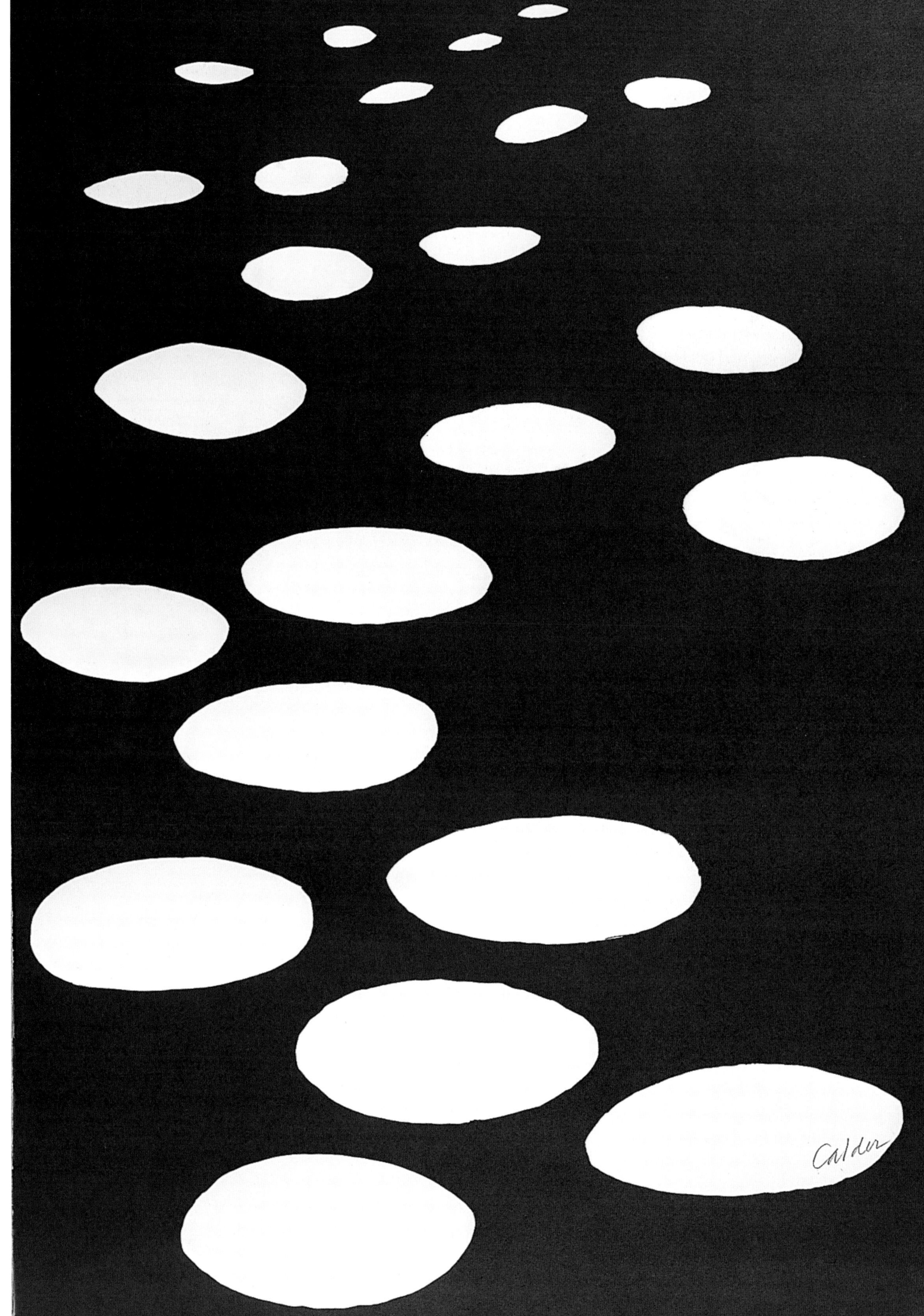
Calder

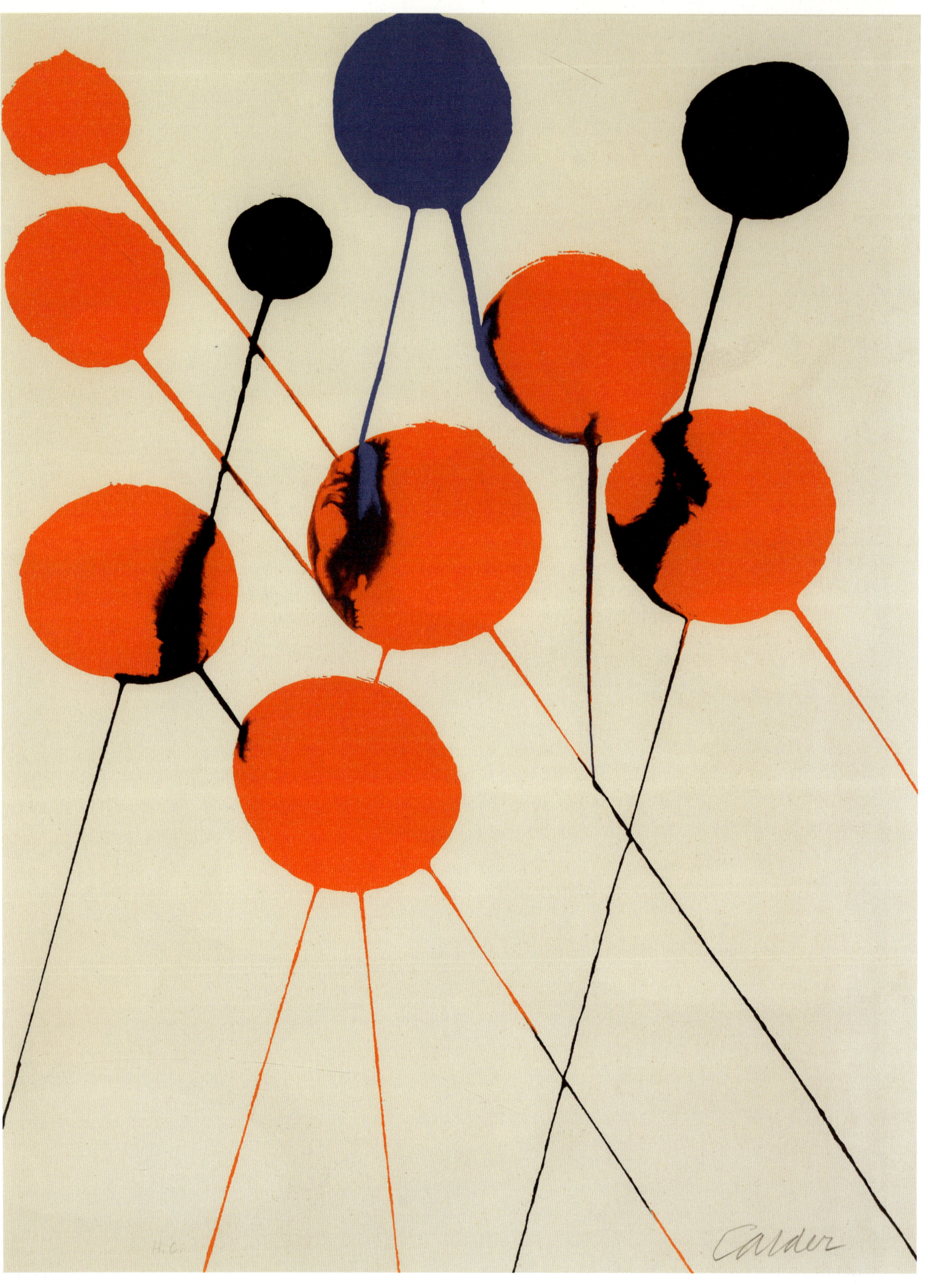

Calder

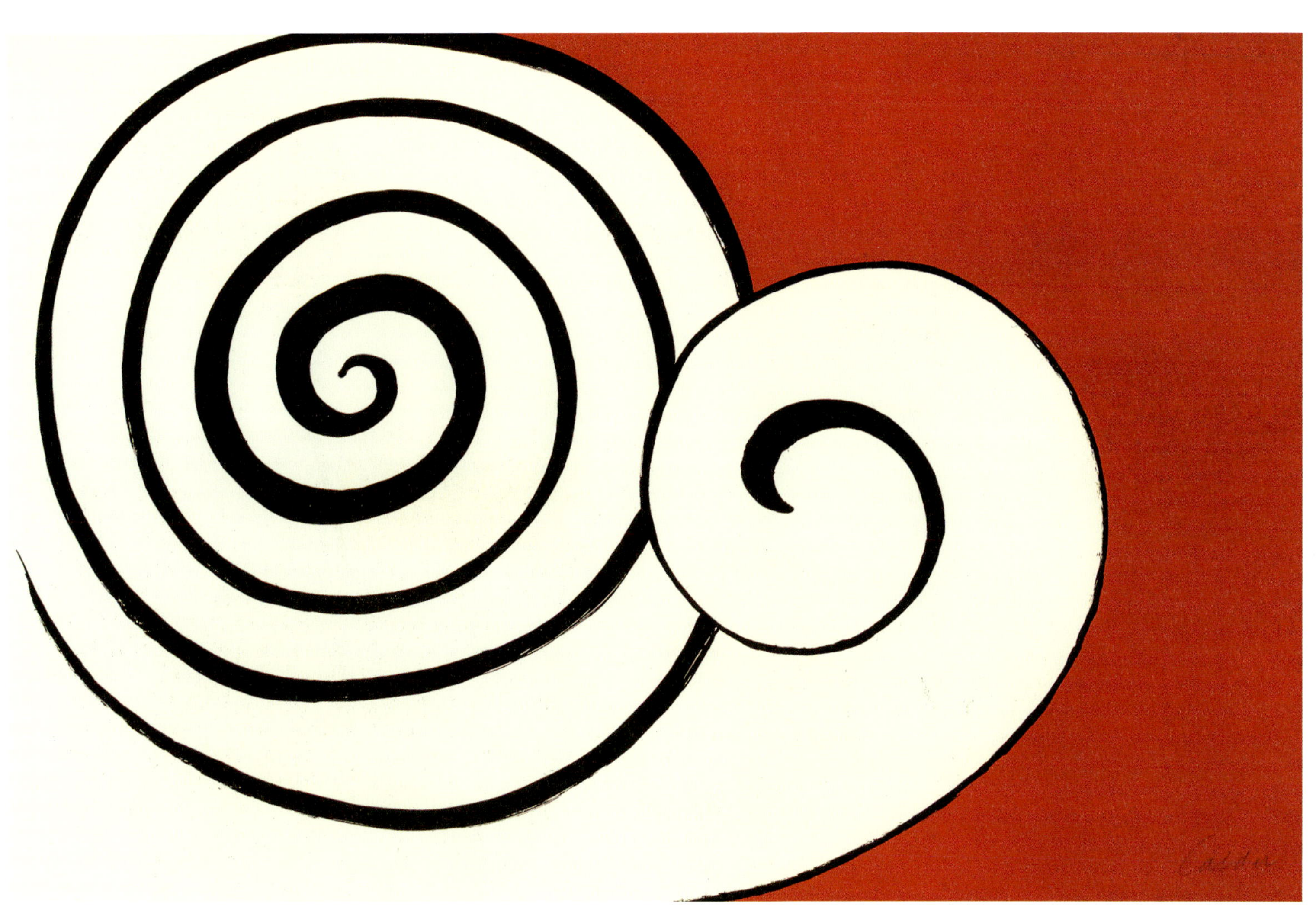

CAT. 108
Alexander Calder (1898–1976)
Dripping Balloons (*Ballons dégoulinés*), 1969
Lithograph, 78 x 58 cm

CAT. 109
Alexander Calder (1898–1976)
Two Spirals (*Deux spirales*), 1974
Original lithograph, 75 x 110 cm

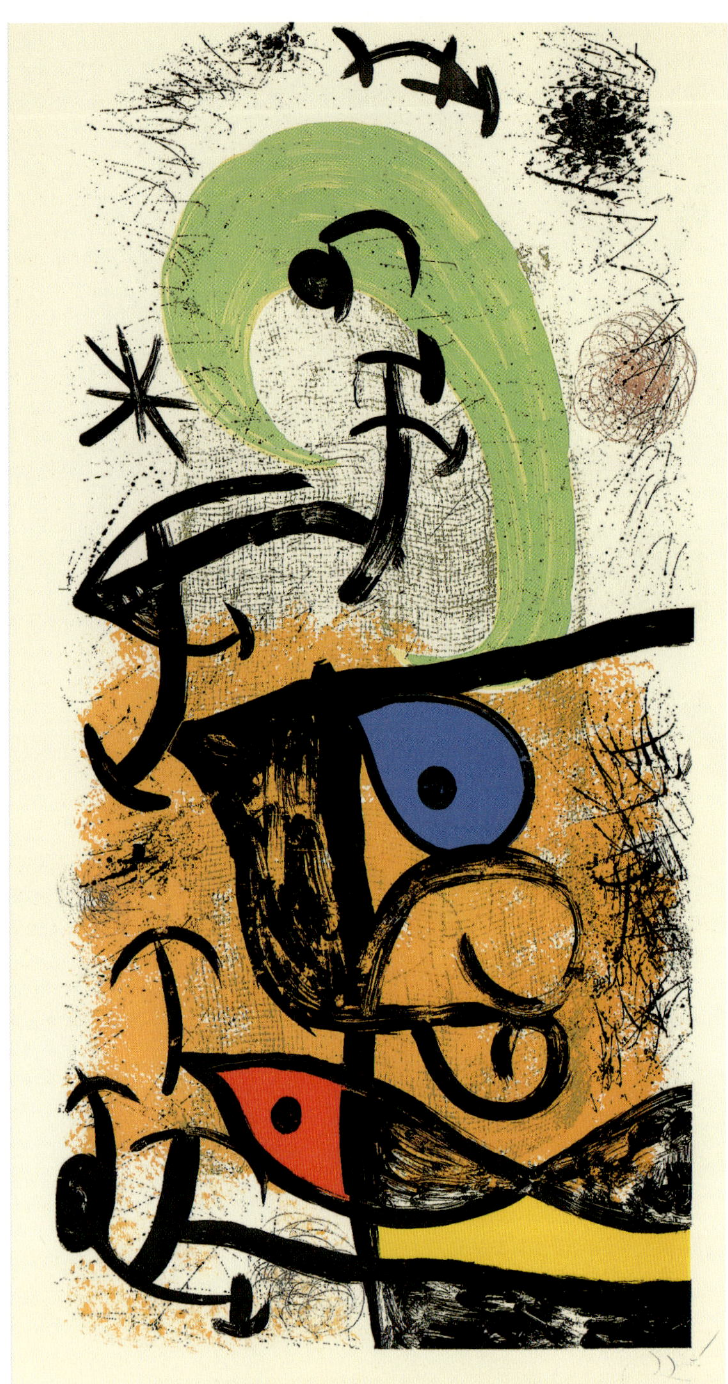

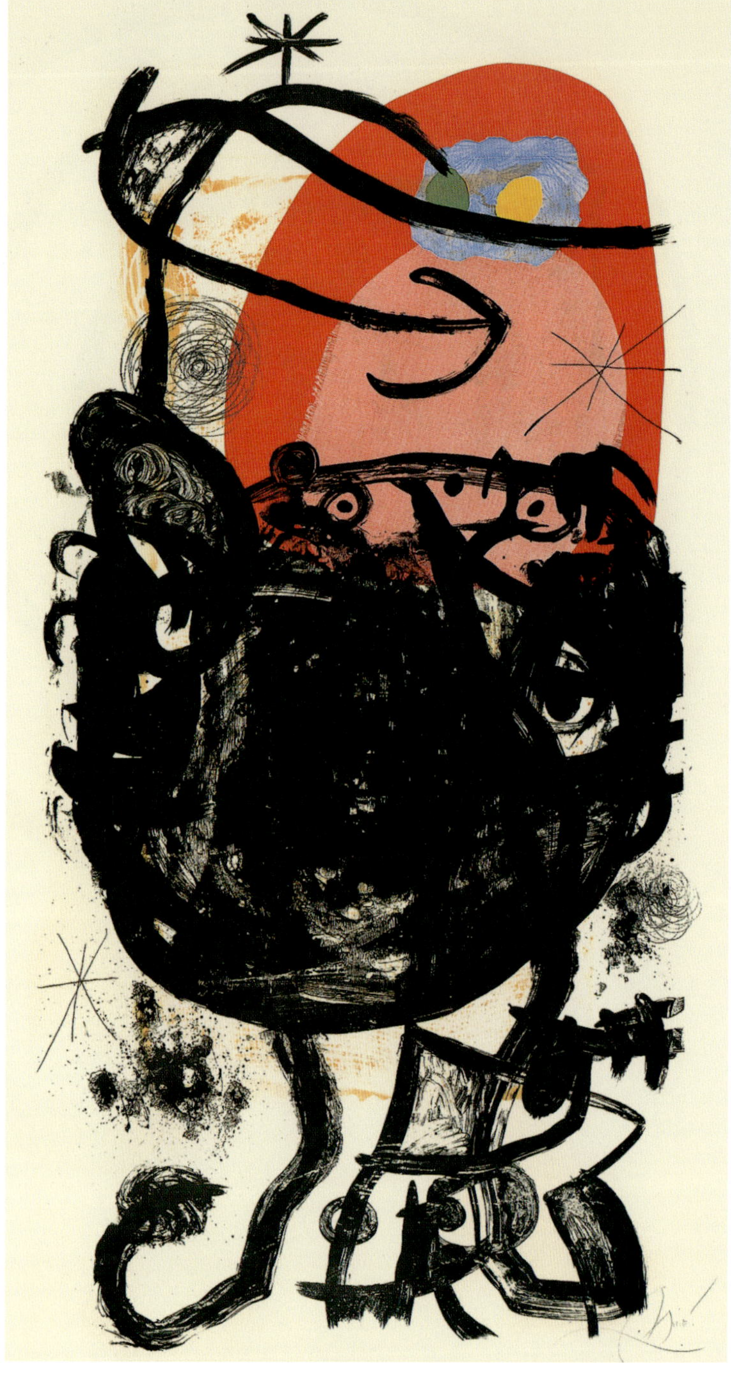

CAT. 110
Joan Miró (1893–1983)
Woman Leading the Moon
(*La Meneuse de lune*), 1975
Original lithograph, 236 x 122 cm

CAT. 111
Joan Miró (1893–1983)
The Hundred-year-old Warrior
(*La Guerrière de cent ans*), 1975
Original lithograph, 232 x 122 cm

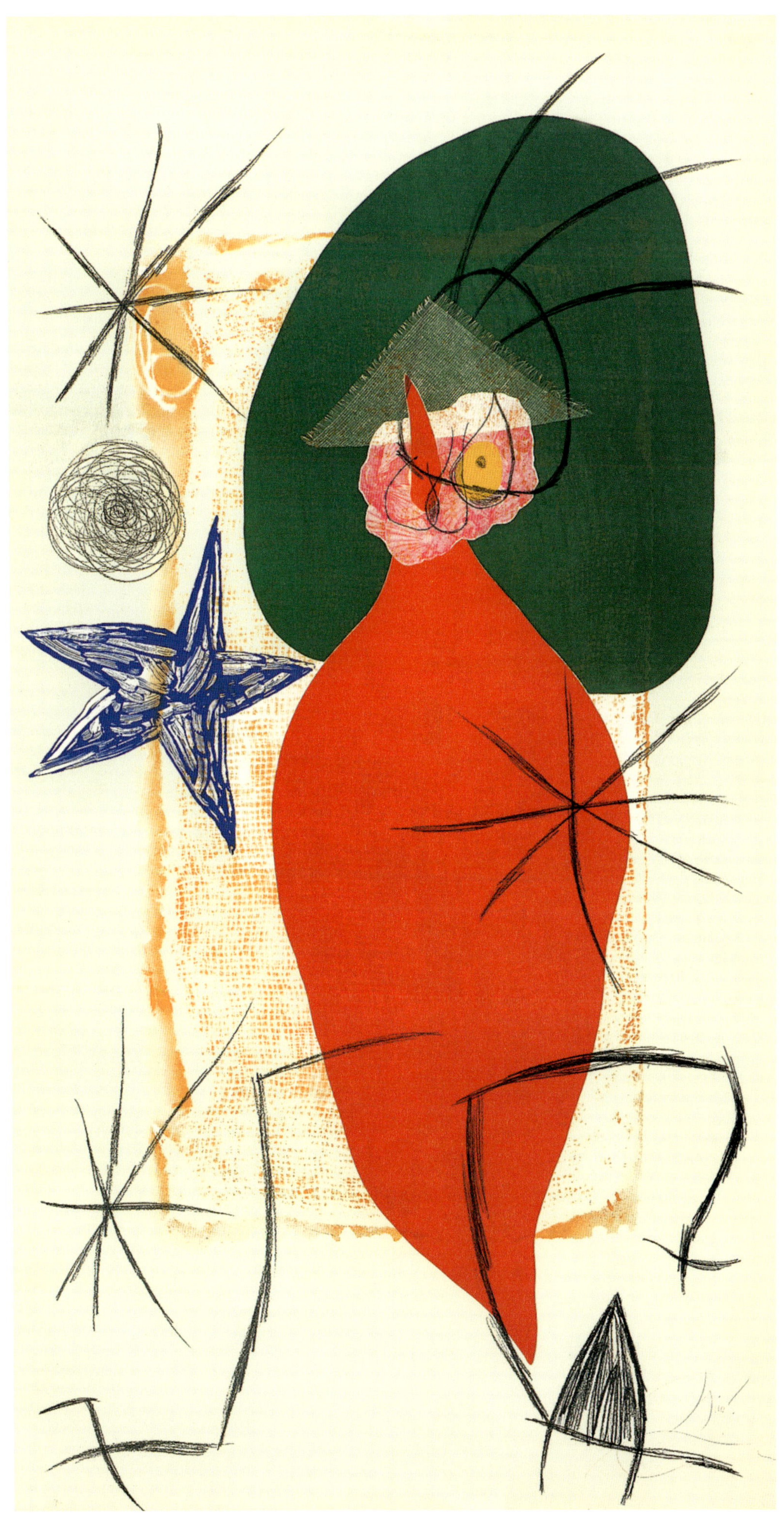

CAT. 112
Joan Miró (1893–1983)
Madwoman with Hot-tempered Pepper
(*La Folle au piment rageur*), 1975
Original lithograph, 232 x 122 cm

Pages 13–31: Introduction

1 Yoyo Maeght, *The Maeght Family: A Passion for Modern Art*, New York, 2007, p. 177.

2 Yoyo Maeght 2007, pp. 11–13.

3 *Bonnard/Matisse: Letters Between Friends*, trans. Richard Howard, New York, 1991, p. 101.

4 Hilary Spurling, *Matisse the Master*, London, 2005, pp. 425, 434.

5 John Russell, *Matisse: Father and Son*, New York, 1999, p. 242.

6 John Richardson, *The Sorcerer's Apprentice: A Decade of Picasso, Provence and Douglas Cooper*, London, 2001.

7 Russell 1999, pp. 110, 146, 201–3.

8 Bram van Velde had to be dropped after his three exhibitions failed to sell.

9 *Georges Braque: Printmaker*, Jennifer Mundy, exh. cat., Tate Gallery, London, 1993, pp. 24–6.

10 Yoyo Maeght 2007, p. 214.

11 Michel Enrici, 'Profession: éditeur', in François Chapon, Michel Enrici and Claude Lefebvre du Prey, *A proximité des poètes et des peintres: quarante ans d'Edition Maeght*, Paris, 1986, p. 27.

12 Nicholas Watkins, *Bonnard*, London, 1994, pp. 63–9.

13 Jean Paulhan, *Braque le Patron*, Geneva and Paris, 1946, p. 29.

14 Sophie Bowness, 'Braque le Patron: Braque and the Poets', in *Braque: The Late Works*, John Golding et al., exh. cat., Royal Academy of Arts, London, 1997, pp. 24–8.

15 Dora Vallier, 'Braque, la Peinture et Nous', *Cahiers d'Art*, Paris (October 1954), pp. 13–24.

16 Georges Braque, quoted in John Golding, 'Braque and the Space of Still-Life', in *Braque Still-Lifes and Interiors*, exh. cat., South Bank Centre Touring Exhibition, London, 1990, p. 9.

17 Georges Braque, quoted in Richardson 2001, p. 186.

18 Alex Danchev, *Georges Braque: A Life*, London, 2005, pp. 100–3.

19 Danchev 2005, pp. 100–3.

20 Jean-Paul Sartre, 'The Search for the Absolute', in *Alberto Giacometti: Sculptures, Paintings, Drawings*, exh. cat., Pierre Matisse Gallery, New York, 1948, pp. 2–22, reproduced in Jon Woods et al., *Modern Sculpture Reader*, Leeds, 2007, pp. 180–8.

21 David Sylvester, *Looking at Giacometti*, London, 1994, p. 7.

22 Jean Genet, *L'Atelier d'Alberto Giacometti*, trans. Charles Penwarden, Paris, 1986, pp. 17, 26.

23 Joan Miró, letter to J. F. Rafols, 18 November 1920, in *Joan Miró: Selected Writings and Interviews*, Margit Rowell (ed.), London, 1987, p. 75.

24 Joan Miró, letter to Michel Leiris, 10 August 1924, in Rowell 1987, p. 86.

25 Alberto Giacometti, quoted in Pierre Schneider, 'Miró', *Horizon*, 1, no. 4 (March 1959).

26 Michel Leiris, 'Joan Miró', *Documents*, 5 (October 1929), quoted in Dawn Ades (ed.), *Dada and Surrealism Reviewed*, London, 1978, p. 217.

27 Nicholas Watkins, 'Miró and the *siurells*', *Burlington Magazine*, 132 (February 1990), p. 93.

28 Jonathan Fineberg, 'Alexander Calder: A Dialog with Europe', *Art Since 1940*, London, 2000, p. 42.

29 Alexander Calder, *Calder: An Autobiography with Pictures*, New York, 1977, p. 130.

30 Elizabeth Hutton Turner, 'Calder and Miró: A New Space for the Imagination', in *Calder/Miró*, Elizabeth Hutton Turner and Oliver Wick (eds), London, 2004, p. 38.

31 Joan Miró, quoted in Rowell 1987, p. 209.

32 Joan Miró, 'Working Notes, 1941–42', in Rowell 1987, p. 175.

33 Joan Miró, 'Working Notes, 1941–42', in Rowell 1987, p. 192.

34 Joan Miró, *Derrière Le Miroir*, 107–9 (June–July 1958), n.p.

35 Nicholas Watkins, 'The Joy of Life', *Art Quarterly* (Summer 2006), pp. 38–42.

36 Yoyo Maeght 2007, pp. 153–8.

37 Jan K. Birkstead, *Modernism and the Mediterranean: The Maeght Foundation*, Aldershot, 2004, p. 61.

38 Watkins 1990, pp. 90–1.

39 Birkstead 2004, pp. 65–6.

40 Henri Maldiney, 'La Fondation Maeght à Saint-Paul', *Derrière Le Miroir*, 148 (July 1964), p. 53.

41 Birkstead 2004, p. 41.

42 Sarah Whitfield, 'Shaping Memory', in *Ellsworth Kelly*, exh. cat., Serpentine Gallery, London, 2006, p. 15.

43 Yoyo Maeght in conversation with Ann Dumas

44 Eduardo Chillida in conversation with Nicholas Watkins, Paseo de Faro 26, San Sebastian, 3 April 1997.

45 Eduardo Chillida in conversation with Nicholas Watkins, 3 April 1997.

Pages 48–61: Bonnard and Matisse

1 Sasha M. Newman (ed.), *Bonnard*, New York and London, 1984, p. 132.

2 Longus, *Daphnis and Chloe*, trans. Paul Turner, London, 1968, p. 17.

3 Nicholas Watkins, *Bonnard*, London, 1994, p. 75.

4 Nicholas Watkins, *Matisse*, Oxford, 1984, p. 199.

5 Henri Matisse, 'Letter to Henry Clifford', 1948, in *Matisse on Art*, Jack D. Flam (ed.), London, 1973, p.121.

Pages 62–95: Miró and Calder

1 Joan Miró, 'Working Notes, 1941–42', in *Joan Miró: Selected Writings and Interviews*, Margit Rowell (ed.), London, 1987, p. 179.

2 *The Touch of Dreams: Joan Miró, Ceramics and Bronzes, 1949–1980*, Veronica Sekules (ed.), exh. cat., Sainsbury Centre for Visual Arts, University of East Anglia, Norwich, 1985, p. 61.

3 Alexander Calder, quoted in Elizabeth Hutton Turner and Oliver Wick (eds), *Calder/Miró*, London, 2004, p. 273.

4 Jacques Prévert, 'Oiseleur du fer', *Derrière Le Miroir*, 156 (February 1966). Translation: 'Mobile above / stable below / just like the Eiffel Tower / Calder's like the tower / making seasonal winds from iron / making timepieces from the wind ...'

5 Jean-Paul Sartre, quoted in *Calder*, John Russell, exh. cat., Royal Academy of Arts, London, 1992, p. 8.

Pages 96–133: Braque and Giacometti

1 Hesiod, *Theogony and Works and Days*, lines 226–60, trans. M. L. West, Oxford, 1988, p. 10.

2 Dora Vallier, 'Braque et la sculpture', in *Georges Braque sculptures*, exh. cat., Galerie Adrien Maeght, Paris, 1985, p. 10.

3 Hesiod 1988, lines 429–62, p. 50.

4 Sophie Bowness, 'The Late Varengeville Landscapes and Seascapes', in *Braque: The Late Works*, John Golding et al., exh. cat., Royal Academy of Arts, London, 1997, pp. 118–19.

5 Alberto Giacometti, *Derrière Le Miroir*, 144–6 (May 1964), quoted in Bowness 1997, p. 119.

6 James Lord, *A Giacometti Portrait*, London and Boston, 1980, p. 52.

7 'Heads', from the dictionary section of *Documents*, in *Undercover Surrealism: Georges Bataille and DOCUMENTS*, Dawn Ades and Simon Baker, exh. cat., Hayward Gallery, London, 2006, pp. 196–203.

8 Jean Genet, *L'Atelier d'Alberto Giacometti*, trans. Charles Penwarden, Paris, 1986, p. 22.

9 Jean-Paul Sartre, 'The Search for the Absolute', in *Alberto Giacometti: Sculptures, Paintings, Drawings*, exh. cat., Pierre Matisse Gallery, New York, 1948, pp. 2–22, reproduced in Jon Woods et al., *Modern Sculpture Reader*, Leeds, 2007, pp. 182–3.

10 Alberto Giacometti, letter to Pierre Matisse, 1950, quoted in Yves Bonnefoy, *Alberto Giacometti*, trans. Jean Stewart, Paris, 1991, p. 349.

11 Yves Bonnefoy, *Alberto Giacometti*, trans. Jean Stewart, Paris, 1991, p. 332.

12 Alberto Giacometti, quoted in Bonnefoy 1991, p. 290.

13 Alberto Giacometti, quoted in Bonnefoy 1991, p. 290.

Pages 134–65: Editions Maeght

1 *Georges Braque: Printmaker*, Jennifer Mundy, exh. cat., Tate Gallery, London, 1993, pp. 24–6.

2 'It isn't the flowers, it's we painters who are more fragile.' Alberto Giacometti, quoted in *Alberto Giacometti oeuvre grave*, exh. cat., Centre d'art contemporain, Château des Adhémar, Montélimar, in association with Galerie Maeght, Paris, 2001, p. 9.

3 Yoyo Maeght, *The Maeght Family: A Passion for Modern Art*, New York, 2007, p. 214.

4 D'Arcy Wentworth Thompson, *On Growth and Form*, vol. 1, Cambridge, 1952, pp. 7, 79.

5 Thompson 1952, fig. 120, p. 395.

6 Thompson 1952, vol. 2, p. 750.

7 Maurice La Belle, *Alfred Jarry: Nihilism and the Theatre of the Absurd*, New York and London, 1980, p. 50.

8 Keith Beaumont, *Alfred Jarry: A Critical and Biographical Study*, Leicester, 1984, p. 116.

9 Pierre Reverdy, *La Liberté des mers*, with original lithographs by Georges Braque, Paris, 1959, p. 13. Translation: 'Murmuring between the / four walls with drop- / lets of blood from thorns.'

10 Reverdy 1959, pp. 64–5. Translation: 'A hand / with rhyth- / mic move- / ment and / no thoughts / flung its five / fingers towards / the ceiling.'

11 Reverdy 1959. Translation: 'It snows on / my roof and / on the trees.'

12 Tristan Tzara, quoted in Mary Ann Caws, *The Inner Theatre of Recent French Poetry*, New Jersey, 1972, p. 51.

13 Jacques Prévert, *Fêtes*, with illustrations by Alexander Calder, Paris, 1971. Translation: ' Mobile above / stable below / just like the Eiffel Tower / Calder's like the tower.'

14 Prévert 1971: Translation: 'Solomon Grundy / born on Monday / christened on Tuesday / married on Wednesday.'

15 Jacques Prévert, *Adonides*, with engravings by Joan Miró, Paris, 1975. Translation: 'All / things considered / in these unhappy times / the mirror shattered.'

16 'Prévert 1975. Translation: '...and God / surprising Adam and Eve / tells them / please do continue / don't let me / disturb you / Carry on as if I did not exist.'

BIBLIOGRAPHY

A Proximité des poètes et des peintres, quarante ans d'édition Maeght, A. Julien-Laferrière, exh. cat., Centre de Création Contemporaine, Tours, and Nordjylands Kunstmuseum, Aalborg, with Adrien Maeght Editeur, Paris, 1986

Ades, Dawn (ed.), *Dada and Surrealism Reviewed*, London, 1978

Alberto Giacometti 1901–1966, T. Stooss and P. Elliott (eds), exh. cat., Royal Academy of Art, London, 1996

Alberto Giacometti oeuvre grave, exh. cat., Centre d'art contemporain, Château des Adhémar, Montélimar, in association with Galerie Maeght, Paris, 2001

Alberto Giacometti: Sculptures, Paintings, Drawings, exh. cat., Pierre Matisse Gallery, New York, 1948

Bastlund, K., *José Luis Sert: Architecture, City Planning, Urban Design*, Zurich, 1967

Beaumont, Keith, *Alfred Jarry: A Critical and Biographical Study*, Leicester, 1984

Bernier, R., 'Miró as Ceramist: Interview with Miró', reprinted from *L'Œil* (May 1956) in *Joan Miró: Selected Writings and Interviews*, Margit Rowell (ed.), London, 1987

Binet, J.-L, 'Retourner à Varengeville; l'atelier de Georges Braque', in *Cimaise*, 235 (April–May 1995), pp. 37–42

Birksted, Jan, 'Where Oppositions Disintegrate and Grow Complicated: the Maeght Foundation', in *The Architecture of the Museum: Symbolic Structures, Urban Contexts*, M. Giebelhausen (ed.), Manchester, 2003

Birksted, Jan, *Modernism and the Mediterranean: The Maeght Foundation* (Aldershot, 2004)

Bonnard/Matisse: Letters Between Friends, trans. Richard Howard, New York, 1991

Bonnefoy, Yves, *Alberto Giacometti*, trans. Jean Stewart, Paris, 1991

Boustedt, B., 'Quand Giacometti plaçait lui-mème ses sculptures', *XXème siècle*, 23 (1969), pp. 22–36

Bowness, Sophie, 'Ben Nicholson and Georges Braque: Dieppe and Varengeville in the 1930s', in *The Dieppe Connection: The Town and its Artists from Turner to Braque*, exh. cat., Brighton Museum and Art Gallery, 1992, pp. 44–49

Bowness, Sophie, 'Braque le Patron: Braque and the Poets', in *Braque: The Late Works*, John Golding et al., exh. cat., Royal Academy of Arts, London, 1997, pp. 24–28

Bowness, Sophie, 'The Late Varengeville Landscapes and Seascapes', in *Braque: The Late Works*, John Golding et al., exh. cat., Royal Academy of Arts, London, 1997, pp. 118–19.

Braque: The Late Works, John Golding, Sophie Bowness and I. Monod-Fontaine (eds), exh. cat., Royal Academy of Arts, London, 1997

Breton, André, 'Constellations de Joan Miró', *L'Œil*, 48 (December 1958), pp. 50–55

Bruzeau, M., *Calder*, Paris, 1975

Calder, Alexander, *Calder: An Autobiography with Pictures*, New York, 1977

Calder, John Russell, exh. cat., Royal Academy of Arts, London, 1992

Campbell, R., 'Alberto Giacometti 1901–1966: A Personal Reminiscence', *Studio International*, 2 (February 1966), p. 47

Campbell, R., 'Homage to a Catalonian: A Personal View of AIA Gold Medalist José Luis Sert', *AIA Journal* (February 1981), pp. 50–53

Caws, Mary Ann, *The Inner Theatre of Recent French Poetry*, New Jersey, 1972

Chambon, C., *La Fondation Marguerite et Aimé Maeght*, Paris: Maeght Editeur, 1994

Chapon, François, *Le Peintre et le livre: l'âge d'or du livre illustré en France, 1870–1970*, Paris, 1987

Chapon, François, 'Aimé Maeght, homme du livre' in *A proximité des poètes et des peintres, quarante ans d'edition Maeght*, A. Julien-Laferrière, exh. cat., Centre de Création Contemporaine, Tours, and Nordjylands Kunstmuseum, Aalborg, with Adrien Maeght Editeur, Paris, 1986, pp. 11–19

Danchev, Alex, *Georges Braque: A Life*, London, 2005

De Courcel, M. (ed.), *Malraux: Life and Work*, London, 1976

Dufrêne, T., *Giacometti, Les Dimensions de la réalité*, Geneva, 1994

Dupin, Jacques, *Joan Miró: Life and Work*, New York, 1962

Dupin, Jacques, *Miró*, Paris, 2004

Dupin, Jacques, and Michel Leiris, (eds), *Alberto Giacometti: Ecrits*, Paris, 1990

Enrici, Michel, 'Profession: éditeur', in *A proximité des poètes et des peintres: quarante ans d'Edition Maeght*, François Chapon, Michel Enrici and Claude Lefebvre du Prey, Paris, 1986, pp. 21–39

Fineberg, Jonathan, 'Alexander Calder: A Dialog with Europe', *Art Since 1940*, London, 2000, pp. 42–85

Fletcher, V. J., *Giacometti 1901–1966*, exh. cat., Hirshorn Museum, Washington, D.C., 1988

Flam, Jack D. (ed.), *Matisse on Art*, London, 1973

Freixa, J., *Josep Lluis Sert*, Barcelona, 1979

Gall, A. and M., *Maeght le Magnifique*, Paris, 1992

Genet, Jean, *L'Atelier d'Alberto Giacometti*, trans. Charles Penwarden, Paris, 1986

Georges Braque, Printmaker, Jennifer Mundy, exh. cat., Tate Gallery, London, 1993

Giacometti, Alberto, *Derrière Le Miroir*, 144–6 (May 1964)

Golding, John, 'Braque and the Space of Still-Life', in *Braque Still-Lifes and Interiors*, exh. cat., South Bank Centre Touring Exhibition, London, 1990, pp. 8–26

Golding, John, 'The Late Works, in *Braque: The Late Works*, John Golding et al., exh. cat., Royal Academy of Arts, London, 1997, pp. 1–14

Hesiod, *Theogony and Works and Days*, trans. M. L. West, Oxford, 1988

Hohl, R., *Alberto Giacometti: Sculpture, Painting, Drawing*, London, 1972

Honisch, D., 'Scale in Giacometti's Sculpture', in *Alberto Giacometti: Sculpture, Paintings, Drawings*, A. Schneider (ed.), Munich, New York and London, 1994, pp. 65–69

J. Ll. Sert and Mediterranean Culture, A. Pizza (ed.), exh. cat., bilingual, Architects' Association of Catalonia and the Ministry of Development, Barcelona, 1996

Joan Miró, C. Lanchner (ed.), exh. cat., Museum of Modern Art, New York, 1993

Lanchner, C., 'Peinture-Poesie, Its Logic and Logistics', in *Joan Miro*, C. Lanchner (ed.), exh. cat., Museum of Modern Art, New York, 1993, pp. 42–5

La Belle, Maurice, *Alfred Jarry: Nihilism and the Theatre of the Absurd*, New York and London, 1980

Leiris, Michel, 'Joan Miró', *Documents*, 5 (October 1929), pp. 263–9

Longus, *Daphnis and Chloe*, trans. Paul Turner, London, 1968

Lord, James, *A Giacometti Portrait*, London and Boston, 1980

Lord, James, 'In Memoriam: Alberto Giacometti', in *L'Œil* (March 1966), pp. 42–46

L'univers d'Aimé et Marguerite Maeght, J.-L. Prat, exh. cat., Fondation Marguerite et Aimé Maeght, Saint-Paul, 1982

Maeght, Yoyo, *The Maeght Family: A Passion for Modern Art*, New York, 2007

Maldiney, Henri, 'La Fondation Maeght à Saint-Paul', *Derrière Le Miroir*, 148 (July 1964), p. 53

Marter, J. M., *Alexander Calder*, Cambridge, 1991

Matisse, Henri, 'Letter to Henry Clifford', 1948, in *Matisse on Art*, Jack D. Flam (ed.), London, 1973, p. 121

Miró, Joan, 'I Dream of a Large Studio' [May 1938], in *Joan Miró: Selected Writings and Interviews*, Margit Rowell (ed.), New York, 1992, pp. 161–2.

Miró, Joan, *Derrière Le Miroir*, 107–9 (June–July 1958)

Miró, Joan, 'Working Notes, 1941–42', in *Joan Miró: Selected Writings and Interviews*, Margit Rowell (ed.), London, 1987, pp. 173–95

Miró, Prat, J.-L., exh. cat., Fondation Pierre Gianadda, Martigny, 1997

Mullins, E., *Braque*, London, 1968

Newman, Sasha M. (ed.), *Bonnard*, New York and London, 1984

Paulhan, Jean, *Braque le Patron*, Geneva and Paris, 1946

Pierre, J., and J. Corredor-Matheos, *Miró et Artigas, Céramiques*, Paris: Maeght Editeur, 1974

Prévert, Jacques, 'Oiseleur du fer', *Derrière Le Miroir*, 156 (February 1966)

Raillard, G., *Conversaciones con Miró*, Barcelona, 1978

Reverdy, Pierre, *La Liberté des mers*, with original lithographs by Georges Braque, Paris, 1959

Richardson, John, *The Sorcerer's Apprentice: A Decade of Picasso, Provence and Douglas Cooper*, London, 2001

Rowell, Margit (ed.), *Joan Miró: Selected Writings and Interviews*, London, 1987

Russell, John, *Matisse: Father and Son*, New York, 1999

Sartre, Jean-Paul, 'The Search for the Absolute', in *Alberto Giacometti: Sculptures, Paintings, Drawings*, exh. cat., Pierre Matisse Gallery, New York, 1948, pp. 2–22, reproduced in Jon Woods et al., *Modern Sculpture Reader*, Leeds, 2007, pp. 180–88

Sartre, Jean-Paul, 'Alexandre Calder, père des mobiles', *Combat* (3 May 1952)

Schlulmberger, E., 'Architecture pour un musée, *Conaissance des Arts* (April 1963), pp. 2–12

Schneider, Pierre, 'Miró', *Horizon*, 1, no. 4 (March 1959), pp. 70–89, 126–7

Schneider, A. (ed.), *Alberto Giacometti: Sculpture, Paintings, Drawings*, Munich, New York and London, 1994

Spurling, Hilary, *Matisse the Master*, London, 2005

Sylvester, David, *Looking at Giacometti*, London, 1994

Thompson, D'Arcy Wentworth, *On Growth and Form*, 2 vols, Cambridge, 1952

The Touch of Dreams: Joan Miró, Ceramics and Bronzes, 1949–1980, Veronica Sekules (ed.), exh. cat., Sainsbury Centre for Visual Arts, University of East Anglia, Norwich, 1985

Turner, Elizabeth Hutton, and Oliver Wick (eds), *Calder/Miró*, London, 2004

Turner, Elizabeth Hutton, 'Calder and Miró: A New Space for the Imagination', in *Calder/Miró*, Elizabeth Hutton Turner and Oliver Wick (eds), London, 2004

Undercover Surrealism: Georges Bataille and DOCUMENTS, Dawn Ades and Simon Baker, exh. cat., Hayward Gallery, London, 2006

Vallier, Dora, 'Braque, la Peinture et Nous', *Cahiers d'Art*, Paris (October 1954), pp. 13–24

Vallier, Dora, 'Braque et la sculpture', in *Georges Braque sculptures*, exh. cat., Galerie Adrien Maeght, Paris, 1985, p. 10.

Watkins, Nicholas, *Matisse*, Oxford, 1984

Watkins, Nicholas, 'Miró and the *siurells*', *Burlington Magazine*, 132 (February 1990), pp. 90–5

Watkins, Nicholas, *Bonnard*, London, 1994

Watkins, Nicholas, 'The Joy of Life', *Art Quarterly* (Summer 2006), pp. 38–42

Whitfield, Sarah, 'Shaping Memory', in *Ellsworth Kelly*, exh. cat., Serpentine Gallery, London, 2006, pp. 7–17

Wilson, Sarah, 'Paris Post-War: In Search of the Absolute', in *Paris Post-War: Art and Existentialism, 1945–55*, Francis Morris (ed.), exh. cat., Tate Gallery, London, 1993, pp. 25–52

Zurcher, B., *Georges Braque: Life and Work*, New York, 1988

1946

René Lacôte, *Où finit le desert*, Paris, 1946. Lithographs by Gilbert Rigaud. 32 x 24.5 cm, 76 pages, 10 illustrations. Edition of 350

Franz Kafka, *Description d'un combat*, Paris, 1946, translated by Clara Malraux and Rainier Dorland, with a Preface by Bernard Groethuysen. Lithographs by Jean-Michel Atlan. 31 x 24.5 cm, 84 pages, 16 illustrations. Edition of 350

1947

Jacques Kober, *Les Vents des épines*, Paris, 1947. Illustrations by Pierre Bonnard, Georges Braque and Henri Matisse. 29 x 22 cm, 24 pages, 3 illustrations based on previously unpublished drawings. Edition of 270

Paul Eluard, *Elle se fit élever un palais…*, Paris, 1947. Woodcuts by Serge Rezvani. 53 x 34 cm, 44 pages, 12 illustrations, decorated dust jacket. Edition of 16

Cahier de Georges Braque 1916–1947 (first edition), Paris, 1947. Lithographs by Georges Braque. 50 x 33 cm, 94 pages, 3 prints, page decorations. Edition of 95

1948

Gilbert Lely, *Ma civilisation*, Paris, 1948. Etchings by Lucien Coutaud. 33.5 x 25 cm, 94 pages, 11 illustrations. Edition of 250

Paul Eluard, *Perspectives*, Paris, 1948. Poems printed on etchings by Albert Flocon. 33.5 x 25 cm, 48 pages, 12 illustrations. Edition of 200

Paul Eluard, *Le Bestiaire de Paul Eluard*, Paris, 1948. Etchings by Roger Chastel. 38 x 31 cm, 192 pages, 88 illustrations. Edition of 196

Cahier de Georges Braque 1916–1947 (second edition), Paris, 1948. Lithograph by Georges Braque. 38 x 28 cm, 94 pages, 1 print, page decorations. Edition of 845

1948–1950

Tristan Tzara, *Parler seul*, Paris, 1948–50. Lithographs by Joan Miró. 38.5 x 29 cm, 118 pages, 78 illustrations. Edition of 250

1950

Milarepa, *Milarepa*, Paris, 1950, translated by Jacques Bacot. Etchings by Georges Braque. 23.5 x 33.5 cm, 42 pages, 5 illustrations. Edition of 100

1955

Hesiod, *Théogonie,* Paris, 1955. Etchings made in 1932 by Georges Braque. 44 x 32.5 cm, 82 pages, 20 illustrations, decorated slipcase. Edition of 150

1958

Frank Elgar, *Résurrection de l'oiseau*, Paris, 1958. Lithographs by Georges Braque. 38 x 28.4 cm, 40 pages, 7 illustrations. Edition of 225

Yves Bonnefoy, *Pierre écrite*, Paris, 1958. Cut-slate engravings by Raoul Ubac. 39 x 29 cm, 54 pages, 10 illustrations. Edition of 125

1959

Pierre Reverdy, *La Liberté des mers*, Paris, 1959. Lithographs by Georges Braque. 57.5 x 39.5 cm, 170 pages, 8 illustrations, text decorations. Edition of 250

André du Bouchet, *Sur le pas*, Paris, 1959. Aquatints by Pierre Tal-Coat. 41 x 38 cm, 64 pages, 18 illustrations. Edition of 200

1960

Georges Ribemont-Dessaignes, *La Nuit, la faim*, Paris, 1960. Lithographs by Georges Braque. 28 x 18.5 cm, 34 pages, 2 illustrations. Edition of 163

1961

Album 19, Paris, 196, with a Preface by Raymond Queneau. Lithographs by Joan Miró. 66 x 51 cm, 54 pages, 19 illustrations. Edition of 75

1962

Christian Dotremont, *Ancienne éternité*, Paris, 1962. Burin engravings by Raoul Ubac. 28 x 18.5 cm, 32 pages, 5 illustrations. Edition of 187

Yves Bonnefoy, *Anti-platon*; André du Bouchet, *La Lumière de la lame*; Jacques Dupin, *Saccades*; Paris, 1962. Etchings by Joan Miró. Three volumes, each 33.5 x 26.5 cm, 40/48/56 pages, 9 illustrations. Each volume printed in an edition of 125

1963

St John of the Cross, *Les Cantiques spirituels de Saint Jean de la Croix*, Paris, 1963, translated by the Reverend Father Cyprien. Lithographs by François Fiedler. 39 x 56 cm, 72 pages, 16 illustrations. Edition of 80

Pierre Tal-Coat, *Traverse d'un plateau*, Paris, 1963. Poem and dry-points by Pierre Tal-Coat. 33 x 26 cm, 29 pages, 7 illustrations. Edition of 75

1964

René Char, *Le Flux de l'aimant*, Paris, 1964. Dry-points by Joan Miró. 51 x 62 cm, 52 pages, 17 illustrations. Edition of 75

1965

Heraclitus, *Sans le soleil*, Paris, 1965. Etchings by Joan Miró. 33 x 27 cm, 52 pages, 10 illustrations. Edition of 75

Jean Giono, *La Charge du Roi*, Paris, 1965. Etchings by Jean Cortot. 19 x 26 cm, 44 pages, 6 illustrations. Edition of 150

1966

André Frénaud, *Le Chemin des devins* and *Ménerbes*, Paris, 1966. Etchings by Eduardo Chillida. 37 x 30.5 cm, 54 pages, 11 illustrations. Edition of 175

1967

André Frénaud, *Vieux pays* and *Campagne*, Paris, 1967. Etchings by Raoul Ubac. 41 x 31 cm, 72 pages, 15 illustrations. Edition of 165

Yves Bonnefoy, *La Poésie française et le principe d'identité*, Paris, 1967. Etchings by Raoul Ubac. 24.5 x 19 cm, 50 pages, 2 illustrations. Edition of 150

Haï-Ku, Paris, 1967, translated by Philippe Jaccottet. Lithographs by Joan Miró. 32.5 x 26 cm, 28 pages, 7 illustrations. Edition of 100

1969

Jerzy Ficowski, *Lettre à Marc Chagall*, Paris, 1969, translated by Suzanne Arlet. Etchings by Marc Chagall. 29 x 20.5 cm, 36 pages, 5 illustrations. Edition of 175

Michel Leiris, *Fissures*, Paris, 1969. Etchings by Joan Miró. 50 x 60 cm, 128 pages, 15 illustrations. Edition of 75

1971

Marcel and Gabriel Piqueray, *Vins puis faons pour les Anzacs*, Paris, 1971. Colour kinetic prints by Pol Bury. 50 x 34 cm, 44 pages, 31 illustrations. Edition of 330

Jacques Dupin, *Proximité du murmure*, Paris, 1971. Etchings by Raoul Ubac. 43.5 x 30 cm, 44 pages, 9 illustrations. Edition of 175

Philippe Denis, *Cahier d'ombres*, Paris, 1971. Lithographs by Joan Miró. 30.5 x 24 cm, 40 pages, 4 illustrations. Edition of 200

Jean-Pierre Lemesle, *Les Bœufs meurent aussi*, Paris, 1971. Lithographs by Joan Gardy-Artigas. 64 x 50 cm, 40 pages, 13 illustrations. Edition of 250

André du Bouchet, *Air*, Paris, 1971. Etchings and lithographs by Antoni Tàpies. 29.5 x 23 cm, 40 pages, 15 illustrations. Edition of 150

Jacques Prévert, *Fêtes*, Paris, 1971. Etchings by Alexander Calder. 46 x 34 cm, 46 pages, 8 illustrations. Edition of 200

1972

Max Hölzer, *Lunariae*, Paris, 1972. Etchings by Pablo Palazuelo. 67 x 52 cm, 36 pages, 8 illustrations. Edition of 150

Pierre Schneider, *Parler de corde*, Paris, 1972. Lithographs by Jean-Paul Riopelle. 48 x 33.5 cm, 42 pages, 14 illustrations. Edition of 75

André Frénaud, *Le Miroir de l'homme par les bêtes*, Paris, 1972. Etchings by Joan Miró. 44 x 33.5 cm, 52 pages, 5 illustrations. Edition of 200

1973

Heraclitus, *Fragments sur le devenir universel*, Paris, 1973, translated by Yves Battistini. Etchings by François Fiedler. 29 x 20 cm, 126 pages, 31 illustrations. Edition of 150

Jorge Guillén, *Mas Allá*, Paris, 1973, translated by Claude Esteban. Woodcuts by Eduardo Chillida. 40 x 33 cm, 64 pages, 16 illustrations. Edition of 150

Friedrich Hölderlin, *L'Unique*, Paris, 1973, translated by André du Bouchet. Lithographs by Bram van Velde. 41.5 x 30 cm, 42 pages, 6 illustrations. Edition of 125

1974

Helmut Heissenbüttel, *Das Reich. Gelegenheitsgedicht Nr 27. 1871–1945*, Paris, 1974, translated by Louis Fessard. Silkscreen prints by Valerio Adami. 51 x 43 cm, 52 pages, 10 illustrations. Edition of 600

René Char, *Le Monde de l'art n'est pas le monde du pardon*, Paris, 1974. Prints by Georges Charbonnier, Wifredo Lam, Joan Miró, Arpád Szenes, Vieira da Silva and Zao Wou-Ki. 34 x 26 cm, 140 pages, 68 illustrations. Edition of 75

Cartes per a la Teresa, Paris, 1974. Lithographs by Antoni Tàpies. 77 x 62 cm, 104 pages, 64 illustrations. Edition of 150

Jacques Dupin, *L'Issue dérobée*, Paris, 1974. Engravings by Joan Miró. 33.5 x 51 cm, 68 pages, 11 illustrations. Edition of 200

Robert Desnos, *Les pénalités de l'enfer* or *Les Nouvelles Hébrides*, Paris, 1974. Lithographs by Joan Miró. 27 x 38 cm, 104 pages, 25 illustrations. Edition of 200

1975

Yves Bonnefoy, *L'Ordalie*, Paris, 1975. Etchings by Claude Garache. 25 x 18.5 cm, 58 pages, 5 illustrations. Edition of 120

Roger Caillois, *Pierres réfléchies*, Paris, 1975. Etchings by Raoul Ubac. 47 x 46 cm, 66 pages, 15 illustrations. Edition of 200

André Martel, *La Géometrille dé ramollisses*, Paris, 1975. Lithographs by Pol Bury. 40.5 x 40.5 cm, 36 pages, 13 illustrations. Edition of 200

Jean Daive, ⅄*, Paris, 1975. Etchings by Antoni Tàpies. 25 x 18.5 cm, 74 pages, 5 illustrations. Edition of 120

Serge Sautreau and André Velter, *Conte rouge pour Paloma*, Paris, 1975. Lithographs by Paul Rebeyrolle. 29 x 33 cm, 48 pages, 16 illustrations. Edition of 175

Bruno de Montalivet, *L'Herbe déracinée*, Paris, 1975. Etchings by Raoul Ubac. 25 x 18.5 cm, 68 pages, 4 illustrations. Edition of 120

Jacques Dupin, *Journal d'un graveur*, Paris, 1975. Etchings and dry-points by Joan Miró. 57 x 45 cm, 3 volumes in a slipcase, each with 18 illustrations. Edition of 75

Charles Racine, *Le Sujet est la clairière de son corps*, Paris, 1975. Etchings by Eduardo Chillida. 25 x 18.5 cm, 52 pages, 5 illustrations. Edition of 120

Charles Juliet, *Au long de la spirale*, Paris, 1975. Lithographs by Bram van Velde. 45 x 29 cm, 32 pages, 5 illustrations. Edition of 200

Michel Couturier, *L'Ablatif absolu*, Paris, 1975. Etchings by Pablo Palazuelo. 25 x 18.5 cm, 74 pages, 5 illustrations. Edition of 120

Jacques Prévert, *Adonides*, Paris, 1975. Engravings by Joan Miró. 40.5 x 33.5 cm, 68 pages, 45 illustrations. Edition of 200

Louis Aragon, *Celui qui dit les choses sans rien dire*, Paris, 1975. Etchings by Marc Chagall. 48 x 37 cm, 134 pages, 25 illustrations. Edition of 205

1976

Claude Royet-Journoud, *Le Travail du nom*, Paris, 1976. Engravings by Lars Fredrikson. 25 x 18.5 cm, 58 pages, 4 illustrations. Edition of 120

Claude Esteban, *Dans le vide qui vient*, Paris, 1976. Etchings by Arpad Szenes. 25 x 18.5 cm, 54 pages, 5 illustrations. Edition of 120

Samir Amin, *Eloge du Socialisme*, Paris, 1976. Lithographs by Paul Rebeyrolle. 57 x 38 cm, 50 pages, 15 illustrations. Edition of 150

Erskine Caldwell, *Le Sacrilège d'Alan Kent*, Paris, 1976, translated by Marcel Duhamel. Etchings by Alexander Calder. 41 x 46 cm, 100 pages, 20 illustrations. Edition of 200

1977

André Malraux, *Et sur la terre…*, Paris, 1977. Etchings by Marc Chagall. 44 x 34 cm, 66 pages, 15 illustrations. Edition of 205

Jean Tardieu, *L'Ombre, la branche*, Paris, 1977. Lithographs by Jean Bazaine. 41.5 x 32 cm, 28 pages, 15 illustrations. Edition of 150

Alain Delahaye, *L'Etre perdu*, Paris, 1977. Lithographs by Jean Bazaine. 25 x 18.5 cm, 48 pages, 4 illustrations. Edition of 120

Pascal Quignard, *Sarx*, Paris, 1977. Engravings by Gérard Titus-Carmel. 25 x 18.5 cm, 56 pages, 6 illustrations. Edition of 120

Alain Veinstein, *Recherches des dispositions anciennes*, Paris, 1977. Etchings by Joël Kermarrec. 25 x 18.5 cm, 92 pages, 6 illustrations. Edition of 120

1978

Carlos Franqui, *Album 21*, Lithographs by Joan Miró. Paris, 1978. 50 x 65 cm, 54 pages, 21 illustrations. Edition of 75

E. M. Cioran, *Shismes*, Paris, 1978. Lithographs by Pierre Alechinsky. 33 x 24 cm, 10 pages, 4 illustrations. Edition of 150

Jean Frémon, *L'Envers*, Paris, 1978. Lithographs by Bram van Velde. 25 x 18.5 cm, 70 pages, 5 illustrations. Edition of 120

André Frénaud, *Joan Miró et l'émancipation définitive de la queue du chat. Fantaisie en forme de boniment pour amuser Joan Miró*, Paris, 1978. Etchings by Joan Miró. 25.5 x 26.5 cm, 28 pages, 3 etchings, illustrations within the text. Edition of 175

Philippe Denis, *Revif*, Paris, 1978. Engravings by Pierre Tal-Coat. 25 x 18.5 cm, 57 pages, 8 illustrations. Edition of 120

Octavio Paz, *Petrificada petrificante*, Paris, 1978, translated by Claude Esteban. Engravings by Antoni Tàpies. 52 x 42 cm, 40 pages, 8 illustrations. Edition of 175

1979

Eugène Guillevic, *Fifre*, Paris, 1979. Lithographs by Pol Bury. 80.5 x 59 cm, 12 pages, 10 illustrations. Edition of 75

André Frénaud, *La Vie comme elle tourne et par exemple avec Pierre Alechinsky*, Paris, 1979. Etchings and illustrations by Pierre Alechinsky. 32.5 x 23 cm, 44 pages, 3 illustrations. Edition of 600

1980

Jacques Dupin, *Sang*, Paris, 1980. Lithographs by Valerio Adami. 43 x 32 cm, 54 pages, 51 illustrations. Edition of 150

Paul Auster, *Unearth*, Paris, 1980, translated by Philippe Denis. Lithographs by Jean-Paul Riopelle. 25 x 18.5 cm, 60 pages, 5 illustrations. Edition of 120

André du Bouchet, *Dans leur voix les eaux*, Paris, 1980. Lithographs by Bram van Velde. 32 x 26.5 cm, 62 pages, 6 illustrations. Edition of 165

Jean-Michel Reynard, *Maint corps des chambres*, Paris, 1980. Engravings by Pierre Alechinsky. 25 x 18.5 cm, 72 pages, 5 illustrations, text decorations. Edition of 120

1981

Philippe Jaccottet, *Beauregard*, Paris, 1981. Engravings by Zao Wou-Ki. 25 x 18.5 cm, 54 pages, 5 illustrations. Edition of 120

Jean Daive, *Tàpies, répliquer*, Paris, 1981. Engravings by Antoni Tàpies. 28 x 20 cm, 58 pages, 4 illustrations. Edition of 200

Alain Veinstein, *Ebauche du féminin*, Paris, 1981. Lithographs by Claude Garache. 29.5 x 21 cm, 98 pages, 7 illustrations. Edition of 200

Joyce Mansour, *Le Grand Jamais*, Paris, 1981. Collaborative lithographs and illustrations by Pierre Alechinsky and Roberto Matta. 33 x 25 cm, 46 pages, 4 prints, illustrations within the text. Edition of 120

1984

Charles Baudelaire, *Chacun sa chimère*, Paris, 1984. Etchings by Warja Lavater. 46 x 34 cm, 54 pages, 7 illustrations. Edition of 50

1985

Julius Baltazar, *A l'infini le sable*, Paris, 1985. Engravings by Raoul Ubac. 25 x 16 cm, 40 pages, 2 illustrations. Edition of 85

1 Pierre Bonnard (1867–1947), *Summer* (*L'Eté*), 1917. Oil on canvas, 260 x 340 cm. Fondation Marguerite et Aimé Maeght, Saint-Paul

2 Pierre Bonnard (1867–1947), *Young Girl Reclining* (*Jeune fille étendue*), 1921. Oil on canvas, 56 x 61 cm. Maeght family, Paris

3 Pierre Bonnard (1867–1947), *Head of a Woman, Portrait of Marguerite Maeght* (*Tête de femme, portrait de Marguerite Maeght*), late 1930s. Pencil on paper, 30 x 23 cm. Maeght family, Paris

4 Pierre Bonnard (1867–1947), *Garden at Vernon* (*Jardin de Vernon*), 1930. Ink on paper, 25 x 32 cm. Maeght family, Paris

5 Pierre Bonnard (1867–1947), *Marguerite and Bernard Maeght*, c. 1944. Pencil on paper, 22 x 28 cm. Maeght family, Paris

6 Pierre Bonnard (1867–1947), *Woman and Child, Marguerite and Bernard* (*Femme et enfant, Marguerite et Bernard*), c. 1944. Ink on paper, 10.5 x 16.5 cm. Maeght family, Paris

7 Henri Matisse (1869–1954), *Portrait of Marguerite Maeght*, 1944. Charcoal on paper, 61 x 47 cm. Maeght family, Paris

8 Henri Matisse (1869–1954), *Blessing to Baudelaire* (*Bénédiction à Baudelaire*), 1944. Charcoal on paper, 40 x 30 cm. Maeght family, Paris

9 Henri Matisse (1869–1954), *Seated Nude* (*Nu assis*), 1944. Charcoal on paper, 62.5 x 48 cm. Maeght family, Paris

10 Henri Matisse (1869–1954), *The Bush* (*Le Buisson*), 1951. Ink and gouache on paper, 149 x 149 cm. Maeght family, Paris

11 Joan Miró (1893–1983), *North–South* (*Nord–Sud*), 1917. Oil on canvas, 62 x 70 cm. Maeght family, Paris

12 Joan Miró (1893–1983), *Blue* (*Bleu*), 1925. Oil on canvas, 64.5 x 91 cm. Maeght family, Paris

13 Alexander Calder (1898–1976), *Bird with Balls* (*Oiseau aux roubignolles*), 1954. Iron wire, 25 x 27 x 18 cm. Maeght family, Paris

14 Alexander Calder (1898–1976), *Bird with Spectacles* (*Oiseau aux lunettes*), c. 1930. Iron wire, 35 x 32 x 18 cm. Maeght family, Paris

15 Joan Miró (1893–1983), *Yellow Vase*, 1941–45. Ceramic, 40 x 22 cm. Maeght family, Paris

16 Alexander Calder (1898–1976), *Constellations*, 1944. Wood, 31 x 7.5 x 4.5 cm. Maeght family, Paris [This work has been withdrawn from the exhibition]

17 Joan Miró (1893–1983), *Light Blue Head* (*Tête bleu clair*), 1944–49. Ceramic, 25 x 18.5 cm. Maeght family, Paris

18 Joan Miró (1893–1983), *Superstition*, 1947. Ink and gouache on canvas, 195 x 430 cm. Maeght family, Paris

19 Alexander Calder (1898–1976), *Personage*, 1946. Oil on canvas, 123 x 114 cm. Maeght family, Paris

20 Joan Miró (1893–1983), *Drawing Dedicated to Paul Eluard*, 1948. Ink on paper, 27.5 x 20 cm. Maeght family, Paris

21 Joan Miró (1893–1983), *Blue Totem* (*Totem bleu*), 1953. Oil on canvas, 300 x 20 cm. Maeght family, Paris

22 Alexander Calder (1898–1976), *Feathers* (*L'Empennage*), 1953. *Stabile mobile*, painted metal, 150 x 284 cm. Fondation Marguerite et Aimé Maeght, Saint-Paul

23 Alexander Calder (1898–1976), *Sumac V*, 1953. *Mobile*, painted metal, 125 x 140 cm. Maeght family, Paris

24 Joan Miró (1893–1983), *Black Vase*, 1956. Ceramic, 51 x 27 cm. Maeght family, Paris

25 Joan Miró (1893–1983), *Large Double-sided Disc* (*Grand disque double face*), 1956. Ceramic, diameter: 59 cm. Maeght family, Paris

26 Joan Miró (1893–1983), *Catalan Bowl* (*Coupe Catalane*), 1956. Ceramic, 28 x 23.5 x 13.5 cm. Maeght family, Paris

27 Joan Miró (1893–1983), *Red Sun Plate with White Enamels* (*Plat soleil rouge émaux blancs*), 1956. Ceramic, diameter: 37 cm. Maeght family, Paris

28 Joan Miró (1893–1983), *Joy of a Little Girl in Front of the Sun* (*Joie d'une fillette devant le soleil*), 1960. Oil on canvas, 130 x 162 cm. Maeght family, Paris

29 Joan Miró (1893–1983), *Birds' Flight at the First Spark of Dawn* (*Vol d'oiseaux à la première étincelle de l'aube*), 1964. Oil on canvas, 162 x 130 cm. Fondation Marguerite et Aimé Maeght, Saint-Paul

30 Alexander Calder (1898–1976), Maquette for *Spider* (*Araignée*), 1959. *Stabile*, painted metal, 40 x 71 x 63 cm. Maeght family, Paris [This work has been withdrawn from the exhibition]

31 Alexander Calder (1898–1976), *Spider* (*Araignée*), 1947. Sheet metal and wire, 32 x 52 cm. Maeght family, Paris [This work has been withdrawn from the exhibition]

32 Joan Miró (1893–1983), Maquette for *Moon Bird* (*L'Oiseau lunaire*), c. 1963. Plaster, 77 x 69.5 x 69 cm. Fondation Marguerite et Aimé Maeght, Saint-Paul

33 Joan Miró (1893–1983), Maquette for *Arch* (*L'Arc*), 1963. Ceramic, 53 x 65 x 22 cm. Fondation Marguerite et Aimé Maeght, Saint-Paul

34 Joan Miró (1893–1983), *The Birth of Day I* (*Naissance du jour I*), 1964. Oil on canvas, 146 x 113.5 cm. Fondation Marguerite et Aimé Maeght, Saint-Paul

35 Joan Miró (1893–1983), *The Birth of Day II* (*Naissance du jour II*), 1964. Oil on canvas, 162 x 130 cm. Fondation Marguerite et Aimé Maeght, Saint-Paul

36 Joan Miró (1893–1983), *The Birth of Day III* (*Naissance du jour III*), 1964. Oil on canvas, 162 x 130 cm. Fondation Marguerite et Aimé Maeght, Saint-Paul

37 Joan Miró (1893–1983), 'Pour Adrien Maeght, en hommage à son travail, 12 mai 1965' ('For Adrien Maeght, in Recognition of His Work, 12 May 1965'), 1965. Wax crayon on paper, 37 x 28.5 cm. Maeght family, Paris

38 Joan Miró (1893–1983), *Poem* (*Poème*), 1966. Oil on canvas, 260 x 175 cm. Maeght family, Paris

39 Alexander Calder (1898–1976), *Five Yellows* (*Cinq jaunes*), 1976. *Stabile mobile*, painted metal, 28 x 50 cm. Maeght family, Paris

40 Alexander Calder (1898–1976), *Cat Snake* (*Le Chat serpent*), 1968. *Animobile*, painted metal, 20 x 7 x 77 cm. Maeght family, Paris

41 Alexander Calder (1898–1976), *Standing* (*Debout*), 1972. *Mobile*, painted metal, 200 x 100 cm. Maeght family, Paris

42 Joan Miró (1893–1983), *Thinking about Sandy, Sandy*, 1973. Gouache on paper, 36 x 79 cm. Maeght family, Paris

43 Joan Miró (1893–1983), *Painting on Table Mat* (*Peinture sur napperon*), 1972. Oil on table mat, 32.5 x 48 cm. Maeght family, Paris

44 Joan Miró (1893–1983), *The Birds of Prey Swoop Down on Our Shadows* (*Les Oiseaux de proie foncent sur nos ombres*), 1970. Oil on cowskin, 250 x 200 cm. Maeght family, Paris

45 Alexander Calder (1898–1976), *Three Yellow Suns* (*Trois soleils jaunes*), 1965. *Mobile*, painted metal, 150 x 400 cm. Fondation Marguerite et Aimé Maeght, Saint-Paul

46 Joan Miró (1893–1983), *Constellation*, 1972. Bronze, 142 x 130 x 44 cm. Fondation Marguerite et Aimé Maeght, Saint-Paul

47 Alberto Giacometti (1901–1966), *Spoon-woman* (*La Femme-cuillère*), 1926. Bronze, 145 x 51 x 21 cm. Fondation Marguerite et Aimé Maeght, Saint-Paul

48 Alberto Giacometti (1901–1966), *Bust with a Sharp Head* (*Buste tête tranchante*), 1927. Bronze, 40 x 35.5 x 7 cm. Maeght family, Paris

49 Alberto Giacometti (1901–1966), *Composition*, 1927. Bronze, 38 x 27 x 25 cm. Maeght family, Paris

50 Georges Braque (1882–1963), *Woman Lying Down* (*Femme couchée*), 1930–56. Oil on canvas, 74 x 180 cm. Maeght family, Paris

51 Georges Braque (1882–1963), *Zao*, for Hesiod's *Theogony*, 1931. Engraved plaster, 187.5 x 129.5 cm. Fondation Marguerite et Aimé Maeght, Saint-Paul

52 Georges Braque (1882–1963), *Zelos*, for Hesiod's *Theogony*, 1931. Engraved plaster, 185 x 98 cm. Maeght family, Paris

53 Georges Braque (1882–1963), *Heracles*, for Hesiod's *Theogony*, 1931. Engraved plaster, 187 x 105.5 cm. Fondation Marguerite et Aimé Maeght, Saint-Paul

54 Alberto Giacometti (1901–1966), *Cubist Head* (*Tête Cubiste*), 1934–35. Bronze, 18 x 25 x 20 cm. Maeght family, Paris

55 Georges Braque (1882–1963), *Ibis*, 1945. Bronze, 18 x 11 x 6 cm. Maeght family, Paris

56 Georges Braque (1882–1963), *Bone and Ovoid Form* (*Os et forme ovoïde*), 1949. Bone and plaster, 18.5 x 18.5 x 16 cm. Maeght family, Paris

57 Georges Braque (1882–1963), *Hymen*, 1939–57. Bronze, 76 x 50 x 35 cm. Fondation Marguerite et Aimé Maeght, Saint-Paul

58 Georges Braque (1882–1963), *Hesperus – Theogony* (*Hespéris – Théogonie*), 1939. Bronze, 41 x 23 x 10 cm. Maeght family, Paris

59 Georges Braque (1882–1963), *Work and Days – Fragment from Hesiod* (*Les Travaux et les jours – fragment d'Hésiode*), 1939–55. Bronze, 25 x 47 x 22 cm. Maeght family, Paris

60 Alberto Giacometti (1901–1966), *Bust of a Woman* (*Buste de femme*), 1945. Bronze, 48.5 x 13.5 x 12.5 cm. Fondation Marguerite et Aimé Maeght, Saint-Paul

61 Alberto Giacometti (1901–1966), *The Forest* (*La Forêt*), 1950. Bronze, 57 x 61 x 49.5 cm. Fondation Marguerite et Aimé Maeght, Saint-Paul

62 Alberto Giacometti (1901–1966), *Cat* (*Le Chat*), 1951. Bronze, 32 x 82 x 13 cm. Fondation Marguerite et Aimé Maeght, Saint-Paul

63 Georges Braque (1882–1963), *The Studio* (*L'Atelier*), 1949. Oil on canvas, 130.8 x 74 cm. The Metropolitan Museum of Art, New York. Bequest of Florene M. Schoenborn, 1995 (1996.403.13a, b)

64 Georges Braque (1882–1963), *The Echo* (*L'Echo*), c. 1953–56. Oil on canvas, 130.2 x 161.9 cm. Nahmad Collection, Switzerland

65 Georges Braque (1882–1963), *Vase of Flowers* (*Vase des fleurs*), 1954. Oil on canvas, 116 x 60 cm. Maeght family, Paris

66 Georges Braque (1882–1963), *Hyacinths* (*Les Jacinthes*), 1959. Oil on canvas, 33 x 41 cm. Maeght family, Paris

67 Georges Braque (1882–1963), *Black Birds* (*Les Oiseaux noirs*), 1956–57. Oil on canvas, 181 x 229 cm. Maeght family, Paris

68 Georges Braque (1882–1963), *Landscape – Fields with Overcast Sky* (*Paysage – les champs ciel bas*), 1956–57. Oil on canvas, 27 x 44.5 cm. Maeght family, Paris

69 Georges Braque (1882–1963), *Storm, Boat on the Pebbles* (*Marine l'orage barque sur les galets*), 1959. Oil on canvas, 24 x 42 cm. Maeght family, Paris

70 Georges Braque (1882–1963), *Plain I* (*La Plaine I*), 1955–56. Oil on canvas, 21 x 73 cm. Maeght family, Paris

71 Georges Braque (1882–1963), *Landscape* (*Paysage*), 1959. Oil on canvas, 21 x 73 cm. Maeght family, Paris

72 Georges Braque (1882–1963), *Landscape with Plough* (*Paysage à la charrue*), 1955. Oil on canvas, 34 x 64 cm. Maeght family, Paris

73 Georges Braque (1882–1963), *Plough* (*Charrue*), 1959. Oil on canvas, 22 x 33 cm. Maeght family, Paris

74 Alberto Giacometti (1901–1966), *Dog* (*Le Chien*), 1957. Bronze, 47 x 100 x 15 cm. Fondation Marguerite et Aimé Maeght, Saint-Paul

75 Georges Braque (1882–1963), *Thoroughbred* (*Pur-sang*), 1955–56. Bronze on stone, 25 x 47 x 22 cm. Maeght family, Paris

76 Georges Braque (1882–1963), *Little Horse* (*Petit cheval*), 1955–56. Bronze, 22 x 19 x 5 cm. Maeght family, Paris

77 Alberto Giacometti (1901–1966), *The House Opposite* (*Maison d'en face*), 1952. Oil on canvas, 69 x 45 cm. Maeght family, Paris

78 Alberto Giacometti (1901–1966), *White House* (*La Maison blanche*), 1958. Oil on canvas, 81 x 65 cm. Maeght family, Paris

79 Alberto Giacometti (1901–1966), *Apples* (*Les Pommes*), 1960. Oil on canvas, 16 x 33 cm. Maeght family, Paris

80 Alberto Giacometti (1901–1966), *Portrait of Reverdy*, c. 1960. Pencil on paper, 24 x 19 cm. Maeght family, Paris

81 Alberto Giacometti (1901–1966), *Portrait of Aimé Maeght*, 1960. Pencil on paper, 48.5 x 31.5 cm. Maeght family, Paris

82 Alberto Giacometti (1901–1966), *Portrait of Marguerite Maeght*, 1961. Oil on canvas, 145 x 95 cm. Maeght family, Paris

83 Alberto Giacometti (1901–1966), *Standing Woman with Arms by Her Side* (*Femme debout bras le long du corps*), 1952. Plaster, 51 x 17 x 9 cm. Maeght family, Paris

84 Alberto Giacometti (1901–1966), *Standing Woman* (*Femme debout*), 1960. Plaster, 24 x 10 x 6 cm. Maeght family, Paris

85 Alberto Giacometti (1901–1966), *Standing Woman with Arms by Her Side* (*Femme debout bras le long du corps*), 1952. Plaster, 23 x 8 x 5.5 cm. Maeght family, Paris

86 Alberto Giacometti (1901–1966), *Standing Woman I* (*Femme debout I*), 1960. Bronze, 270 x 54 x 36 cm. Fondation Marguerite et Aimé Maeght, Saint-Paul

87 Alberto Giacometti (1901–1966), *Walking Man I* (*L'Homme qui marche I*), 1960. Bronze, 183 x 26 x 95.5 cm. Fondation Marguerite et Aimé Maeght, Saint-Paul

88 Georges Braque (1882–1963), *Waltz* (*Valse*), 1960. Ceramic, diameter: 27 cm. Maeght family, Paris

89 Georges Braque (1882–1963), *White Bird* (*Oiseau blanc*), 1961. Ceramic, diameter: 24 cm. Maeght family, Paris

90 Georges Braque (1882–1963), *Profile* (*Profil*), 1960. Ceramic, diameter: 28 cm. Maeght family, Paris

91 Jean Cassarini (1910–2004), *Pierre à feu*, 1944. Book, 24 x 22 cm. Maeght family, Paris

92 Georges Braque (1882–1963), *Théogonie*, text by Hesiod, 1955. Book, 53 x 38 cm. Maeght family, Paris

93 Georges Braque (1882–1963), *La Liberté des mers*, text by Pierre Reverdy, 1959. Book, 57.5 x 39.5 cm. Maeght family, Paris

94 Georges Braque (1882–1963), *La Nuit, la faim*, text by Georges Ribemont-Dessaignes, 1960. Book, 28 x 18.5 cm. Maeght family, Paris

95 Joan Miró (1893–1983), *Sans le soleil*, text by Heraclitus, 1965. Book, 33 x 27 cm. Maeght family, Paris

96 Joan Miró (1893–1983), *Parler seul*, text by Tristan Tzara, 1948–50. Book, 38.5 x 29 cm. Maeght family, Paris

97 Alexander Calder (1898–1976), *Fêtes*, text by Jacques Prévert, 1971. Book, 46 x 34 cm. Maeght family, Paris

98 Joan Miró (1893–1983), *Adonides*, text by Jacques Prévert, 1975. Book, 40.5 x 33.5 cm. Maeght family, Paris

99 Georges Braque (1882–1963), *Teapot and Lemons* (*Théière et citrons*), 1949. Original lithograph, 50 x 65 cm. Maeght family, Paris

100 Georges Braque (1882–1963), *Leaves, Colour, Light* (*Les Feuilles couleurs lumière*), 1953. Original lithograph, 97.5 x 60 cm. Maeght family, Paris

101 Georges Braque (1882–1963), *The Chariot II* (*Le Char II*), 1953. Original lithograph, 50 x 65 cm. Maeght family, Paris

102 Alberto Giacometti (1901–1966), *The Dog* (*Le Chien*), 1954. Original lithograph, 53.5 x 44 cm. Maeght family, Paris

103 Alberto Giacometti (1901–1966), *Self-portrait* (*Autoportrait*), 1965. Original lithograph, 65.5 x 50.5 cm. Maeght family, Paris

104 Alberto Giacometti (1901–1966), *Walking Man* (*L'Homme qui marche*), 1957. Lithograph, 76.5 x 57 cm. Maeght family, Paris

105 Georges Braque (1882–1963), *Bird in Foliage* (*L'Oiseau dans le feuillage*), 1961. Original lithograph, 80.5 x 105.5 cm. Maeght family, Paris

106 Alexander Calder (1898–1976), *Low Tide* (*Marée basse*), 1969. Lithograph, 76 x 115 cm. Maeght family, Paris

107 Alexander Calder (1898–1976), *Saucers in the Dark* (*Soucoupes dans le noir*), 1969. Lithograph, 109.5 x 74 cm. Maeght family, Paris

108 Alexander Calder (1898–1976), *Dripping Balloons* (*Ballons dégoulinés*), 1969. Lithograph, 78 x 58 cm. Maeght family, Paris

109 Alexander Calder (1898–1976), *Two Spirals* (*Deux spirales*), 1974. Original lithograph, 75 x 110 cm. Maeght family, Paris

110 Joan Miró (1893–1983), *Woman Leading the Moon* (*La Meneuse de lune*), 1975. Original lithograph, 236 x 122 cm. Maeght family, Paris

111 Joan Miró (1893–1983), *The Hundred-year-old Warrior* (*La Guerrière de cent ans*), 1975. Original lithograph, 232 x 122 cm, Maeght family, Paris

112 Joan Miró (1893–1983), *Madwoman with Hot-tempered Pepper* (*La Folle au piment rageur*), 1975. Original lithograph, 232 x 122 cm. Maeght family, Paris

113 Henri Matisse (1869–1954), Invitation to the opening reception of the inaugural exhibition at Galerie Maeght, Paris, 6 December 1945. Paper, 24 x 32 cm. Maeght family, Paris (ill. page 15)

114 Aimé Maeght and André Breton, 1947. Photograph. Maeght family, Paris (ill. page 17)

115 The Fondation Marguerite et Aimé Maeght, Saint-Paul, designed by Josep Lluís Sert 1957–64. Photograph. Maeght family, Paris (ill. page 27) [This photograph has been withdrawn from the exhibition]

116 Galerie Maeght, Paris, inaugural exhibition, December 1945. Photograph. Maeght family, Paris (ill. page 34)

117 The catalogue for the 'Exposition internationale du surréalisme en 1947', Galerie Maeght, Paris, 1947, with cover design by Marcel Duchamp. Book. Maeght family, Paris (ill. page 34)

118 Arte shopfront, Cannes, 1939. Photograph. Maeght family, Paris (ill. page 35)

119 Stationery for Arte Publicité. Paper. Maeght family, Paris (ill. page 35)

120 Joan Miró wearing his *Superstition* at the 'Exposition internationale du surréalisme en 1947', Galerie Maeght, Paris, 1947. Photograph by Louise Bourgeois. Fondation Marguerite et Aimé Maeght, Saint-Paul (ill. page 36)

121 Performance at the 'Exposition internationale du surréalisme en 1947', Galerie Maeght, Paris, 1947. Photograph. Fondation Marguerite et Aimé Maeght, Saint-Paul (ill. page 36)

122 Adrien and Jules Maeght at the Arte printing house, 1994. Photograph. Maeght family, Paris (ill. page 38) [This photograph has been withdrawn from the exhibition]

123 Florence Maeght's visitors' book, with a felt-tip drawing of Florence by Alexander Calder, 1969. Book. Maeght family, Paris (ill. page 39)

124 Henri Matisse (1869–1954), *Deep Mirrors* (*Miroirs profonds*), on the cover of *Pierre à feu*, 1947. Book, 24 x 21 cm. Maeght family, Paris (ill. page 40)

125 Pierre Bonnard and Aimé Maeght. Photograph. Maeght family, Paris (ill. page 48)

126 View of Calder exhibition at Galerie Maeght, Paris, 1954. Photograph. Maeght family, Paris (ill. page 64) [This photograph has been withdrawn from the exhibition]

127 Aimé Maeght and Alexander Calder at Le Mas Bernard, Saint-Paul, 1966. Photograph. Maeght family, Paris (ill. pages 66–7) [This photograph has been withdrawn from the exhibition]

128 Alberto Giacometti in his studio, Paris, 1963. Photograph. Maeght family, Paris (ill. page 96)

129 Aimé Maeght and Georges Braque, 1948. Photograph. Maeght family, Paris (ill. page 98)

130 Georges Braque (1882–1963), Sketchbook, 1916–47. Book, 50 x 33 cm. Maeght family, Paris (ill. page 99)

131 Alberto Giacometti (1901–1966), *Braque on His Deathbed* (*Braque sur son lit de mort*), 1 August 1963. Pencil on paper, 29.5 x 29 cm. Maeght family, Paris (ill. page 100)

132 Alberto Giacometti (1901–1966), *Bust of Diego* (*Buste de Diego*), 1955. Plaster, 27.5 x 11 x 20.5 cm. Maeght family, Paris (ill. page 100)

133 Adrien Maeght in front of 'La Pilar' press, signed by Joan Miró, in the engraving studio at Saint-Paul, August 2006. Photograph. Maeght family, Paris (ill. page 137)

134 Aimé Maeght placing sculptures in the Giacometti courtyard, Fondation Marguerite et Aimé Maeght, 1967. Photograph. Maeght family, Paris (ill. pages 2–3)

135 *Derrière Le Miroir* covers, 1946–82. Book covers, 38 x 28 cm. Maeght family, Paris (endpapers)

136 Alberto Giacometti (1901–1966), 'Gris, brun, noir...', original essay about Braque's flower paintings, 1952. Paper, 21 x 29.4 cm. Fondation Marguerite et Aimé Maeght, Saint-Paul (not illustrated)

137 Film of Bonnard, Maeght family, Paris

138 Film of Matisse, Maeght family, Paris

139 Film of Giacometti, Maeght family, Paris

140 Film of Braque, Maeght family, Paris

BENEFACTORS OF THE ROYAL ACADEMY OF ARTS

ROYAL ACADEMY TRUST

Major Benefactors
The Trustees of the Royal Academy Trust are grateful to all its donors for their continued loyalty and generosity. They would like to extend their thanks to all those who have made a significant commitment, past and present, to the galleries, the exhibitions, the conservation of the Permanent Collection, the Library collections, the Royal Academy Schools, the education programme and other specific appeals.

HM The Queen
The 29th May 1961 Charitable Trust
Barclays Bank
BAT Industries plc
The late Tom Bendhem
The late Brenda M Benwell-Lejeune
John Frye Bourne
British Telecom
John and Susan Burns
Mr Raymond M Burton CBE
Sir Trevor Chinn CVO and Lady Chinn
The Trustees of the Clore Foundation
The John S Cohen Foundation
Sir Harry and Lady Djanogly
The Dulverton Trust
Alfred Dunhill Limited
The John Ellerman Foundation
The Eranda Foundation
Ernst & Young
Esso UK plc
The Foundation for Sports and the Arts
Friends of the Royal Academy
Jacqueline and Michael Gee
Glaxo Holdings plc
Diane and Guilford Glazer
Mr and Mrs Jack Goldhill
Maurice and Laurence Goldman
Mr and Mrs Jocelin Harris
The Philip and Pauline Harris Charitable Trust
The Charles Hayward Foundation
Heritage Lottery Fund
IBM United Kingdom Limited
The Idlewild Trust
The J P Jacobs Charitable Trust
Lord and Lady Jacobs
The Japan Foundation
Gabrielle Jungels-Winkler Foundation
Mr and Mrs Donald Kahn
The Kresge Foundation
The Samuel H Kress Foundation
The Kirby Laing Foundation
The Lankelly Foundation
The late Mr John S Latsis
The Leverhulme Trust
Lex Service plc
The Linbury Trust
Sir Sydney Lipworth QC and Lady Lipworth
John Lyons Charity
John Madejski OBE DL
Her Majesty's Government
The Manifold Trust
Marks and Spencer
Ronald and Rita McAulay
McKinsey and Company Inc
The Mercers' Company
The Monument Trust
The Henry Moore Foundation
The Moorgate Trust Fund
Mr and Mrs Minoru Mori
Robin Heller Moss
Museums and Galleries Improvement Fund
National Westminster Bank
Stavros S Niarchos
P F Charitable Trust
The Peacock Trust
The Pennycress Trust
The Pidem Fund
The Pilgrim Trust
The Edith and Ferdinand Porjes Trust
The Porter Foundation
Rio Tinto plc
John A Roberts FRIBA
Virginia Robertson
The Ronson Foundation
The Rose Foundation
Rothmans International plc
Dame Jillian Sackler DBE
Jillian and Arthur M Sackler
Mrs Jean Sainsbury
The Saison Foundation
The Basil Samuel Charitable Trust
Mrs Coral Samuel CBE
Sea Containers Ltd
Shell UK Limited
Miss Dasha Shenkman
William and Maureen Shenkman
The Archie Sherman Charitable Trust
Sir Hugh Sykes DL
Sir Anthony and Lady Tennant
Ware and Edythe Travelstead
The Trusthouse Charitable Foundation
The Douglas Turner Trust
Unilever plc
The Weldon UK Charitable Trust
The Welton Foundation
The Weston Family
The Malcolm Hewitt Wiener Foundation
The Maurice Wohl Charitable Foundation
The Wolfson Foundation
and others who wish to remain anonymous

Patrons
The Royal Academy is delighted to thank all its Patrons for generously supporting the following areas over the past year: exhibitions, education, the Royal Academy Schools, the Permanent Collection and Library and Anglo-American initiatives, and for assisting in the general upkeep of the Academy.

Secretary's Circle
The Lillian Jean Kaplan Foundation
Mrs Coral Samuel CBE

Platinum Patrons
Mr and Mrs William Brake
Mr and Mrs John Coombe
Mr and Mrs Patrick Doherty
Mrs Helena Frost
Lady Getty
Mr Leif Hoegh
Mr Frederik Paulsen
Mr and Mrs David Shalit

Gold Patrons
Sir Ronald Cohen
Lady Gosling
Michael and Morven Heller
Lady Hobson MBE
Sir Sydney Lipworth QC and Lady Lipworth
Mr and Mrs Ronald Lubner
Professor and Mrs Anthony Mellows
Lady Rayne
Mrs Stella Shawzin
Mr James B Sherwood

Silver Patrons
Mrs Denise Adeane
Mrs Leslie Bacon
Alain and Marie Boublil
Mrs Gary Brass
Mrs Elie Brihi
Mrs Debbie Burks
Sir Charles and Lady Chadwyck-Healey
Sir Trevor Chinn CVO and Lady Chinn
John C L Cox CBE
Mary Moore Danowski
Mr and Mrs Maurice Dwek
Benita and Gerald Fogel
Mr and Mrs Eric Franck
Jaqueline and Jonathan Gestetner
Patricia and John Glasswell
Mr and Mrs Alan Hobart
Mr and Mrs Jon Hunt
Mrs Pauline Hyde
S Isern-Feliu
Mr and Mrs Fred Johnston
Mr and Mrs Joseph Karaviotis
Mrs Aboudi Kosta
The de Laszlo Foundation
Lady Lever of Manchester
Mr and Mrs Mark Loveday
Mr and Mrs Richard Martin
The Mulberry Trust
Mr and Mrs D J Peacock
Mr and Mrs Kevin Senior
The Countess of Shaftesbury
Mr and Mrs Andrew Shrager
Richard and Veronica Simmons
Jane Spack
Sir James and Lady Spooner
The Lady Henrietta St George
Mrs Elyane Stilling
Sir Hugh Sykes DL
Group Captain James Tait
Mr David Teitelbaum

Bronze Patrons
Abstract Select Ltd
Mr and Mrs Gerald Acher
Agnew's
James and Julie Alexandre
Mr Derrill Allatt
Mr Peter Allinson
Artvest Limited
Edgar Astaire
Jane Barker
Mrs Yvonne Barlow
Stephen Barry Charitable Settlement
James M Bartos
The Duke of Beaufort
The Bellinger Donnay Charitable Trust
Mrs J K M Bentley/Summers Art Gallery
Konrad O Bernheimer
Dame Elizabeth Blackadder RA
Sir Victor and Lady Blank
Mrs Marcia Brocklebank
Mr and Mrs Charles H Brown
Jeremy Brown
Lord Browne of Madingley
Mrs Alan Campbell-Johnson
Mr F A A Carnwath CBE

Jean and Eric Cass
Mr and Mrs George Coelho
Mrs Carole Cohen
Denise Cohen Charitable Trust
Carole Conrad
Mrs Cathy Corbett
Mr and Mrs Sidney Corob
Thomas Corrigan OBE
Julian Darley and Helga Sands
The Countess of Dartmouth
Ms Davina Dixon
Dr Anne Dornhorst
Lord Douro
Sir Philip Dowson PPRA and Lady Dowson
Lord and Lady Egremont
Mary Fedden RA
Mr and Mrs David Fenton
Bryan Ferry
Mrs Donatella Flick
Mrs George Fokschaner
Lord and Lady Foley
Mrs Pamela Foster-Brown
Mrs Jocelyn Fox
Mr Monty Freedman
Arnold Fulton
Michael Godbee
Nicholas and Judith Goodison
Piers and Rosie Gough
Peter and Kate De Haan
David and Lesley Haynes
Mr Andreas Heeschen
Mr and Mrs Christoph Henkel
Mr and Mrs Jonathan Hindle
Anne Holmes-Drewry
Sir Martin and Lady Jacomb
Mrs Raymonde Jay
Mr Harold Joels
Fiona Johnstone
Dr Elisabeth Kehoe
Mr D H Killick
Mr and Mrs James Kirkman
Norman A Kurland and Deborah A David
Joan H Lavender
Mr George Lengvari and Mrs Inez Lengvari
Mrs Rose-Marie Lieberman
Miss R Lomax-Simpson
The Marquess of Lothian
Mr and Mrs Henry Lumley
Sally and Donald Main
Mr and Mrs Eskandar Maleki
Mr and Mrs Michael RA and Jose Manser
Mr Marcus Margulies
Mr and Mrs Stephen Mather
Miss Jane McAusland
Christoper and Clare McCann
Gillian McIntosh
Andrew and Judith McKinna
Zvi and Ofra Meitar Family Fund
Lakshman Menon and Darren Rickards
Mrs Michele Michell
Mrs Michael Moore
James Moores
Mrs Alan Morgan
Dr Ann Naylor
Mrs Ann Norman-Butler
North Street Trust
Mrs Flin Odfjell
Hilary O'Neill
Mr Georg Von Opel
Mr Michael Palin
John H Pattisson
Mr Philip Perry
David Pike
Mrs Godfrey Pilkington
Mr and Mrs Anthony Pitt-Rivers
William Plapinger and Cassie Murray
John and Anne Raisman
Mr and Mrs Ian Rosenberg
Lady (Robert) Sainsbury
Mrs Sirkka Sanderson
H M Sassoon Charitable Trust
Carol Sellars
Dr Lewis Sevitt
Mrs Lesley Silver
Alan and Marianna Simpson
Mr and Mrs Mark Franklin Slaughter
Brian D Smith
Mr and Mrs David T Smith
Mrs D Susman
Mrs Mark Tapley
Lord and Lady Taylor
Miss M L Ulfane
Mrs Norah de Vigier
John and Carol Wates
Edna and Willard Weiss
Anthony and Rachel Williams
and others who wish to remain anonymous

Benefactor Patrons
The Peter Boizot Foundation
Mrs Mary Graves
The Lord Marks of Broughton
Lord Rothschild
Sir Anthony and Lady Tennant
and others who wish to remain anonymous

BENJAMIN WEST GROUP PATRONS

Chairman
Lady Judge

Platinum Patron
Dean Menegas

Gold Patron
Lady J Lloyd Adamson

Silver Patrons
Mrs Adrian Bowden
Mr and Mrs Paul Collins
Brian and Susan Dickie
Kim Dunn
Dr Yvonne von Egidy-Winkler and Mr Peter Philip Winkler
Charles and Kaaren Hale
Lady Judge
Scott and Christine Morrissey
Elaine and David Nordby
Mr and Mrs John R Olsen
Wendy Becker Payton
Frank and Anne Sixt

Bronze Patrons
Ms Ruth Anderson
Mrs Alan Artus
Tom and Diane Berger
Mrs Michal Berkner
Wendy Brooks and Tim Medland
Mrs J Morgan Callagy
Debra Cajrati Crivelli
Mr and Mrs Gunnar L Engstrom
Cyril and Christine Freedman
Mr Roy Hill
Madeleine Hodgkin
Suzanne and Michael Johnson
Sarah H Ketterer
Mr and Mrs H A Lamotte
Charles G Lubar
Mr and Mrs Patrick Mahon
Neil Osborn and Holly Smith
Lady Purves
Carole Turner Record
Mr and Mrs K M Rubie
Sylvia Scheuer
Mr and Mrs Thomas Schoch
John and Sheila Stoller
Mrs Betty Thayer
Frederick and Kathryn Uhde
John and Amelia Winter
Mary Wolridge
and others who wish to remain anonymous

SCHOOLS PATRONS GROUP

Chairman
John Entwistle OBE DL

Platinum Patrons
Mr Campbell Rigg
Matthew and Sian Westerman

Gold Patrons
Mr Andrew Hanges
Mr and Mrs Paul Myners

Silver Patrons
Lord and Lady Aldington
John Entwistle OBE DL
Mr Philip Marsden

Bronze Patrons
Ian and Tessa Ferguson
Julia Fuller and David Harding
Professor and Mrs Ken Howard RA
Pickett
Peter Rice Esq
Anthony and Sally Salz
Mrs Inge Borg Scott
Mr Ray Treen
and others who wish to remain anonymous

CONTEMPORARY PATRONS GROUP

Chairman
Susie Allen

Bronze Patrons
Mrs Alan Artus
Viscountess Bridgeman
Dr Elaine C Buck
Miss Camilla Bullus
Debbie Carslaw
Jenny Christensson
Mr Gus Danowski
Mary Moore Danowski
Helen and Colin David
Chris and Angie Drake
Dr Yvonne von Egidy-Winkler
Lawton Wehle Fitt
Belinda de Gaudemar
Ms Soma Ghosh

Elizabeth Griffith
Mrs Selima Gürtler
Caroline Hansberry
Mrs Susan Hayden
Mazen and Mireille Masri
Sharon Maurice
Marion and Guy Naggar
Angela Nikolakopoulou-Koulakoglou
Maria N Peacock
Mr Andres Recoder and Mrs Isabelle Schiavi
Rosanna Wilson Stephens
John Tackaberry
Britt Tidelius
Mr and Mrs Nicholas Whyatt
Cathy Wills
John and Amelia Winter
Manuela and Iwan Wirth
Mary Wolridge
and others who wish to remain anonymous

Trusts and Foundations
The Albert Van den Bergh Charitable Trust
The Peter Boizot Foundation
The Bomonty Charitable Trust
The Charlotte Bonham-Carter Charitable Trust
The D'Oyly Carte Charitable Trust
C H K Charities Limited
The Coutts Charitable Trust
Alan Cristea Gallery
The Dovehouse Trust
The Gilbert & Eileen Edgar Foundation
The Fenton Arts Trust
The Flow Foundation
The Joseph Strong Frazer Trust
Goethe Institut London
Heritage Lottery Fund
The Emmanuel Kaye Foundation
The Kindersley Foundation
The Kobler Trust
Lapada Association of Art and Antiques Dealers
The David Lean Foundation
The Leche Trust
The Leverhulme Trust
The Maccabaeans
The Marsh Christian Trust
The McCorquodale Charitable Trust
Margaret and Richard Merrell Foundation
The Millichope Foundation
The National Manuscripts Conservation Trust
Newby Trust Limited
The Old Broad Street Charity Trust
P F Charitable Trust
The Peacock Charitable Trust
The Stanley Picker Charitable Trust
The Pidem Fund
The Edith & Ferdinand Porjes Charitable Trust
The Privy Purse Charitable Trust
Mr and Mrs J A Pye's Charitable Settlement
The Radcliffe Trust
The Rose Foundation
The Archie Sherman Charitable Trust
The South Square Trust
Oliver Stanley Charitable Trust
Peter Storrs Trust
Sir Jules Thorn Charitable Trust
Celia Walker Art Foundation
The Spencer Wills Trust
The Harold Hyam Wingate Foundation
Hazel M Wood Charitable Trust
The Worshipful Company of Painter-Stainers

AMERICAN ASSOCIATES OF THE ROYAL ACADEMY TRUST

Burlington House Trust
Mr and Mrs James C Slaughter

Benjamin West Society
Mrs Walter H Annenberg
Mr Francis Finlay
Mrs Nancy B Negley

Benefactors
Mrs Deborah Loeb Brice
Mrs Edmond J Safra
Mr and Mrs Albert H Small
The Honorable John C Whitehead
Mr and Mrs Frederick B Whittemore

Sponsors
Mrs Russell B Aitken
Ms Britt Allcroft
Mrs Katherine D Findlay
Mrs Sylvia K Hassenfeld
Mrs Henry J Heinz II
Mr Arthur L Loeb
Mr and Mrs Hamish Maxwell
Mrs Lucy F McGrath
Ms Diane A Nixon
Mr Arthur O Sulzberger and Ms Allison S Cowles
Mr Vernon Taylor Jr
Mr and Mrs Dave Williams

Patrons

Ms Helen Harting Abell
Mr and Mrs Steven Ausnit
Mr Donald A Best
Mrs Edgar H Brenner
Mrs Mildred C Brinn
Mrs Benjamin Coates
Mrs Mary Sharp Cronson
Anne S Davidson
Ms Zita Davisson
Mrs June Dyson
Mrs Barbara Fox-Bordiga
Mr and Mrs Lawrence S Friedland
Mr and Mrs Leslie Garfield
Mr C Hugh Hildesley
Dr Bruce C Horten
The Honorable and Mrs W Eugene Johnston
Mr William W Karatz
The Honorable and Mrs Philip Lader
Mr and Mrs Daniel Leab
The Hon. Samuel K Lessey Jr
Ms Barbara T Missett
Mr and Mrs Wilson Nolen
Mr and Mrs Jeffrey Pettit
Cynthia Hazen Polsky and Leon B Polsky
Lady Annie Renwick
Mr and Mrs Peter M Sacerdote
Ms Louisa Stude Sarofim
Mrs Frances G Scaife and Mr William G Dagit
Mr and Mrs Stanley De Forest Scott
Mrs Frederick M Stafford
Mr and Mrs Stephen Stamas
Ms Joan Stern
Ms Brenda Neubauer Straus
Ms Elizabeth F Stribling and Mr Guy
   Robinson
Mr Martin J Sullivan
Mr and Mrs Lewis Townsend
Dr and Mrs Robert D Wickham
Mr Robert W Wilson

Donors

Mr James C Armstrong
Mr and Mrs Stephen Bechtel
Mr Constantin R Boden
Mr and Mrs Philip Carroll
Mr and Mrs Reginald B Collier
Ms Jody Donohue
Mr and Mrs William J Doody
Mr Robert H Enslow
Mr Ralph A Fields
Mr and Mrs Christopher Forbes
Mr and Mrs Gordon P Getty
Mrs Betty N Gordon
Mr O D Harrison Jr
Mr and Mrs Gurnee F Hart
Mr and Mrs Gustave M Hauser
Mrs Judith Heath
Ms Elaine Kend
Mr and Mrs Nicholas L S Kirkbride
Mr and Mrs Gary Kraut
Mr Henry S Lynn Jr
Ms Christine Mainwaring-Samwell
Ms Clare E McKeon
The Honorable and Mrs William Nitze
Mrs Charles W Olson III
Mrs Nanette Ross
Laura Christman and William Rothacker
Mr Mark Schneider
Mrs Martin Slifka
Mrs Sharon Tedesco
Mrs Judith Villard
Mr and Mrs William B Warren

Corporate and Foundation Support

American International Group, Inc.
Annenberg Foundation
Bechtel Foundation
The Blackstone Charitable Foundation
The Brown Foundation
Gibson, Dunn & Crutcher
The Horace W Goldsmith Foundation
Hauser Foundation
Leon Levy Foundation
Loeb Foundation
Henry Luce Foundation
Lynberg & Watkins
Sony Corporation of America
Starr Foundation
Thaw Charitable Trust

CORPORATE MEMBERS OF THE ROYAL ACADEMY

Launched in 1988, the Royal Academy's
Corporate Membership Scheme has proved
highly successful. Corporate Membership
offers benefits for staff, clients and community
partners and access to the Academy's facilities
and resources. The outstanding support we
receive from companies via the scheme is vital
to the continuing success of the Academy and
we thank all Members for their valuable
support and continued enthusiasm.

Premier Level Members

A. T. Kearney
Accenture
The Arts Club

Bain Capital
The Bank of New York Mellon
Barclays PLC
Booz & Co.
CB Richard Ellis
Deutsche Bank AG
E.ON
Ernst & Young LLP
GlaxoSmithKline plc
Goldman Sachs International
Hay Group
HSBC plc
Intercontinental London Park Lane
King Sturge
Kleinwort Benson Private Bank
LECG Ltd
Lombard Odier Darier Hentsch
Northern Trust
Schroders plc
Smith and Williamson
Sotheby's
Standard Chartered

Corporate Members

All Nippon Airways
Arcadia Group plc
BGC Brokers L. P.
Bibendum Wine Limited
BNP Paribas
The Boston Consulting Group
Bovis Lend Lease Limited
British American Business Inc.
British American Tobacco
Calyon
Capital International Limited
Christie's
Citi
Clifford Chance
Concateno Plc
Control Risk Group
Curzon Partnership LLP
Denton Wilde Sapte
Diageo plc
Doll
Eurohypo AG
F & C Asset Management plc
GAM
Heidrick & Struggles
House of Fraser
Insight Investment
ITV plc
John Lewis Partnership
JPMorgan
KPMG
Lazard
Lehman Brothers
London College of Fashion
Louis Vuitton
Man Group plc
Mizuho International plc
Momart Limited
Morgan Stanley
Navigant Consulting
Nedrailways
Novo Nordisk
Osborne Samuel LLP
Pentland Group plc
Rio Tinto plc
Roger Vivier
The Royal Society of Chemistry
SG
Slaughter & May
Theo Fennell
Timothy Sammons
Trowers & Hamlins
Veredus Executive Resourcing
Weil, Gotschal & Manges
Windsor Partners Limited

Sponsors of past exhibitions

The President and Council of the Royal
Academy would like to thank the following
sponsors and benefactors for their generous
support of major exhibitions in the last
decade:

2008
2008 Season supported by Sotheby's
Vilhelm Hammershøi: The Poetry of Silence
   OAK Foundation Denmark
   Novo Nordisk
240th Summer Exhibition
   Insight Investment
*From Russia: French and Russian Master
   Paintings 1870–1925 from Moscow and
   St Petersburg*
   E.ON

2007
Paul Mellon's Legacy: A Passion for British Art
   The Bank of New York Mellon
Georg Baselitz
   Eurohypo AG
239th Summer Exhibition
   Insight Investment
Impressionists by the Sea
   Farrow & Ball
Premiums and RA Schools Show
   Mizuho International plc

RA Outreach Programme
   Deutsche Bank AG
The Unknown Monet
   Bank of America

2006
238th Summer Exhibition
   Insight Investment
Chola: Sacred Bronzes of Southern India
   Travel Partner: Cox & Kings
Premiums and RA Schools Show
   Mizuho International plc
RA Outreach Programme
   Deutsche Bank AG
Rodin
   Ernst & Young

2005
China: The Three Emperors, 1662–1795
   Goldman Sachs International
*Impressionism Abroad: Boston and French
   Painting*
   Fidelity Foundation
*Matisse, His Art and His Textiles: The Fabric
   of Dreams*
   Farrow & Ball
Premiums and RA Schools Show
   The Guardian
   Mizuho International plc
*Turks: A Journey of a Thousand Years,
   600–1600*
   Akkök Group of Companies
   Aygaz
   Corus
   Garanti Bank
   Lassa Tyres

2004
236th Summer Exhibition
   A. T. Kearney
*Ancient Art to Post-Impressionism: Masterpieces
   from the Ny Carlsberg Glyptotek, Copenhagen*
   Carlsberg UK Ltd
   Danske Bank
   Novo Nordisk
The Art of Philip Guston (1913–1980)
   American Associates of the Royal Academy
   Trust
The Art of William Nicholson
   RA Exhibition Patrons Group
*Vuillard: From Post-Impressionist to Modern
   Master*
   RA Exhibition Patrons Group

2003
235th Summer Exhibition
   A. T. Kearney
*Ernst Ludwig Kirchner: The Dresden and Berlin
   Years*
   RA Exhibition Patrons Group
Giorgio Armani: A Retrospective
   American Express
   Mercedes-Benz
*Illuminating the Renaissance: The Triumph
   of Flemish Manuscript Painting in Europe*
   American Associates of the Royal Academy
   Trust
   Virginia and Simon Robertson
Masterpieces from Dresden
   ABN AMRO
   Classic FM
Premiums and RA Schools Show
   Walker Morris
*Pre-Raphaelite and Other Masters: The Andrew
   Lloyd Webber Collection*
   Christie's
   Classic FM
   UBS Wealth Management

2002
234th Summer Exhibition
   A. T. Kearney
   Aztecs
   British American Tobacco
   Mexico Tourism Board
   Pemex
   Virginia and Simon Robertson
*Masters of Colour: Derain to Kandinsky.
   Masterpieces from The Merzbacher
   Collection*
   Classic FM
   Premiums and RA Schools Show
   Debenhams Retail plc
   RA Outreach Programme*
   Yakult UK Ltd
*Return of the Buddha: The Qingzhou
   Discoveries*
   RA Exhibition Patrons Group

2001
233rd Summer Exhibition
   A. T. Kearney
*Botticelli's Dante: The Drawings for Dante's
   Divine Comedy*
   RA Exhibition Patrons Group
*The Dawn of the Floating World (1650–1765).
   Early Ukiyo-e Treasures from the Museum
   of Fine Arts, Boston*
   Fidelity Foundation

*Forty Years in Print: The Curwen Studio
   and Royal Academicians*
   Game International Limited
*Frank Auerbach, Paintings and Drawings
   1954–2001*
   International Asset Management
Ingres to Matisse: Masterpieces of French Painting
   Barclays
Paris: Capital of the Arts 1900–1968
   BBC Radio 3
   Merrill Lynch
Premiums and RA Schools Show
   Debenhams Retail plc
RA Outreach Programme
   Yakult UK Ltd
Rembrandt's Women
   Reed Elsevier plc

2000
1900: Art at the Crossroads
   Cantor Fitzgerald
   The Daily Telegraph
232nd Summer Exhibition
   A. T. Kearney
*Apocalypse: Beauty and Horror
   in Contemporary Art*
   Eyestorm
   The Independent
   Time Out
Chardin 1699–1779
   RA Exhibition Patrons Group
The Genius of Rome 1592–1623
   Credit Suisse First Boston
Premiums and RA Schools Show
   Debenhams Retail plc
RA Outreach Programme
   Yakult UK Ltd
The Scottish Colourists 1900–1930
   Chase Fleming Asset Management

1999
231st Summer Exhibition
   A. T. Kearney
   John Hoyland
   Donald and Jeanne Kahn
John Soane, Architect: Master of Space and Light
   Country Life
   Ibstock Building Products Ltd
Kandinsky
   RA Exhibition Patrons Group
*LIFE? or THEATRE? The Work of Charlotte
   Salomon*
   The Jacqueline and Michael Gee
   Charitable Trust
Monet in the Twentieth Century
   Ernst & Young
   Premiums
   Debenhams Retail plc
   The Royal Bank of Scotland
RA Schools Show
   Debenhams Retail plc
RA Outreach Programme
   Yakult UK Ltd
Van Dyck 1599–1641
   Reed Elsevier plc

* Recipients of a Pairing Scheme Award,
managed by Arts + Business. Arts + Business
is funded by the Arts Council of England and
the Department for Culture, Media and Sport

Other sponsors
Sponsors of events, publications and other
items in the past five years:

Carlisle Group plc
Country Life
Derwent Valley Holdings plc
Dresdner Kleinwort Wasserstein
Foster and Partners
Goldman Sachs International
Gome International
Gucci Group
Rob van Helden
IBJ International plc
John Doyle Construction
Martin Krajewski
Marks & Spencer
Michael Hopkins & Partners
Morgan Stanley Dean Witter
Prada
Radisson Edwardian Hotels
Richard and Ruth Rogers
Strutt & Parker